OUT OF THE DARK

OUT OF THE DARK

Linda Caine and *Robin Royston*

This edition published 2003
by BCA
by arrangement with Transworld Publishers
a division of The Random House Group Ltd

Second Reprint 2003

CN 110032

Typeset in 11/14pt Caslon 540 by Falcon Oast Graphic Art Ltd.

Printed in Great Britain by
Mackays of Chatham Ltd, Chatham, Kent

This book is dedicated to my husband, Chris, my children, Gary and Christy, my sister, Annette, and my brothers Brendan and Clive.

Also to Linda McCormack, who spent many hours listening to me, holding my hand when I was afraid to sleep, playing badminton and going for walks with me on good days. Linda, when I telephoned you for the last time, to say goodbye, I told you that Robin and I were going to dedicate this book to you. I wish you had lived to read it, but you know the story because you lived it with me. Thank you, my dear friend.

ACKNOWLEDGEMENTS

Linda Caine

I have been blessed with a rich and eventful life. Some of these events have been painful and difficult, others magnificent almost beyond description. The writing of this book has been a remarkable story in its own right, and has taken me from America to England and Zimbabwe, and back again. Sometimes, looking back and immersing myself in it all again was almost more than I could bear. I wondered whether I should just let it all go, and move on with my life. But this thought did not last long, for my story is one of victory – not so much my own, but rather of those who did not give up on me, even when I was on the verge of giving up on myself.

Had it not been for the following people, my story would not have been told. I am profoundly grateful to them all.

My husband, Chris, and children, Gary and Christy: thank you for persevering with me through the dark years, and encouraging me to complete this book.

My sister, Annette, and brothers, Brendan and Clive: thank you for your support and prayers over the years.

Robin Royston, my psychotherapist and now my good friend: thank you for walking with me and helping me to unravel my past, and for your patience, optimism and insight.

Louise Orpin, my dynamic friend: thank you so much for all your encouragement over the years.

The staff at Ticehurst House Hospital between 1989 and 1991, particularly Roger Smith, Linda McCormack, Dympna Boyce, Noel Taggart and Bo Mills, for your care and understanding. Also Joe, Bridget, Beryl, Joseph, Liz, Sheila, Leonie, Sally and Tina, for your support.

The staff at Chaucer Hospital between 1989 and 1991: particularly Sally McGregor, Carol Trigger, Janet Hobson, Penny and Uno.

Dr Stefani: thank you for being so patient, and for not giving up on me.

Mark Lucas of Lucas Alexander Whitley, my literary agent: thank you for your steadfast confidence in my story, and for putting the wheels in motion to make this book the best it could be. Also to Peta Nightingale, for a great last rewrite!

Michael Robotham: thank you for weaving this complex story together so incredibly well.

Transworld Publishers: thank you for your patience, and for your vision for this book.

Grateful thanks to my Christian friends, for praying for me. In particular, Ben and Joan White, and Martin and Gail Collings, for their wise counsel. Thank you, Jenny Walker, Jill Poulson and Lu Sunderland, for your specific prayer.

Most of all I am grateful to God, who brought all these people into my life at exactly the right time.

Robin Royston

I would like to thank all those to whom Linda has already paid tribute, in particular Mark Lucas and Michael Robotham. And also special thanks to the staff at Ticehurst Hospital and The Chaucer Hospital. Being able to share the load, to laugh to ease the at times unbearable tension, and to go home at night knowing the strong, capable arms of Roger, Dympna and Noel would carry her through yet another dark journey was deeply reassuring. They would be there to encourage her, tease her and keep her safe. There were so many who travelled with us, and I cannot name them all. The same applies to Carol Trigger, who had no fear of doing what was needed. And to Sally MacGregor, who first set out on the road with Linda.

I must mention especially Linda McCormack. We have worked together for many years and she was perhaps the most professional of us all. Had I known what fate had in store for her, perhaps I would have understood better. She had an almost unlimited capacity to stay with people, with their journey, until they reached the far shore. We have passed through some awful territory together, but she never looked to escape or turn back. She was always there when the rest of us would have gone home, encouraging or just being with someone in their pain. Her touch was remarkable, judging the distance to keep between herself and the patient in so subtle a way. She could move in and out of that space and allow them to find their own way, or push on with her own determination if that was what was needed.

Thanks are due to Louise Orpin, whose energy and intuition made the right connections at the right time.

Also to Margaret Cudmore, Ticehurst's General Manager, who allowed me the space to follow my nose, and my secretaries: Janet Hobson, Pat Young, Sue Baynham and Sue Glover.

Finally, to Rena Proud, who always had faith.

1

JANUARY 1988

Linda Caine

The buzzing is too muffled to wake me completely but too loud to ignore. How long will Gary let it ring? I can picture him in his bedroom upstairs, buried in his duvet so that only his dishevelled brown hair is visible. I know exactly what he's done – put the alarm clock under his pillow. That son of mine could sleep through World War Three. I wonder what dream he's woken from this morning. Has he been slaying dragons, or scoring the winning try at Twickenham? What worldly wrongs has he put right since I kissed him goodnight? The sound stops suddenly. Gary has found the 'snooze' button and given himself another ten minutes before the alarm rings again.

Chris shifts beside me and I can feel the warmth of his chest against my back. I turn quietly and look at him. His face is pressed against the pillow and his lips are slightly parted. A few streaks of grey are visible in his black hair. We have been married for fourteen years but first met each other in primary school. Like most boys he didn't think much of girls back then, but that soon changed. Now I could happily lie beside him for ever.

Upstairs, Gary's alarm clock buzzes again. This time he manages to ignore it totally. Slipping out of bed, I pull on a pair of jeans and a thick woollen jumper. As I sit on the bed, lacing my sneakers, Chris opens one eye.

'Why did we get Gary an alarm clock?' he asks, sleepily.

'So that he'd get out of bed in the morning.'

'It hasn't worked.'

'Obviously.'

There are paint pots and throw rugs piled near the top of the stairs. Wallpaper samples stand upright in a roller tray, next to my spirit level and cordless drill.

Downstairs in the kitchen, I find Christy sitting at the breakfast table, studying the side panel of a cereal box. She is already dressed in her school uniform and has her dark hair in a ponytail.

'Have you seen how much salt they put in this?' she says earnestly.

'No.'

'I really think we should choose a cereal with less salt.'

'OK.'

Being lectured on healthy eating by an eight-year-old is fairly normal in our household. Christy is our moral compass – declaring which brands of tuna we should buy (to save dolphins) or insisting that we only eat free-range eggs. Sometimes I look at her and wonder if she hasn't skipped a few years of childhood.

With the kettle about to boil, I yell up the stairs: 'Gary Caine, if I have to come up there and drag you out of bed then you'll be gated after school. Do you hear me? There'll be no going to Stacey's house or to the park. You have five minutes.'

I don't bother waiting for a reply. Somehow Gary always knows how to judge his morning appearances to perfection, or at least to within an inch of being OK. How can my children be so different? Christy is always ready for school on time, homework done and school bag packed, whereas any moment now Gary will come leaping down the stairs, shirt hanging out, hair uncombed and school tie scrunched in his breast pocket. He'll pour too many cornflakes into his bowl so they spill out when he adds the milk. Then he'll wipe his mouth on his sleeve, scoff his toast in four bites and give me the most angelic smile imaginable.

As if on cue, he appears, slides onto a chair and reaches for the cereal box. He pours too many cornflakes into his bowl and I stifle the urge to laugh.

Gary is small for his age but if he's like my two brothers he'll suddenly spurt when he hits seventeen. I know he gets teased about his size, but he makes up for it with his boundless energy. In between each mouthful of cereal he beats out a rhythm on the table with his fingers. Chris looks up from his newspaper. 'Do you have to do that?' He disappears behind the newspaper again.

In mid-chew Gary taps the back of the paper as if knocking at a door. 'Hey, Dad.'

Chris looks over the top of the page.

'I need five quid.'

'What for?'

'The bus trip on Saturday.'

'Why didn't you tell me last night?'

'I forgot.'

Chris sighs in frustration and opens his wallet. Over the years he's learned to go with the flow when it comes to Gary. Chris works as a solicitor in Canterbury and drops Gary at school on his way to work. I always smile when I see them leaving the house – one the image of orderliness in his suit and polished shoes, the other still combing his hair as the car pulls out of the driveway.

I look at my watch. 'Five minutes, Christy.'

'Can we go now? I have a book I want to get from the library.'

'Sure.'

We walk out to the car together. In total contrast to Gary (and much to his disgust) Christy is tall for her age. She's just a few inches shorter than I am and like Gary has a smattering of freckles on her nose, particularly in the summer. I think freckles look cute, but they both hate them.

My little dark blue Metro has ice on the windows and I let it idle for a while with the heater running. I hate the cold. When it snowed last December, we took the kids sledging on Chestfield Golf Course. When we got back, I tried to make hot drinks for everyone but my hands were so cold I couldn't put my fingers together to pick up the spoon.

I keep telling myself it's because I grew up in a hot country. I'm just not used to the cold. That's why we bought such a big house. If I was condemned to living months of the year inside to stay warm, then I needed a sense of space.

Christy's school is in Swalecliffe, about two miles away. The round trip takes only fifteen minutes – barely enough time for the ice to melt on the side windows.

Back at the house I put on my painting clothes – a pair of tracksuit pants and one of Chris's old business shirts. The shirt is too big so I roll the sleeves up over my wrists. Then I make myself another cup of coffee, grinding the beans and pressing down the plunger. Too many people treat coffee like fast food. For me it's an indulgence.

My favourite time of day is that moment when I sit on the staircase with a coffee, listening to the silence of an empty house and planning my day. First I'll finish sanding the windowsills and skirting boards in the art room. I should have time to paint them before lunch. Then I'll set up the jigsaw and start cutting the shelving for my art cupboard. I picked up the wood on Saturday.

I have great plans for my art room. I want an extra two desks and chairs, as well as paper and pens, so that Gary and Christy can come in whenever they want to be creative. And I want lots of room to put all the bits and pieces that I collect when they catch my eye or remind me of a particular moment. I can never go for a walk without coming back with rocks, flowers or pieces of wood. I tear pages with pictures I like from magazines, and collect pebbles from streams.

The world is full of pictures that imprint themselves on my mind, waiting for me to put them on paper. Things like the patterns on the petals of a flower, or the texture of wood or a creeper wound around a barbed-wire fence.

Ever since I can remember, I've been fascinated by patterns and colours. I love the way certain colours clash when put together by man, yet look stunning when found together in nature.

On wet days I can stare endlessly at puddles, mirrors in the earth, which reflect things perfectly on a clear day, but fragment them when it's windy or rainy. I love the soft green moss that grows from nowhere on wet rocks and wood near waterfalls and streams. And how spears of new grass look almost fluorescent in the aftermath of a bush fire.

Most of the bits and pieces I've collected over the years have been lost or left behind when we've moved from place to place. But I still have a pebble from a waterfall in Africa and a stone from the ocean bed off the South of France. The water was so clear that day I could see my shadow below me as I swam. It made me feel like I was flying.

Whenever I fall in love with a place, I bring a piece of it home with me. I also press a few strands of my hair beneath a rock or let them loose on the wind. It probably sounds eccentric, but I love to know that a part of me will always be in 'my' places, and that I have a part of them with me.

A gallery in Faversham has started showing some of my paintings – mostly flowers and animals. Occasionally I get a commission, but to be honest I don't like them. Whenever someone asks me to do a painting, I find myself getting anxious and uptight. The end result is always far duller and less inspiring than when I paint from my imagination.

As I finish my coffee I hear a whimper from the laundry. Poor Sammy, I've forgotten about him. I open the door and a ball of black fur comes bouncing into the kitchen, skidding on the smooth floor and back-pedalling furiously to stop colliding with the table.

Sammy is a poodle who thinks he's a lion. He stands at the door, looking at me expectantly.

'It's too cold out there,' I tell him, feeling guilty.

He whines.

'Oh, come on, Sammy, we have work to do.'

The dog spins and races past me to the first landing.

'Up! Up!' I say.

Sammy goes tearing off up the stairs, heading for the top floor.

'Stop!'

He spins to face me, trembling with anticipation.

'Down!'

He bounds down the stairs.

'Up!'

'Stop!'

'Down!'

I sometimes try to trick him by using funny accents, or mixing up my commands, but poodles are pretty bright. We play the game for ten minutes until Sammy is exhausted. He curls up on the old sheet covering the art room floor, while I start painting.

Occasionally, he nuzzles my leg or puts his head in my lap. He doesn't like the paintbrush in my hand. I think he remembers being accidentally speckled with white emulsion and having chunks cut out of his fur.

The house has been transformed in the past twelve months. Walls have been stripped, bathrooms retiled and carpets laid.

When we first saw this place, Chris called it a dump.

'I can fix it,' I declared.

'It's falling apart.'

'It isn't falling apart. It's just cosmetic. Get rid of the wallpaper, rip up the carpets . . .'

'It isn't worth the effort.'

For a week I badgered and coerced him into coming back for a second look. 'Just look at the space,' I told him. 'Try to imagine everything painted white.'

'I keep thinking of the cost.'

'I can wallpaper. I can paint.'

Eventually, I wore him down. Now he loves the space as much as I do. Sometimes I get downhearted at how much work still has to be done, but I love watching the transformation. The third floor has two huge bedrooms, which belong to Gary and Christy. Chris and I sleep on the middle floor, which also has a guestroom, study and my art room.

At first I concentrated on the back living room and the kitchen. For the difficult jobs, I had help from Mel, a retired builder whom I met through the church.

Chris and I joined the Swalecliffe Free Church in the early eighties. It was founded by the Baptists but is non-denominational and Bible-based. It has a wonderful free worship session on Sunday evenings, when anybody can say a prayer out loud or ask others to pray about something. Some people sing and others speak in tongues. If you start a song you never finish it alone.

Now I'm involved in the church youth group. I meet with the other group leaders every Wednesday night to pray and work out what we're going to teach at Sunday School. I find it really challenging because the children are constantly asking me questions and I have to go looking for the answers. My life is really busy at the moment. Apart from the redecorating and church, I play badminton once a week and the occasional game of squash with friends.

When we first left Rhodesia and arrived in England it was a real struggle emotionally and financially. Chris had to study in his spare time and do his articles all over again. Now he's a partner at his legal firm. We don't have to worry about money any more. We can afford this house and school fees and the occasional holiday.

Chris works long hours and thrives on the challenges of being a lawyer. He has about twenty staff working under him. I'd be terrified by that sort of responsibility, but he gets excited about it. We are such different creatures. Chris is outgoing and gregarious, well educated and not intimidated by clever people, while I'm shy and reclusive, with a fear of standing out in a crowd. His world is full of lawyers, academics and senior clergymen (his firm represents the Archbishop of Canterbury), while I love art, poetry and nature.

It's funny because Chris doesn't normally like artistic people. He thinks most of them are neurotically 'searching' for themselves, with their heads in the clouds. 'How will they see the meaning of life through all the incense they burn?'

That's the sort of thing you'd expect a solicitor to say, but he's just teasing me. Chris likes things to be structured and stable – just like the law. His childhood was like that and it has carried on. Not like me. I've moved house thirty-two times in my life. The sands shifted under my feet so often that I had no sense of security or stability . . . not until I met Chris.

After I finish painting the skirting boards, I make myself a coffee and a sandwich, and I sit on the stairs, cradling the mug in my hands, feeling the heat soak into my fingers.

My mind begins drifting. It just seems to float off and leave me sitting there. I look at my watch and it's almost 3 p.m. Two hours have passed. Where did they go? It can't have been a daydream or I'd have remembered something about it. The time has simply vanished and left no trace.

Christy! School! I'm going to be late.

Still in my painting shirt, I grab my car keys. I pull out of the driveway and turn right, past the small post office and butcher's, and head towards the main road, Thanet Way, half a mile away. I slow for the roundabout and wait for a gap in the traffic. Every so often I glance at the clock on the dashboard. There are puddles by the side of the road. When did it rain? What else have I missed?

Passing under the railway bridge, past Swalecliffe station, I signal to turn left into Herne Bay Road. Waiting in a queue of traffic, I have a sense that time has gone missing in the past. I can't be sure. It's so hard to know unless I have somewhere to be . . . like today. I pass a school crossing and the lollipop lady in a yellow dayglo vest waves me through. It takes me several seconds to respond. I'm still in a daze. What's wrong with me today?

The road outside Swalecliffe Primary School is locked solid. Cars are double-parked as mothers strap children into the back seats. Bright yellow raincoats are shaken out, umbrellas are folded and windows begin to fog.

Christy has walked half a block to the corner of Kemp Road where I normally park. She's been standing alone, waiting for me. She clambers in beside me and tosses her school bag onto the back seat. She gives me a hug and I squeeze her for a little longer than normal. As we go, she studies me closely.

'Good timing,' she says, matter-of-fact.

'I was almost late.'

'You're never late, Mum,' she says, laughing. The rain has plastered strands of hair to her forehead, where her hood hadn't quite covered her.

'Are we going shopping tomorrow?' she asks.

'If you want to.'

'Can we have a cappuccino?'

'Uh huh.'

This is our Saturday morning ritual. With Gary at school for the half-day and Chris at the office or playing squash, Christy and I have the mornings together. We go shopping at Tesco's in Whitstable and afterwards have cappuccinos and slices of cake in their in-store café. I love spending time with my children one-on-one. That's when I hear all their thoughts and dreams.

Gary's favourite place is a restaurant called The Barn, which has an enormous thatched roof. We always sit at the front window over-looking the street and each have a ploughman's lunch. Blue Stilton for me and Cheddar for Gary. He loves the soft white middle of the French bread, while I love the crusts, so we swap chunks of bread.

Gary has a knack of making life look easy. When he first picked up a squash racket or rode a horse, he showed amazing natural ability. Christy has to work harder and listen to her teachers, but her persistence pays off. She's becoming a better rider than Gary because she works for it.

Christy is shaking my arm. 'It's green, Mum.'

I look at the traffic lights.

'You were away with the pixies,' she says with a smile.

'I'm sorry.'

It had happened again. Time was slipping away from me. I can't remember pulling up to the lights. It's as though someone hit a pause button and I froze while the world carried on.

When we get home, Christy gets changed and I make her a snack. She dips digestive biscuits into her hot chocolate and tells me about her day. She can sense that I'm distracted.

'Can I take my chocolate upstairs?' she asks. 'I want to listen to a tape.'

'OK, but keep the volume down.'

'Always,' she answers without looking back.

I go back to my painting. I have to wash out the brush because the bristles have gone stiff. That's what happens when you get distracted.

Starting on a windowsill, I work hard to get a straight edge. The trick is not to put too much paint on the brush. There's a noise outside and it makes me jump. I freeze. Looking out the window, I see a man put his ladder against the wall of the guest bedroom. My heart is racing.

I jump up and close the curtains. Running into Chris's office, I pull down the blind and then draw the curtains in our bedroom. Afterwards, I press myself against the wall on the landing where nobody can see me. A voice inside my head is saying, 'Don't be stupid, Linda. It's just the window cleaner.'

In the same breath I remember the top windows are open. Christy is playing in her room. I start to panic all over again. My voice is shaking as I call up the stairs, 'Sweetheart, don't get a fright if anyone appears at the window. It's just the window cleaner.'

'OK,' she sings back.

Taking a deep breath I try to calm down. Back in the art room I write a cheque for the cleaner. My hands are shaking so much that I have difficulty signing my name.

What's happening to me?

My panic attack over the window cleaner makes Chris laugh. I laugh too.

'You are strange,' he says, giving me a hug. Then he pours himself a drink and loosens his tie. Gary and Christy are in the TV room. I can hear the theme music of *Home and Away*. I strain pasta in the colander and watch the steam mist up the windows above the sink. I wonder if I should tell Chris about how I lost track of the time and nearly forgot about Christy.

He knows I've been struggling for a while. Some days are like swimming through mud. A blackness leaks into my thoughts and everything moves in slow motion around me. I have to force myself out of bed in the mornings and return to it exhausted at night.

What reason do I have to be depressed? I have a successful husband who loves me; two bright, talented children; a lovely house; my faith in God . . . That's why I get so angry at myself. I have a great life.

Yet there seems to be a dark undercurrent – something I can't fathom, or put my finger on. It's not just about being depressed. I seem to be haunted by images that flash into my head and leave me breathless and struggling to cope. It's as though a bolt of lightning illuminates a scene for a split second before the darkness snatches it away again. And that blast of light burns the scene into my brain.

Sometimes I see myself lying beneath the water, staring up through the fingers of a hand, spread across my face, over my mouth and nose. At other times, I see a pair of eyes staring furiously at me; eyes that want me dead; eyes that look straight through me as though I don't warrant the space I take up. I've tried to draw these eyes. I have page after page of sketches, but I never draw the face, just the eyes. If I shade the background, the eyes seem to be peering out of the darkness at me.

As a child I was terrified of the dark and of falling asleep. Now I'm getting frightened again and I'm almost thirty-seven years old. Sometimes when I'm scared of falling asleep I lie close to Chris so that I can feel him breathing. It reminds me of when I was a little girl. If I had nightmares I used to run into Dad's room and lie in the little 'cave' between the blankets and his broad back.

The flashes have been getting worse. It's as though I've forgotten something important and I'm being dragged down by dark thoughts. Some days the bleakness is suffocating and I go through the motions from morning till night.

On Sunday mornings at church, I pray for things to get better. But even Jesus seems distant now. What's wrong with me? Why do I feel so dead inside? Why am I jumping at shadows and having time vanish?

One day, after the service, I ask our new pastor, Ben White, if we can talk.

'Sure. Whenever you want.'

My eyes begin filling with tears.

'What's wrong?'

'I don't know. I feel awful and I don't know why.'

Ben takes me to a quiet corner and we talk about what might be wrong. Ben is middle-aged with a soft voice. He once studied to be a doctor before he felt called to the ministry.

'Have you talked to Chris?' he asks.

'I've tried. He's really busy at the moment.'

'What about your doctor?'

I shake my head.

'I think there is something evil in me.'

'I seriously doubt that.'

'Then what's happening to me?'

He doesn't answer. Instead he suggests that I come and see him every week. 'We'll study the Bible and pray. In the meantime, I think you should also see a doctor. Tell him that you've been feeling depressed.'

A wave of panic squeezes my throat. Deep down I know that I'm cracking up. What if they say I'm an unfit mother? They might take Gary and Christy into care. They might lock me up . . .

I don't go and see a doctor. Instead, I keep telling myself how wonderful my life is, and try to pull myself together.

2

JANUARY 1989

Linda Caine

How shall I die if that time comes? I need to know these things. They have to be planned. Yet even as I ask the question, another voice inside me says, accusingly: 'How can you do this to your family?'

I answer back, 'What good am I to them when I'm like this? They'll be better off without me.'

It has been a year since I started talking to Ben, and I have the makings of a plan. It has to seem like an accident. I can't bear Chris, Christy and Gary knowing the truth. The idea came to me a few months ago as I drove home from Tesco's in Whitstable with the weekly shopping.

Thanet Way is a busy road, notorious for accidents. Every so often a sad little bouquet of flowers will appear, tied to a streetlight, or left at the base of a tree. At one point there's a steep drop on the left side of the road, down to a football field. The road is so high you can see the tops of the trees. With a good speed up, my little blue Metro would fly over the edge. Nobody would suspect. Nobody commits suicide in a car loaded with shopping. It will look like just another accident on Thanet Way.

I can't explain how helpless the last twelve months have made me feel.

But the worst part is the depression. It's like a huge black suffocating cloud. I'm always exhausted and I can't concentrate. I've tried again to talk to Chris but he has such an analytical mind: he deals in facts not feelings.

'What more can I do to make you happy?' he asks.

'Nothing. I don't want anything more.' I *know* how lucky I am and that just makes me feel even worse. Chris puts his arms around me and I start to cry. Nothing seems to help. I don't know *why*. At that moment, I almost tell him about my thoughts of suicide. Just as I open my mouth Gary appears at the door. He wants to know if Chris will come to his rugby match on Saturday. I turn my face away so that he doesn't see me crying.

Chris gives me a look which says, 'Can it wait, love?'

As he goes to talk to Gary I feel desperately lonely. I know that it's not Chris's fault. He's a strong, practical man, who's used to seeing a problem and finding a solution. He's *not* used to dealing with depression.

I still have my weekly Bible studies with Ben and Joan White. These sessions are the best I feel all week. Ben and Joan understand depression. It's such a relief not having to explain things to them. I told Ben about the flashes I get in my mind of being held under water. Since then he's been even more insistent that I see my family GP.

'Don't be frightened of medicine, Linda. It's a God-given thing.'

I haven't mentioned the time lapses. I keep making excuses for them. Yet deep down I can't shake the fear that I'm going mad. I keep thinking about St Augustine's – the local mental hospital. A friend of mine once went there. She said it was such a bleak place that her feelings of depression and helplessness were only made worse.

When I mention this to Ben he tells me to stop. 'You *won't* be put in St Augustine's. Your doctor will probably just give you anti-depressants. It's no different to taking pills for high blood pressure . . .'

Ben asks me if I've said anything to Chris.

I shrug. 'He knows something is wrong, but he can't understand why. That's the difficulty with depression – unless you've been through it you can't possibly know what it's like.'

A few weeks later Ben asks if he can come and see me at home. He wants Chris to be there. He brings a book with him called *Anxiety and Depression*, written by Professor Robert Priest, a psychiatrist. I can see Chris starting to fidget. He's uncomfortable with the whole subject and just wishes it would go away. Ben sits down next to him and I make us some coffee.

When I come back into the lounge Chris is looking at the book. Ben is leaning over him, pointing to something. I put the tray down and sit quietly next to Chris. I skim the headings of the pages. One of them says, 'The Psychological Symptoms'. There's a list of sub-headings below it: 'Sadness. Loss of Interest. Loss of Energy. Loss of Concentration. Morbid Thoughts. Guilt. Unworthiness.'

It's as though someone has written a book about *me*.

Over the next few days Chris reads the book and is totally absorbed. He keeps reading bits and pieces aloud to me at night when we're lying in bed. I think it helps him enormously because he realizes that it's not his fault. It also gives him a role. He can be supportive and understanding when I'm tired and struggling.

Day after day, I try to make a stand; to consciously count my blessings; to think positively. I keep re-reading chapter three of the book: 'Self-Help Ways of Overcoming Anxiety and Depression'.

Chapter four is entitled 'When to Go to Your Doctor'. I can't face that one.

Rational people don't contemplate suicide but I'm no longer rational. I have become short-tempered, irritable, anti-social and almost agoraphobic. I snapped at Gary yesterday for having lost a sweatshirt. I really sounded off and I could see he was shocked. Later I found the sweatshirt in the washing basket.

It's a small thing. Most of the time I simply don't care any more. The darkness inside me is so complete that I've forgotten what the light is like. Death has to be better than this.

Ben knows that I'm suicidal. For months he has been counselling me and recommending books for me to read. Joan sometimes joins us and we all talk. We've been praying and reading passages from the Bible together but nothing has changed. It's not their fault. I won't go and see a doctor. I'm too frightened of being locked away.

'Suicide is *not* the answer,' says Ben. 'It's running away from the problem.'

'Don't you understand . . . I *am* the problem. It's *me*. I'm poisoning my children's lives. I'm dragging them down with me . . .'

'Go and see a doctor, I beg you.'

'I can't.'

Ben leans forward and fixes his eyes on mine. 'You must promise me one thing,' he says. 'If you reach the end, you must call me first . . . before you do anything. Will you promise me that?'

I nod and wipe away my tears.

On the drive home I feel happier than I have in months. It's as though I've taken back control of my life. Suicide isn't a *fait accompli* – it's a last resort. And if it comes to that, it won't be anybody's fault. It will just mean that I can't cope any more. The song on the car radio is the old Louis Armstrong classic 'Wonderful World'. Maybe he's right.

Christy helps me peel the vegetables for dinner. She wants to know if she can perm her hair. According to her, she'll soon be the only girl in southern England who hasn't had it done.

'I think you're exaggerating.'

'No, I'm not.'

'But you have beautiful hair.'

'It's boring.'

I wonder who she'd ask these questions if I was dead? Who would put her hair in a ponytail, or help her go shopping for clothes? There are hundreds of little things that Gary and Christy would have to learn to do themselves. I should get them ready . . . just in case.

Over the next few weeks I make a conscious effort to make them less reliant on me. Am I preparing them, or releasing myself? A bit of both perhaps. There are small things I can do, like leaving their washed and folded clothes on their beds so they learn to put them away themselves. I teach Christy to put her hair in a ponytail and how to iron her school uniform. Gary starts to polish his own shoes and put his dirty plates straight into the dishwasher.

When it comes to meals I know they'll be fine without me. Christy has become a vegetarian and taken to cooking for herself.

Gary, like his father, loves fast food and prefers pizzas or fried chicken to anything I cook.

That night, as I tuck Gary and Christy into bed, I listen to their prayers.

My father recently had a heart attack and nearly died. Christy's prayers concentrate on keeping him well.

'God bless Granddad and make his heart strong so he won't have another heart attack,' she says. In her floral pyjamas and surrounded by soft toys, she looks young and vulnerable. 'Is Grandpa going to die?' she asks.

'One day.'

'But I don't want him to die.'

'I know. But death isn't really such a sad thing. It just means that one of us is going to heaven and will be waiting for the rest of us to arrive. It's like when we all go into town and arrange to meet at the pancake place for supper. We might go our separate ways, but we all know we'll meet up in the end at the pancake place. Heaven is the same – it's where we'll all be together some day.'

I tuck the duvet under her chin and kiss her on the forehead. She snuggles up with Noon-Noon and Nin-Nin, her toy bunnies.

Afterwards, in my art room, I sit and think about what will happen if I die. I picture their lives without me. I don't picture their grief. I can't go that far. Instead, I see them coping. Surely it's far better for them to suffer a short, sharp shock and get on with life, than to be dragged down by me.

A couple of days later, I fetch Gary from St Edmund's and find him standing next to the lecture hall, with his head bowed against the wind. He's quieter than usual as we drive home. Gary isn't one to sulk. His coat is pulled around him, with the collar up. He presses his chin to his chest.

'Are you angry because I was late?'

'No.'

'Are you feeling all right?'

'I'm fine. I've just had a lousy day.'

'You want to talk about it?'

'No.'

I back off and leave him alone. He'll talk to me when he's ready. When we reach the house, I unlock the front door and Gary walks inside. A strap from his shoulder bag catches on the door handle. I see him wince in pain as the strap stops him suddenly. As he turns to disentangle the bag he lets go of his coat. There's an ugly graze on his throat that he's been trying to hide.

I go cold. 'Gary, what's that?'

He sees me looking at his neck. 'Mum. Please. Just leave it.'

'What happened to your neck?' My voice sounds sharper than I want it to be. I know that several boys in his class have been teasing him about his size and pushing him around. Gary might be small but he doesn't back down.

He tells me what happened. The bullies had been pushing him around all day – bumping into him or trying to trip him as he walked between classes. Some of the girls had thought it was funny and started to laugh.

That's when Gary blew up.

'Did you try to ignore them?' I ask.

'I told them to leave me alone. They kept pushing me.'

'What did you do then?'

'Next time they pushed me I pushed them back. Then I hit one of them.'

I sigh and take a closer look at his neck. 'That's what they wanted you to do. That's why they teased you in the first place . . . because they *wanted* you to react.'

'I know. But it's hard. I can't do *anything* without them pushing me around or calling me names.'

His shirt is torn and grubby and the graze on his neck is raw. It looks like a burn. There's also a bruise near his collarbone. I feel myself getting angry. I want to punish whoever did this. I hate bullying. With the right advice and encouragement, children can solve most problems by themselves, but bullying is something different because it's the work of cowards and thugs.

First thing next morning I make an appointment to see Gary's housemaster later in the day. Mr Barnard is a tall, good-looking teacher, well liked by the students. I've met him once before at a parents' evening. He ushers me into his office and listens sympathetically as I tell him what happened. I want to say that Gary has enough to cope with at home without being bullied at school, but I stick to one problem at a time. I'm a little worried that I'll be dismissed as an over-protective, panicky mother, but Mr Barnard is really nice. He's noticed the problem already.

'I've been thinking how best to deal with it. If I openly warn the boys responsible, it could turn other boys against Gary. Kids often have a strange sense of duty when it comes to sneaking on their mates.'

'But it's gone too far.'

'I know.'

When I leave Mr Barnard's office, I'm confident that he'll do what he can to stop the bullying. Even so, as I drive out the side entrance of the school, I wonder who would have sorted this out if I wasn't around. Who would Gary have turned to? It gives me a sharp jolt. How can I possibly leave my children? Who'll look after them when they're sick? Who will solve their problems and listen to their dreams? They need their mother.

SATURDAY, 25 FEBRUARY 1989

Where are the doves today? I miss them when they don't come to pick up the scraps I leave in the garden. I read somewhere that there are one hundred billion birds on the Earth. That's fifty for every human being, yet it's amazing how rarely we seem to notice them.

I could never keep a wild bird in a cage. They're meant to fly against the sky, not stare at it from behind wire. My favourite bird is the fish eagle. They call it the 'voice of Africa' because it has such a haunting and distinctive call. It's a sound from my childhood, just like the village drums and the hammering of rain on tin roofs.

'So what are we going to do today?' I ask Christy, as I turn away from the living-room window.

She's sitting at the table drawing invisible patterns on the table-cloth with a teaspoon.

'Let's go shopping,' she says hopefully.

'What with? You've spent all your Christmas money.'

She scowls. At nine years old, Christy seems to believe that she has all the answers and life has become rather boring.

'I think we should clean out Nibbles's hutch,' I suggest.

Christy screws up her nose.

Nibbles is a gorgeous bundle of fur that lives in a wooden summer house in the garden.

'Come on, it won't take long,' I say, finishing my coffee. 'You grab the old newspapers and I'll get the straw.'

'Oh, Mu–um!' she complains. 'I don't *feel* like doing it now. I'll do it later.'

'No, we'll do it now.'

Outside, frost has dusted the lawn like icing sugar and frozen droplets of water cling to the clothesline like threaded beads. Christy lags behind me, carrying old newspapers in her arms. The cold pinches her cheeks, turning them pink. She's wearing the colourful jumper I knitted for her, along with black leggings. Her hair is tied back in a loose ponytail.

Nibbles hops to the front of his hutch as we open the door. He's a Netherlands Dwarf rabbit, with tiny ears that flatten against his head when you stroke him. Christy sometimes takes him for walks around the garden on a leash. I'm sure he thinks he's a dog.

I glance around the summer house. Bits of straw and food have fallen through the wire and collected on the floor.

'This really should have been done a week ago,' I say.

Christy is lingering near the door. 'Mum! I *don't* want to do this *now*,' she says, with an exaggerated sigh.

I can feel myself getting irritated. 'He's your rabbit, and I'm trying to help you.'

I turn just in time to see her pull a face as she mouths the words silently back at me. At that moment the world slows down. A roll of newspaper is clenched in my hand. I watch it swing around and hit Christy in the face. Her head snaps back and she loses her balance. Her eyes are wide with shock as she stumbles backwards. Tears are starting to form. She blinks them back, but not for long.

I drop the paper and hear it flutter to the floor. My mouth opens but no sound comes out. What can I say?

'Christy.' My voice sounds very far away.

I reach towards her, but she ducks under my arm and runs out of the summer house. I try to call her but can't get the words out. Instead, I watch her run across the lawn and into the house, moving in slow motion. I look at my hands. Newsprint has blackened my fingers. What have I done?

Forcing myself to move, I try to run, but it's painfully slow. With each step my world seems to be falling apart around me, crumbling like a cheap film set. Someone, somewhere, has slammed a door and the painted backdrop has toppled over. There is nothing solid behind the façade.

My mind seems to be speeding up, as my body slows down. I will myself to go on, desperate to find Christy and tell her . . . tell her . . . tell her what? What will I say? I have no excuses. I reach the french doors and step inside. Then I suddenly stop in the TV room. I stand perfectly still.

I don't know what to call such a moment. Life-changing? Life-ending? My mind has become absolutely clear. Clearer than it has been for a long time. I have lashed out. I have hurt someone I love. How can I trust myself? Something evil is inside of me.

I don't know how long I stand in the TV room. When I begin moving again, I don't try to rush. Calmly, I climb the stairs and find Christy crying on her bed. I put my arms around her, but feel a strange detachment. Inside I'm numb and empty. I love her desperately and have never been more sorry, but at the same time I feel as though I'm already somewhere else.

'Sweetheart. I'm *so* sorry.'

Christy looks up at me. A few loose strands of hair are plastered to her cheek, wet with tears. I brush them aside.

'Dad and Gary are going to be home soon,' I say. 'I need to go to the shops to pick something up. I am going to leave you here. I want you to stay in your room. Don't go downstairs. Don't answer the door. Don't answer the phone.'

She gives me a puzzled look, blinking away the last of her tears. I have never left her alone before.

'OK, Mum,' she says in a small voice. I hug her goodbye.

Downstairs I call Ben White, my pastor. Punching the numbers with a steady hand, I wait until I hear his voice.

'Hi, Ben . . .' My voice falters. 'I just wanted to tell you that I'm leaving.'

'Where are you going?'

'You know where I'm going.'

'Wait!' The sense of urgency in his voice is unmistakable.

'No. Ben, I only called because I promised you I would, and to say thank you for everything you've done for me. And ...' my voice breaks, 'to ask you to help my family.'

'Wait. Let me come over. Let me talk to you.'

'No. I've just hit Christy. Something snapped. I can't do this any more.'

'Please let me come over.'

'No. I'm sorry. I must go now.' I put the phone down.

I can picture Ben weighing up his options. If he tries to reach me by car he'll have to cross the Thanet Way roundabout. Even if he drives like a maniac, I'll be at the roundabout first. He won't know which way I've gone.

As I walk out the front door I hear the telephone ringing. Ben, no doubt. I close the door and turn towards the driveway. The engine is still cold by the time I reach the roundabout. I turn left up Thanet Way, knowing that I'm safe now.

The drive to Tesco's will take me ten minutes. Fallen leaves swirl in the slipstream of speeding trucks and lorries. They all seem to be travelling too quickly. A few brave souls are out walking their dogs on the muddy paths between the trees.

Ben may have reached the house by now. I know Christy won't answer the door. She'll stay in her room until Chris and Gary arrive. I hate leaving her alone. What if something were to happen to her? What if the house catches fire? What if someone . . . My heart skips a beat. I remember a story in the local newspaper about two young girls who were raped when their mother left them alone in a house in Canterbury. What if Chris and Gary are late getting home? What if they stop off for a milkshake? What if Gary has sport and Chris stays to watch him? Instead of being home in half an hour, they might be two or three hours.

I can't risk leaving Christy alone for that long. I *have* to make sure somebody is with her. Scanning the roadside, I look for a phone box. I have Ben's number in my head. If he hasn't already left I can tell him to look after Christy – to stay at the house even if she doesn't open the door. I pull off the road at a phone box. Fumbling for change, I reach for the handset and realize it's been torn off by vandals. I stare at the frayed wires incredulously. It's not meant to happen like this. I have it all planned. Now my absolute clarity is starting to blur. I need a telephone. Where can I find one? Tesco's

. . . the petrol station near the entrance to the carpark . . . surely it has a phone. I drive in a daze. Confusion and panic are breeding among the butterflies in my stomach.

When I pull up at the service station my hands are shaking so much I have trouble putting the nozzle into the tank. The cashier is just a teenager, with a mouthful of chewing gum and a pop magazine in her lap.

'Do you have a public phone?' I ask, trying to sound normal.

She motions towards Tesco's. 'They're inside the door.'

I can't get Christy's face out of my head as I drive across the carpark. I have to make sure she's safe.

The supermarket is packed with Saturday morning shoppers. I'll have to make the call in full view of everyone. As soon as I start speaking I'll cry. I know it. I don't want anybody to see me.

'Come on, Linda, pull yourself together. What are you going to do?'

I need to find a phone in a less public place.

Racking my brain I remember the Christian Literature Crusade shop in Canterbury. It has a quiet area downstairs with a telephone. Looking at my watch, I see it's after one o'clock. Canterbury is fifteen minutes away. If they're looking for me, nobody will think of the bookshop.

I talk to myself as I drive, telling the traffic to get out of the way. Everybody seems to be on the road today. My knuckles are white on the steering wheel but my mind is clear again. I turn through the gates to Canterbury Cathedral, past the commissionaire and into the precinct carpark near Chris's office. It's a five-minute walk to the bookshop, out of the cathedral gates, past Debenham's and across the square. I keep my head down as I weave through the crowds.

At the CLC shop I slip inside and straight down the stairs, past the cards and calendars. The Sunday School materials are in the basement. The telephone is in the corner near the coffee pot.

I dial the number and it only rings once.

'Ben . . .' I begin.

'Linda, where are you?' Ben's voice is urgent.

I cradle the handset in both hands and whisper, 'I'm not telling you. I haven't changed my mind. I just want you to go and get Christy. Please make sure that she's OK.'

'She's fine. Tell me where you are. Let me come and talk to you.'

'Just look after Christy. I have to go now. I'm so sorry.'

As I lower the phone, I hear him shout, 'Linda, Chris knows!'

It feels as though someone has punched me in the stomach. I put the phone back to my ear. 'What do you mean he knows?'

'I went to your house and Chris had just arrived home. He said that you'd gone shopping. I told him the truth . . . I told him what you were going to do . . .'

'But I trusted you!' I say accusingly.

'They would have found out, Linda. They would have known deep down.'

'You betrayed me.'

'Please let me come. I only did this because I care about you. You can get through this.'

I put the phone down and start to cry. Curling up on a chair, I hug my knees and sob uncontrollably. I still want to die. I *have* to do it! Only now my family will know the truth. A suicide, is a suicide, is a suicide . . .

Finding a pad I begin writing a letter to Ben and Joan. I say how sorry I am and ask them to forgive me. I plan to leave the letter with Fred, who looks after the bookshop. He can drop it at Ben's house on his way home. Summoning my courage, I climb the stairs. Fred is standing behind the cash register. I hand him the letter. 'Can you make sure that Ben gets this?'

'Linda, can we talk? You look upset.'

'Sorry, Fred, I need to go.'

'Is something wrong? Let me help you. At least let me pray with you.'

I don't want him phoning Ben, so I follow him into his office and we pray. When he's finished I thank him and leave quickly. I keep my head down, hoping he doesn't follow me. One thought keeps echoing in my head – Chris *knows*! He'll call the police. They'll be looking for me. Maybe they've already found the car, or set up road-blocks.

As I reach the precinct carpark I stop and begin browsing in shop windows. I use the reflection to see if anybody is standing near my car. It seems OK. I move quickly and slide into the driver's seat.

My hands are shaking. It takes me ages to get the key into the ignition. As I begin driving, a thought occurs to me. What if they're watching the roads out of Canterbury? How will I get to Thanet Way? Then I realize that it doesn't matter. My plan isn't a secret any more. At any moment they're going to stop me. Then they'll lock me up in St Augustine's and throw away the key.

I don't know where I'm going. I drive aimlessly, turning left and right, trying to clear my head. Suddenly, I realize that I'm near the police station so I turn quickly into a side road that leads to a hotel parking lot. I pull up, but realize the Metro can still be seen from the road. It *has* to be hidden.

I drive on, out past the tannery to a roundabout and onto a road leading out of Canterbury. Around every corner I expect to see a police car. Where will I go? I'm not thinking about suicide any more. I'm so confused. Taking a sharp left turn, I head along a narrow road that flanks a school. A rag-tag string of girls on a cross-country run are circling the sodden sports field. The backs of their shirts are splattered with mud thrown up by their heels.

I stop in a side street and park between two cars, hoping no-one will notice the Metro. I need time to clear my head. Still clutching the steering wheel, I rest my head on my forearms. The windows are open. The cold will help me concentrate. But I'm so tired . . . so, so tired.

I don't know how long I sit there. I can't remember the time passing, or thinking about anything. It's like a black hole. The only thing I'm sure about is the fading light and the bitter cold. My hands and fingers are blue and I have to rub them together to get feeling in my fingertips. It takes me ages to reverse the car and negotiate my way back down the road. As I near the roundabout I see the Victoria Hotel opposite me. Christy and I sometimes go there for chocolate sundaes as an afternoon treat. The hotel parking area is shielded from the road by a high wall.

I pull inside and park in a tight spot between other cars. I've come to a decision of sorts that's aimed at giving me time. I want twelve hours to think. Just the night. Hopefully, I'll work out what to do by then.

At the reception desk, a chatty and cheerful woman begins

telling me about their special offer of two nights for the price of one.

'I just want one night,' I say, barely holding myself together.

'It's the same price.'

'That doesn't matter.'

'You might change your mind.'

'OK, OK, whatever you think . . .' I hand her a credit card, but my hands are so cold that I can't hold the pen to sign the slip. I'm frightened she'll think I'm forging my signature. Instead she smiles and begins handing me brochures for hotel amenities.

When I reach the room, I collapse on the bed. Relief washes over me. I have a tiny pocket of space and time to get myself together. Do I still want to die? Yes, I think so. No, I don't know any more. I can't hold on to any one thought for more than a few seconds. What can I do about Gary and Christy? What will happen to them? What will they think of me? Will Chris tell them?

Drawing a deep hot bath, I lie in the tub and begin thawing out. But instead of being able to think, I'm exhausted and drained. I just want to sleep. Maybe that will clear my mind. Getting out of the bath, I get dressed again and lie down. Exhaustion overcomes me, and I pull the quilt around my body protectively.

The telephone rings next to the bed and I jump. For a few seconds I don't recognize the hotel room. I pick up the phone.

'Thank goodness you're all right.'

It takes me several seconds to recognize the voice. It's my friend Gail Collings.

'But . . . how did you know . . . how did you find me?' I stammer.

'God told me,' she says.

She tells me how Chris had been ringing all our friends, asking if anyone knew where I might be. The police had told him to stay at home near the phone in case I called. Gail and her husband Martin had started praying, asking God to help them to find me. That's when Gail remembered the Victoria Hotel. She and I some-times treated ourselves to an ice-cream here after we'd played squash.

'Lin, I want to come over and see you. We need to talk.'

'No. Just leave me.'

'What are you doing?'

'I'm thinking. I just need tonight. I need time to think.'

'Can I at least tell Chris you're OK?'

'No, please. He'll only try to find me.'

'I know what you're going through,' says Gail. 'I've been there too.'

I can't stop my tears. 'I don't know if I can go on.'

'Yes, you can. You take one day at a time.'

I tell Gail about what has happened during the day. She listens and makes reassuring noises. I know she's frightened of letting the call end. But I'm tired . . . I have to sleep.

'You won't do anything silly,' she says.

'I promise . . . as long as you don't tell Chris that I'm here.'

We go on like this, extracting promises, until she finally says goodbye. Ten minutes later there's a knock on the door. I feel angry and betrayed. Grabbing my car keys, I run to the window and slide it open. Just as I'm about to jump, Gail shouts through the door.

'Linda, it's me. I'm by myself, I promise you.'

I open the door and we burst into tears, hugging each other.

'I thought we were friends,' she says angrily. 'Why didn't you come to me first? Why did I have to wait for God to tell me where you were?'

Suddenly, she stops shouting and we both get the giggles. Sitting on the bed, I half laugh and half cry. I'm just so pleased to have someone with me.

For the next three hours we sit on the bed and talk. We swap stories about how awful depression can be and how pointless life can seem. We also talk about suicide and all its ramifications. She asks me to promise to call her if I still feel suicidal in the morning, and allow her another chance to talk to me. I give her my word. Gail doesn't want to leave, but she has to trust me. I feel sorry for poor Martin, her husband, sitting at home, sworn to secrecy. He and Chris are good friends. He will know that Chris won't understand how he could keep a secret like this.

After she's gone, I lie awake, unable to sleep. By morning my mind has cleared enough for me to realize that I can't go through with this. I can't leave my children emotionally scarred. I always said that I'd never be like *my* mother; that I'd never leave *my* children. Look at me now!

*

At seven in the morning I call Chris.

'Where are you?'

'At the Victoria Hotel.'

'Wait there.'

'No. I'm coming home.'

'No. Just wait there. Don't get in the car. Will you please wait there? Promise me.'

'OK.'

When I answer his knock, I almost don't recognize the man standing in the hallway. He looks grey, with black rings under his eyes. I doubt if it's possible to look more shattered. I tell myself to make a mental image of Chris's face and store it away. Then if ever I contemplate suicide again, I could bring the image to mind and realize what impact my death would have.

Chris takes over. With his arm around my shoulder, he pulls me against his side as if scared to let me go. We walk to his car and drive home in silence. Gary and Christy are being looked after by friends.

'Why didn't you call me? Why didn't you tell me?'

'I've been trying to tell you.'

He shakes his head and seems silently to curse himself. 'You told me things were bad, but I didn't realize . . . not this bad.' He rubs his eyes. 'I just want to help . . . but I don't know what to do. I don't know what's wrong . . .'

How can I explain it to him when I don't understand it myself? I just want the world to stop. I don't want to talk, or cry, or rationalize how I feel. I'm dead inside. I've given up.

Chris is saying something about taking me to see a doctor first thing in the morning. I hear the words, but feel nothing. Let them lock me away in St Augustine's. They can throw away the key. Anything has to be better than living like this.

3

MONDAY, 27 FEBRUARY 1989

Robin Royston

Loose change jangles in George's pockets as he sits down. He smoothes out his crumpled trousers and fidgets with his small, neat hands. Although he's been coming to see me for nearly six months George never looks entirely relaxed when he sits opposite me. Like a lot of people he thinks it is my job to solve his problems. After all, he is paying me!

'How was your week?' I ask, hearing him sigh.

'Lousy.'

'Why?'

'Same old story. I'm normally pretty easy-going, but my boss expects too much of me.'

George grows more and more irritated and frustrated as he talks about his work and the unfair pressure he is placed under. 'Then I had this stupid dream this morning,' he says.

'Tell me about that.'

'This man was being really horrible to a kid. He was shouting at him and threatening him. The kid was pretty pathetic. He looked as though he'd cry if you even looked at him.'

George dismisses the dream with a wave of his hand.

'Was the kid like you, or the man?' I ask.

'Neither.'

'Did they remind you of anyone?'

He shakes his head and thinks for a minute. 'Well, the man was a bit like my father.'

'In what way?'

'My dad used to get angry and bully me.'

'So could the child be you?'

'No, not a chance.'

'Why are you so sure?'

'Because he was wearing a Manchester United football shirt. I hate football.'

'So why the shirt?'

'How should I know?' says George, getting irritated. 'It's just a stupid dream.'

Straight away he regrets the outburst. He doesn't want me to get the wrong impression about him.

After a long silence he says softly, 'My son supports Man United.'

'Which son?'

'Peter – the middle one.'

I know that George has a troubled relationship with Peter. We have talked about it before but George invariably stops the conversation dismissively.

'He never does what he's told, that boy. And he's weak, weak as water. I don't know where he gets it from . . .' He shakes his head. 'It's just a stupid dream . . . nothing to do with me.'

George hates being pushed like this. He quietly fumes until the end of the session. George and I both know that he is a bully. He is his father's son, but will never admit it. Instead it is always going to be his son's problem.

Normally this is my last session of a Monday. I can get away by 6.50 p.m. and be home by eight. But a last-minute request has come in from a local GP asking if I can see a new patient.

The small psychiatric department at the Chaucer handles exclusively outpatients and the occasional day patient. The Chaucer has two general wards, one medical and the other surgical, but neither provides beds for psych admissions because of the problems that can arise when you mix such people with general hospital patients.

The psych department has a sister, Carol Trigger, a nurse counsellor, Penny Steel, and Janet, the receptionist/secretary. They are a close-knit group and I rely heavily on them all.

I have ten minutes' grace before my new patient arrives – just enough time to phone Lynn to see if she wants me to pick anything up on my way home. As she answers I can hear the TV in the background and Mike singing along. Emma is in the high chair and no doubt smearing mashed food over herself.

'Are you going to be late?' Lynn asks, nursing the phone in the crook of her neck as she spoon-feeds Emma, who is eleven months old.

'I'll be home by nine.'

'Be careful of ice on the roads. It's freezing. Do you know that nice pullover I bought for Michael? The one with all the colours. It's gone missing at the nursery.'

'I'm sure it will turn up.'

She turns her head and calls out, 'Michael, it's Daddy. He wants to say goodnight!'

I can hear him running from the lounge. At three, he shouts because when he holds the phone to his ear, the mouthpiece seems too far away.

'Mum wants me to eat broccoli,' he complains.

'It'll make you strong.'

'You say that about spinach.'

'It's the same with all that green stuff.'

'What about carrots?'

'They help you see in the dark.'

'But I'm scared of the dark.'

'All the more reason to eat carrots.'

I leave him pondering this and tell him to give Emma a hug for me. I can picture him screwing up his face in disgust. He has yet to fully accept this interloper.

I hate not being home to say goodnight to them. The long hours are a legacy of a huge mortgage. A year earlier, in 1988, just after Emma was born, we'd moved from a two-bedroom flat into a house near Tunbridge Wells.

At 7 p.m. I walk along the corridor to the nurses' station. There are several chairs against the wall, which act as my waiting room. A couple have arrived and they are sitting quietly. The woman doesn't look up as I introduce myself. She is attractively dressed in trousers and a jumper, but her eyes are red and swollen. I invite them into the consultation room and go through the formalities of confirming names and addresses.

Chris Caine wears a well-cut, dark grey suit, white shirt and something that could be an old school tie. He looks like a man who is used to being in control of any given situation. But this is new to him and he isn't as sure of himself.

He has a letter from the family's GP, Terry Stefani.

> *Dear Robin,*
> *re: Mrs Linda Caine – 9/3/1951.*
> *Thank you very much indeed for seeing this lady so urgently. She is an extremely pleasant woman and, on the face of it, her life could not be sweeter at the moment. She is happily married, financially secure and has two nice children. Yet increasingly she has felt life too difficult to cope with and has begun to prepare her children for her own death in their prayers together.*
>
> *Her mood has swung from periods of deep despair to at best when she just copes. She now admits that for the past ten months she has been gradually going downhill.*
>
> *I have not started her on an antidepressant yet as I thought you could assess her first. She seems to be seriously suicidal and may require admission. Nevertheless, I see very positive features with her caring family and the support that she is receiving from her pastor. I would be most grateful for your help.*

Linda glances at me only briefly. She leans against Chris, with her head on his shoulder and her eyes staring at the floor. Her long hair has fallen across her face, but she doesn't brush it aside. It is like a shield that she can hide behind. She has long, restless fingers, with the nails cut short. She appears to wear no make-up, but has obviously brushed her hair and taken some care with her clothes. These are important signs. Despite being distraught and bewildered, Linda still has enough presence of mind to take care of her appearance.

Clinical depression is quite different from the blues everyone feels at one time or another. It is more debilitating and dangerous. Apart from being sad, sufferers can become preoccupied with suicide, or plagued with guilt and a sense of worthlessness. They can have difficulty thinking clearly, remembering, or taking pleasure in anything.

'How are you feeling?' I ask.

Linda flinches slightly and pinches the skin on her wrist until I can see the red pressure marks on her skin.

'How have you been sleeping?'

'You've been waking up a lot,' prompts Chris.

'How long has it been like that?' I ask.

There is no answer, but an overriding impression of passivity and acceptance. Chris tries to help her. He comes across as a very pleasant, articulate man, who is at a total loss to understand what has happened.

'In the past few weeks, when you've been feeling really low, did you have a poor appetite or overeat?'

'She hasn't been eating much at all,' says Chris.

'Have you lost weight?'

Linda nods.

For the next thirty minutes, I continue through a series of questions dealing with fatigue, loss of energy, poor concentration, inappropriate guilt and thoughts of death.

'In the past few weeks have you been thinking about hurting yourself?'

'Yes.'

'Do you still want to kill yourself?'

'Yes.'

Linda seems detached, as if talking about a third person rather than herself. She speaks with a slight accent, which I can't quite place. Everything about her posture seems to say 'I'm sorry', and her movements appear to be exaggeratedly slow. At one point, she starts crying and covers her face with her hands. 'I just want to die,' she whispers.

There is a lot we still don't know about depression. Psychologists, psychiatrists and neuro-biologists are still debating whether it is caused by biological processes, such as a chemical imbalance in the brain, or some experience in life that affects the mind. It is a subject of immense complexity and one about which I have very few firm conclusions.

Regardless of the initial trigger, it's clear that depression involves biochemical changes in the brain. In essence, these chemicals carry messages and allow brain cells to 'talk' to one another. When something causes a change in their levels, it can give rise to a whole range of mental problems.

This is why antidepressants are so valuable in normalizing a patient until we can discover if there are important psychological factors involved in their problem. Such drugs can help restore the balance of certain chemicals in the brain or flatten the mood swings.

I explain this to Chris and Linda. 'These should also, hopefully, help you sleep,' I say.

'Will they make her feel better?' Chris asks, almost pleading for a positive response.

'I hope so. It will take a few weeks before they have any effect. In the meantime, I want Linda to come into the Chaucer as a day patient. We'll keep an eye on her during the day and she can go home in the evening. Once the drugs start to kick in, we'll review the situation.'

Linda simply nods. I doubt if she can summon the energy to kill herself at this moment. She looks beaten.

'Won't these drugs just make her artificially normal again?' asks Chris.

'No. They should help her feel like her old self. More able to cope.'

'And then she'll get better?'

'That's the aim. Once she feels a little better we'll either start searching for any underlying issues, or simply support her until she's able to cope.' I give them both a reassuring smile.

I sense that Chris wants more – a full diagnosis or an instant solution – but it is too early to identify the cause of Linda's depression. He thanks me and supports Linda as she rises. He keeps his arm around her as they walk down the corridor towards the main entrance. I stay back and write a note to the admissions staff for Tuesday, informing them of Linda's arrival.

Then I pack my things in my battered briefcase, leave the note on the psych sister's desk and join the evening traffic. I'd promised Lynn that I'd be home by nine, but it is already 8.30. Another reheated meal awaits. Then I'll poke my head into Emma's and Mike's rooms and watch them sleeping. Mike will be lying flat on his back, with his arms and legs outstretched, while Emma sleeps on her side with her hand near her mouth.

THURSDAY, 2 MARCH 1989

Linda Caine arrives at the Chaucer each morning just after nine. Chris drops her at the main entrance and she doesn't make eye contact with anybody as she comes down the corridor. I want Linda to be a day patient because it means that she can be supervised for those hours when Chris is at work and her children at school. She needs to be protected from herself until the antidepressants have time to work.

Carol Trigger, the psych sister, is a gentle Scottish woman, with a wonderful lilting accent. She tries to get Linda involved in relaxation exercises, or listening to music. Linda also brings stationery to write letters and a sketchpad and pencils, but rarely does anything other than sit by herself, staring out the window. Somebody keeps watch on her throughout the day and gives her opportunities to chat or interact, but Linda seems happier to be withdrawn and alone.

On each of my visits to the Chaucer I make a point of seeing her. We sit opposite each other in the consulting room, with the desk to one side. Normally I ask her general questions about her sleeping, her appetite and moods. I want to understand her in the context of the present day. What is happening in her life at *this* moment? Why is she struggling to cope? It means learning all I can about her marriage and her children. Is she healthy? Does she have many friends? What are her interests?

Linda rarely initiates conversation and her answers tend to be short and monosyllabic. I am trying to draw up a picture in my mind of Linda and how she has arrived at this point in her life. Sometimes she looks at me like a startled deer. Her entire appearance has a soft doe-like character. Although clearly attractive, she has a face that seems almost too childlike to have the sort of established characteristics we associate with age.

Silence can be a great pressure or a great comfort, depending upon the circumstances. Sitting a little distance away, I try to give Linda plenty of personal space. At the same time I use my voice and posture to make her feel more at ease.

I begin by talking about general things. 'It must be very difficult at the moment. I can see you're nervous about being here. Some people who I talk to are much more uncomfortable than others. They fear that I'm going to judge them, or become annoyed if they don't have the answers. I'm not going to do any of that, Linda. I know it's awkward for you. I know you're embarrassed about what happened. But I just need to find out a little more about you.'

She seems to be consumed by a mixture of sadness and regret. She is self-conscious about causing such a 'fuss'.

'I understand how you feel, Linda. Things just seem wrong at the moment, don't they? You feel like you're thinking in slow motion and getting up in the morning is a real effort. You're crying a lot either at nothing or something that normally would be insignificant. When you smile it feels stiff and awkward, as if your muscles are frozen . . .'

Linda looks up at me, with her eyes wide.

'You feel as though there's a glass wall between you and the rest of the world. You're anxious and jumpy. You have these thoughts of death or suicide, which you think would be a welcome relief . . .'

Linda begins crying.

'I'm right, aren't I?'

She nods.

'I'm here to help you. I know what you're going through and how you're feeling. But I still need your help. I need you to tell me about your life . . . what it's like, what friends you have, how your children are: all of these things.'

Linda nods. We are beginning to establish something. Concentrating on the present day, I ask about her hobbies, interests, marriage, family and faith. Primarily, I am looking for potential problem areas such as a bereavement, or marital turmoil, or illness, or drug use, that might have put Linda under stress.

Yet the life she describes is idyllic. Through her church and the youth group she helped to establish, she has made a lot of friends. She loves Chris and has devoted herself to Gary and Christy. There are no health or financial issues. For nearly a year she has known something is very wrong, frighteningly wrong, but has tried desperately to hold things together.

Over the next three weeks I manage to see Linda twice a week. When the antidepressants begin to take effect, she is able to concentrate for longer periods and think about the future. Linda looks at the world with the eyes of an artist. She shows me some of her drawings from the previous few months. Some are simply of eyes staring out of the page, or of unseeing faces. They are immensely powerful.

'How do you decide what to paint?' I ask her during one of our sessions.

She shrugs. 'Nature. Animals. Pictures in my head. I don't think I'm a good enough artist to put on canvas exactly what I see. If I could, then I think people would think I was exaggerating.' She laughs for the first time since I've met her.

'When I was young, living in Africa, I used to ride my horse or walk along dry riverbeds before the rains came. I used to look for weathered stones and driftwood, worn smooth by the current. One of my favourite places was sitting on an old gnarled log under a weeping willow near the Gwelo River. The log may have been dead but it was full of life. Tiny ants marched in trails, spiders wove webs in the cracks and caterpillars crawled along the branches. I could spend all morning lying on that log.'

'Where in Africa did you grow up?'

'Rhodesia.'

'Do you miss it?'

Her sad smile says it all.

'What do you miss most?'

'The sense of space . . . the smell of rain . . . the isolation . . .' Her voice trails off.

'When did you leave?'

'In 1976.'

'Have you been back since?'

'Just once, in 1981.'

'Why did you leave?'

'The war. There didn't seem to be a future for whites in the new Zimbabwe. Chris was working as a lawyer and part of his job was to help defend the black independence leaders who were in jail. One of these men told him that whites would never be welcome in Zimbabwe under black majority rule. I think that was the final straw. We knew that we had to leave.'

Linda tells me the story of her great-uncle, William Harvey-Brown, the first in her family to live in Africa. He was a well-known writer, hunter and naturalist in America, working for the Smithsonian Institution, when in 1889 he took part in an expedition to Africa to study a total eclipse of the sun. He invited his younger brother, Arthur Houston-Brown (Linda's grandfather), to join him.

Afterwards, Arthur went back to America, but William stayed on. The scramble for Africa had started and all the European powers were racing to carve up the continent. William joined the pioneer corps being assembled by Cecil Rhodes to cut a road into Mashonaland and start a white settlement (Salisbury) to the north of the Limpopo River. He was one of the original pioneers of Southern Rhodesia and received his payment in land. He called his property Arlington Heights and it covered an area that is now Harare International Airport.

Back in America, Linda's grandfather went to Princeton University and gained degrees in electrical and civil engineering. Later he helped electrify the New York tramways. But in the mid-1890s his brother convinced him to return to Africa. Both of them became ranchers and miners in Rhodesia, with mixed success. By the time Linda was born, the family's land holdings had been broken up and sold.

Linda talks a lot about her father, but not her mother. When I ask her, she shrugs. 'She left when I was eight. I don't remember much about her.'

I wait for her to say something else. She seems to be racking her brain for a memory.

'For a while, my family lived in an old boarding house in Gwelo called the Park Hotel. We had one large, long room divided by two big cupboards. My sister and brothers and I slept in the area behind the cupboards, which had a bed in each corner. It was very dark because there were no windows in our half of the room. On the other side of the cupboards, Mum and Dad had a double bed, a small table and a window that overlooked the back garden. It was a bleak place with low-watt bulbs and echoing floors. It had long, dark passages that I used to hate.

'One Christmas morning, I found a teddy bear at the end of my bed. He was plump and beautiful and I named him Dumpy. Straight away I looked for my old teddy bear so that they could play together. I couldn't find him and grew quite desperate. He'd been with me for as long as I could remember.

' "Where is my teddy bear?" I asked.

' "You've got a new one," my mother said.

' "Yes, but where is my real one?"

' "He was old and dirty so I threw him away. Now you have a nice new friend."

'I started to sob uncontrollably. "I want my bear, I want my bear . . ."

' "Don't be silly," she said dismissively. "All teddy bears are the same."

'She was wrong, of course, but I couldn't tell her that.'

'Why not?' I ask Linda.

'She wouldn't have listened. I punched Dumpy, and left him in the dark side of the room – the ultimate punishment.

'I remember the day she left,' she says now, her voice becoming detached and unemotional. 'I was lying in bed in our room at the Park Hotel. I hadn't been well. I saw my mother standing in the doorway holding a suitcase and wearing a beige coat. The sunlight was on her hair and she looked very beautiful. My sister Annette always told me how soft our mother's hair was. I asked her where she was going.

' "To the hospital."

' "Are you sick?"

'She didn't answer.

' "How long will you be away?"

' "Just a few days."

'That was it. She didn't kiss me goodbye, or leave a note on the table – nothing. That was thirty years ago.'

She falls silent and gazes out the window of the consulting room, across the playing fields of the local school.

'How do you feel about your mother now?' I ask.

Linda shrugs. 'It was a long while ago.'

'Have you seen her since then?'

'Four times.'

There is no hint of anger or regret in her voice. Perhaps there had been once, but in the midst of her depression Linda can't summon up the emotion again.

I ask Linda what happened after her mother left. She tells me how she and Annette were sent off to a Christian holiday camp for several days, living in tents in a dusty field outside of Gwelo.

'I wet the bed every night and cried myself to sleep. After three days the missionaries called Dad and asked him to come and fetch me. He said we weren't going back to the Park Hotel. We were going to live in a proper house with lots of bedrooms and bunk beds. I was so happy. Now we could live like other families.

'Apparently we'd lived at the same house before – 5 Maple Avenue – when I was younger. I don't remember anything about that time.'

Linda grows a little agitated at having forgotten details like this. She seems to want to put everything in place to make it easier to understand.

'When did you realize that your mother wasn't coming back?' I ask.

'Dad made us sit down on the bed next to him, Annette on one side and me on the other. "She's gone away. She's never coming back," he said.

' "Why? Is she dead?" I asked.

' "No. She's just not coming back."

' "Where are Brendan and Clive?" Annette asked.

' "She's taken them, but I'm going to get them back," he said, sounding angry. "I don't care what she wants, but she's not breaking up this family."

'I knew at that moment that my life would never be the same again. Something had changed and it couldn't be changed back. I burst into tears.'

Linda has been staring out the window and seems to forget I am even in the room. I don't interrupt her chain of thought. I can always go back and ask questions later.

'Brendan and Clive came home within a few days. Brendan kept asking me why Mum had gone away and when she was coming back.

' "Maybe tomorrow," I kept telling him. I didn't have the heart to tell him the truth. This went on for months until one day I snapped, "Don't ask me any more, OK? She's gone. She's never coming back."

'He looked at me with his huge blue eyes and I felt terrible. I wanted to bite my tongue off.'

Linda looks up self-consciously. She apologizes for waffling on, but then remembers something else.

'After Mum left, Dad took all of us to see the sea for the first time. We went by train and it took about three days to reach Fishhook in South Africa. Dad sang songs along the way, like "Blue Moon" and "Keep Your Sunny Side Up". Each time the train stopped, dozens of street vendors would crowd the platforms selling nuts, fruit and maize biscuits.

'When I first set eyes on the Indian Ocean, the sheer size of it frightened me. The horizon seemed higher than the land and I expected the water to sweep in and carry us away. I was a pretty good swimmer, but I wasn't used to waves and backwash. I got dumped quite badly.

'I have an abiding image from that holiday. My dad is standing waist deep in the water, with his back to the sea, looking at us playing on the sand. He is silhouetted against the sky, happy, strong and vibrant. But I can see a wave coming behind him and in my mind I know it's going to knock him over and carry him away from us.

'I panic and call out as the wave hits him. Water explodes all around him and his body shudders. But he stays there, like a rock. I felt then that he would be there for ever. Nothing could ever knock him down.'

4

SATURDAY, 4 MARCH 1989

Linda Caine

Chris has been following me around all week. If I go to the kitchen he finds some excuse to come and talk to me. At other times, I hear his footsteps on the stairs behind me.

'I'm really OK, you don't have to guard me.'

'I know. I just needed to wash my hands.'

I know he's lying, but I don't care.

Every morning, when he wakes up, he looks at me as though searching for a sign that I might be happier. I can't look into his eyes. I'm scared of what I might see. A lack of hope? Disappointment?

The last few days have been strange because I keep thinking I shouldn't be here. I shouldn't be folding the washing, or making the beds. I'm supposed to be dead. Chris hasn't told Gary and Christy what really happened last Saturday. He just said I was upset and sad. Since then I've tried to seem happy and 'normal' around them, but I feel so helpless. It's as though my mind has slipped out of gear and is running in neutral. I can't hold my thoughts together.

Each morning when I go to the Chaucer, I tell myself, 'Right, I *will* do something today. I'll write a letter, or draw something, or read a book.' But when I get there, I just sit and stare out the window. I managed to sleep today, but I'm still exhausted. Poor Chris, he looks even worse than I do. He's had to do the school runs every morning and afternoon, as well as drop me off at the Chaucer and pick me up again. His secretary, Margaret, has been rearranging appointments and apologizing to clients.

'Hey, team, how about a Gandhi special for supper?' he says.

Gary and Christy don't have to be asked twice. The Gandhi is our favourite Indian restaurant. Chris orders over the phone and collects the take-away fifteen minutes later. We set out a feast on the coffee table – lamb tikka, sag bhaji and chicken, with nan bread all round.

My mind is still in neutral, but I go through the motions of eating and watching a movie on TV. I think all of us are grateful for the distractions. The end of the movie takes me by surprise. Has it been two hours? Chris gets up and switches the TV off.

'OK, you two. Brush your teeth and get up to bed.'

There's not a murmur of complaint from Gary and Christy. This is what it's been like lately. No arguments about bedtime, homework done, rooms tidy, school bags ready each morning. I know why. They're on their best behaviour because of me. Isn't it strange: my children are doing exactly as I've always wanted, but I feel guilty instead of happy.

On Friday I spend another six hours in the Chaucer sitting like a vegetable. By the time I get home I'm determined to do *something* worthwhile. Kneeling on the lawn, I start pulling dandelions and weeds out of the garden. The next thing I remember is the dusk. Where did the time go? Next to me is an impressive pile of weeds. At least I've managed to do *that*!

I pick out a few large dandelions as a treat for Nibbles. When I open the door of the wooden summer house I hear him shuffling in his hutch. A rake has fallen over from behind the door. As I bend down to pick it up, I see the roll of newspaper on the floor. It's still lying where I dropped it after I hit Christy. I stand there, frozen in time, staring at the paper. The reality of last Saturday almost overwhelms me. It wasn't a dream! It was real!

After a while, I force myself to stand and put the dandelions in Nibbles's cage. My hands are shaking as I close the door.

Back in the kitchen Chris finds me clutching the sink with both hands.

'What's wrong?'

'Nothing.'

'You're shivering.'

'I'm OK.'

'Go and sit down. I'll get you a glass of wine.'

He leads me to the lounge like a child. I listen to him opening a bottle. I don't deserve him.

MONDAY, 20 MARCH 1989

After three weeks as a day patient, I'm allowed to stay at home. Twice a week I have appointments at the Chaucer. Eventually, I start driving myself, which gives me a great sense of achievement because it means I can do school runs again.

I'm also trying to stay on top of the housework, but there's a pile of unwashed laundry and another of ironing. I'm normally on top of everything, but nowadays I'm so slow. It takes a whole weekend to do chores that used to occupy a morning.

I didn't go to church on Sunday. I haven't been since the breakdown. Last Wednesday I went to see Ben and Joan. I didn't know what I was going to say. As it turned out, I just kept telling them that I was sorry. There were no recriminations. They hugged me and said they were praying for me.

Ever since the suicide attempt, I've been avoiding people. I don't want to play squash, or badminton, or go shopping. Even when I go to the supermarket, or the corner store, I pray that I don't run into anyone I know. The thought of having to maintain a normal conversation terrifies me. I haven't the strength or the energy. I know what I'm doing. I'm hiding. I'm scared they'll all notice something wrong with me.

On Mondays and Thursdays I drive to the Chaucer to see Dr Royston. I still don't know what to make of him. I can't place him in life. Is he young and prematurely grey, or is he old with a young face? His clothes give no clues – he wears a suit and tie. The only thing that sets him apart from the other consultants I see arriving at the hospital is his shock of rather wild grey hair. I don't know why exactly, but I trust him. He listens. Mainly he wants to know about how I'm coping at home. He asks about Gary and Christy. Do they get on well together? Who do they take after most? Where do they go to school? He's interested in my painting and wants to see some of my drawings. A couple of times, he's asked me about my dreams, but I couldn't remember any.

'That's OK. But if you *do* remember, I'd like to hear about them. Some people find it helps to keep a notepad and pen beside their bed. They jot down a few words if they wake in the middle of a dream. It can help you remember.'

I don't know anything about psychotherapy. I don't know what he expects of me. At the moment, we just seem to talk. There doesn't seem to be any set plan or list of topics he wants us to cover. I arrive and we chat about the weather or the traffic. Then he gets me to talk about what I've been doing and how I've been feeling. I guess he's trying to see if the drugs are working.

On the first day of spring I can hear schoolchildren playing on the sports field outside. I stand at the window, watching them chase each other, filling the air with laughter. Dr Royston is watching me, saying nothing. He doesn't seem to mind long silences.

'What are we doing here?' I sigh.

'Talking.'

'What good will that do?'

'I'm trying to understand you. I know you think these problems of yours have come out of the blue, but I suspect it may not be that simple. You have the answer. It might not seem that way, but it's inside you.' He taps the side of his head and joins me at the window.

A green caterpillar is crawling along the window ledge, lifting its middle and sliding forward. It reminds me of when I was a child, sitting on the old log on the Gwelo River, watching the insects that lived in the cracks and crevices.

Dr Royston wants to know about my family so I tell him about my dad and my brothers Clive and Brendan, my half-brothers Sean and Jemal, and my sister Annette.

'What did your father do?' he asks.

'He sold insurance. He went away a lot and I was always afraid that he wouldn't come back.'

'What made you think that?'

'I don't know. He used to say to me, "Don't worry, darling, at eight o'clock when you go to bed, just look at the moon and say goodnight to me. I'll be looking at the same moon and saying goodnight to you." I wrote a poem about it:

> *'Don't worry darling,*
> *I* will *be home soon.*
> *Remember at eight*
> *To look at the moon.*
> *Say, "Goodnight, Daddy"*
> *– I'll say goodnight too*
> *And I'll look at exactly*
> *The same moon as you.'*

'What happened after your mother left?' he asks.

I tell him how Dad kept working and travelling because we needed the money. Meanwhile, Annette tried to be a substitute mother. She used to rush home from school to give Clive his bottle and make sure that Brendan and I bathed and brushed our teeth. It was her job to make sure that everything was OK, just in case the social workers called around to check up on us.

We had a succession of white housekeepers who looked after us. I didn't like most of them. I liked the black staff – Kaderi, our cook, his wife Helena and the gardener, Aaron.

Helena was a beautiful, round lady who had a smile that was like the sun rising. She adored her two fat little children who adored her right back. As she cleaned or prepared food, they clung to her skirts, or played nearby. Sometimes she paused to play a clapping game with them, or chase them around the trees. At other times she sat and cradled them, singing in a soft, crooning voice.

If she saw me sitting in the branches of the mulberry tree, she'd say, 'What you doing up there, missy?'

'Nothing.'

'You come down and eat with us now.'

I'd jump down and squat beside the fire. Helena let me share their sadza and roast flying ants.

My voice breaks as I talk, and I realize I'm close to tears. Dr Royston hands me a tissue.

'It sounds as though you were quite a tomboy,' he says.

'I didn't know the colour of my feet until it rained and I ran through the wet grass.'

He laughs. His voice has a soft reassuring rhythm like a familiar song or a nursery rhyme.

I start telling him about Prince, my horse. I was thirteen years old and already tall for my age. Riding had become my passion.

Annette, Brendan, Clive and I shared a small, fat pony called Tinker and took turns riding him. He was bow-legged and pigeon-toed in his back legs. He couldn't go faster than a slow canter, but he was ours and we loved him.

One weekend in 1964 I needed Tinker for a Pony Club meeting, but it was Brendan's turn to ride him. I pleaded with him to swap days, but he wouldn't do it. Normally, I wouldn't have minded, but I'd promised my friend Sheryl that I'd be there. She didn't have a phone so I couldn't call her.

I was furious at Brendan. I pleaded with Dad to get involved.

'Lindy, listen to me,' he said, trying to calm me down. 'A friend of mine has two horses that haven't been ridden for ages. He told me that you kids were welcome to ride one.'

I couldn't believe it. 'When? Where? Can we go now?'

'I don't know how you're going to do it by tomorrow,' he said. 'The farm is five miles out of town and he doesn't have a horsebox.'

'I could ride. If we leave really early, I'll have enough time to ride back into town and give the horse a rest before Pony Club in the afternoon.'

Dad laughed at my enthusiasm and feigned surprise when I threw my arms around his neck.

Up early the next morning, I dressed in jeans, boots and a T-shirt. My hair was always tied back in a ponytail and rarely washed. Dad drove me out to the farm and dropped me near the stables. His friend was a middle-aged hobby farmer, who worked all week in town. He wore John Lennon-style glasses that made him look cross-eyed because they were too small for his round face.

Showing me the saddle and bridle, he pointed out the path to the paddock.

'You might need these,' he said, handing me a battered tin full of horse cubes. 'Just rattle them. Take the horse with the shorter mane. The other one is very headstrong. He threw his last rider.'

I glanced at the bridle in dismay. The buckles had rusted and the leather had hardened under a layer of dirt and mould. Who would let such a thing happen? Finding some saddle soap, I began scrubbing. Most of the dirt would have to wait until later when I could take it all apart.

Hefting the saddle over my arm, I set off along the path. It was barely eight o'clock and already the sun stung my forearms. The farmer hadn't mentioned how far I had to walk. The saddle and bridle grew heavier and twice I had to stop and rest.

When I arrived, one of the horses was obscured by trees and the other was just a speck on the far side of the paddock. I rattled the can of cubes and the nearer horse lifted his head and began walking towards me. He was a chestnut gelding, so thin that his ribs and hips stuck out like sticks in a sack. He reminded me of Don Quixote's Rosinante.

He trotted right up to me and reached forward to get the cube in my outstretched hand. His ears came forward and the right one tilted sideways and inward until it almost touched his left. I reached out and patted his neck. A cloud of dust rose in the sunlight.

What will they say at the Pony Club?

Glancing into the distance I wondered about the other horse. I rattled the cubes again, to no response.

'Shhhhh, steady, boy,' I whispered, as I threw the saddle on the gelding. He began jogging sideways as I tried to mount him, but I managed to settle on his back.

An astonishing transformation took place as we trotted down the path towards the shed. This dusty, unkempt bag of bones no longer shambled. Instead he danced beneath me, with his neck arched and ears pricked forward. It took all my strength to hold him. He wanted to run. He felt so alive.

I glance up self-consciously. Dr Royston is still looking at me intently. I feel relieved. Whenever I start telling him a story I'm afraid he'll get bored, or tell me to move on. Maybe I'm wasting his time.

He pours another cup of coffee and leans back in his chair. 'You were telling me about Prince,' he says.

I didn't know his name then. I rode him back to the shed and started grooming his coat. Beneath the dust and mud I found he was a rich red chestnut colour, with a mane so long that it draped over his neck. I remembered what the farmer had said and wondered if I should go back and check the other horse in the paddock. No, this horse intrigued me. He had real spirit and a spark in his eyes. Much later, I learned that he'd languished in that paddock for nearly ten years, without supplementary feeding or anybody riding him.

Saddling him again, I tried to walk down the driveway, but he wanted to jog, with his neck arched and his knees lifting high like the Hackney show horses. I shortened the reins and kept talking to him. We rode towards town along the wide stretch of land between the farm fences and the road. Everything seemed to fascinate him; his ears were pricked forward and he looked this way and that. He was like a coiled spring, waiting to be let loose. I knew I should get him into town quickly to let him rest for a few hours, but another part of me wanted to give in to him and let him run.

About a mile and a half from the stables, I stopped holding him back. As I loosened the reins he began to canter. Within moments, his stride lengthened into a gallop. We were flying. Through broken scrub, across ditches and uneven ground. I held his mane and laughed. His hooves barely seemed to touch the ground. This was the most amazing ride of my life. After about half a mile I had to take a short cut over a railway line. I should have let him run earlier because he showed no sign of slowing down. I shortened the reins and tried to pull him in, but he had the bit between his teeth.

We were close to the road by now. Trucks and cars whizzed by. I tried to turn him back towards the bush, hoping he'd get tired and run himself out. He fought me. With all my strength I pulled his head around until it was almost against my knee, but still only managed to turn him slightly away from the road. His pace didn't slacken.

I looked up and saw strands of wire catch the sun. The railway line had been fenced off to prevent people walking on the tracks. It was too late to turn him away. I let his head go. Bravely, he tried to jump, but we were too close, going too fast. The world turned upside down. I remember seeing the sky blacked out by the gelding above me. I thought, 'Please don't land on top of me.'

Then my head exploded.

I don't know how long I was unconscious. I woke up with something tugging at my ankle. At first I wasn't sure what had happened. Then I saw the gelding grazing near me. The reins were caught around my ankle. I lay and watched him for a while, relieved to see that he wasn't limping. Slowly, I moved my arms and legs to make sure nothing was broken. My head hurt, but there was no blood.

I stood up and led the gelding up and down. He still moved freely. Then I looked at the fence. Only the top strand had broken. I went and stood next to it. The strands were about twelve inches apart and four were still intact. He had cleared four feet at a run-away gallop with only a few moments to prepare himself.

Any thought of going to the Pony Club had gone. Instead, I rode slowly to the showgrounds, where we stabled Tinker. A set of practice jumps had been set up in the arena. Lightweight wooden poles were balanced on white-painted drums. Pausing before the first jump, I set myself and gently clicked my tongue. In a handful of strides he was over the first and turning to approach the second hurdle. This horse didn't just jump, he flew! All I had to do was point him in the right direction and stay on his back.

That night I couldn't sleep I was so excited. Dad called his friend in the morning to ask if I could keep him at the stables for a couple of weeks.

'She's taken the wrong horse,' he said. 'That horse is unrideable.'

Dad could see me shaking my head.

'She's confident that she can handle him,' he said.

I nodded forcefully.

Dad accepted full responsibility and thanked him again for lending us the horse. 'Has he got a name?' he asked. 'Prince? That's nice. I'll let her know.'

Over the next few weeks I experimented with different bits on the bridle. I was never totally in control riding Prince, but I didn't mind that. There was something in his spirit that I didn't want to subdue. He never shied away from a jump, or baulked at a new challenge.

Pretty soon I was begging Dad to buy him for me. He was in such bad condition that we picked him up for a very good price. I groomed him every day and gave him extra food but he didn't gain a lot of weight. He had too much energy.

After school or first thing on Saturday morning, I ran the quarter mile to the paddock where Prince was kept. As soon as he heard my whistle, he transformed himself from a rangy, shambling creature into a dancing steed. He nuzzled my pockets for the carrots and apples that I normally brought. Prince seemed to sense that I needed to escape from things at home. I gave him space to run and I knew he wouldn't stop until *he* was ready.

Sometimes, I rode alongside the railway tracks where firebreaks had been cleared on either side. The steam trains were fired by coal and the slightest spark could set the bush alight. The train from Gwelo to the smaller town of Selukwe carried passengers as well as freight. Prince and I would start along the firebreak. He knew what was coming and would dance sideways, tossing his head until the train caught up. Then I let him have his head and his stride lengthened. Leaning from the open carriage windows, the passengers would cheer us on as we jumped logs and ditches. I threw my head back and laughed, my shirt billowing and hair flying.

What a magical time. The world stood still. Nothing else existed except for Prince, me, and the train racing through the bush.

As I finish, I fall silent. Dr Royston says nothing. He waits for the memory to fade and my eyes to meet his.

'I'm sorry.'

'Why are you apologizing?'

'I've been prattling on.'

'No. You've been telling me a story.' He pauses and looks at me intently, as if capable of reading my thoughts. My coffee has grown cold.

'What happened to Prince?' he asks.

I can feel my eyes mist over. 'I don't know if I can do this.'

'Take your time.'

It's silly really – crying after all these years. I must have been fourteen by then. I woke up very early one morning to the sound of men talking. They weren't speaking English, so I couldn't understand what they were saying, but I heard the urgency in their voices. Kaderi, our cook, was talking to another man. He mentioned the name 'Philemon' and then 'Prince'.

Philemon was in charge of the stables at the showground. I leapt out of bed, and Dad caught me as I ran up the passage.

'What's happened?' I pleaded.

'It's Prince. He's sick. They think it's colic.'

I tried to wrestle out of his arms. 'Let me go! Let me go! I have to see him.'

'Sshhhh, Lindy. I'll call the vet. You go and get dressed.'

Soon we discovered that someone had come to the stables during the night and fed Prince mealies (dry maize). Some time afterwards Prince had broken out of the stable or been let out. It was a hot night and the maize was dry. Prince had grown thirsty and had a lot to drink. Now the maize in his stomach had started to swell.

When I arrived, a groom was leading Prince in circles around one of the holding yards, trying to keep him moving. The gelding was in obvious pain. He kept stopping and kicking at his stomach with his back legs. I knew enough about colic to know we had to keep him moving and hope the blockage in his system would move. I took over from the groom and kept walking with Prince until the vet arrived.

He took Dad to one side for a quiet word. 'I want to hear it too,' I demanded. Dad agreed. The vet told us the maize had compacted in Prince's stomach. 'To be honest, I don't think he can survive. He's in a lot of pain. I think we should put him to sleep.'

'You can't,' I cried. 'No!'

Dad had his arms around me. He and the vet looked at each other.

'Can't we at least try?' Dad asked him.

The vet called for some warm water. He gave Prince an enema as well as an injection. Then he told me, 'You must keep him moving. He can't lie down. I'll come back in three hours. If he falls before then and can't get up, call me straight away.'

Dad had to go to work soon after that. I walked Prince from one side of the showground to the other, talking to him constantly. I told him how the people on the Selukwe train would miss us if we didn't race them any more. And about all the lovely things that we'd find on the riverbed when it dried up after the rainy season.

Every so often Prince paused and kicked violently at his stomach. He lay down and rolled once before the vet came back at 11 a.m. I was able to coax him to his feet again quite quickly. Apart from a few droppings he still hadn't managed to pass the mealies. Prince didn't try to kick this time as the enema mixture was pumped into him. He was too exhausted. The vet put his hand on my shoulder.

'Young lady, I know you love this horse, but colic is a terrible way for him to die. But I guess while he stays on his feet there's a chance the blockage will break up. Keep him walking. I'll come back at four.'

We walked some more – back and forth across the showground. Prince carried his head lower now and gave muffled grunts when he stopped to kick at his stomach. He fell again, and took longer to get up this time. When the vet came back I knew he was surprised to find Prince still on his feet, let alone able to walk. He pumped Prince's stomach and went away again.

Time seemed to slow down. Prince carried his head lower and lower as the day wore on. I put his head over my shoulder, trying to carry some of the weight for him. With my ear against his neck, I could hear his deep, soft groans. I felt so helpless. Dad came back after work. He walked alongside us for a while but then had to go home to look after Annette, Brendan and Clive.

As darkness fell there was just the light from the tack room and the fire outside Philemon's house. I could hear the low murmur of voices around the fire. Every now and then Philemon came and checked on us as we walked. Prince fell and rolled twice more. Each time it took longer for him to rise. I begged him to live. I don't know when the emptiness began seeping into me. Perhaps when I began stumbling as well and I had to keep resting from the weight of his head on my shoulder.

Blindly, we stumbled from one side of the field to the other. His low groans had become deep grunts. He had difficulty keeping his balance. Thinking it might help him if he could have a short rest, I walked back to the stables and leaned him against the poles that separated the stalls. I stood and supported him on the other side. By then it was almost midnight.

Dad and Annette arrived. Prince suddenly took a couple of steps, then shuddered. His knees began to buckle. I leaned hard against him, trying to support his weight, but I couldn't hold him up. As he fell, I had to jump backwards so as not to be crushed. Then I knelt beside him in the dust, stroking his ears and the soft skin between his nostrils. I begged him not to die. My fingers felt wet. In the dim light from the lantern in Philemon's hand, I saw blood on my hands.

Prince's eyes were open, but unseeing. He didn't respond to me any more. I knew I had lost him and I couldn't bear it. I cried and held his head. Dad put his arm around me and said, 'Let him go now, Lindy. He tried so hard, but you must let him go now.'

I couldn't. I loved him too much to let him go. Before Dad took me home, I cut a piece of Prince's mane so I would always have a part of him with me. I still have it.

Robin Royston

Linda is crying as though Prince died only yesterday and not twenty-four years ago. Brushing the tears away with the back of her hand, she tries to hide her face.

I look at the clock. It has been a long session, but a very important one. From my growing knowledge of Linda's life, her relationship with Prince transcended almost all the others in her childhood, apart from perhaps that with her father. By comparison, the loss of her mother seems nowhere near as traumatic as the death of her horse.

She shed no tears when she told me of her mother leaving. She has barely even acknowledged the role that she played in her childhood. And while the housekeepers came and went, Prince was one of the few constants in her life. What was missing in her everyday life that made this relationship so important? Why is she still grieving?

She wipes her eyes with a tissue and blows her nose. Pushing back her hair, she makes a conscious effort to pull herself together. I can tell that she is admonishing herself. She thinks it silly and childish to be crying over something that happened so long ago. Yet to my mind the death of Prince has a resonance that has carried on until the present day. I can't help feeling that I am part of a similar drama. Linda is like her horse – deeply wounded, walking round and round in agony. She can see no reason for her pain and no treatment that can take it away. I have to keep her on her feet, to keep her moving forward. The answer lies within her. It invariably does.

Linda doesn't have an identifiable psychiatric disorder such as schizophrenia or bipolar disorder. And although the anti-depressants have made a slight difference, she hasn't responded to them as well as I'd hoped.

The pattern of her moods has begun moving me away from thinking that her depression is caused by biological factors that will respond to drugs. Her mood changes too quickly, for one thing. One minute she is fine, able to laugh at one of my feeble jokes, the next racked by sobs when I touch a 'landmine' hidden beneath the surface.

She still struggles to cope with the everyday stresses of living. And if these grow to be too much for her, she will almost certainly become suicidal again.

Nothing has emerged in the present day that can explain her feelings. There has been no bereavement, or trauma. Her marriage is strong. There are no financial worries, or health problems. All of this suggests that the root of her emotional turmoil and depression might lie in her past. It could be something that she doesn't realize affected her so dramatically. It's not unusual for people to shrug off hardship, sadness or grief and get on with their lives, but have these things impact upon their lives in ways they can't imagine, even years later.

The fundamental basis of psychoanalysis and psychotherapy is that all of us possess an unconscious. It's what a lot of people call our sub-conscious mind. It's a part of our mind that we're not usually aware of, but it has a huge influence over what we do and who we are.

By talking to Linda about her past and the present and asking her about her dreams, I am trying to discover what might be going on beneath the surface in her unconscious mind. I know this seems strange to Linda. But the unconscious mind *is* quite strange. It doesn't operate according to the rules of common sense.

The human brain has developed over many thousands of years, but the cognitive part, which is the most highly evolved, is the newcomer. It's remarkable how quickly our thinking has been able to separate itself from the rest of our mind. Human beings can think in the abstract, even think our feelings into submission, or make up all sorts of convincing reasons for the dreadful things we do. We have developed a 'laterality' in our brains, so that some processes are carried out on the left side (for example, language, reading, writing and talking), while others are performed by the right side of the brain (for example, artistic abilities). The two sides usually work together and 'co-operate', but they can be in opposition. Somewhere in the middle of this complex system of thinking and feeling are our memory circuits. No wonder the mind is so prone to conflict.

Linda has managed to calm down. 'I'm not getting any better, am I?' she asks. 'Why can't I pull myself together? Chris, Gary and Christy are hurting and all I can think about is me, me, me. I'm so sick of myself.'

Here is a real self-loathing. Where has it come from?

'You are beginning to allow yourself to feel,' I tell her gently. 'I'd call that progress.'

'I don't know what's worse – being able to feel or being numb.'

'Being able to feel,' I reassure her. 'Because it makes us who we are.'

She nods and gives me a brave smile.

5

JUNE 1989

Linda Caine

On some days, for no reason, I get shaky. That's when I totally avoid contact with people. I take the phone off the hook and park the car away from the house. I close the curtains and don't answer the doorbell. I don't know what I fear. Not being able to cope? Breaking down in public? Having madness seen in me? Three months have passed since I drove away from the house intending to die. Nothing has taken the blackness away. I still struggle with the simplest of tasks, even having a sick child for the day.

Gary is upstairs. He's home from school with a high temperature. Normally I feel like tying him down to keep him still, but he's spent most of the day in bed, or playing on his computer. He's only had two cup-a-soups and three pieces of dry toast since dinner last night. That's not like Gary at all.

I've been shaky all day. It got so bad this morning I telephoned Carol Trigger at the Chaucer. Sometimes I find it's enough just to speak to her and I relax. She suggested I go in for a coffee, but I have Gary to look after. I could have called Chris, but he has enough on his plate without any tearful messages from me.

His firm is considering shutting down most of the Canterbury office. Some of the partners feel it doesn't generate enough of a profit to warrant keeping it open in its present form. They want to reduce it to being just a small office, serving just the Archbishop of Canterbury and the Dean and Chapter. This would mean laying off practically all the staff. It would also mean that Chris would have to go to work in London instead of Canterbury most of the time, which he would hate. Each time there's a partners' meeting in London, Chris comes home drained and exhausted. He's drinking more and I know he's keeping the worst news from me.

I've been trying to tell Dr Royston about the flashes that I sometimes get when I turn on a tap or have a bath. Each time I get to the important details of the story my emotions overwhelm me. I end up sobbing and shaking my head. I hate my weakness. We've wasted two entire sessions like this. I can't hold on to the memory – if that's what it is. I can't hold on to Dr Royston or the Chaucer. My mind just slides away into blankness.

I think I'm wasting everybody's time, but Chris keeps telling me to give it time. That's the problem. Everybody seems to think that I *have* time. But I keep picturing my head as one of those old-fashioned bombs with a spluttering and spitting fuse. Instead of one fuse there are dozens of them, some burning faster than the others. I don't know how to put them out.

At that moment the doorbell rings. I'm standing on the landing, but I can't remember if I was going upstairs or downstairs. I think really hard.

'That's the door, Mum,' says Gary, peering over the banister.

I put my finger to my lips, signalling him to be quiet. Why am I telling my son to be quiet? What's the matter with me? I creep down the stairs and stand behind the curtains in the lounge. I can peek through a narrow space in the drapes to see who's outside. It's a lady from the church. I don't want to talk to her. I don't want to talk to anyone.

She rings the doorbell again. I look towards the stairs. 'Please don't come down, Gary,' I whisper to myself. 'Just stay in your room. Please, stay in your room.'

When she's gone, I collapse on the sofa and wait for my heart to stop racing. I don't want to make conversation, or try to act normal. I don't want people pitying me or making sympathetic noises or wondering what's wrong with me. I just want to be left alone.

*

The next morning I suffer a complete blank. When I come round I'm in the car driving on an unfamiliar road. It's a real shock. I pull over and try to think. Where am I? Where have I been? I turn the car around and drive back, hoping to recognize somewhere familiar. After about ten minutes I come to the Chaucer Hospital turn-off. Suddenly, I remember that I have an appointment with Dr Royston. I'd left home early because I wanted to have a coffee with Carol Trigger. Sometimes we sit and chat because it helps me relax before my session with Dr Royston.

I park the car at the Chaucer and walk to the psychiatric department. I can't find Carol. Penny Steel, the nurse counsellor, says good morning and asks how I am. I open my mouth to tell her what's happened, but I can't get the words out. I know I'm going to cry. Suddenly the phone rings and Penny turns to answer it. It's Carol calling to say that she's running late.

'Oh, Linda's here now,' says Penny, glancing at me and smiling. 'She's looking so much better today that I'm going to take her to the cafeteria.'

She puts the phone down and marches me off. At the cafeteria I try to tell her what happened. Tears start forming and Penny slams her hand down on the table. 'Linda, pull yourself together,' she barks, sounding like an old-fashioned schoolmarm.

I freeze and feel like a child. I don't say a word.

I wait in the corridor. Dr Royston breezes through the main doors, full of smiles and the joy of spring. His jokes don't cheer me up. I tell him about my drive to the Chaucer and 'coming to' on a strange road. He asks me to retrace things in my memory. What is the last thing I remember?

'Leaving the house . . . backing out of the driveway . . . I don't really know . . .'

'What time was that?'

'About 9.30.'

'And what time did you come to?'

'About twenty-five minutes later. I can't have blacked out. I was driving the car.'

'OK,' he says, 'let's leave that for a while. How have you been feeling?'

I tell him about the past few days, how I've been hiding away from people.

'I keep putting off things like taking books back to the library or shopping for groceries. I don't want to meet anyone, or talk to anyone.'

Dr Royston has such a reassuring voice that I begin to relax. I make another attempt at telling him about the flashes in my mind. But as soon as the image starts to form it slips away. I bite down hard on my lip until I can taste the blood. The pain helps me concentrate. But I can't hold on. It isn't there any more. I could scream I'm so frustrated.

At the end of the session Dr Royston gives me his home telephone number.

'If you start to panic, or things get really bad, I want you to call me. It doesn't matter if it's day or night.'

I look at the piece of paper and get all emotional. I've come to rely on Dr Royston. That's why I'm so terrified that he might write me off as a lost cause. One day he'll say, 'Enough is enough.' That's why I won't abuse his trust. I'm not going to call him at home unless I've reached the very end.

Back at home I spend most of the afternoon tidying up my art room. Then I sit down and begin writing.

Dr Royston, I am writing these thoughts down because when I'm with you I have trouble getting the words out. When I lie down to sleep, or when I'm awake, the things that have happened in my past keep coming into my mind.

A lot of these memories disturb me, but I can't stop thinking about them. I try to keep busy, but I can't concentrate. I end up just feeling sort of numb and dead inside.

When I come to see you, I try to hold on to the memories that disturb me, so I can tell you about them. I'm hoping they might be relevant to why I'm in such bad shape at the moment.

When I've gone through black times in the past, I've always been able to find the reason and it helps me get through it. This time there doesn't seem to be any particular cause – just an overwhelming feeling of hopelessness.

I sit there with you with my emotions swinging wildly, from feeling very foolish and childish, to extremely distressed. I can't explain why.

That's why I've decided to try writing my thoughts down – however nonsensical and out of sequence they come – to see if you can find some rhyme or reason for them.

Afterwards I look at what I've written. The sentences seem very childlike. For a fraction of a second I contemplate ripping out the page and throwing it away. No, I'll keep it. Maybe it will help me get my thoughts straight.

6

TUESDAY, 20 JUNE 1989

Robin Royston

Pigeons flutter out of the way as I stride across the concourse of Charing Cross station. I make the train for Tunbridge Wells with a few minutes to spare. My psychotherapy seminar in London didn't finish until late and then I couldn't get a taxi.

As the train pulls away and crosses the Thames I look up the river towards Westminster. The banks of the river are dotted with brightly coloured barges and every lamppost has a hanging basket of flowers. I love this time of year. The long twilights are made for walking.

The train rattles through south-east London and I flick through the pages of the *Evening Standard*. In the foreign news briefs there is a paragraph about a famine in Ethiopia. I think of Linda. She has a great love for Africa, which comes across in the stories she tells about the landscape and the people. To me it has always seemed to be a place where danger and beauty exist in harmony. I like Linda. She isn't manipulative, or self-seeking. She has no hidden agenda. She wears her pain apologetically, as though she doesn't want anyone's sympathy or help.

I have roughly sixty patients I am seeing regularly and Linda's condition concerns me more than any of the others'. She doesn't seem to be getting any better. If anything, her state of mind has become far more dangerous and unpredictable. She seems devoid of hope and certain of her imminent death. This is more than just a question of depression. Powerful psychological factors are at work although I am no closer to understanding the cause.

Whenever we begin discussing anything sensitive, Linda immediately starts to struggle. I try to get her to slow down and take her time. If we can't charge into the core of the problem, we will work our way in from the edges, picking off pieces as we go.

So far I've flagged certain things in her history that are worth looking at more closely. Her mother leaving is one of them. Although Linda dismisses this as being unimportant, I would be surprised if it didn't impact enormously on an eight-year-old child. And even if the leaving, in itself, wasn't that significant, the early relationship behind that moment must have been crucial.

Linda describes herself as a 'loner', who escaped into the bush on her horse at every opportunity. She remembers suffering from nightmares and being afraid of the dark. She has also described suffering what her family called 'hallucinations' after her mother left. Annette would sometimes find her standing as still as a statue staring into space.

'She sometimes had to push me over to bring me round,' Linda says. 'And they'd say, "Linda's a million miles away," or "Look at Linda daydreaming again." '

Most children have idiosyncrasies – they're scared of the dark, or have nightmares, or wet the bed, or daydream. It might have no significance at all. I simply don't know enough.

When I arrive at Tunbridge Wells station I walk to the squash club where I left my car. At home Lynn sits with me at the kitchen table as I eat a late dinner. I tell her about the seminar and listen to her stories about Mike and Emma. Mike has done a painting for me, which is proudly displayed on the refrigerator door.

Being married to a very intuitive woman can be difficult sometimes. Lynn knows I am concerned about a patient and she guesses it is Linda.

'So what's your opinion, Dr Royston?' she asks light-heartedly.

'I think she's in trouble.'

'Why?'

'I don't know. She's like one of those plants that when you just touch them they explode and the seeds go everywhere.'

'So what lies behind it?'

I shrug. 'It's as though there's something in her mind that wants to get out but each time we move closer she just falls apart.'

Three days later, on 23 June, I have a phone call from the Chaucer. Linda has suffered a major breakdown. She has phoned the psych unit after a sleepless night and Carol Trigger has suggested she come into the hospital. They sit in the lounge and chat, but Linda can't concentrate. She has little idea of where she is and why she is there, according to Carol. Eventually she falls asleep in the lounge.

Carol calls me. 'I'm really worried about her. She needs to be admitted. I've called Ticehurst. They can take her as a voluntary patient. I've also spoken to Linda's insurance company. They're faxing an emergency form for you to sign.'

'How are you going to get her there?'

'I'll drive her.'

'Good.'

I know Ticehurst well. I have worked as a consultant there since 1986, spending Tuesdays and Fridays dealing with outpatients. Although I have access to beds at the hospital, until now I have never had to admit an inpatient.

Ticehurst was built as a private mental hospital in 1792. It was named after the nearby village, less than a mile to the south. Back then it was the sort of place where rich people put their schizo-phrenic sons, or mad Uncle Arthur, or geriatric Aunt Mildred. As recently as twenty years ago it was more like an up-market health spa than a mental hospital. Now the emphasis is on pro-active intervention and treatment, with serious therapeutic programmes. Ticehurst doesn't have the star reputation of a place like The Priory in Roehampton, but it still attracts its fair share of the rich and famous, if not the publicity. Private patients need a lot of money to afford the fees, or in Linda's case private medical insurance.

Two hours later Carol calls me again. Linda has been admitted into Ticehurst.

'How was she when you left?'

'Curled up on the bed, lost in her own world. I tried to explain what was happening, but I don't know how much she understood. I said that you'd come when you could.'

'I'll try to see her tonight.'

I thank Carol and wish her a pleasant weekend. My own is now less certain.

After seeing my last patient I drive the forty-five miles from Canterbury to Ticehurst. Linda is sleeping when I arrive and I decide not to wake her. Instead I go home and plan to call the hospital in the morning.

All evening I keep thinking about Linda. I know that she'll be anxious about her new surroundings and worried that she's let people down. I also know how upset her family will be.

'Why don't you go and see her tomorrow?' Lynn says.

I look surprised. 'It's Saturday.'

'I know, but you're only going to let it bother you all weekend. Go and see her. I'll take Mike and Emma to the park in the morning. We can all do something together in the afternoon.'

Saturday morning has its own rituals in our house. Mike will crawl into our bed at around six, while Emma sleeps peacefully next door in her cot, curled up beneath a small duvet covered in bright colours and stars. At seven I go downstairs to give Mike his cornflakes and find cartoons for him on the TV. Then I make some plunger coffee.

'Do you want marmalade or Marmite on your toast?' I ask Mike.

He looks up at me very seriously. 'Sorry, Daddy, I can't want it.'

Lynn and I laugh. 'So you don't want toast at all?'

'Can't want it,' he repeats. I sense another catchphrase being coined.

I leave home just after nine for the drive to Ticehurst. Twenty minutes later the car swings through the stone gates and follows the curving asphalt road for a hundred yards until the main building comes into view. Built on a ridge, overlooking the patchwork fields of neighbouring farms, the hospital looks like a strange cross between a stately home, a country house hotel and a health farm. The exterior walls are ghostly white in the overcast light. They rise

64

three floors to where the buttressed stone looks almost like battlements.

Once through the front door to reception, I pass through the double doors that lead onto the acute ward on the ground floor. The rooms are built around each side of a central courtyard. There are about twenty-eight beds in all, administered by a small number of trained staff and a larger number of assistants. On the first floor, above the acute ward, is the Young Persons Unit for children and adolescents. Tucked away at the back of this floor are the rooms where I see my outpatients each week.

On the second floor is a ward for the elderly as well as the administration area. The hospital kitchens are on the ground floor, adjacent to the oldest and perhaps slowest lift ever built.

Roger Smith stands in the doorway of the nursing station, filling the frame. Roger, a psychiatric nurse, does night duty and is a tall man with a wonderful sense of humour. He was born in England but went to Australia as a child migrant. Perhaps he and Linda can share their love of wide open spaces.

'Have you forgotten what day it is?' he says. 'I thought you had a family.'

'I just want to look in on Linda.'

'Ah yes. We've had her under close obs [observation]. That one's fighting demons.'

'How has she been?'

'Distressed . . . weepy . . .'

'Has anyone managed to talk to her?'

Roger shakes his head. 'She's in Room 31.'

I head down the corridor and stop at a door opposite the lounge. Knocking gently, I open it slightly. Linda lies curled on the bed, hugging her knees. Her hair has fallen over her face.

The room is quite basic with a bed, side table, wardrobe and chest of drawers. A chair is squeezed into a corner near the window. The overall effect is that of a hotel room, with freshly laundered sheets and a bathroom that smells of pine-scented disinfectant.

'How are you feeling?'

She pushes hair from her eyes. 'Like a failure. Poor Chris. I've let him down.' Her eyes are red-rimmed and she speaks with one hand hovering near her mouth.

'He'll understand.'

I pull the chair closer to the bed and sit down.

'How did you sleep?'

'OK.'

'Did you have dreams that you can remember?'

She shakes her head. 'Is it important? You've asked me that before.'

'Dreams can often tell us things about what's going on beneath the surface, in the unconscious.'

I can see Linda feels slightly uncomfortable with this idea. Perhaps it sounds rather New Age and alternative to her.

'Have you ever heard of Carl Jung?' I ask.

Linda nods uncertainly.

'Well, I'm a Jungian psychotherapist. There are many theories about dreams but no-one has ever come up with any real answer about why we have them and what they mean. Dreams have many different possibilities,' I tell Linda, giving her my own humble opinions. 'Some clearly try to solve a problem that the dreamer is struggling with, some seem to contain a memory from the past for whatever reason and some, however much we try to understand them, seem to lead nowhere. Some reflect our emotions in symbols, like a fire for anger or a wild animal for energy. Unfortunately, there is no code we can use – no dictionary of dream symbols. All we can do is look for the clues and see what sense we can make of each dream.'

I ask Linda if she remembers the magic mirror of many fairy tales.

She nods.

'Whenever someone looks in the mirror it tells them about the future, or the past. Sometimes it reveals secrets and conspiracies. I think dreams can be like that. Like another "mind", sometimes wiser, sometimes evil, but one that each of us should get in tune with.'

'But what does that mean for me?' she asks.

'Your mind is like a little boat on the vast ocean. It has started sinking and we don't know why. The only way to find out is to look under the water and see what caused the hole. The unconscious is like the sea. You and I are on a journey and your boat is sinking. At the moment there's no sight of land, but if we keep looking and stay afloat then maybe a favourable wind or a helpful current will carry us to shore. We need help from your unconscious.'

I explain Jung's theory about 'big dreams' that are very powerful and may even help shape our lives. These often have great meaning but they can be obscure and difficult to understand. They can stay with people all their lives.

As we continue chatting, I explain to Linda the benefits of being in Ticehurst. For one thing, it will mean our sessions can be longer. I won't have other patients waiting and she won't be pressured by the clock to get something out in the open. Nor will she have the day-to-day pressures of being at home. She can totally relax, sleep, read, or go for long walks.

'There are no locks on the doors. Chris and the kids can come and see you at any time. You're a voluntary patient. You can leave whenever you want.'

She seems far more relaxed when I leave. I drop into the nurses' station and leave a note for the staff. I don't want anybody trying to take a detailed history from Linda, or to put pressure on her to take part in the daily programmes of group therapy sessions, exercises or outings. Linda must be given the time and space to get her thoughts together. Then perhaps whatever demons lie inside her might finally be ready to come out.

7

SUNDAY, 25 JUNE 1989

Linda Caine

Trolleys clatter along the corridor, the wheels bouncing over the cracks in the nylon carpet. They're handing out the medications again. Four times a day they come around. It's the medical equivalent of the old-fashioned tea trolley.

A nurse taps on the door and says hello. She's wearing a crisp white shirt and black trousers. She hands me the pills in a little plastic beaker and waits until I've swallowed them. As the door closes another voice in the corridor says, 'Next time, Martha, if you want to take your clothes off, please do it in your room.' Someone mumbles a reply. Maybe it's Martha.

I haven't left this room since I arrived. I lie here, curled up, worrying about Chris and the children. I've let them all down. It would have been better for all of us if I'd driven off the Thanet Way. It would be over . . . done with.

As the trolley rattles onwards down the corridor, I hear footsteps.

'It's only me,' whispers Chris, putting his head around the door. He gives me a smile and pushes the door closed. He's carrying a small suitcase with some of my things.

'I also brought you these,' he says. The bunch of carnations is wrapped in cellophane, with a red plastic ribbon around the stems.

I start to cry. 'I'm sorry . . . I'm sorry . . . I tried so hard . . . but I just couldn't cope.'

He puts his arms around me. 'I know. It's not your fault.'

For a long while we hold each other and I try to draw strength from him. I feel so pathetic and weak. I have the perfect life and I'm screwing it up for everyone.

'This is nice,' he says, glancing around the room. I agree with him. It doesn't feel like a hospital room. The furniture is dark wood, and the curtains are thick and heavy in warm, comforting colours. I have my things around me, and there are relaxing chairs to sit in.

'How are Gary and Christy?' I ask.

'Fine. We're all fine.'

'Is everything OK at the office?'

'Absolutely.'

I know he's trying to reassure me. I've seen him use the same tactics on clients who come to him for help. He tells them not to worry and then does the worrying for them.

Chris is pacing the room, unsure of what to do. Hospitals give him the creeps. They always have. Even when Christy was born he couldn't wait until visiting hours had ended and he could get outside.

'Do you want to go for a walk?' I ask. He looks relieved.

I put on my shoes and we start walking down the corridor. Can Chris guess it's the first time I've done this? A handful of patients are sitting in the lounge. Each seems to inhabit a different space, without acknowledging that anyone else is around them. A middle-aged woman in a floral skirt bustles between them, cleaning ashtrays and dusting the tables. I think she must be a cleaner until somebody says, 'For God's sake, Agnes, just sit down.'

A solid-looking young man with a crew cut is sitting and staring at a half-finished jigsaw. One hand holds a piece in the air, as if he's about to put it down. But nothing happens. It's as if he's frozen in place. Nearby, two young women, one little and one large, are nodding to each other, but saying nothing. One of them has wet cheeks and the other has bandages on her wrists.

Chris walks so close to me, I can feel his arm against mine. He doesn't want to be here. Near the main door, a young man in a tracksuit shambles towards us. His eyes are half closed and he's muttering to himself. Chris tries to avoid eye contact. He wants to flatten himself against the wall.

I feel myself getting anxious. Am I one of them, I wonder? Is this where I'm going? Will they medicate me into non-existence? Am I going to become a twitching, tongue-flapping prisoner of some new drug? Please, God, no. I couldn't live like that.

Yet instead of wanting to run away, I know that I have to stay. Ticehurst frightens me, but it's also somewhere safe. Nobody is judging me here. Nobody has any expectations. Maybe there's something to be said for being mad.

Outside, I put my hand through the crook of Chris's arm and we start walking. It is a clear, warm day and I enjoy the scent of the earth and the light breeze on my face.

'I don't want to leave you here,' Chris says. 'I can't bear the thought of you being here.'

'It's not so bad. I feel safer here.'

'Safe from what?'

'I don't know . . . Myself.'

He can't hide the pained expression on his face.

Not far along the path we come across a bench made from a half-log, under the branches of a tree. Somebody has carved graffiti into the wood: 'Sex drugs and a bacon roll'.

Nearby is a makeshift lawn tennis court. The net droops sadly and in the centre someone has left a pair of trousers. Looking closer, I see a bra in the nearby hedge and a matching pair of white knickers in the compost heap. The rest of the clothes are strewn across the grass. We look at each other and laugh as I tell Chris about Martha. Any moment I expect another naked patient to come streaking through the trees.

'Dr Royston wants me to write down my dreams,' I tell Chris.

'Why?'

'He thinks dreams are sometimes important.'

I expect Chris to be sceptical but instead he says it couldn't hurt. Then I realize that he's so desperate for me to get better, he'll grab at any lifeline. He's not the sort to believe that dreams are windows to the soul. He's the son of a military man – one of the tough love brigade who believe men don't cry and emotions can't be trusted.

The sun disappears and the temperature falls. Chris notices me shivering and insists we go back inside. We almost reach my room when someone begins screaming further down the corridor. It's a horrible, wild, helpless sound. I cover my ears.

'You can't have this,' mutters Chris.

'It's OK, really.'

'No, it's not.'

He goes looking for a member of staff and I hear him talking. 'What are you doing about that noise? It's upsetting my wife.'

Linda McCormack, a nurse and counsellor, puts him in his place. 'The person screaming is also upset. We're trying to find out why.'

Somewhat chastened, Chris comes back to my room and sits on the bed.

'Maybe you could bring Christy and Gary next time,' I suggest.

'I thought it might upset you.'

'I'd still like to see them.'

He nods and glances at his watch. It's a long drive back to Chestfield.

'I'll come tomorrow,' he says, giving me a kiss. 'And I'll tell Gary and Christy that you'll phone them.'

My feet feel chilled, so I decide to thaw them out in a bath. Linda McCormack shows me to the best bathroom. As I walk inside I look down at the tub and suddenly panic. I see myself under water, with a hand over my face. Gasping for breath, I grab hold of the sink to stop myself falling.

Linda McCormack puts her arm around me. 'Are you all right?'

'I think so . . . I'm fine now.' I take a deep breath.

'What happened?'

'I wish I knew.'

She offers to stay with me for a while. 'I'll face my chair away from the bath if that makes you feel better.'

I feel embarrassed but thank her. Linda McCormack is in her early thirties, slim and attractive with short blonde hair and blue eyes. She sits facing the door, asking me questions to keep me occupied.

As I get undressed and take off my bra, the foam cup slips out.

Linda notices the scars across my chest. She says nothing, but I feel self-conscious. I feel I should tell her what happened.

'I had a mastectomy when I was fourteen years old.'

'That's young.'

'I'd just started wearing a bra, which I hated. I noticed a lump in my right breast. I told Annette, my sister, but made her promise not to tell anyone else. Of course, she went straight to Dad. I was furious.'

'I'm sure Annette thought she was doing the right thing.'

'I guess so. The doctor said it was probably just a large cyst but the only way to be sure was to operate. When they opened me up they found a large pear-shaped tumour that was fibrous. The surgeon left me on the operating table and went outside to talk to Dad.

' "I've already started the operation," he explained. "If the tumour is cancerous then she could die because the cancerous cells were released when I cut into it."

' "Can't you do a biopsy?" Dad asked.

' "We don't have the facilities. The samples have to be sent to South Africa."

'The risk that the tumour was malignant must have seemed too great. They decided to give me a mastectomy.

'When I came round the pain was terrible. I looked down and saw all the bandaging. I assumed the lump had gone and everything was OK. The next day a nurse came to change the dressing. She unwound the bandages, then carefully began to remove the large inner pad that had become stuck to my chest. As she freed it, I realized the lump I had thought was my breast was actually just the wadding. With shock, I saw that my right breast was flat, and mottled black and blue. I was stitched from the centre of my chest across to the side of my ribcage, then up to my armpit. A tube stuck out of the top of the incision, with a safety pin attached to the end.

The nurse pulled the top of the tube and snipped off about an inch from the end. I felt sick. As she attached the safety pin back to the end of the tube, I asked her why it was there.

' "To drain fluid from the operation," she replied, matter-of-factly. 'The safety pin is to make sure the tube doesn't slip back inside you. I'll cut a bit off the end each day until it's all out."

' "Is my breast going to grow back?" I asked.

She hesitated, then continued wrapping the new bandage around me. "Somebody will talk to you later," she said. I assumed the answer must be yes, because she had been non-committal. It was two days before somebody gave me a straight answer, but not an explanation.'

Linda McCormack shakes her head sympathetically. 'Was it malignant?' she asks.

'No. Benign.'

'So you didn't need a mastectomy?'

'No.'

Linda McCormack looks at me in disbelief.

'Before I left the hospital a nurse gave me two little sponge cups to fill my bra. That was the total follow-up.'

'You must have been devastated.'

'Not really. It would have been more traumatic if it had happened later. As it was, I was more interested in horses than breasts at that age. My main complaint was that I couldn't ride Prince for a couple of months after the operation.'

'What about boyfriends?'

I laugh. 'They took a while to discover me. I used to get self-conscious when I went swimming. I'd have a wet patch on my right side where the rest of my swimsuit had dried except for the sponge cup. That's when I began growing my hair long so I could drape it over my shoulder and cover that side of my swimsuit.'

'That's clever,' she says, handing me a towel.

I've decided that I like Linda McCormack. When I first met her I thought she was cool and detached, but now I can see her warmth. She's a good listener and seems to care.

'I'm going to be your key-worker,' she says.

'What does that mean?'

'Dr Royston can't always be here so I'm going to liaise with him. If you need someone to talk to, I'll be here for you.'

I like that idea. I wrap myself in a dressing gown and we walk back to my room. I have so many questions I want to ask, yet I feel too exhausted. I curl up on the bed and she puts a blanket over me. I don't remember her leaving.

*

Dr Royston is coming down the corridor. I can hear him saying hello to people and being cheerful. He always seems so positive and upbeat. It's probably part of the job description. He pulls up a chair with his back to the window. I sit cross-legged on the bed, leaning against the wall with a pillow behind my back.

We chat for a while about how I'm feeling. Then he steers the conversation back to my childhood. I don't know what he's hoping to find. I guess things started to unravel about a year before I had the mastectomy. Dad had to go away on business and he couldn't find a housekeeper at short notice. Eventually, he hired a young woman called Connie, who came from one of the townships on the outskirts of Gwelo. Connie was of mixed race; 'coloured', in southern African terms. She had two children of her own.

'Once Connie arrived, she never left,' I tell him, sounding resigned rather than bitter. 'She was only six years older than Annette and the two of them bonded and became friends. I didn't warm to her in the same way. Maybe I was jealous. I could see that Dad liked her a lot. Up until then *I'd* always been his girl.

'I started spending more and more time away from the house, riding horses and exploring the bush. My school grades collapsed and I went from an A-stream student to a C-stream student in less than a year. Perhaps I was trying to punish Dad. I could see he was falling in love with Connie.'

I glance up at Dr Royston to make sure he's still listening. He seems interested, so I carry on.

A lot of kids used to meet at the stables in the afternoon and go riding. I used to join them sometimes. There were Jane and Richard, who were the mayor's children, along with another boy called Eddie and the Butt brothers, John and Michael. We were all about the same age. We played lots of different games on horseback. In one of them you tucked a scarf into the back of your jeans and the others had to chase you and yank it out. One day someone suggested that we play kiss-catchers. The rules were pretty much the same, but whoever you caught you could kiss.

The boys seemed to pick on me. I was quite flattered. But when I turned up at the showground the next day there seemed to be an atmosphere. When I went into the tack room to fetch Prince's saddle, Jane slipped in behind me and told me that their mother had found out about our game. I was being blamed for leading the boys astray, and she and Richard had been told they were not to ride with me any more. I can't be sure but it probably had something to do with the whispers about Dad and Connie. You see, racism was a fact of life in Rhodesia – so much so, that I didn't really think about it much until then.

A divorced white man and his children living under the same roof as an attractive coloured girl was definitely taboo. I didn't notice most of the gossip or hear the rumours. Annette noticed it more. She and I were totally different as sisters. Her shoulder-length hair was dyed blonde, and she had brown eyes. She was about five foot six, with a great figure and lots of boyfriends. By comparison, I was the gawky, gangling kid sister – Gwelo's very own Calamity Jane.

One Saturday night, when I was about fourteen, Dad told Annette to take me out to a dance. I think he wanted me to be more feminine and get out of my scruffy jeans for once. Annette wasn't very happy about having to take me along, but Dad insisted. She went through her wardrobe and found me a Chinese-style dress made of shiny material with a high collar. It was short and very figure-hugging.

Annette curled my hair and did my make-up. She even lent me a pair of her shoes. The dance hall had been done up with bunting and balloons. A large banner was strung across the stage announcing 'Miss Gwelo 1965'. I didn't take any notice. I just wanted to get through the night without doing something clumsy. Dad used always to say, 'If there is nothing for Lindy to fall over, she'll fall over her own feet.' He was right. But when it comes to dancing I have a good sense of rhythm. It's only when I get embarrassed or think people are watching me that I stiffen up and trip over myself.

I was nervous, but began to relax as I listened to the music. The beat was so strong that I could feel the vibrations in the table as I leaned on it. I closed my eyes and lost myself in the music. At one point I went to the toilet and then heard people shouting my name. Someone said, 'You've got to go up. You've been chosen to go in the competition.'

'What competition?'

'Miss Gwelo.'

I laughed, but they were serious. Apparently a panel of judges had been walking around the dance floor choosing girls for the beauty pageant. My first reaction was to run. I dashed back into the toilet and locked myself in a cubicle. Annette came storming in and hammered on the door. 'What are you doing? They're calling your name.'

'No. It's a mistake. They must mean you.'

'Don't be silly. You *must* come out *now*. Everyone's waiting.'

Ten girls were standing at the front of the hall. One of them, Colleen Dale, was in my year at school. We were both fourteen, but all the others were aged sixteen and seventeen. I didn't raise my eyes as I joined them. I was handed the number eleven, which I had to hold in front of me.

The master of ceremonies had a booming voice and I flinched when he announced each of the contestants' names. Everybody knew who was going to win. Moira Felsmith was Gwelo's perennial beauty queen. She had blonde hair, a gorgeous smile and a Marilyn Monroe-type mole.

The dance floor was cleared and seats were pushed back against the walls to create a big open space in the centre of the hall. Then the music restarted and each contestant had to walk around the outside of the dance floor. I wasn't used to wearing high heels and was terrified that I'd fall over in front of everyone. But a strange thing happened. The song had a very strong drumbeat and it gave me a rhythm to walk to. I began to relax as I stepped in time to the beat, and even gave Annette a little wave as I walked past.

Returning to the stage, we all stood in a line holding our numbers. I could see Moira's million-dollar smile. They awarded third place first and then Moira's name was called; she had come second. She looked devastated. I saw surprise register on people's faces. Nobody could believe she hadn't won. Including me. Who could beat Moira? I glanced down the line of girls as a drum began rolling and the judge called for quiet.

He said, 'The winner of Miss Gwelo 1965 is – number eleven.'

I heard a squeal from Annette, whose hands were covering her mouth. What's she on about? I looked down. Even upside down, there was no mistaking the number eleven. It was me! Surely there had to be some mistake.

'Will Linda Houston-Brown please come forward,' said the judge.

I nervously edged a few steps forward. At any moment I expected them to say, 'I'm sorry, we didn't mean number eleven.'

I had to sit on a chair that was meant to be the throne. Moira was standing next to me. The crown was too big and it slipped over my head and rested on my ears. Eventually they managed to balance it. They also put a pale blue 'Miss Gwelo 1965' sash over my shoulder. A photographer from the local newspaper wanted to take some pictures. I wasn't allowed to move my head otherwise the crown would fall over my face. He told me to cross my legs but my dress was so short that I kept tugging it down.

The story ran the next day but without a photograph. I discovered why when I went to the office to order some prints. In every picture Moira looked poised, confident and lovely, while I had a fixed and frozen smile as I tugged down my dress.

'That's a lovely story,' says Dr Royston.

'Do you think so?'

'Like a fairy tale.'

I shrug. 'Boys weren't queuing up to take me out, if that's what you mean.'

He laughs.

'It's true. I felt like the ugly duckling. I was five feet nine and my body embarrassed me.'

'Others saw you differently.'

'I suppose so.'

I can still remember when Dad decided to give me the birds-and-the-bees talk. He called me into his room and put on his important tone of voice. 'Do you know how babies are made?'

I knew the mechanics, of course. I figured it was the same way as puppies were made. People did much the same thing, said Dad, struggling to find the right words. I don't know who was more embarrassed, him or me.

'If you have any more questions, you should ask Annette,' he said.

'OK. Sure.' I just wanted to get away.

It was times like that when I realized how difficult it was for Dad, trying to bring up daughters.

Robin Royston

Throughout the entire session Linda has been nursing a notebook and running her fingers along the spine.

'I've written down a dream,' she says nervously. 'Sorry about the spelling and punctuation. I've never been very good at that sort of thing.'

I take the book from her and begin reading.

There is a swimming pool – a very small one – rectangular and too small to dive into. There are two children in the pool, both of them girls, and they wear clothes instead of swimming costumes. They are both floating face-down under the water. One of them turns over and her face is bloated. I am afraid because she looks as though she is dead.

I say so to a man with dark hair who I realize is standing next to me. He laughs and says that they are just pretending. He pushes another girl into the pool to show me. The girl is slightly podgy and she sinks under the water and puffs out her cheeks until she has the same bloated expression on her face.

Both the other children in the pool have disappeared. The man with black hair begins laughing and making moves to push Annette in. She joins in and is also laughing, but in a resigned way. The pool is so small that I am afraid she'll hit her head on the side.

The man turns to me. He is still laughing but I feel cold and frightened inside. I don't like him. I pull away and walk around the corner. The dark-haired man appears again and he keeps trying to stick something – a soft, green, jelly-like shape – on the sloping part of the wall above me so that it will melt and drip on me. I keep trying to dodge out of the way.

'It seems so silly,' says Linda, self-consciously. 'But it's the first one I've really been able to remember.'

'Apart from Annette, do you recognize anyone in the dream?' I ask.

'No.'

'What about this man with black hair?'

She shakes her head.

'Did your father have dark hair?'

'Yes, but it's not him.' She sounds sure. 'What does it mean?'

I shrug. 'Your guess is as good as mine.' Then I notice her frowning. She has expected something more.

'Analysing dreams isn't straightforward. They're rarely literal. They're full of symbols and things that represent other things. That's why I look for patterns in dreams – symbols or characters that are repeated. It takes time.'

I can see what she is thinking. She doesn't have time. She has been in Ticehurst for five days and feels guilty about being away from Chris and her children. Nothing has been resolved. She isn't getting any better. All she seems to know for sure is that Ticehurst makes her feel safer.

Linda has barely been out of her room since she arrived here. Several times I've suggested we have coffee in the lounge, but she prefers to talk in her room. Sometimes I think she is frightened of getting herself into situations or conversations where people expect something from her. She isn't ready for that.

Ticehurst has a full programme of therapy sessions, workshops and physical activities. There are art and craft classes, as well as excursions by minibus to the local swimming pool, or shopping trips to local towns. The staff put no pressure on Linda to get involved, but they let her know she is welcome to join in.

By her second week at Ticehurst Linda seems to have improved. She has become much brighter and more animated. On 5 July the nursing notes read:

Seen by Dr Royston. Mood at present seems brighter and not as weepy as when first admitted. Appears to be sleeping better. Spending her time mainly in bedroom, occupying herself with various activities, i.e. reading, writing, designing cards, games, etc . . .

The following day, Roger Smith has written:

Remains in reasonable spirits – in fact is quite happy. Loves the warm weather. Went for a brief walk this afternoon and showed me her favourite place in the grounds – a tree stump set in the hedge of circular walk, opposite front door. Says it reminds her of Africa.

*

Late that same afternoon I sit down with Linda for another session. I notice that she's personalized her bedroom with some photographs from home. All her art and craft equipment is neatly stacked in the wardrobe.

She wants to know about the medication she is taking.

'Temazepam is a sedative. It's designed to help you sleep more soundly, without always waking up during the night.'

'Is that all?'

'Yes.'

'You won't ever give me anything without me knowing, or hypnotize me, will you?'

'No. What makes you ask?'

'It's just that I'm frightened.'

'Why?'

'Well . . . the thought of being given drugs that I don't know about, or being hypnotized to try to find out about anything I may have forgotten, frightens me.'

I leaned forward and looked directly into her eyes. 'Linda, I can't look inside your head without you being there. We're in this together. I'm just like your travelling companion.'

She seems to like this idea. Whatever happens, she won't be alone.

After the coffee arrives we start talking about her childhood again. Somewhere in her background, I expect to find feelings of rejection. Her mother abandoned her and then her father fell in love with someone she wasn't sure of.

'I don't know why I was so uneasy about Connie,' says Linda. 'Perhaps it was jealousy. I always assumed that she was married because she had two children of her own. One day she came to work covered in bruises. Somebody had beaten her up. Dad told her not to go back. He offered to protect her. After that she started sleeping at our house.

'I had a nightmare one night and went tearing down the hall to Dad's bedroom. He wasn't there. I stood in the passage, feeling frightened and unsure. I woke Annette and she helped me look, but we couldn't find him anywhere.

'I called our next-door neighbour, Mrs Leach. She was a Christian, who once gave me baking lessons to make up for the fact that I didn't have a mother.

' "Dad's gone. We can't find him anywhere," I told her. And she said, "Have you told the housekeeper?"

' "No."

' "Well, go and wake her."

'I went down the hallway and knocked on Connie's door. When nobody answered I pushed it open. I could see Dad's silhouette lying in bed next to her. They were both asleep. I went back to the phone and told Mrs Leach it was OK. Dad was with Connie.'

Linda shakes her head at her own naivety. The next morning she told her father what had happened and he turned white. He made her call Mrs Leach again and apologize for having woken her in the middle of the night. 'Tell her that I was sitting on a chair next to Connie's bed. Connie had been sick and I was making sure that she was all right.'

'The hardest part was having to lie for him,' Linda recalls. 'One of Dad's favourite sayings was, "Never ever promise a lie". It meant that sometimes you can twist the truth a little, or manipulate things with white lies, as long as you don't mean any harm or hurt people. But if you make a promise, it has to be true, and you should never tell big lies. Dad was asking me for a big lie and it hurt.

'My dad was an incredible man,' says Linda. 'Despite being raised in a racist country he had been resolute from the year dot that colour made no difference, we were all equal. He drummed this into us in everything he said and did. "Never take anyone for granted," he said. "Never be demeaning or talk down to someone. Show each person the same respect that you expect them to show you." '

'He sounds like a man ahead of his time.'

'He had his faults . . . but he never stopped trying.'

Despite his beliefs, the reality of life in Rhodesia was one of seg-regation and prejudice. Having a coloured housekeeper was acceptable, but having her live under the same roof as a divorced white man was entirely different. When the family went to the cinema with Connie, she had to sit in the back four rows, which were reserved for blacks, and they had to sit in the fifth row from the back to be near her. Afterwards, at the café next door, the fam-ily couldn't sit with Connie at a table inside, because she was coloured. In protest they all stood outside and drank their sodas with her.

If she went into the café on her own, she had to give way to any white person who walked in and let them be served first. And if she took the bus, she had to sit in one of the rear four rows, even if the rest of the bus was empty.

'Connie was an attractive, vibrant woman, with a great sense of personal style,' says Linda, 'but at the same time she seemed bitter or angry at her life. I don't blame her.

'One day Dad said that he wanted to talk to Annette and me. We sat on the bed next to him, one on each side. I had the same sinking feeling as six years earlier when our mother left.

' "I want to know what you think about Connie," Dad said. "She's really grown to love you and I hope that you love her too."

'I could see where this was heading. I looked at Annette. She was staring straight ahead. Her lips were thin lines.

' "We've fallen in love and want to get married," Dad said. "But I want your blessing. If you don't want me to marry her, I won't."

'Both of us wanted him to be happy so we told him what he wanted to hear. I thought Annette was OK with the idea, but she wasn't. She liked Connie, but she knew the ramifications far better than I did. A mixed race marriage would make us social outcasts.'

Keith Houston-Brown married Connie in secret in Salisbury. Soon afterwards he lost his job with the insurance company. Ironically, the colleague at work who encouraged him to marry was the man who took his position.

'Dad couldn't get another job. Nobody would employ him because he'd married a coloured woman,' Linda says bitterly. 'And if he didn't find work, the social workers were going to take us away . . . all of us children.

'We had to lay off the domestic staff and Dad bought a battered old van with a broken back window. Connie used to cook cauliflower leaves and other dishes that were eaten in the townships by the urban poor. She even boiled brown paper to make a concoction that looked like tea.'

Keith Houston-Brown decided it was time to leave Rhodesia. If they weren't welcome in a country run by a white minority, then perhaps they should go to a country controlled by the black majority. Surely Zambia, having gained its independence, wouldn't discriminate against a mixed race family.

Linda says, 'I was ambivalent about leaving Gwelo. Prince had died. My grades were terrible. My only regret was leaving Annette behind. She was sixteen years old and had convinced Dad to let her leave school and get a job in the post office.

'On the day we left I hugged her goodbye and felt numb inside. I couldn't believe we were leaving her.

'I now had a stepbrother and stepsister, Danny and Pat, who were six and four. They had lived in the townships while Connie had been our housekeeper and only occasionally had she brought them to visit. I barely knew either of them.

'We packed up all our things in the small van. Dad drove, and Connie sat in front with little Pat on her lap. Brendan, Clive, Danny and I lay in the back, on top of our belongings. It was really squashed.

'As we set off towards Zambia I waved to Annette until we were around the corner and I couldn't see her any more. Then I peered out of the broken back window, watching Gwelo disappear into the dusty haze. Black farm workers dotted the fields and women balancing containers of water and paraffin on their heads swayed as they walked along the narrow tracks between plots of maize and sugar cane. Would Zambia be any different, I wondered. I was the eldest now. I had to look after the others.'

Linda carries on with the story. She seems to have forgotten about me being in the room.

Linda Caine

Brendan and Clive were ten and seven years old. Brendan had fair hair, pale skin and a splattering of freckles on his nose. He had a wicked sense of humour and would tease his younger brother mercilessly. Clive was far quieter and more contemplative. He was small for his age, with brown hair and brown eyes. He could climb trees like a monkey.

On the first evening we reached Victoria Falls and stopped at a campsite. Lying in bed that night I finally realized that Annette wasn't coming with us. I cried myself to sleep. Next morning there were problems at the Zambian border. Our immigration papers weren't in order. Dad and Connie decided to go on ahead to Lusaka to fix things up. They left me in charge of the children, giving me enough money to buy food.

We had a rondavel (round house) at the back of the campsite, overlooking the railway track. Beyond the tracks lay lush rain forest, created by the spray from the falls. There were no fences or turnstiles in those days. Anybody could wander to the edge and peer into the Devil's Cataract. Clouds of spray billowed into the clear blue sky and the ground shook with the power of the water.

Brendan and I went hunting with a pellet gun and shot a guinea fowl for dinner. But mainly we lived on cereal, toast and sandwiches, along with fruit that I bought from street vendors outside the campsite. Eventually someone at the campsite noticed there were no adults with us and complained to the manager. We were ordered to stay within the campsite and the guards at the front gate were told to stop us leaving.

After that we didn't use the front gate any more. We slipped through the back fence and across the railway line to play in the rain forest. I bought some food from the camp store each day, so nobody suspected we were sneaking out.

Dad and Connie were already on their way back. Unfortunately when they reached the border the white Rhodesian customs officials took offence at a white man emigrating to a black-ruled country with a coloured woman. They stripped the van, unpacking everything, taking off the wheels and letting down the tyres. I'd never seen Dad so upset. We patched the van together but it broke down before we reached Choma in Zambia. We had it towed into town and Dad went in search of spare parts. Meanwhile, the rest of us checked into a small hotel.

We went to lunch in the cafeteria. The first course was soup, with a piece of bread. Danny didn't want his bread, so I asked him if I could have it. Connie glared at me angrily and said no. I couldn't understand why she was so upset. I asked Danny again.

'No, it's Danny's,' said Connie, getting angrier.

'But he doesn't want it.'

She started shouting. 'Just because you're white don't think you can have everything.' Everybody in the dining room could now hear. I tried to calm her down, but she started to scream. 'We're not in Rhodesia now. Who do you think you are? Just because you're white doesn't mean you can have everything on the table any more.'

Burning with embarrassment, I walked out, but she followed me, still yelling. The other children trooped after us, back to our rooms. Finally I turned to Connie and shouted, 'What's wrong with you? Danny didn't even want it.'

She swung her hand and slapped me hard across the face. She turned to walk out. 'How *dare* you hit me!' I shouted. She turned, grabbed me by the hair and pulled my head forward. She began hitting me on the back of my head until I thought I might black out. Rolling backwards onto a bed, I kicked my legs, sending her sprawling onto the floor. In a blind rage, I picked up a bedside table and held it over her head.

'You're frightened now, aren't you?' I said coldly.

She nodded. Her arms were raised, shielding her face.

'Don't *ever* hit me again. And *don't* talk to me like that.' I held the table over her, with my arms trembling, then I threw it to one side. Connie grabbed Danny and Pat by the hands and fled. They locked themselves in the room she was sharing with Dad.

Brendan and Clive stayed with me. I knew I was in deep trouble, but I just felt numb inside.

Dad came back at dinner time. He and Connie sat with Danny and Pat in the dining room. Brendan, Clive and I sat a few tables away. I could hear Connie saying 'She's mad, Keith. She threatened to hit me with a table. She's mad.'

Hearing my side of the story later, Dad was caught in the middle. He asked me to apologize to Connie 'to keep the peace'. I said she needed to apologize to me as well, for shouting at me in front of everyone, and then hitting me repeatedly. Dad sighed deeply, and I felt terrible as he left me and returned to his room. I heard his voice, deep and pleading, through the adjoining wall, but could not make out the words. Then Connie's voice rose above it, shrill and angry. I lay down and covered my ears.

We completed the journey to Lusaka the next day in an uneasy silence.

From the moment we set foot in Zambia, Connie had changed. She was no longer looked upon as a second-class citizen. The roles had been totally reversed.

8

SUNDAY, 16 JULY 1989

Linda Caine

The clock beside my bed has red numbers that glow in the dark.
It's 5.15 a.m. Why do the minutes seem to take longer at night than
during the day? Gary and Christy are coming to visit me today. I'm
looking forward to seeing them, although I'm anxious about how
they'll react. How can they possibly understand what's happened?

They arrive mid-morning and there are hugs all round.
Everybody is trying to be bright and positive.

'How about we go for a walk?' says Chris, still hating his
surroundings. 'We've been stuck in the car for an hour and a half.'

'Isn't it raining?'

'Not any more.'

We all agree and head outside, relieved to be in the open air.
Nobody knows what to say. As we walk in silence towards the rose
garden, I try to break the ice.

'I suppose you've been living on takeaways.' I ruffle Gary's hair.

'No. Dad's a really good cook.'

'Is he now!' I feign surprise.

'Yeah. He cooked us supper last night.'

'What did you have?'

'Baked beans on toast.'

'Goodness me, I'd better be careful or I'll be out of a job.'

Chris laughs and starts chasing Gary up the path. Christy runs after them.

Later, as the children play amid the trees, Chris falls into step beside me.

'How are you doing?' he asks, rubbing my back.

'I don't know. Some days I think I'm feeling better, but then I crash again.'

He hesitates, then continues, 'Do you think it will be much longer before you can come home? I don't want to put pressure on you – you must stay as long as you need – but we all miss you. Gary and Christy keep asking me when you're going to come home. I don't know what to say . . .' He falls silent.

'How much do they know?'

'I've told them bits and pieces. We're doing OK. I'm dropping Gary off at school and picking him up after work. Liz is taking Christy on the school run.'

'How about your work?'

'I can handle that, but I miss you. I want you to come home.' He suddenly gets angry at himself. 'I promised I wouldn't say that. I'm sorry. I didn't mean to put pressure . . .'

'Chris, it's OK. You should always be honest with me. I'm so sorry. I'm really trying. I wish I had answers for you . . . I wish . . .'

He puts his arms around me and we stand in the middle of the path, holding each other tightly.

'Hey, guess what? There's a horse in the paddock over there,' says Christy, emerging from the trees.

Wiping my eyes, I give her a smile. 'Well, let's get some grass for him.'

Later, as we say goodbye, we get caught in another long silence. Gary kicks at a car tyre with his shoes and then gives me a hug. 'I love you, Mum. I *wish* you could come home.'

Christy has brought me two of her toy bunnies to look after for her. 'They want to stay with you,' she says. 'You have to look after them until you come home.'

She gives me a brave smile, but her eyes are shining.

With my heart aching, I clutch the toy bunnies to my chest as they drive away. I can't do this to them any more. I *must* get better. I *must* go home.

MONDAY, 17 JULY 1989

After spending all morning in my room, I decide to get out and do something. There's a group therapy session in the long room near the old chapel. Linda McCormack has told me a little about these sessions. She says they teach coping mechanisms and how to deal with problems and mix with people. In truth, I just want to be left alone. I don't *want* to mix with people. But I know I need to try.

I walk down the corridor and peer into the long room. Chairs have been set up in a circle. I'm early, so I look out the window at the garden, sneaking glances at people as they arrive. About a dozen people turn up, young and old, male and female. Some look devastated, while others seem completely normal. I recognize Agnes, the lady from the lounge. She has a wonderfully clipped English accent and a voice like a schoolmarm. 'Goodness me, look at all these long faces,' she says. 'It doesn't hurt to smile.'

The session is led by a tall handsome Dutchman called Martin, who is training to be an occupational therapist or counsellor.

'Today we're going to talk about the fight or flight response,' he says, in a thick accent. 'When we begin to panic, or get anxious, we must make a decision. When should we fly and when should we cope?'

He gives each of us a sheet of paper to take notes. A couple of people keep interrupting and asking questions. Others sit and look blankly at the sheet of paper, and don't try to participate. 'Now, if you are going to cross a road and see a rabbit in your path, you are not going to run,' says Martin. 'You know how to deal with a rabbit. It will run away, or you will step over it. There is no need to run. But if you are going to cross the road and you see a massive eighteen-wheel juggernaut bearing down on you, you will certainly have an erection and run.'

Agnes almost chokes and bursts out laughing. The whole room wakes up and dissolves into laughter. Martin sits there looking very pleased with himself.

'You mean a "reaction"?' asks Agnes.

'Yes, erection,' says Martin, unable to get his accent around the vowels.

We burst out laughing again.

*

Dr Royston arrives at 6 p.m. He always phones ahead if he's going to be late.

'How did you sleep?' he asks.

'A little better.' I'm sitting on the bed, hugging my knees.

'Does that mean you're feeling better?'

'I think so. I'm still frightened.'

'Do you know why?'

I shrug. 'Just when I start feeling better, the blackness comes back. Everything becomes futile. I think I'm just wasting time until the inevitable happens.'

'The inevitable?'

'Until I die.'

'Do you still want to die?'

'Sometimes. I've always had the notion that suicide is an escape. I know it sounds strange, but death is like the ultimate release. There have been times in my life when I've said to myself, "If things get any worse, I can always commit suicide." '

I look up at him, expecting to see shock or disappointment. Instead, he doesn't react at all.

The coffee arrives and I pour. Dr Royston begins reading my dream notes.

I am carrying a handful of marbles. I fall over and drop most of them. They roll all over the place and I am very annoyed as I look for them and pick them up. I think Gary and Christy help me find them.

'Well, for once I was able to interpret my dream,' I say, in a serious voice.

Dr Royston tilts his head and gives me a questioning look.

'Well, I've lost my marbles. That's why I'm here.'

He laughs at my attempt to be light-hearted. 'I'm sorry, Linda, but that would be too easy. You're as sane as I am – which might not be saying much. You can't write off your problems that easily.'

Robin Royston

The past few days have been better for Linda. She has started taking long walks in the grounds, enjoying the warmer weather. Hopefully, she is now strong enough to tackle the issue that has been our stumbling block for weeks. Ever since our last sessions at the Chaucer, Linda has tried and failed to tell me about the 'flashes' in her mind. These disturbing images are so powerful that she struggles to breathe and feels her mind sliding. There is clearly something in her mind that wants to get out, but each time we move closer it slips away. She talks of being 'far away', as though she travels to a different place in her mind.

Knowing that she feels secure at Ticehurst, I hope that Linda can finally find the means to explain to me what happens and what she sees. She sits on the bed, clutching her knees, with her chin cradled between her kneecaps. Starting at the very beginning, she describes being pregnant with Christy and suffering from terrible morning sickness, not just in the mornings but all day. She couldn't keep anything in her stomach except oranges.

Gary was two years old and a handful at the best of times. Linda was also child-minding a little girl for a friend, which doubled her workload. One night, after Gary was in bed, she ran herself a deep, hot bath. As she turned on the tap a picture flashed into her mind that was so powerful and unexpected it took her breath away. She had to lean against the tub to stop herself falling in.

Linda's voice begins shaking and her sentences come in snatches, between gulps of air and sobs. She becomes so distraught that it takes ten minutes before she can carry on. Eventually she describes what she saw: the image of a young girl being held under the water in a bath.

'Each time I get the flash, it's as though it's happening all over again,' sobs Linda. 'It's always the same – I'm under the water. I can't breathe. What does it mean? Am I insane?'

In total it takes Linda more than two hours to tell me about the incident. There are moments when I wonder if I should stop her because it is just too painful for her. But overriding this is the knowledge that it is better out than in. She buries her face in her hands and her whole body shakes as she describes turning off the tap and sitting in the middle of the bathroom floor, trying to work out what had happened. It felt as though someone had pushed her under water and held her there.

'Later I tried to rationalize what had happened. I was tired. I hadn't managed to keep any food down all day. That's what happens when you get run down – you start imagining things. I told myself all I really needed was a good night's sleep. I didn't tell Chris. I was too shocked and embarrassed. I thought maybe there was something wrong with me.

'From then on I tried to dismiss what happened, but the same "flashes" kept coming back to me over the next few months. They were so powerful and vivid that it took me hours to recover. When I finally told Chris, it was because I thought there was something evil in me.' She starts to cry again.

'How did Chris react?'

'He thought I was over-reacting, that I was under stress. He tried to help, but I knew he didn't understand.'

She sits still and silent for a long moment before beginning again. 'Sometimes the flashes come two or three times a day. At other times I'll go weeks without one. They went away after Christy was born. I thanked God. But I knew they were still there ... beneath the surface ...'

'And now you're having them again?'

She nods and looks at me imploringly. 'Did it really happen, Dr Royston? Is it something I should remember?'

'When did the flashes start again?'

'About a year ago.'

'When you started getting depressed?'

She nods.

'And the image is always the same?'

'Yes. I wish I could see a beginning or an end. Then maybe I'd know if it was a memory or something I've just imagined.' Her voice rattles.

'Are you frightened of water?' I ask.

'No. I love swimming. But I've always been terrified of being held under water. I used to go crazy if people ducked me in a swimming pool or grabbed my legs and pulled me under.'

I can see that Linda is exhausted and emotionally drained. She curls up on the bed and becomes distant. I turn off the light and close the door behind me.

'Keep a close eye on her tonight,' I tell Roger Smith. 'She's opened up a lot today, and it will have made her vulnerable.'

On the drive home I think about Linda's 'flashes'. What do they signify? Are they memories? Has someone held Linda under water?

Water seems to be a recurrent feature. The swimming pool dream featured two girls floating face down under the water. One of them was bloated as though dead. The truth is that I'm no closer to understanding the cause of the images, or why they have returned to Linda so powerfully. This is frustrating and serves only to increase my anxiety over her.

Linda Caine

Ever since Dr Royston left, I've been shaky and unsure. I'm angry because I can't cope. And in the back of my mind, I keep telling myself, if I'm not better next week I can always commit suicide. Chris calls me this evening. I'm still tearful from the session with Dr Royston. Chris keeps asking me what's wrong, but I can't tell him.

'Why can't you talk to me?' he says, getting frustrated. 'I'm your husband, for goodness' sake.'

I start to cry and he apologizes.

'I'm sorry. I just feel so helpless.'

'It's not your fault. It's *me*. I'm the problem.'

Afterwards, I know Chris calls the ward and talks to the night supervisor. He wants to make sure that someone keeps watch on me.

It's a difficult night. I wake at 4 a.m. and can't get back to sleep. I finally order some coffee and try to get my thoughts together. Dr Royston is coming this afternoon. I feel very unsettled, and although I know that there are staff I can talk to, the sense of isolation and loneliness seems to press in on me. I can't rid myself of the feeling that I will be engulfed by my fear if I don't make myself do something positive. But how? The suggestion is always that it would be beneficial if I started mixing more. I don't want to do this. I'm frightened of being with people or finding myself in a situation that I can't get out of. But the staff are gently and persistently encouraging. I don't want to let them down. And in spite of how I think it must appear, I do want to get better.

So later that morning I force myself to go to another group therapy session. This time a different therapist is in charge. She arrives last and shuts the door to fit an extra chair into the circle. As the door closes it's like a switch flicking inside of me. I can feel a wave of panic rising like vomit in my oesophagus. I keep telling myself not to be stupid, but panic overwhelms me and I feel myself break out in a cold sweat. I want to run. I don't know why. I just know I have to get out.

I start trying to leave quietly, but the therapist is blocking the door with her chair. She asks me if I'm all right. I can't answer. I squeeze past her and try opening the door. She puts her hand on my shoulder. I want to scream. I can't breathe. Run, Linda, run! Next minute I'm in the corridor. I push through the side door and swing right, across the driveway and onto the path that circles the grounds. I run and run, taking no notice of where I'm going.

The trees blur. The path twists and turns. My lungs are aching from lack of oxygen, but I keep running. When I finally stop it takes me a while to recognize where I am. I've been here before. It's the path at the far end of the hospital grounds. The trees cast deep shadows and the bark on the trunks is pitted and worn. Doubled over, gasping for breath, I try to clear my head, but my mind keeps sliding. Nothing makes sense. Why am I here? Who is after me? I shiver and look down. A dark stain covers my grey track pants. I've wet myself.

I feel frightened and embarrassed. Maybe I've gone too far this time. Maybe Dr Royston will give up on me. I need time and a place to think. There's a hollow beneath a hedge, just off the path. The midday sun is slanting through the trees. I curl up on the dead leaves. It's dry and warm.

The sun is much lower when I wake. My legs are stiff and leaves and dirt are stuck to my pants. Where am I? I feel my mind beginning to slide again. I can't remember what happened even a few moments ago. There's a barbed-wire fence inside the hedge. The barbs are stained with rust. In slow motion I put my wrist over one of the barbs and press it down. I move my arm back and forth in a sawing movement, watching the blood leak down my fingers and drip onto the ground. One drop, two drops ... ten drops ... twenty ...

The pain helps to clear my head. I don't feel shaky any more.

I start walking along the path. Eventually I reach a lane that borders the hospital grounds. The bitumen is potted and scarred, with newer patches of tar filling the holes. I walk aimlessly, unsure of what to do next.

I hear a car coming ...

Robin Royston

As I round a bend near the northern boundary of Ticehurst, I see Linda standing beside the narrow road. She wears a light-coloured top and grey track pants. Her eyes have a faraway frightened look. I stop the car and she stares directly at me with no hint of recognition. Strands of loose dark hair are plastered to her forehead. She looks towards the trees and then back to me.

'It's me. Dr Royston.'

She stares hard at me.

'What's wrong, Linda?'

Then she suddenly takes off. Her ankles kick in the air as she sprints back down the road. I can't reverse fast enough to keep up with her. By the time I turn the car round she has disappeared.

The staff at Ticehurst have told me that Linda has gone missing. Roger Smith and Linda McCormack have launched a search of the grounds. Meanwhile, I drive my car up and down the nearby roads, feeling like a parent who has lost a child. Linda could be injured. She could have cut herself, or be hanging from a tree. I push these thoughts out of my head and keep searching the trees. Whenever I come to a break in the hedges or a farm gate, I pull to the side of the road and call Linda's name.

After forty minutes, I catch a glimpse of her through the trees, walking parallel to the road. This time she stops and seems to recognize my car. Even so, she appears to be caught in two minds about whether to run. I know that any sudden movement will scare her.

'Hello, Linda.'

She doesn't answer.

'It's cold out here. How about we go back and have a coffee?'

'Will they lock me away?' Her voice is on the verge of breaking.

'No.'

'So they won't send me to St Augustine's? They won't turn me into a zombie?'

'No. Just get in the car.'

'How can I be sure?'

'Trust me.'

Slowly, I lean across and open the door. At the same time I quickly take an inventory, looking for any signs of injury. Her trousers are stained and damp. She holds the sleeves of her jumper in the balls of her fists. Linda edges towards the car and nervously sits down. She turns her face away from me.

Back at Ticehurst, I help her to her room. I wait while she goes to the bathroom. I know she has cut her wrists, but she is too embarrassed to let me know. The cuts are superficial, inflicted by something jagged rather than sharp. I let her clean herself up while I wait for the coffee. When she comes back into the bedroom, she doesn't look at me. She sits on the edge of her bed, keeping her back to me.

'Next time you go for a run, you'll have to remember your trainers,' I say, trying to lighten the mood.

She doesn't answer.

'You should really let a nurse see those cuts.'

Again she says nothing.

'You want to tell me what happened?'

She shakes her head.

'I'm not going to be angry or disappointed. I'm only trying to help.'

She hugs her knees.

'Did it make you feel better, cutting yourself?'

She nods.

'Why?'

'I was trying to clear my mind. I couldn't think straight. I was standing next to a fence . . . I saw the barbed wire . . . I pushed my wrist into a barb . . . The pain cleared my head and I started to come back . . .'

'Where were you?'

She shrugs. 'I don't know . . . somewhere far away.'

She looks at her wrists. 'What will Chris say?' she sobs. 'I feel so dead inside.'

She hesitates, then continues. 'Last night I tried to write down how I feel. It came out in verse:

> 'It's black, it's black, it's black, I said
> A living darkness in my head
> With an appetite that must be fed
> Satiated – when I am dead.'

I know that yesterday's session was tremendously hard on Linda. Part of the reason she is struggling is because she has no sense of what we are doing in these sessions, talking about events that cause her enormous pain.

How can I explain the therapeutic process? I know that Linda likes stories and I tell her one from a holiday that I took in Spain with my stepson Simon, aged thirteen, and my brother and his two teenage boys. We stayed in a villa near Marbella and the backdrop was a mountain that soared above the coastline. I had been eager to climb it ever since we arrived and I promised the boys we'd go hiking.

We set off at around ten in the morning. My brother would take the road to the summit and pick us up later in the afternoon. It was mid-August and the sun had already pushed temperatures into the high thirties. The big wide track grew gradually steeper for the first thirty minutes of climbing. Dressed in trainers, shorts and T-shirts, we stopped regularly to drink from our water bottles.

The path curved around the side of the mountain, up a steep incline and then abruptly stopped. I looked upwards at the peak, framed against the blue sky, and down at the great bowl beneath us. We were surrounded by knee-high scrub that was sharp and nasty. Given our clothes, it would cut our legs to ribbons.

We were all silent.

'What now, Dad?' asked Simon.

The thought of going back and taking the road which wound for miles up the mountain didn't appeal to us. Then I noticed a small track, just wide enough for us to walk in single file through the scrub. It twisted so often that I couldn't see more than a few yards in front of us, making it impossible to know exactly where it was leading.

'It seems to be heading for that rocky outcrop,' I said.

'That's not the way we want to go,' said one of the boys.

'I know. How about we go a little way and see? We can always come back if it's no use.'

We began following the goat track, which led in a truly eccentric fashion up the mountain. Sometimes it came back on itself, sending us down the mountain, but inevitably it began to climb again.

By late afternoon we had struggled across and up the great bowl leading to a narrow, very steep climb to a ridge. The goat track began to flatten out a little as it finally led us to the summit and the end of our journey.

When I finish the story I pause. I can see Linda trying to grasp the point. 'That's what we're on,' I say. 'A goat track. We have to trust it, wherever it goes, no matter how rocky or steep it becomes, or how many times it seems to be leading us away from our goal. We have to trust that it will get us there.'

'How?' she asks imploringly.

'There is no map. I don't know the way. Don't imagine that I have some special knowledge or technique. If we follow whatever path unfolds, the unconscious will hopefully lead us to the end.'

This idea of trusting the process is very Jungian. He said that there were times when you had to trust the unconscious and others when you had to stand against it. In Linda's case, I have to allow her dreams to unfold and hope they lead us to safety. This isn't guaranteed, of course. Goat tracks don't always lead to the summit.

'I think you should rest,' I say, getting to my feet. A shadow of fear flits across her face. She doesn't want me to leave.

'It's going to be fine. Trust the process.'

'I'll try.'

Dropping by the nurses' station on my way out, I find Roger Smith making himself a coffee.

'None of us saw that one coming,' he says. 'How is she now?'

'Settled.'

'Why did she run?'

'The trigger seemed to be when the therapist closed the door during the group session. Linda panicked and needed to get out. She thought she was being boxed in, with no means of escape.'

'So why didn't she recognize you?' Roger asks.

'She was dissociated. I doubt if she realized where she was.'

I have seen Linda become withdrawn during a session, but never to the point where she couldn't recognize me. She has talked of feeling 'far away' as though she can't reach people or they can't reach her. Why does she have such feelings? Is she escaping from something? If so, then the 'far away' place must also be a trap. Why else would she cut her wrists in an attempt to stay in the 'real' world?

I have seen patients mutilate themselves for many reasons. Some cut themselves to relieve tension. Others believe the bleeding is ridding them of 'bad blood' or some unnamed evil. A few are addicted to the 'buzz' they get from the endorphins (the body's natural pain-killers) flooding their bodies.

In this case, I am confident that Linda didn't attempt to commit suicide. Nor was she trying to punish herself. Clearly, it has something to do with her dissociation and was a genuine attempt to 'clear' her mind.

The verse she has written is interesting. Although it clearly describes her depression, the blackness seems to be remarkably active. She describes it as 'living' and I imagine it as being like a black hole, sucking everything into itself.

Jung was the originator of the term 'complex'. Nowadays it has entered popular speech and we talk of 'inferiority complexes' and 'little man complexes'. According to Jung we all have 'unconscious complexes' that occasionally surface. On a very simplistic level these cause us to do things that seem totally out of character. By touching an unconscious complex, we disturb the normal flow of our conscious lives. It's like a ship going through a minefield. If it touches a mine the explosion will cause damage that may be minor or could sink the ship completely. Some complexes are small and cause only minor disturbance, such as nail biting or a tendency to overeat. Others are more serious and can have a profound impact upon the sufferer.

The human ego, or consciousness, is constantly battling against these 'unconscious complexes', which have a habit of returning, however hard we fight to hold them off. To diminish their power (or empty a complex), we first have to make sense of them. What is the energy they contain? Where does this energy come from? In Linda's case I fear we are dealing with a very large, very dangerous complex. I witnessed her lose her balance totally and become distant, inaccessible and inarticulate. I fear I may have to learn to trust the goat track almost as much as Linda.

9

Robin Royston

Perspiration drips from the end of my nose and I lean against the back wall of the squash court. Mike watches me from behind the glass on the balcony. I promised to give him a quick game when I finished.

'Frank's a goner, Mike,' I say, blowing hard. The score is two games all. 'I'll just put him to the sword as soon as I get my breath back.'

'Yeah, right, Dad.'

Frank laughs. 'You'd better not watch, Mike. Your dad's gonna cry when he loses this one.'

I love squash. It's such an elegant game when it's played well, all about angles and moving people around. A sport like tennis I find frustrating because when you really let fly at the ball it goes pinging out. With squash you don't have that problem – you can hit the ball as hard as you like. That doesn't mean it's all power. Sometimes you slow it down and rely on touch. I didn't take up squash until my mid-thirties, when soccer became too hard on my knees and cricket took up too much of a weekend. With a young family, I needed something practical and time-saving.

Mike started hitting the ball when he was only two years old. I wish that I'd started playing at his age. I'd love to be really good at this game. Although I can be very competitive in matches, most of the time I'm relatively laid back when I'm playing friendlies. For an hour it gives me a chance to clear my mind of all the demands of the job.

Frank has been a friend for about five years. Both of our wives are called Lynn and they met through playgroups and children's parties. Frank and I discovered that we both played squash and now we're members of the same club.

He's one of those people who doesn't give a second thought to me being a shrink. Not everybody is like that. There's a familiar pattern to most conversations at dinner parties or barbecues.

'And what do you do?'

'I'm a doctor.'

'Oh (with interest), are you a GP or do you specialize?'

'I'm a hospital doctor.' (At this point I hope the subject will change.)

'What line are you in?'

'I'm a psychiatrist.'

'Oh, how interesting,' they say, or simply, 'Oh.'

From that moment the entire tone of the conversation alters. A lot of people are suspicious of psychiatry or 'therapy'. They think it's somehow rather self-indulgent, or unnecessary. Looking 'too deeply' is seen as a bad thing, or certainly something to be avoided. Other people are wary, thinking I have strange perceptive powers that enable me to see right through them by reading their body language, for example, or analysing their every utterance.

Twelve years ago, in 1977, I dabbled in a very different career, its success limited only to the fact that it led to my meeting my wife, Lynn. I had just finished my medical degree and house jobs, and had a brief window of freedom before I specialized in anaesthetics.

I was sharing a flat with a friend in south London. Max was into acting and used to drag me along to various acting classes. One weekend he booked us into Battersea Arts Centre for a weekend workshop.

Lynn was studying to be a drama teacher. Tall, brown-haired and lovely, she had a wonderful smile and a gift for intuition. We were thrown together in various exercises, all of which she excelled at.

I knew it was the end of showbusiness for me when Max got us both a job as magicians launching a new series of simple magic tricks at Harrods and John Lewis. After a week performing at John Lewis I was bored silly, but Max had volunteered us to perform at street parties for the Queen's Silver Jubilee.

With Lynn as my beautiful assistant I arrived at Kennington on a sunny afternoon to find a huge audience of children and a group of rather bored mothers – all from nearby high-rise blocks.

My first trick involved a banana that had been secretly pre-cut so I could magically slice it up with my wand. It was a pretty weak trick, but rendered even worse by the fact that it had been shown on children's TV only a week earlier. My act died at that moment. The kids began running riot, stealing the prizes and various bits of equipment. Trying to salvage my pride, I attempted my one genuinely decent trick. A ten-year-old boy stood right in front of me, watching the trick carefully. He had a crewcut and a fake tattoo on his arm. At least I thought it was fake.

Somewhat distracted, I completed the trick with a flourish. 'And the card you chose was the seven of hearts!'

He looked at me with utter disdain. Clearly, it was the wrong one. 'You're fucking rubbish!' he said amid the pandemonium. Only he and I were aware of how true that statement was.

That was enough for me. Laughter may indeed be the best medicine, but I decided to stick to the kind of doctoring I knew best.

While Lynn continued her degree, I went to work at St Stephen's Hospital in Chelsea. After several months of training I had my first night on call unsupervised in anaesthetics. It was so quiet that I wandered down to the doctors' mess and watched some sport on TV.

My bleeper went off. There was an emergency in casualty. I expected a cardiac arrest or a road accident. Instead the scene that greeted me will stay with me for ever. There were bodies lying on trolleys in the corridors because the beds were full. Nurses and doctors were dashing from one new arrival to the next, pinning pieces of paper to patients' clothing to say what treatment had been given. It was mayhem.

The IRA had exploded a bomb at the Ideal Home Exhibition at

Earl's Court. It had been placed in a rubbish bin and, mercifully, the injuries were mostly to legs and feet rather than heads.

I went from trolley to trolley, putting up intravenous lines and intubating patients. It was so chaotic, I struggled to take it all in. To make matters worse, I remembered that Mum had talked of going to the Ideal Home show that weekend. I suddenly wondered if she could be among the wounded.

A patient was rushed into theatre with his leg hanging off. He kept pleading with the surgeon, 'I play rugby. Don't take my leg.' Each time I tried to put the mask over his face, he pushed my hand away. 'Please, save my leg.'

I lost count of how many operations we did that night. Still very inexperienced, I was comfortable putting patients under for the operations, but the surgery was long and hard. At one point, a patient began breathing faster. I knew he was reacting to the surgery and the operation was only just beginning.

I had to get him deeper under, but already he was beginning to tighten his vocal chords. I wasn't sure of what to do. Suddenly Trottie, an experienced anaesthetist, appeared at my elbow. It was her day off but she'd heard about the bombing on the radio and come straight into work.

'A bit of analgesia, I think,' she said as she drew up some pethidine. The patient's breathing slowed and the chords relaxed.

At 5 a.m. the consultant surgeon sent out for a takeaway for all the staff. Most of us had been working twelve hours straight. For the survivors of the bombing, there would be many more operations ahead. Most would bear the scars for the rest of their lives.

A few weeks later, I saw the young rugby player leave the hospital. He walked on crutches and his wife carried his bag. He had lost his leg below the knee. I couldn't get his desperate pleas on the night of the explosion out of my head, and struggled to imagine his anger and confusion now.

Lynn and I had been together three years when we left on a long-awaited adventure, backpacking across the Middle East to India and possibly Australia. Studying anaesthetics had been part of the plan. It meant I could travel the world and earn good money.

Just before we left Lynn gave me a book, *Memories, Dreams,*

Reflections, by Carl Jung. It is about Jung's journey of discovery as an analyst and the theories he developed about the human psyche and the unconscious. As I read I became fascinated by the link between the mind and the body. Not everything is simple and rational about human experience. It can't be reduced to a set of scientific rules. Up until then I had always assumed that I'd follow in the footsteps of my older brother, Chris, and be a medical doctor. But the idea of healing the mind instead of the body appealed to me. Jung was interested in where people came from and what shaped their personalities. He pulled me along, opening up my mind to possibilities.

During the next nine months, as we travelled through Iran, Afghanistan and Pakistan, I read more of Jung's collected works. By the time we returned to England, I knew that I wanted to be a psychotherapist.

By chance I discovered that Dr Gerhard Adler, who had trained directly under Carl Jung, was running a training course in London. I wrote to him and explained that I wanted to be a Jungian analyst and psychotherapist. Dr Adler managed to arrange a meeting, and I began my analytic training three months later.

There are relatively few medical psychotherapists in Britain. Most therapists aren't trained as doctors, though the hybrid of being both a psychiatrist *and* a psychotherapist is traditionally sound. On a practical level, it gives me a detailed knowledge of the limitations and boundaries of both the drugs and the therapy. And from a career point of view, it has enabled me to get a post within the NHS as a consultant psychotherapist and also to work as an independent practitioner at private hospitals.

It is four days since Linda ran away from the group therapy session. She still feels guilty about causing so much trouble and is highly self-critical.

'I had another dream,' she whispers. 'I didn't write it down because at first I wasn't sure if I'd been asleep or awake.'

'What did you decide?'

'I must have been dreaming. I thought I'd woken up. I was in my room and I suddenly felt as though I wasn't alone – there was something very evil with me. I don't know if it came through the window or the door. I don't even know if it had a form – it was just there and it wanted me to die. It wanted me to commit suicide.

'I tried to switch on the light to make the evil go away. I leaned over to the lamp on the left side of my bed. The evil was hovering over me. I couldn't find the switch at first and when I did, I pressed it and the bulb sparked and popped. The light went off. The evil was mocking me – wanting me to die.' Linda's whole body shakes.

'When did you realize you were dreaming?' I ask.

'I began trying to make myself wake up. It took enormous effort. This thing didn't want me to wake up. Finally I managed to lean over to the light. When the room lit up I felt enormous relief.'

What is this thing that wants her dead? It sounds almost demonic. Clearly this 'evil presence' is somehow connected to her suicidal feelings. It is like a malevolent energy in her unconscious that wants to destroy her. Very importantly, this energy lives separately within Linda's mind. It is like a cancer that feeds off her, but doesn't belong. In days gone by, people would have talked about 'possession' and 'evil spirits'. These are just old-fashioned ways of describing 'unconscious complexes'.

I am fascinated by her confusion between dream and reality; the notion that she tried desperately to wake herself up and had to fight her way out of the dream. Again it brings to mind the idea of a black hole within her psyche that is sucking everything into it. I don't share these thoughts with Linda. For the moment, it is more important that we continue the process of looking back at her life, piecing together the separate events. In order to make sense of her current problem I have to understand what it has evolved from. Only then can we hope to find the underlying pattern and the reason for her self-destructive urges.

Nursing a coffee cup and with her legs tucked underneath her, Linda begins telling me what happened when the family arrived in Lusaka. She turned fifteen a few days later.

Linda Caine

Dad had rented a big rambling house, with cement floors and an Aga stove in the kitchen. The landlord, Mrs Hugo, tried to renege on the lease when she discovered that Connie was coloured. She accused Dad of being deceitful.

'I didn't realize that you had to specify colour in Zambia,' he said pointedly. 'I thought it was against the law.'

The house was very basic but I loved the huge garden. It had mango trees and a large reservoir on one side where I used to go swimming. I'd dive in and float on top because I hated my feet touching the mud and ooze on the bottom, which felt like it would suck me under.

In Gwelo there had been total segregation, but my new school, Kabulonga Girls' High, was different. There were only six white girls in my class of forty-three – the rest were black, Asian or coloured. Despite the mixed classes, the girls tended to hang out with their 'own'. Whites with whites, blacks with blacks, etc. My difficulty was having a white father and a coloured stepmother. People couldn't work out where I belonged.

I became friends with Mundia and Supiwe, two black girls who came from one of the high-density urban estates. We'd sit together during break-times and in class.

The white girls couldn't understand why I was spending time with the 'Kaffirs' as they called them. They also used to complain about finding half-naked black girls from the poorer villages using the basins in the girls' toilets to wash themselves before school. Somebody scrawled graffiti on the toilet wall: 'Why don't you Kaffirs go back to your kayas (homes).' Angry at the insult, the black girls boycotted classes and stormed out of the school in protest. The headmistress tried to stop them leaving and I heard that one of the girls knocked her down.

I was on my way to school slightly late when I saw them streaming out of the school gates. They were marching to the Ministry of Education, demanding that whoever wrote the graffiti be found and expelled.

For those of us left behind – white girls and Indians – the atmosphere in the classroom was tense. The teachers tried to run the lessons as normal but a few hours later, during biology, we heard the girls returning. They were chanting slogans, slamming doors and overturning benches.

Our biology teacher, Mrs Phipps, was a tiny woman, with the

mannerisms of a bird. As the mob drew closer she ushered us into a small storeroom at the front of the classroom and locked the door.

'Stay away from the window and don't make a noise,' she said.

The black girls stormed into the classroom. I could hear Mrs Phipps trying to reason with them. 'You've made your point,' she said. 'Why don't you go home and let everything calm down?'

They were calling her a racist and accusing the teachers of having one rule for white girls and another for blacks. I huddled in the corner of the storeroom, staring up at the small patch of blue sky visible through the window. We were only allowed out once the mob had cleared. And the teachers told us to stay away from school for a couple of days until things settled down.

From that day onwards the atmosphere at school changed. The black girls took control. When they marched along the corridors the white girls had to jump clear, or risk being beaten. Mundia and Supiwe no longer sat with me during break-time. They wouldn't even catch my eye. I felt sorry for them because I knew they were afraid. The three girls responsible for the graffiti were caught and expelled. That left only three whites in my class including me. Towards the end of term I discovered that the others were leaving. I faced being the only one left.

I pleaded with Dad to let me leave school. 'I'll get a job, like Annette. I'll pay rent . . .' He wouldn't even consider it. I was only fifteen.

After seven months in Zambia, Dad had become a branch manager for Prudential Insurance. We had bought a property with five acres and a house in Kudu Road, just down the road from the school. Dad and Connie had one of the large bedrooms at the front and I had the other. Both had double doors leading onto the veranda. Our new baby brother, Sean, also slept in the house, while the other four kids bunked in a separate building.

The surrounding countryside was open and flat, with a small airstrip and a black shantytown in the distance. We couldn't see the hessian and tin shacks, but I'd see the children in bare feet and rags getting condensed milk and penny buns from a small general store down the road.

I was desperately unhappy. I hated school and I hated being at home. Most of the time I made myself scarce, but Connie used to complain to Dad that I didn't help around the house and was lazy. He tried to be the peacemaker but Connie ruled the house and his life. With the arrival of Sean, the family set-up had changed yet again. I loved my new little brother, but I felt surplus to requirements.

I was still terrified of the dark and of falling asleep. Sometimes I'd pay Brendan or Clive to sleep with me because I was so frightened of being alone at night. I started skipping classes at school. I had lots of places where I used to hide instead: the mango or banana groves behind the house; an ancient cooling tower; and one of my favourites, the old water tank half hidden in the branches of a huge avocado tree at the back of our place.

The water tank was round but sat on a square base, which meant each of the corners formed a ledge. I could sit there, with the avocado leaves all around me, invisible to the world. Nobody could see me, but I could see them. I can't tell you how much I loved that place. All my life I've loved hiding places – secret spots that only I knew about. Places where nobody could find me. They had to be outside, in the open, where I could see all around me.

A girl called Gene lived in the property behind us. She went to a different school, but I'd seen her at the movies. Boys were always talking about her because she looked sixteen when she was only twelve. Gene was far worldlier and wiser than I was, but we became good friends.

Lusaka's first disco was started by a Jewish guy called Dan who rented a school hall every Friday night. Gene and I went along. Her mum would drop us off and my dad would pick us up, or vice versa. Neither of them realized, of course, that we could drink at the disco. Gene was very outgoing, but I always found it difficult to be around people. To disguise it I headed straight to the bar and drank a couple of brandy and Cokes, one after the other. Then I could float on the music and forget about everybody else. It was like listening to the drumbeat at the Miss Gwelo contest – the music took me away.

Dan had hired three girls as go-go dancers for the disco. 'We can do better than that,' said Gene scathingly. We convinced Dan to let us try out and then spent a week practising at home. I couldn't have done it without Gene. She had enough confidence for both of us.

Having come up with a routine – most of it copied shamelessly from *Hollywood a-Go-Go*, a popular TV show – we auditioned for Dan.

Without even asking how old we were, he hired us. The following Friday we began our career as go-go dancers. Gene didn't seem to have a doubt in the world. She had a fabulous sense of rhythm, and didn't appear to be nervous about going on stage at all. I loved dancing but, more than ever, I needed the brandy and Coke to calm my nerves. The resident band, The Crusaders, did mainly covers and we danced to records during their breaks. We did sets of four songs and then the band took over again. Dad didn't seem to mind my part-time job. I think he was relieved that I had found a friend.

My insecurity and lack of confidence didn't match the image I portrayed on stage, gyrating to the music, in figure-hugging clothes. Gene and I introduced the mini-skirt to Lusaka. One of our outfits had cut-away sleeves, with a turtle neck, tight-ribbed bodice and a blue and black striped mini-skirt with a belt.

Being a go-go dancer made me feel special. During breaks I'd climb to the top of a ladder on the stage, behind the curtains. It was like sitting on top of the water tank; I could watch the world below, without having to take part.

At Christmas I went back to Gwelo to see Annette. She seemed to have her life really sorted out, with a good job at the post office and a room in a large boarding house nearby. She had enough money to pay her board and still go out every weekend. Her husband, Stewart, was an English rocker who had a motorbike, leather jacket and greasy hair. Dad hated him but that didn't stop Annette from marrying him.

I loved being back in Gwelo and I didn't want to return to Zambia after the holiday. I rang Dad and told him that I was going to stay and get a job, just like Annette. He began wheezing and choking. Connie took the phone off him and screamed at me. 'He's having a heart attack. You're killing your father.'

I couldn't be sure if Dad was genuinely having a heart attack. He could be very melodramatic sometimes. Annette knew she would be blamed if I stayed, so she made arrangements for me to return to Zambia.

Two days later, we hugged goodbye at Gwelo railway station and I boarded the train for Salisbury. Desperately unhappy, I couldn't hold back the tears. I didn't want to go back. I wanted to stay with Annette. I sat in the old-fashioned carriage and stared out the window at the bush I used to ride through.

At a place called Hunter's Road, the train slowed down and stopped briefly at a bush siding. It was in the middle of nowhere. Nobody got on or off. In the darkness I slipped off the train. Hiding in brush, I watched the guard wave his lantern and heard the whistle sound. The train pulled away.

Alone, miles from anywhere, I lay down on the siding and stared into the heavens, searching for shooting stars. I probably should have been scared. The sounds of the insects and animals were amplified by the night air. I could hear baboons in the trees and warthogs in the undergrowth.

Hours later another train stopped, this time heading for Gwelo. As I jumped on board the conductor spied me. He wanted to know what a white girl was doing in the middle of the bush at that time of night. I made up a story about leaving something behind in Gwelo. He was really nice and let me sit in the conductor's room for the rest of the journey. He even gave me some of his tea and sandwiches.

It was still early in the morning when we arrived back at Gwelo station. I walked to Annette's boarding house, but knew she'd still be sleeping. Rather than wake her, I locked myself in the bathroom down the hall and went to sleep in the empty bath. When the sun came up I knocked on her door and begged her to let me stay. She was furious. She called Dad and made an excuse for me. Then she arranged another ticket and made me promise to stay on the train.

I can't tell you how miserable I felt arriving back in Zambia. Soon things got even worse. When the holidays ended I went back to school, but immediately started skipping classes and forging sick notes. I spent hours hiding out in the old cement cooling tower at the back of our property.

The tower used to keep things cool in the days before iceboxes and electric fridges. Now it was full of insects and there were doves nesting in the roof. I used to have drawing paper and pencils in my school bag. I'd sketch things. Or lie down and watch the birds soaring on the hot air currents.

Nothing was going to knock that cooling tower down, not even the thunderstorms that made the walls shake and whipped the trees in all directions. An eerie darkness would descend over the landscape, lit up briefly by flashes of lightning. When I left my tower each afternoon, I smoothed the dirt and leaves so that nobody would see I'd been there. It didn't matter in the end. Dad found out that I was bunking off school and tried to force me to go back.

We had a huge row and I told him how much I hated living at home. He slapped me across the face. It was the first time he'd hit me since I was put over his knee as a child. I turned around and screamed at him, 'Why didn't you just let me go to an orphanage? It would have been much better than all this.'

He flinched and his eyes misted over. He walked out of my bedroom and I heard him start to cry. I wanted to die. How could I have hurt him like that?

He came to me the next day and said that I could leave school.

Robin Royston

Linda stares into the cold dregs of her coffee as if hoping they might reveal something more. She seems disappointed and at the same time relieved.

From my point of view the session has been revealing enough. In particular I am interested in her relationship with her father. Partly I wonder if they were drawn together as a legacy of the mother leaving. Other things are notable: her sense of being uprooted and taken away from the place where she grew up; the struggle in her relationship with Connie.

Three or four times Linda referred to her 'hiding places'. She said: 'All my life I've loved hiding places – secret spots that only I knew about. Places where nobody could find me.'

Why? What was she hiding from? And why did her hiding places always have to be places where she could see if anyone was approaching?

One of the most positive aspects of the session was how bright and animated Linda became. The deadness in her voice of the previous few days had gone. Instead she laughed at her stories of go-go dancing and wearing mini-skirts that scandalized the locals. I had a brief glimpse of what she must have been like as a teenager.

10

THURSDAY, 20 JULY 1989

Linda Caine

The aerobics instructor Leonie has the sort of permanently sunny disposition that belongs on breakfast TV. She bounces into the old chapel just before eight each morning, carrying her portable tape deck and selection of tapes.

I really like Leonie. For half an hour each morning she jollies us along, telling us to 'Lift those knees . . . breathe deeply . . . don't forget to flex . . .'

It's the only time I mix with the other patients. I don't go to the lounge and I've only been to the dining room once. I ordered a salad but was so nervous I almost choked when I tried to swallow. Since then I've been eating my meals in my room. The food is surprisingly good, which is a waste because I have very little appetite. When I know Chris is coming, I make sure that I order something he likes, such as steak or an omelette.

The old chapel has become my favourite place. It has a huge vaulted ceiling, with stained glass in the higher windows. At certain times of the day the sun angles through these windows and dust particles dance in the beams of light. Apart from the morning aerobics classes, the chapel is barely used. Plastic chairs are stacked up in one corner and the wooden floor needs a polish. The gym equipment is pretty basic – a treadmill and a few exercise bikes. But there's a badminton net and a box full of assorted racquets, shuttlecocks and balls.

I played badminton with Linda McCormack after she coaxed me out of my room. It was fun. She squeals whenever she almost reaches a shot and it makes me laugh. She's actually not a bad player, although she's pretty rusty.

It was Linda McCormack who told me about these morning exercise classes. The first time I came along I didn't speak to anyone, or even make eye contact. Now I'm starting to relax a little. I'm on nodding terms with some of the patients, but most of them seem to come and go. Agnes is still here. She acts more like a member of staff than a patient. She's always complaining that exercise will be the death of her, but she turns up every morning.

There's another lady, Elizabeth, who can't be left alone or she'll kill herself – at least that's what Agnes says. Apparently, Elizabeth was once a very high-powered secretary, married to a wonderful man. They both retired together, but within weeks her husband died. After that she just fell apart.

Another patient, Jimmy, is a schizophrenic in his early twenties. He arrived on my floor in the same week I did. I know him well enough to say good morning or good afternoon, using his name. He smiles and waves. Jimmy is quite overweight and he wanders around barefoot, which upsets some of the older patients. In the lounge he sits on his favourite chair and props his bare feet on the coffee table, almost inviting criticism. Maybe he's trying to relieve the boredom.

Dr Royston says it's OK for me to spend a night away from Ticehurst. Chris is picking me up this afternoon. He's booked a hotel nearby because I want to be close to Ticehurst . . . just in case. I feel safe here. Maybe that's a problem. I've heard of people becoming 'institutionalized' and not wanting to leave. But when I think about Chris, Gary and Christy I know that isn't true of me. I miss them too much.

Chris arrives at four and we head off. He's wearing a shirt that I bought him last Christmas. Every so often he glances across at me as he drives, making sure I'm OK. We head down narrow country roads towards Rye, passing through little villages. A country cricket match is under way. Tea is being set up on trestle tables in the shade of the trees.

'So where are we going?'

'Somewhere special.'

'A surprise?'

'Sort of.'

On the drive Chris chats about work and general things. He's still fighting to save the Canterbury office. It must be doubly hard trying to hold things together at work and at home.

'Christy won a prize for her art project,' he says, changing the subject.

'Wonderful.'

'Yes. She ended up doing a papier-mâché model. You know the sort of thing. You start with a balloon and you cover it with paper soaked in glue. She really wanted you to be around to help her paint . . .' He stops in mid-sentence and apologizes.

'It's all right. You don't have to apologize.'

'They're both doing their homework in your art room. I hope you don't mind.'

'Of course not. That's what it's for.'

Suddenly I feel very homesick. I always had visions of Gary and Christy doing their homework in the art room, or simply coming in to draw or paint. I want to be there with them.

The hotel used to be an old brewery and has a big round oast house converted into rooms. Our room has a big canopy bed with loads of pillows. It's lovely but I can't help feeling anxious. We take a walk in the garden before dinner and I keep telling myself that nothing is going to happen. Ticehurst is just down the road. Grow up, Linda. Pull yourself together.

That evening at dinner I make a real effort for Chris's sake. It's the first time in three weeks that I've been around so many people. I keep glancing up every so often, expecting to find people staring at me. I know it sounds stupid, but a part of me thinks people are going to recognize that there's something wrong with me. They'll know where I've been living . . . what I've done.

My steak looks great, but my stomach is in knots. I try to calm down by telling Chris about playing badminton in the old chapel.

'When you come home maybe we can all go to Herne Bay Pier and have a game,' he says. 'Just like we used to.'

'That's a good idea.'

We both take a sip of wine. 'I'm sure I'll be home for the holidays.' As soon as I say the words, I start to panic. The school holidays! What if I haven't improved?

My knife slips out of my fingers and clatters onto the floor. The people at the next table turn and look at me. My hands are shaking as I lean down and pick it up. My face is burning. It takes all of my willpower not to run out of the room.

'I'm so sorry,' I whisper to Chris.

'I don't want you worrying about the school holidays,' he says.

'Why?'

'I've talked to Mum and Dad and they've invited Gary and Christy for the holidays.'

'To the Isle of Man?'

'Yes. Just for a couple of weeks. I'll drop them at the airport and Mum and Dad will pick them up at the other end.'

'Are they old enough to fly alone?'

'Gary's almost thirteen. And they'll be together.'

Chris keeps telling me what a good idea it is. I guess he's right. But why do I feel so guilty? It shouldn't have come to this. My children are about to spend longer away from home than at any time in their lives and it's all because of me.

Chris is also suffering. It's not just *my* life that's falling apart. My breakdown has shaken everything that he's worked so hard to build – a career, a family, financial security. I can't give him any guarantees or make any promises. Right now I think he'd be better off without me.

It takes me ages to fall asleep. Even with Chris beside me I feel nervous. When I finally drift off I have a terrible dream. I'm in a house with a swimming pool. It's a nice pool, but the water is very dirty. A girl gets in and begins to swim around. I follow her but feel uncomfortable in the dirty water, so I turn to swim back to the ladder.

The girl reaches the ladder before me and climbs out of the pool. As I grip the rungs and begin to climb up, a small frog hops into my mouth. I get a fright and open my mouth wider in order to get my fingers inside to pull the frog out. But as I do so, more frogs hop into it. Panicking, I hold onto the ladder with my left hand so that I won't fall back into the pool. I try to pull the frogs out of my mouth with my right hand. My mouth is full and I can't get a grip on the frogs because they're so slippery. I feel one begin to slide down my throat. My mouth is full of slime and I'm beginning to choke. A man standing next to the pool just watches me.

I wake in panic, staring blindly into the darkness, with my heart thumping. My jaw is clenched open and my first instinct is to run. Chris is asleep beside me.

At Ticehurst I would have turned on the light and sat up for a while. But I don't want Chris to know how frightened I am. I don't want to hide things from him, but he's got too much to worry about already. I lie down and listen to him breathing. It's nice having him so close.

That next afternoon, back in my room at Ticehurst, I tell Dr Royston about the dream. It's still so vivid that I almost gag when I mention the frogs and forcing my mouth open, trying to get the slime from my throat.

'It's a horrible dream,' he says.

'But what does it mean?'

'Did you recognize the man standing next to the pool?'

'No.'

'Did he remind you of anyone?'

'No.'

'How old was he?'

'Young.'

'A teenager?'

'No, older than that ... maybe in his thirties.' I struggle to remember. I can't picture his face. Maybe I couldn't see it in the dream. It's so frustrating.

'Don't try to force things. They'll come in good time,' says Dr Royston.

I wish I could read his thoughts. What does he *really* make of the dream? Is there something he's not telling me? Sensing my frustration, he changes the subject and asks about what happened when I left school in Lusaka.

I tell him about my first job. It was in the accounts department of Van's Motors, a local garage. My boss was Mr Van Eck, but everybody called him Mr Van. Customers' accounts would be sent upstairs and I'd enter the details using an old Olivetti accounting machine. At the end of each month I'd print out the statements and post them off.

I was still go-go dancing with Gene on the weekends. One night she introduced me to a guy called Tony, who I really liked. He was about eighteen and I was still fifteen. We went on a date and he tried to touch my breast. I didn't want him to, but he was good looking and seemed really nice. I guess I didn't want to lose him.

'Come on, I'm not going to do anything else,' he whispered. We carried on kissing and things suddenly seemed to snowball. I know he had sex with me, but I don't really remember it.

It's strange because I don't think I even remembered it at the time. Other girls had told me how they climbed the walls in pain with their first experience, but I remember being numb and confused; not being able to think clearly.

Afterwards Tony walked me home. He kept asking if I was OK.
'Yes.'
'Did I hurt you?'
'No.'
I kept thinking, why don't I remember?

I only went out with Tony a couple more times after that. I still really liked him, but I didn't want him touching me any more. It's hard to explain, but his touch had somehow changed. It seemed urgent . . . insistent . . . it made me feel panicky and cold inside.

Soon I realized that when it came to having sex, what I really liked was being held and cherished rather than the act itself. Unfortunately, most of the boys I went out with didn't see things the same way. After a while I stopped caring. If I liked someone and wanted to be with him for a while, I just switched my mind off when he began to go further. I reasoned that we both got what we wanted. He got to have sex and I had someone to hold me.

Annette arrived in Lusaka not long after that. Her marriage had broken down and she was eight-and-a-half months pregnant. She shared a room with me at first, but when Tanya was born she moved into one of the rooms at the back of the house.

One afternoon at Gene's house I met a young guy called Mike Louw. He was about six feet tall, with dark hair, brown eyes and a baby face. He had a great sense of humour and made me laugh. Unfortunately, he was going out with someone else.

A few weeks later, on my way home from work, I dropped into a butcher's shop around the corner from the garage. I chose a strip of biltong and waited at the cash register.

Then a voice said, 'Well, look who it is . . .'

Mike Louw was grinning at me across the counter.

'Do you work here?'

'I manage this butchery. How do I look in an apron?'

I laughed.

'Can I come and see you?' he asked.

'What about your girlfriend?'

'Oh, that didn't work out.'

Mike called me and we began dating. He was lovely. In particular he seemed to understand my need to get away from the house. The tensions at home were terrible and I could do nothing right in Connie's eyes. My silences drove her crazy. Soon after Christmas Connie and Annette had a fight and my sister moved to a boarding house with Tanya. Annette had a job as a receptionist with a transport company and would drop Tanya at a crèche each morning.

Because of the tension at home, Dad said it would be best if I left as well, so I moved in with Annette. He said he would come and visit us when he could, but we shouldn't tell anyone because if it got back to Connie she would be angry. I knew the situation was difficult for him and he was trying to balance it as best he could, but I still felt betrayed.

Annette and I shared a tiny room at the boarding house. There was just enough space for a single bed each and a baby's cot. Annette had to wash Tanya's nappies in the bath we shared with others down the passage.

I was still dating Mike, who seemed to really care about me. I still dreamed of moving back to Gwelo, but Mike said he wouldn't let me go, which was sweet.

A few months later, Annette and I found a six-berth caravan for rent in a caravan park just outside Lusaka. Accommodation was so scarce that even the caravan was more than we could afford. Mike's younger brother, Robbie, also needed somewhere to stay, so he and Mike moved in with us.

The dining table flipped over to form a double bed and there were four smaller bunk beds at the back. The awning also had a bed and a TV. It was wonderful to have our *own* space. We could cook, eat and do what we liked. We were like a family. I adored little Tanya and we all shared looking after her.

I don't know what the other people in the caravan park thought about us. We were all so young. Mike and Annette were eighteen, I was sixteen, Robbie was fifteen, and little Tanya just a few months old. Everything seemed to be falling into place. I loved Mike and we had a lot of fun together – dancing at the disco, going to the movies or to the river at weekends. Whenever we went anywhere he always held my hand. At dances he wouldn't let me go to the bar. Instead, he'd leave me in a corner while he fetched the drinks.

At first I thought it was quite old-fashioned and charming to have to ask his permission when someone wanted to dance with me. Even his friends had to ask him first. And whenever Mike felt as though I'd been dancing too long with someone, he would suddenly walk in between us, signalling the end. As time went by he became even more possessive. If another man looked at me, Mike would get sulky and angry. He drank too much and accused me of flirting.

'Maybe if we got engaged things would be better,' he said. 'People would know you're committed to me.'

'But they know that already,' I told him.

'It's not enough.'

Mike loved me very much, I didn't doubt that, but his jealousy worried me. After every fight or angry outburst, he'd say, 'Getting married will solve it all. I'll know that you really love me.'

Naïvely, I believed him. Maybe he was right.

Robin Royston

Linda pauses as though unsure whether to continue. I know immediately that we've reached a stumbling block. She is staring out the window, recalling events from long ago. Her muscles have tightened and her respiration has changed. She has taken the front of her T-shirt and scrunched it into a ball in her fist.

'Do you want to have a break?' I ask.

She shakes her head and takes a sip of water. 'I don't want to stay here. I want to go home. That's why I have to get this out.'

'OK.'

'I fell pregnant while we were at the caravan park. I was sixteen. The stupid thing was that I was terrified to tell Dad. I knew he would be very disappointed in me, and angry with Mike.'

'What happened?'

'Mike was becoming very possessive. He absolutely didn't want a baby. I was frightened.' Linda covers her face with her hands. I know the tears are coming.

'Mike told a woman at the butchery. She gave him a contraption that looked like a large syringe and told him how I should use it. He made it sound easy. I didn't want to do it . . .' Her shoulders are shaking.

'I didn't know what I wanted. How was I going to have a baby and work? I'd seen Annette struggling with Tanya. She earned more than I did. I couldn't afford a crèche.

'So I did it. I thought I just had to do it once and it would all be over and I would be back to normal. It was really painful. But nothing happened. I was so naïve.

' "The baby didn't come," I told Mike. He talked to the lady at work and the message came back, "For goodness' sake, tell her to keep trying. Sometimes it can take a few weeks." '

Linda wipes her cheeks with the backs of her hands. 'I wanted to change my mind,' she said. 'I wanted to have the baby, but I was afraid that I'd already damaged it. I had visions of it being born with something wrong. So I kept using the device.

'It took about three weeks. By then I was in constant pain. My stomach was distended and I kept getting terrible cramps. I thought I'd damaged myself permanently . . . that I could never have children . . . I just wanted to die.

'Then one night it happened. Annette had gone out to the movies. Mike had been in a bad mood and stormed off to get drunk somewhere. Robbie had gone out. I was lying in the bath when I started bleeding heavily. I had never felt such pain. I managed to get back to the caravan where I began to haemorrhage. I couldn't get back to the toilet so I sat on a bucket. There was no telephone, but I didn't have anyone to call, anyway.'

Linda's voice is now a whisper. She sits with a pillow hugged tightly to her chest, and speaks between gasping sobs.

'When Mike came home he was very drunk,' she continues. 'He looked into the bucket and realized what was happening. Do you know what he did?'

Linda looks at me just briefly. 'My baby was dead and I was in agony, but he just said, "At last." Then he fell over and hit his head on the chest of drawers because he was so drunk. I didn't know if I hated him or loved him then. I felt so alone. I dragged him to bed and lay next to him. I put his arm around me but I don't think he even knew I was there.'

Linda falls silent, seemingly lost in her own thoughts. 'You asked me once if I could remember when I first felt really deeply depressed,' she says, without looking up.

'Yes.'

'It was then. I remember not wanting to be alive any more.'

'What happened?'

'A few weeks after the miscarriage I had an argument with Mike. We were in the annexe of the caravan and I picked up a razor and cut across my wrist. It all happened in slow motion. My wrist flowered open but I didn't feel any pain. I expected to bleed all over the place and die, but I didn't cut deeply enough.

'Mike pulled the razor off me and told me I was being stupid. Afterwards, when he'd gone, I felt absolute despair that I couldn't do it. It was like how I felt when I left the house that day after hitting Christy . . . I was a total failure. I couldn't even kill myself properly.'

Again she lapses into silence. Still clutching a pillow, wet from her tears, she seems to have given up all over again. I want to tell her how important the session has been, but I know she isn't really listening. She is too exhausted.

As I leave her to rest, I contemplate this earlier evidence of depression. Linda once told me that suicide has been her 'friend' for as long as she can remember. Now I understand what she meant. But the only way of knowing if we've discovered the reason for Linda's condition is to wait and see. Now that these issues have been brought into the open, hopefully their power will be diminished. That's the theory at least.

But while I'm obviously struck by how awful this must have been for Linda, and find it hard to imagine how difficult it would be for a young girl to cope with this level of trauma, I am not convinced that we have found the reason. The dream Linda recounted causes me concern. The connotations of the slime in her mouth, choking her, are horribly sexual. Who is the man standing by the pool watching her? Her father? Mike? Or is it someone else?

11

TUESDAY, 25 JULY 1989

Linda Caine

At night I sometimes go to the old chapel and work out on the treadmill and exercise bike. I keep the light off because I don't want anybody wandering in. Instead, I leave the door slightly ajar, which gives me just enough light to see.

I've invented my own game, which I've christened 'Ticehurst Squash'. Two sides of the chapel have no windows and the floor is polished wood. Using a sponge ball and a badminton racquet I can send the ball ricocheting against the smooth walls. Mostly I have the old chapel to myself. I can really work up a sweat playing Ticehurst Squash. Every time I miss the ball I have to run after it across the floor.

'There you are,' says Dympna. She's standing in the doorway with her hands on her hips. Her hair is swept back into a neat French roll.

Dympna has a soft, lilting voice with a gentle Irish accent that sounds like music. Mostly she works on night duty, and I love to have her sit and talk with me when I have trouble sleeping. I know she's not just here because it's a job she has to do: she really cares about people.

'Come on, Sarah is going to play the piano.'

'Who's Sarah?'

'A patient. She's in the lounge. Come and have a coffee.'

My first reaction is to say no. Dympna knows I'm not one for mixing with people.

'Just come and listen,' she says in her soft Irish accent. 'That's all you have to do. I'll even get you some hot chocolate.'

As we walk down the passage, I realize how much smaller Dympna is than I am. She barely comes up to my shoulder. I normally only see her when I'm sitting down and she brings me coffee. She makes the best frothy coffee I've ever tasted.

In the lounge I try not to make eye contact with anyone. Dympna sits me down and gets me a hot chocolate. 'I'll just be a minute,' she says.

She comes back leading a young girl by the arm. The girl is only fifteen, but looks even younger. Her blonde hair touches her shoulders and her eyes are half closed. She's so heavily medicated that she seems to be sleepwalking.

Sitting at the piano, Sarah stares straight ahead. For a moment I think she's forgotten what she's going to play, but then she begins. Her fingers seem barely to touch the piano keys. She casts a spell. Nobody moves or makes a sound. I've never heard a sonata played so beautifully.

For fifteen minutes I listen to this angel playing. As she finishes, the lounge erupts in applause, but Sarah doesn't acknowledge the ovation. She keeps staring straight ahead, as though she can't hear a thing. One of the nurses leads her away. Sarah gazes blankly at the faces around her.

'How long has she been here?' I ask Dympna.

'She arrived about three days after you did.'

'What's wrong with her?'

Dympna shakes her head. 'I can't tell you that.'

The following day I find Sarah wandering in the passage by herself. Normally I'd just walk on by, but I know she shouldn't be on her own.

I put my arm around her. 'Are you all right?'

She's a million miles away, in another world. So I turn her around and lead her back. A nurse appears, looking for her. 'There you are, Sarah. You shouldn't wander away like that.'

As I let go of Sarah's hand something registers in her eyes. She seems to focus on my face and make a mental image. Up until then I doubted if Sarah knew what day of the week it was, but this is different. A few days later I see her again in the corridor, I rub her shoulder and she smiles at me. She remembers. She's like a bird with a broken wing. I want to wrap her up and keep her warm until she's well again.

In four days from now I'm going home. I hope I'm ready. I feel quite uncertain and in some ways it feels too soon. But I want to be home when Gary and Christy get back from the Isle of Man. We can spend what's left of their summer holiday together. Dr Royston seems happy enough for me to go. We've chosen 29 July as my last day. Before then, I want to get through the story of marrying Mike and what happened afterwards.

It's a glorious summer's day. We go for a walk in the grounds and I show him my favourite place, the tree stump in the hedge, opposite the entrance to the hospital. Dr Royston isn't really wearing walking shoes, but he doesn't seem to mind. The turf is soft underfoot and the paths are starting to dry after yesterday's rain.

I begin telling him about my wedding to Mike in November 1968. Connie made me a lovely wedding dress. Dad's next-door neighbour, a German film-maker, let us borrow his big fancy white car. He drove Dad and me to the church.

As the car pulled up outside the main doors, Dad said, 'Lindy, are you sure you want to do this?'

'It's a heck of a time to ask me that,' I said.

I think he was worried about how young we were. I also think he felt partly responsible, as though he'd pushed me into this by telling me to leave home.

Mike wanted me to be blond on my wedding day. I went to the hairdresser and they tried to dye my hair. The result was a disaster. I ended up walking down the aisle with bright ginger hair in curls piled high on top of my head. Mike was horrified.

We couldn't afford to go on a honeymoon, but Gene's mum and stepfather paid for us to spend a night in a fancy hotel in Lusaka. At the wedding reception, a business contact of Dad's asked me to dance. I knew Mike didn't like him very much.

I looked across at Mike, to see if it was OK. He seemed ambivalent so I went ahead and danced. From that moment he wouldn't speak to me for the entire reception. On the drive to the hotel I asked him what was wrong.

'You danced with Dave.'

'Well, I asked you first.'

'You know I hate him.'

'That's why I asked you.'

'You should have just said no.'

'OK, next time I will, but you should have said something.'

As we reached our room, Mike stormed past me into the bathroom and slammed the door. He must have taken a couple of beers from the reception because he lay in the bath drinking them.

I sat down on the bed and asked myself, 'What have I done?' I had signed away my life. For better or for worse, the vicar said. Although Mike's jealousy bothered me, he had never been so manifestly unreasonable. Marriage was supposed to make it better. He wouldn't have to be jealous.

Soon after we married Mike left the butchery and started work as a car salesman. He had a company car and we moved into a large three-bedroom house in a farming area on the outskirts of Lusaka. For the first time we had a little money to spare – not a lot, but at least we didn't have to watch every penny.

All of Mike's friends were still bachelors and he enjoyed going out with them, being one of the boys. He seemed happier leaving me at home because it meant he didn't have to worry about keeping an eye on me.

About a year after we married Mike took me to a party thrown by some friends, Mark and Jennifer. Mark had an eye for the ladies and Mike didn't trust him at all. As usual, Mike isolated me and took me onto the veranda. There were loads of people inside. Mike went to get us a drink and Mark saw me sitting by myself. He came over and chatted to me. Just then Mike returned. He was cold and angry. He shoved my drink at me without even acknowledging Mark's presence.

Mark backed off, but it was too late for me.

'Was he making a pass at you?' Mike demanded.

'No. He asked me if I wanted a drink.'

'But *I* was getting you a drink.'

'Mark didn't know that. He saw me sitting here alone.'

'You're lying.'

We left the party immediately and went home. I started getting ready for bed, but Mike didn't want to let it go. He kept accusing me of lying and wanted to know what Mark had said to me. I couldn't remember the exact words, which made Mike even more convinced that I was covering up. Suddenly, he grabbed my arm and swung me. I lost my balance and my head hit the wall. I woke up on the floor with Mike leaning over me.

'I'm sorry. I'm sorry. I'll never do it again,' he said, as he cradled my bruised face. He was crying. I'd never seen him so upset. I felt sorry for him.

I made him a coffee and told him that it was OK. He kept saying it would never happen again. I believed him.

'You probably think I was very naïve and foolish,' I say, glancing at Dr Royston. He's sitting on the log with his hands pressed flat by the weight of his legs.

'No, I think you were in love.'

'Bad choice, huh?'

'We all make them.'

Across the road, in the field beyond, a dairy herd is being mustered for milking. The farmer's voice carries on the breeze as he gently coaxes the cows home. I love the countryside. I see things to paint and draw everywhere, in the veins of a leaf and the petals of a flower. I think if I could choose to be anything at all, I would be a wildlife artist.

Dr Royston hasn't said anything to interrupt my train of thought. I hope he's enjoying being outside. I know so little about him and he knows so much about me. It seems unfair. I want to know why he does this job. Doesn't it get him down? Doesn't he feel that people unload all their problems onto him? I'm the same. I want to leave all my troubles behind me when I leave Ticehurst. I want Dr Royston to pack them in a box and toss them into the incinerator.

'You were talking about Mike,' he says gently. I can't tell if it's a question or a prompt.

I continue the story. Mike slowly began closing the world around me, making it shrink to fit only the two of us. First he said that it made him feel better if he knew who I was going to see or who I spoke to on the phone. Soon, I couldn't even contact my family without asking him first. At dinner each evening, he'd quiz me about my day, wanting to know every detail of what I did and to whom I talked. The more I hesitated or stumbled, the more difficult the questions became. I had to remember entire conversations word for word, or Mike would accuse me of lying and keeping things from him.

At the same time, Mike was still going out a lot with his mates and drinking heavily. They'd play snooker and go to discos. Sometimes he came home very late, or not at all. I don't know if he was faithful. You know how it is – you hear rumours. There was one particular girl I heard about. By then I felt like saying to her, 'If you really want him, you can have him. I'm not going to put up a fight.'

I also began to wonder if some of the fights that I had with Mike were manufactured. Maybe he wanted to get me out of the way. 'Push off. I don't want you any more,' he'd say, and pack me off to Annette's. Then the next day he'd come and fetch me. Meanwhile, I knew he'd been out all night.

We'd been married for more than a year when Mike's younger brother Robbie moved back in with us. For a while this seemed to calm Mike down. But one night Robbie went out to the drive-in with a friend and they had an accident on the way home. Robbie was only seventeen and didn't have a licence, but his friend had let him drive. The car had left the road and rolled.

I waited until Mike came home a couple of hours later and we rushed to the hospital in Lusaka. Robbie was lying on a stretcher in the emergency department. He was unconscious, and blood spattered from his nose and mouth as he breathed.

'Why aren't you helping my brother?' Mike screamed, bringing people running. 'How long has he been here? Where are the doctors?'

Mike's face was white. 'I want a doctor here *now*,' he yelled, as he held Robbie protectively.

Within minutes Robbie had been rushed into an examination room. Curtains were pulled around the bed. Mike and I sat outside. Doctors and nurses dashed to and fro, giving him transfusions and trying to stem the internal bleeding.

Finally I heard a doctor say, 'His lungs have collapsed, he's drowning in blood. Stop the transfusions.'

The doctor came out and told us that Robbie was badly injured and they had done all they could.

'I think you should go home,' he said. 'We'll call you if there's any change in his condition.'

'We don't have a phone,' I said.

'We'll send a vehicle.'

In the early hours of the morning a car arrived. Mike insisted that he go alone. Robbie died before Mike arrived at the hospital. He had never regained consciousness.

When Mike came home, he went to Robbie's bed, took his pyjamas and hugged them in his arms. Rocking back and forth, he crooned, 'It's all right, Robbie. It's all right.'

He slept on Robbie's bed that night. He wouldn't let me comfort him.

From then on, Mike's behaviour became even more un-predictable. His drinking grew worse and his jealousy intensified. He wanted me to have a baby – a boy that we could call Robbie. It was as though Mike thought this would somehow bring Robbie back.

Soon afterwards we moved to a small town called Kalomo, two hours' drive from Lusaka and seventy miles from Livingstone. Mike said he wanted to get away from Lusaka for a while, but I think the real reason was to isolate me. Kalomo is a dry, dusty, one-horse town, with a general store, a hotel and a couple of garages. One of Mike's uncles owned the garages and another had a farm outside of town. Mike started working as a mechanic and odd-job man. Once a week I did the books at the garage to earn extra money, but eventually that stopped. Mike didn't trust the staff.

We lived in an old farmhouse ten miles from town. It had no electricity or telephone and the nearest neighbours were about four miles away. With Mike at work, my only company was Pedro, who cooked and helped me in the house. He, his wife and their eight children lived in a small house down the sandy road and farmed their plot of mealies.

Pedro was a small man (no more than about five feet four) in his mid-fifties with greying hair. He worked in the morning, cleaning the house and doing the washing. In the afternoon he went home, then returned most evenings to cook dinner for us.

My only other companions were two boxer dogs, a Rhodesian

ridgeback, two cats and my parakeet, Jeremiah. I loved the isolation. It was such a peaceful place. Sitting on the veranda wall (my favourite place) I had a panoramic view of the bush for miles around. The only hint of life was the dust that rose in the distance when cars bounced along the dirt road leading from Kalomo to the various farms along the way.

Parks and gardens are nice, but they can't touch the emotions like the wild. One of the things I loved most was listening to the sounds of the bush. The cry of the fish eagle is one of the most haunting and beautiful sounds you will ever hear. And at night, the deep groan of a lion makes your hair stand on end.

Just outside Lusaka there was a snake centre, which paid money for snakes that were then milked for their venom to make antivenene. Mike began collecting puff adders, which he kept in open-top forty-five-gallon drums until he had enough to take to the centre. I wasn't happy about the arrangement. The drums seemed too small and claustrophobic.

Initially, we had two snakes. Mike almost tripped over one of them going to the outhouse one morning. It was a magnificent specimen, so thick and sleek. Puff adders only grow to about three feet long and this one was so thick that I suspected it might be a pregnant female. She was very mellow and Mike could lift her out on a small hooked wire and stroke her back. I thought him foolish because puff adders can strike forwards and sideways with lightning speed. The second snake was much smaller and more aggressive.

Concerned that the drum might get too hot, I checked on the snakes periodically, peering inside and letting my eyes become accustomed to the shadows. The smaller snake would attack a wad of plastic wedged in a hole at the base of the drum. It was angry and I didn't blame it, being trapped like that, but it was strange seeing this tiny snake working its poison into the plastic. It disturbed me. It was futile because the snake was too small to force the plastic out and sad because it seemed to know that freedom lay beyond it. I found an empty swimming pool near the derelict original farm-house and convinced Mike it was a much better place to keep the puff adders. We put logs and grass in the bottom, creating our own snake pit.

A few weeks later, I awoke suddenly in the night. I lay for a second, staring into the darkness, and wondering why I'd been wrenched from sleep to a confused alertness. And then I felt it – a thousand hot needles being jabbed into my skin.

'Ants,' cried Mike, already on his feet.

I jumped out of bed and began frantically trying to brush them off, dancing and shaking. The army ants were crawling in my eyes, ears and nose, under my clothes and through my hair. The room filled with an eerie, high-pitched sound. The ants were warning each other of attack. The more we tried to get them off, the more ferocious they became. The pain was excruciating.

Mike fumbled for the candle and matches on his side of the bed. He finally managed to light the candle and, in the dim glow, the walls, floor and ceiling seemed to be alive.

The army had turned on us. This is how the ants overpower and kill even large animals. Cattle will stop or roll on the ground, trying to shake them off, but wave after wave of ants will attack in their tens of thousands. They crawl into the nose, ears and eyes, driving the poor animal crazy until it drops from exhaustion.

Grabbing a torch, Mike found four buckets, filling each with water and paraffin. Then we pushed the bed away from the wall and put a bed leg into each bucket. Climbing back onto the mattress, we stripped the sheets and blankets and shook them, flicking away the ants.

I could hear the cats and dogs growing frantic in the next room.

'We have to save them,' I cried.

Mike leapt onto the floor and opened the door. Calling the animals onto the bed, we had to hold them down one by one to brush the ants off them. All the while, I tried to calm them and stop them panicking and jumping back into the sea of angry insects. Meanwhile, Mike danced and hopped outside the house. He opened the door to the chicken coop and chased the chickens out. Then he found Pedro and gave him some paraffin to protect his family.

For the rest of the night we huddled on the bed with the animals. The paraffin water kept the ants from climbing the legs of the bed, but they still dropped from the ceiling. In the grey early dawn light, the room looked surreal. The ants were so thick on the floor that they moved almost like a liquid, filling every crack, hollow and empty space. I danced over the cement floor to get my clothes, hearing the bodies crunch underfoot. Then I jumped onto the bed and shook my jeans and shirt free of ants before putting them on.

I stayed on the bed with the animals, while Mike went into town and bought more paraffin and some ant-killer. When he returned he poured a ring of paraffin around the house, while I sprayed an area of the ground with ant-killer to create a sanctuary. Mike set the paraffin alight and the ants went crazy. Initially, they broke ranks and surrounded the fire, but kept a distance. Many ants inside the ring turned back to fight. They formed a teeming barrier inches thick on the ground.

Complicating matters was the danger of starting a bushfire. The surrounding scrub was tinder dry and the fire could easily get out of hand. We kept circling the house every few minutes, carrying wet towels and buckets of water to beat down the flames. I had my jeans tucked into socks and boots, but the ants still managed to get inside. Every so often, we would jump back into our safe 'island' surrounded by ant-killer and frantically beat the ants off our legs. Mike helped me clear my shirt and I did the same for him. Although it was painful, we couldn't help laughing at each other as we danced around, shaking and slapping our clothes.

For half an hour the army seemed in chaos until their unseen generals marshalled them into ranks again. As the fire began burning itself out, leaving a blackened ring, the column of ants started marching again, this time around the house. Mike put a thicker ring of paraffin just inside the first burnt ring. It was ready to be lit if the ants tried to cross again.

We still had to clear the ants from the house. Thankfully, the fire had drawn many of them outside, answering the call to attack. After Mike had gone to work, I sprayed the house from top to bottom with ant-killer. Then I swept the poisoned ants into piles and carried them outside, adding them to the ring of paraffin as a deterrent. When it was all done, I stood watch on the veranda, ready to light the paraffin if they tried to cross the line. Meanwhile, the column of ants kept marching around the house, their lines stretching off into the distance.

It was an incredible sight. Each ant was about half an inch long and red in colour. They moved in columns three to twelve inches wide that sometimes separated and joined up again. The formations were as slick as any military drill. If I tapped a stick into the middle of their ranks, the high-pitched noise would begin again. All the ants nearby would turn and attack the stick.

It took three days for the column to pass. Every night at dusk we burned the ring of paraffin and poured a fresh ring. Then I sat on the veranda wall – safe on my island – and watched them.

When the danger had finally passed, I went to check the old swimming pool. The snakes were dead. The ants had stripped the flesh from their bones. A couple of chickens wandered back to the house a week or so later. I was surprised that any had survived.

The dogs and cats were traumatized. For weeks the cats would only sleep on top of the cupboards in our bedroom and the dogs had to be forced from our bed to sleep on the floor. They became totally paranoid and would jump up and tear about the house if so much as a fly settled on them.

Although I loved the solitude and peace, Mike's jealousy and irrational behaviour grew worse. Annette visited occasionally, bringing news of the family, but it was obvious that Mike wasn't happy until she'd gone.

Occasionally he took me to the Sports Club at Kalomo to see a film or to watch him play snooker. I had to stay with him, sitting to one side reading a book or looking out the window. I had to be careful about who I looked at or spoke to. If I left the room to go to the toilet, Mike would come with me and wait outside, or he'd stand at the door of the snooker room, keeping one eye on the game and the other watching for me to come back. I could hear laughter and the thwack of balls from the tennis courts. Sometimes Mike let me watch the tennis, but I was frightened that somebody might come and talk to me and then Mike would make me pay for it later.

He came home from work one day and demanded to know who had visited me during the day.

'Nobody. I've been here alone apart from Pedro.'

'You lying bitch,' he roared. His face was twisted into a horrible mask.

He dragged me into the kitchen and held me over the bench. He put a butcher's knife to my throat and screamed, 'Who visited here today?' White spittle clung to the corners of his mouth and I could smell the alcohol on him.

'Nobody, I promise. Please, Mike. Nobody has been here.' I begged him to stop but he wouldn't listen. He held his arm in front of me and sliced it open with a knife. I felt the splashes of blood on my face as he squeezed his fist tight. The blood dripped into my eyes and hair.

He let me go and shouted out the kitchen door for Pedro. Poor old Pedro came running up to the house. He stopped at the door, horrified by the scene.

'Who was here today, Pedro?' Mike demanded to know.

'Nobody, Bwana.'

'Don't lie. I've seen the tyre tracks in the driveway. Somebody came here.'

Pedro thought about this for a moment. The whites of his eyes were huge as he saw me standing with blood running down my face.

'Nobody came here, Bwana, except you. You came home for lunch.'

A cloud of doubt passed across Mike's face. He stormed outside and examined the tyre tracks. Then he slowly walked to the car and crouched to examine the tread. They were the same. Feeling numb inside, I picked up a cloth and began cleaning Mike's blood from the kitchen counter. He sat on the veranda and stared at his feet, ignoring the beautiful sunset. Later that night he came to bed. I lay awake in the darkness with my back to him.

'I'm sorry,' he whispered. 'I'll try harder not to be so jealous. I'll never hit you again, I promise.'

'You're driving me away,' I said.

Mike shook his head. 'If I ever lost you I'd kill myself.'

We had been through a lot together and I cared about him deeply, but I knew I didn't love him any more. He frightened me too much. But then he would cling to me like a child, promising he would not hurt me again, and asking me not to leave him. My heart would go out to him, my resolve to leave would falter, and I'd stay, naively hoping this really would be the last time he hit me.

I only retaliated once. I don't remember what happened to set him off. He shouted at me and pushed me around, then backhanded me across the face so hard that I fell. As he turned away from me, something inside me snapped. I picked up a plate from the small table next to me, and threw it. It bounced off him and smashed against the wall. He spun around, and the shock in his eyes turned to disbelief and then fury. Crossing the floor in a stride, he kicked me in the side. He had never kicked me before, and I curled into a ball to protect myself. He stood over me for a while, his breath coming in gasps, as he fought to control himself.

Then he turned abruptly, went to the bathroom and turned on the taps. I heard him undress and get into the bath. Quietly, I threw my things into a suitcase and ran out to the car. I didn't know how to drive. Mike had once tried to teach me, but I kept stalling the engine because I was so nervous. The car had a dodgy alternator and was difficult to start. It was like a scene from a movie. I sat there, desperate to get away, turning the ignition over and over. Every sound was amplified by the darkness.

'Please start. Please, please, please . . .'

Mike came out of the house with a towel around his waist. He started running towards me. The engine spluttered into life and I slammed my foot down, spinning the tyres. He chased me down the sandy road, screaming my name.

I was so terrified of stalling that I didn't get out of first gear until I got to the main Kalomo road. I bounced over the dirt road, skidding around the bends. I knew the alternator was fading. The headlights were growing dim. How long would the battery last? I had to cross a bridge which had no side-rails and was just wide enough for the car. By the time I arrived at the bridge the lights were failing and I couldn't see properly. I was terrified of driving off it into the water. At any moment I expected the engine to die, leaving me stranded in the middle of nowhere. I would not be able to continue on foot because there were lions in the area.

Somehow I managed to reach town and the railway station. The next train didn't leave until mid-morning. I went back to the car and turned the key in the ignition. Nothing happened. The engine was dead. Unsure of what to do next, I walked through the bush until I reached Mike's uncle's house. I told him what had happened and he let me stay the night.

In the morning Mike arrived. I don't know how he managed to get in – maybe he walked the ten miles. He was coldly angry.

'I want my car keys,' he said. His lips were bloodless thin lines. He walked to the nearest garage, picked up a tow-truck to collect the car, had it mended and drove off to work without saying another word. I told his aunt and uncle about the violence. That evening, Mike's uncle took him to one side and warned him not to touch me. He probably saved my life.

When Mike apologized to me that evening I didn't feel sorry for him any more. When he begged me to stay, I felt no warmth or compassion. Something inside of me had died.

'I can't go on like this,' I said, very calmly. 'I'm afraid of you.'

'I'm sorry.'

'That's not going to be enough. We've tried a lot of things to make this better, but none of them have worked.'

He tried to convince me of his new plan. We'd move to Ndola in the Copperbelt to be nearer to his family. He'd get a new job. I knew it wasn't going to work.

'I think we shouldn't see each other for a while,' I said. 'We both need some space . . .'

'Don't leave me,' he pleaded. 'I won't do it again.'

'I'll stay with Annette in Lusaka for a few months.'

I was surprised when Mike agreed. It seemed too easy. He was still going to Ndola where he'd find himself a job and somewhere to stay. Then we'd get together and discuss our future.

Annette collected me on Saturday, but two days later Mike came to Lusaka and told me he had changed his mind.

'You're coming to Ndola. It'll be different there, you'll see.'

'No, Mike. We need time to think.'

'Go and get your things. You're coming with me *now*.' He grabbed my arm but I held my ground.

'Not this time. You go to Ndola. Sort things out and then we'll decide.'

He hesitated and I braced myself for a beating. Instead, he pushed me away and stormed out, wheel-spinning down the driveway in his car.

I felt weak with relief. I couldn't deal with his violence any more.

*

Next morning I went to Dad and Connie's place to tell them what had happened. We were having tea when Annette arrived with one of Mike's best friends, Johnny. The moment I saw their faces, I knew something was wrong.

'Where's Mike?'

Annette took me into the next room and put her arms around me. 'He's dead.'

The ground beneath me suddenly began to shift. Annette was trying to tell me what had happened, but I couldn't take it in. I couldn't breathe. How could he be dead? I only saw him a few hours ago. I ran outside into the garden and kept running. The shock and sadness were suffocating.

Annette found me. 'He was drunk,' she said. 'He must have decided to take off to Kalomo. He crashed through a roadblock at the Kafue Bridge and hit a stationary truck. He died before they got him to hospital.'

'I'm sorry, Dr Royston. I'm always crying around you.' The sun is behind him, creating a silhouette. I can't see his eyes.

'Don't apologize,' he says.

'Do you know, I can't remember the date that Mike died. I know it was in August. Isn't that terrible?'

He doesn't answer.

'At his funeral I had to sit in the front pew at the church. That's what widows are supposed to do. I could hear them walking down the aisle, carrying his coffin. I didn't want to see it. They set it down right in front of me. I had the same awful feeling of not being able to breathe. I stood up to run, but someone grabbed me and held me down by the shoulders. They made me sit.

'"That's not Mike," I said out loud.

'Someone whispered for me to be quiet. It was like being in a bad dream. After the church service we drove to the cemetery. The long line of cars crawled past a golf course and I looked across these beautifully mown fairways and saw people playing golf in the sunshine. I couldn't understand why they weren't affected. Didn't they realize that Mike was dead? Why was the world still turning?

'At the cemetery they gave me a handful of soil to throw on the coffin. I couldn't do it. I couldn't bury him. People began filing past, each tossing handfuls of dirt that rattled on the casket lid. But I held on to my dirt. I couldn't throw it.

'Mike had a watch that he really loved. His family asked me if I wanted to keep it, but I said no. They buried it with him. I kept thinking about the watch still ticking in the coffin, even though Mike was dead. What do you make of that, Dr Royston?'

Robin Royston

Linda opens her hands in exasperation. The wounds on her wrists have started to heal and she no longer needs bandages. Although she's stopped crying her cheeks still shine wetly. And her T-shirt is creased where she has worried it with her hands.

Linda's story is getting darker each time we shine a spotlight into her past. She has suffered terribly at the hands of a violent husband and was widowed at the age of twenty. In my experience, events such as these often point to a much bigger, more complex picture, and we are still at the stage of taking the pieces out of the box.

'How do you feel about Mike's death now?' I ask.

'Guilty.'

'Why?'

'Because I don't remember the date.'

'Is that all?'

'And I've always had this question mark in my head about whether it was my fault.' She pauses as if trying to find the right words. 'I'm 90 per cent convinced that he was drunk and he lost control at the wheel. But you have to ask yourself . . . you know what I mean. The fact that he crashed through a barrier, crossed over the bridge and drove into that truck. I'll never know if it was deliberate or not. He told me he would kill himself if I left him.'

She begins crying again. 'Do you know what I keep asking – what if I'd gone back to him . . . would he still be alive?'

Here is the question she has been wrestling with for nearly twenty years. I can't answer it for her. From where I sit – as an observer – Mike's fate seems pretty inevitable. It appears that he was on a mission to self-destruct, and would, in all likelihood, have taken Linda with him had he lived.

Clearly, there is a lot of still-unresolved feeling wrapped up in his death. But how important is this in her present troubles? How much of what happened then is responsible for the way Linda is haunted now? I just don't know the answer. Perhaps if she can now make sense of her chaotic emotions things will begin to ease.

I don't want her to leave Ticehurst, but I understand her reasons. Her family need her.

12

SATURDAY, 29 JULY 1989

Linda Caine

My bags are packed and sitting on the bed. Chris is coming to pick me up this morning. On the one hand I don't want to leave Ticehurst, yet I know I can't stay here for ever. My life is outside.

Gary and Christy are still on the Isle of Man at Chris's parents'. I've been sending them letters and cards. Sammy the poodle is there too. Once I get home and settled again, I want to bring them back. I want us to be a family again. I still feel shaky sometimes, but on the whole I feel better than when I arrived here five weeks ago. I know I'm not out of the woods, but let's hope that it's all downhill from here. At least I'll still be seeing Dr Royston twice a week at the Chaucer.

Dympna knocks on the door. 'Sarah wants to know if she can come and say goodbye.'

'OK.'

Although I've barely spoken to Sarah, I know there's a bond between us. Whenever she's playing the piano in the lounge, I stop what I'm doing to listen. And I still rub her shoulder when I see her in the passageway.

She edges into my room looking shy and confused. Her features are so fine that I imagine her as a pencil sketch that some artist has forgotten to fill in. Without saying a word, she holds out her hand

and gives me a tape. It's a recording of the sonata I first heard her play.

She raises her eyes for the briefest moment and then lowers them.

'How did you learn to play the piano like that?' I ask.

'I started when I was five years old.'

'You must have practised every day.'

She shrugs.

'How did you remember this piece without the music?'

'I once had to learn it for a recital.'

'It's beautiful. It goes straight to the heart.'

Sarah glances around my room and notices my guitar. I know she wants to say something.

'I don't play very well,' I tell her. 'Not like you.'

When the time comes for her to leave, I give her a hug and thank her again for the tape. As she walks away, I notice that she isn't shuffling so much. Maybe they've reduced her medication or perhaps she's getting better. I hope so.

Chris picks me up at 10 a.m. He's so happy that his mood is infectious. On the drive home we make plans for the future. We decide that in December we'll go to South Africa and spend Christmas with my younger brother Brendan and his family. I haven't seen Brendan in eight years.

When we arrive home, Chris tells me to close my eyes. He leads me through the front door and into the formal lounge.

'You can open them.'

I gasp with surprise. He's set up a gym, with an exercise bike and a jogging trampoline.

'*Wow!*' I turn and hug him. 'When you decide to do something, you don't spare the horses, do you!'

He laughs as I jump on the exercise bike and begin pedalling. 'I read that exercise can elevate the mood,' he explains. 'It's really good for people with depression. It'll be good for both of us. We can have exercise evenings instead of watching television!' His pleasure and relief at being able to do something specific to help is obvious, and I jump off the bike and hug him again.

I wander around the house, rediscovering how much I love this place. And I keep going into Gary and Christy's rooms just to sit on their beds and look at their things. I've missed them so much.

That night they call from the Isle of Man. Christy breaks down and sobs, 'I want to come back. Please let us come home.'

She makes it sound as though we've banished them. I can feel my heart breaking. Then Chris shows me a letter that arrived a few days earlier from Gary. He'd written, 'I'm trying to be good but Grandpa keeps getting me into trouble. Can we come home now? We'll be really good and quiet, I promise.'

I want to cry, but I'm too angry. This is ridiculous. I want my children.

First thing on Monday morning, we book our flights to the Isle of Man to bring them home. We leave a couple of days later. All through the flight I feel a mixture of excitement and anxiety. And as I walk down the aircraft steps and cross the tarmac, I try to catch a glimpse of Gary and Christy.

I see Gary first. He's running between people towards me. Christy is close behind him. They reach me and throw their arms around me. I have to fight back tears so I don't embarrass them.

After two days we fly back to England together. It's great to be home again. At the same time, I can sense a shift. A huge unstated burden has been placed on Gary, Christy and Chris. They're tip-toeing around me, not wanting to create any stress. I can imagine Chris drumming it into them, 'Mum's feeling better, but you must be extra good. Don't give her any trouble . . .'

My children are so afraid of 'not being good' that they're not being themselves. Christy in particular has changed. I can see her eyes questioning whether she really knows me any more. I'm trying to spend more time with her, like making her favourite biscuits. She loves baking. I invite her to make marzipan fruits so we have time to talk.

'Is there anything you want to ask me?' I ask her.

'Like what?'

'I don't know. Is there something you want to know about Ticehurst and why I was there?'

'No. Dad told us.'

'What did he tell you?'

'That you're depressed about things . . . things that happened a long while ago that you can't forget. He said that you're getting better.'

She doesn't look directly at me. She looks past me, towards the window. I know something is bothering her. She used to be able to talk to me.

Finally she asks, 'Do you love Dad?'

'Of course I do. Why do you ask?'

She chews her bottom lip and lowers her eyes.

'Is something wrong, Christy?'

She shakes her head but not convincingly. Finally it comes tumbling out. 'If you love Dad, why were you married to someone else before him? It means you loved someone else first. How could you do that?' There's a hint of accusation in her question.

So that's it. Now I realize what's wrong. Christy's naive view of romance and love doesn't have room for more than one husband. She imagines that love is for ever, and that someone can have only one true soulmate. Ever since she discovered my earlier marriage she has been questioning how much I love her father.

'My first husband died,' I tell her softly. 'I was only twenty.'

'Did you love him?'

'For a time.'

'But he used to beat you up.'

I'm shocked that she knows this. Why has Chris told her?

'The man I married drank a lot and when he drank he became a different person. He wasn't the same person I'd married.' I watch closely to see if Christy understands. 'He died in a car accident many years ago. Then I met your dad again and we fell in love.'

Christy nods and I put my arm around her. 'Until you and Gary came along, I didn't think I could love anyone as much as I love your dad.'

Later that night, when the children are asleep, I tell Chris what happened.

'Why did you tell them about Mike and the violence?' I ask angrily. 'Why did they need to know that?'

'I had to tell them something. I couldn't just say you were depressed.'

'Why not?'

'Because they thought it was *their* fault. They thought *they'd* done something wrong. By telling them about Mike, I made them see that it was something else . . . that you've had a hard life . . . and that maybe it's something in your past.'

I can see his point, but it doesn't change things. I hate the idea that my children might treat me any differently. I'm not going to break if they hug me. I'm not going to fall apart if they do childish things or fight or argue or be themselves. When I get a chance, I sit down with Gary and ask him how he feels about me having been married once before. His reaction is very different to Christy's. Instead of doubting me, he's angry at Mike.

'I wish he wasn't dead,' he says.

'Why?'

'Because then I could find him and punish him for what he did to you.'

His fists are clenched at his sides and I can sense his helplessness. He has no outlet for his anger and frustration. How long can he keep it bottled up?

So we're all damaged by this. Chris seems to have aged in the past year and he's drinking more than he should. He's always watching me for the slightest sign of something being wrong. I'm acutely aware of the burden I'm forcing them to carry.

Twice a week I drive to the Chaucer to see Dr Royston. These are still my best days. I come away from our sessions feeling much more confident that I can cope with the world.

This one particular morning, I'm on a narrow stretch of road that twists through the woods towards Canterbury. A lorry rounds a corner much too quickly and crosses onto the wrong side of the road. My little Metro has nowhere to go. In that fraction of a second I wrench the wheel and swerve. I close my eyes, expecting to hear the crunch of metal before I die. Somehow the truck misses me and my Metro finishes up off the road, almost parked in a hedge.

My heart is thumping. How close was that? Then the irony dawns on me. Here was an opportunity to kill myself 'legitimately', when any witness would have said it was an accident, but instead I pulled away and saved myself. When I tell Dr Royston what happened he doesn't seem surprised at all. 'Our desire to live is normally stronger than any other,' he says.

'Does that mean I don't really want to die any more?'

'No. It means that at that moment in time, you wanted to live.'

I can tell Dr Royston anything and it's still OK. I trust him completely. He always asks me how I'm coping and I tell him about the days since I saw him last. I'm managing to keep the house running OK and I'm able to ferry the kids back and forth to school. But the reality is that I'm still struggling. Some days are just awful. I live inside a suffocating black cloud that doesn't let in any light. From the moment I wake up until I go to bed, I go through the motions of living, when all I want to do is to stop existing entirely.

If I'm lucky I can sleep at night, but even that small pleasure is often denied me. I lie awake, with my heart pounding, frightened of falling asleep. Because as I do, I see the flashes . . . a hand covers my mouth and nose . . . I can't breathe. I jump with shock, and a cold sweat covers my body. It's as though if I fall asleep the hand will come. So I stay awake, staring into the darkness.

I don't wake Chris. He's got enough on his plate without worrying about me. He thinks I'm getting better. He thinks it's all in the past now. If he knew the truth, I don't know what he'd do. I don't want to find out.

I show Dr Royston a dream that I had on Sunday night.

I am on a very muddy path that becomes a tunnel with a low ceiling. I have to crawl along on my stomach and the mud is wet and slippery. Coming to a large pool of water I lose my nerve and stop, but some people crawl up behind me saying excitedly, 'Come on, I love stalking horses!'

I let them pass me then follow them into the water, which goes deeper and deeper. The people turn, going around a sort of island, and back to the path. I follow, but the water is thick with very deep and slippery mud. I can't get a foothold.

It is too thick to swim and I feel myself begin to slip under. Although the water is very muddy, I can somehow see underneath. I see the woman in front of me slip under as well.

A man who has gained a foothold on the path laughs and, taking hold of her, he pulls her out of the water. I hope that he'll pull me out as well, but he doesn't seem to realize I need help. I can't breathe, or get out by myself.

Desperately, I try to attract their attention, but they don't seem to notice me struggling. I begin to slip deeper under the mud.

Dr Royston says the same imagery keeps coming up in my dreams – the muddy water, not being able to breathe, dying in the deep end of the pool. He's always looking for patterns and themes, but I can't see anything.

'The dirty water and not being able to breathe are quite symbolic of what you're going through now,' he says.

'In what way?'

'You think you're going to drown because you can't cope. You feel like you're going under, that everything is getting on top of you. Or there's something underneath the dirty water that you can't see, but it frightens you . . . you're slipping deeper into the mud.'

'How do I stop it?'

'Sometimes you have to go through the dirty water to get to the other side.'

'What if I drown?'

'We have to hope that doesn't happen.'

I start telling Dr Royston what happened after Mike died. I went to live with Annette for three or four months in the Standard Chartered Bank flat in Lusaka. More than anything else, I wanted to get away from Zambia, away from anything that reminded me of Mike. To make matters worse, his friend Johnny was spreading a story that I had killed Mike as surely as if I'd put a gun to his head and pulled the trigger.

Five weeks after Mike's funeral, I flew to Salisbury in Rhodesia for a holiday. I stayed with my cousin Trish, my uncle Don's daughter, whom I'd met a few times and written to while we were growing up. Trish had a lovely flat in a tree-lined street near the city centre.

It was a difficult time in Rhodesia. The independence struggle or terrorist campaign (depending on your point of view) had been a vague backdrop to my teenage years. It was like watching the storm clouds on the horizon in the weeks before the rains arrive. The lightning and thunder could be seen and heard in the distance, but the storm never seemed to arrive.

The white minority in Rhodesia had clung to power while elsewhere in Africa former colonial rulers were granting the indigenous people independence, or at least the vote. Zambia had won its freedom in October 1963, a couple of years before we arrived. Two years later, the Rhodesian government, led by Ian Smith, made a Unilateral Declaration of Independence (UDI), cutting itself adrift from Britain, which had been encouraging it to negotiate with black nationalist leaders.

In reality, Rhodesia had never been a British colony, but a 'protectorate' of the mother country. Even so, Britain responded by imposing economic sanctions and seizing assets. The United Nations adopted similar tactics. Black nationalist groups such as ZANU and ZAPU, which had been banned in Rhodesia, began conducting a low-level bush war from exile in neighbouring Zambia and Mozambique. They launched raids across the borders, attacking farms and government outposts.

In my six years away, I hadn't taken much notice of these 'troubles'. Perhaps living with the repercussions of a mixed marriage had taken my mind off the bigger picture. My only concerns were the rumours that the border between Zambia and Rhodesia might close because of the war. If it happened suddenly, I could be trapped, unable to get back to Zambia.

In Salisbury it was hard to believe that the country was at war. Life in the leafy northern suburbs appeared to be idyllic and uncomplicated. The sports clubs were full every weekend, with people playing cricket, golf, tennis, badminton and basketball. There were social days and picnics.

Trish didn't like leaving me alone in her flat during the day so she asked her fiancé, Barry, to look after me. Although I appreci-ated their concern, I wasn't very good company after what I'd been through. Barry wanted to take me swimming. I had visions of a crowded public swimming pool, but he said it was a private pool that belonged to a friend of his. We drove through Highlands, a lovely suburb of Salisbury. The houses had sweeping lawns and long drives. Eventually we pulled up in front of a sprawling home with a wrap-around veranda. A young man waved to us.

'Is that Chris Caine?' I whispered to Barry.

'How on earth do you know him?'

'We went to school together.'

Chris and I had been in the same class at Cecil John Rhodes School in Gwelo from the age of ten to twelve. I remembered he wasn't very impressed by girls back then. One particular day the boys from several classes had to combine for woodwork and the girls for domestic science. Chris didn't want any girls sitting at his desk, so he spat on his seat as he left. The last time I saw him was when I was fourteen. We bumped into each other in town and spent the afternoon together. Chris wrote to me but I lost his letter during the move to Zambia.

As I walked across the lawn I could see that he didn't recognize me. He was also surprised by my age. Barry had told him that I was a widow and obviously he had expected an elderly lady. He stood there, a little embarrassed.

'You don't recognize me, do you?' I said.

He looked puzzled and I took pity on him and told him.

'You were always an "A" student,' I said. 'I suppose you're doing law or medicine.'

'Law,' he replied, self-consciously. 'I remember thinking you were a snob,' he said. 'You were always so rigid when you walked and you didn't talk much.'

We both laughed.

It was like stepping back in time as we talked about Mrs Kirk, our class teacher, and Mr Crowley, the sadistic master who was always giving the boys 'six of the best'. Names from long ago drifted in and out of the conversation.

The swimming pool reflected the blue of the sky and a man in a white uniform crossed the lawn carrying a tray with tea and scones, clicking his tongue in annoyance at the three yellow Labradors following him.

It was a wonderful day and over the next couple of weeks Chris and I saw a lot of each other. He and Barry would come over to Trish's flat and we'd go to the George Hotel for a drink, or to a party, or to my favourite place, Mermaids' Pool. This was in the bush, a few miles out of Salisbury, where a waterfall cascaded down huge rocks into a large pool. Chris was a perfect gentleman.

One night we drifted from party to party, because I didn't like places that were too crowded. Somebody bought a bottle of brandy on the way and we passed it around as we danced. I found myself drinking far more than I should. I seemed to be living in a bubble where everything in my life was unreal. I was happy, but that only made me feel guilty. Mike had only been dead seven weeks. I knew my happiness couldn't last. I was due to leave for Zambia in a day or two. Feeling melancholy and overwhelmed, I went outside and lay on the grass, staring up at the clouds moving across the deep purple sky. Patches of stars would appear and disappear.

It was a hot night, with a lovely breeze. Chris came and sat next to me. For a long while he said nothing. He leaned closer and then hesitated. It was almost as though he wanted to kiss me, but was afraid. Suddenly he found his courage and gave me a sweet kiss. I said nothing, but he started saying my name over and over again as I lay there. It was like a dream – a beautiful evening, an African sky and a lovely young man saying my name over and over, as though I was really special.

I held on to that moment for a long time afterwards. It was like a snapshot that I kept in my mind, the way some people keep photographs in their wallets. I thought it could never be anything more than a fond memory. Chris and I came from such different places. Almost all of my friends came from broken homes or dysfunctional families. He was one of the few people I knew whose father and mother were still happily married and living together. He was well educated, gregarious, with dozens of friends. I was a loner, who left school at fifteen and hated crowds.

Chris was very close to his mother and he couldn't understand why I had never tried to find mine. I think he imagined some wonderful reunion.

'I haven't seen or spoken to her in twelve years,' I told him.

'Do you know where she is?'

'No. The only reason I know she's alive is that she used to send me birthday cards before we moved to Zambia. She'd put in the exact number of shillings to match my age.'

'When did she stop doing that?'

'When I was fourteen or fifteen.'

'Don't you ever think about her?' he asked incredulously.

'Sometimes, I suppose. I used to wonder what she looked like now. I remember her as being very beautiful. I used to say to myself that one day I'd find her and just watch her from far away . . . simply to see what she looks like.'

'Don't you want to talk to her?'

'No.'

'But she's your mother.'

'She stopped being my mother a long while ago.'

Chris was excited about looking for her, but I wasn't really interested.

'Well, what if we just find her and then you decide?' he said.

I shook my head but he sensed I was weakening.

I flew back to Lusaka a day later. I would have loved to stay in Salisbury and I promised myself that I'd return as soon as I could arrange it.

In the meantime, I was back working at Van Motors and living with Annette. I mentioned to her that Chris was trying to find our mother. She was quite surprised and a little wary. Being two years older than me when it happened, Annette knew a lot more about the divorce than I did. Dad had burdened her with enormous responsibility and told her things that perhaps a father shouldn't tell his daughter.

'Mum said she would only take the boys, not us,' Annette said, wanting me to know what I was getting myself into.

'What do you mean?'

'Dad showed me the letter from her attorney. I saw what was written: "Mrs Houston-Brown says you can have the girls because they have always been closer to you. She will take the boys if you pay her." But Dad wouldn't. Whatever happened, he said we mustn't be separated. He was going to fight to keep us together. He didn't have to fight very hard. The boys were back with us after just a few days.'

I don't know why I reacted so badly to this news. Why should I care after all these years? But I *did* care. My mother had not only abandoned me, she hadn't even tried to keep me. She only wanted Brendan and Clive if Dad paid child support.

Three weeks later, I went back to Salisbury. It was great to see Trish, Barry and Chris again. We went out to the George Hotel on Friday night and Chris kept smiling at me, as though he had a secret.

'What are you so happy about?' I asked.

'I've found your mother.'

I must have looked totally shocked. For a brief moment, I think Chris wondered if he'd done the right thing.

'She's living in Mtoko – about an hour's drive from here. She and her husband run the local post office and the social club.'

'How did you find all that out?'

'A friend of mine did a stint at the army base in Mtoko. He says everyone in town knows Marion and Peter.'

Chris was pleased with his detective work, but I didn't share his enthusiasm. Why should I risk being rejected by my mother twice? What if she hung up when I called? What if she didn't want to see me?

The man she was now married to had lived down the veranda from us at the Park Hotel. He and my mother had an affair, according to Annette. She saw them together. Dad found out when they were seen together at the racetrack. That's when Dad told her to leave. Even when I told Chris this much of the story, he still thought I should call her.

'What do you have to lose? She's not part of your life now. Even if she doesn't want to see you then nothing changes. But what if she does? What if she's been hoping and praying all these years that you'll get in touch with her?'

I dialled the number and held the phone with both hands to stop it shaking. Each time it rang, I wanted to hang up. A woman answered.

'Is that Marion?' I asked.

'Yes. Who's speaking?'

'Ah . . . well . . . it's Linda . . . your daughter.'

There was a long pause.

'Hello, Linda.'

'A friend of mine found your number . . . I thought . . . I hope you don't mind me calling?'

'Not at all. Goodness, it's been so long. You must be nineteen years old now.'

'Twenty.'

She sounded nice. I don't know what I expected, but I didn't think she'd sound so nice. Making conversation was like stepping over eggshells, not wanting to crush the years that separated us. She didn't know me. I had a million and one questions that I wanted to ask. What happened? Why did she go? What had she been doing all her life?

'Can I come and see you?' I asked. I seemed to blurt the question out, almost without thinking. She hesitated for a moment. I didn't know whether she really wanted to see me, but she said yes. Perhaps she knew how much courage it had taken for me to pick up the phone and call her.

The following weekend Chris and I drove to Mtoko. We planned to have lunch and perhaps stay the night. In the hot and dusty main street the cars were parked nose to the kerb. The bright sunlight made the shade of the trees even deeper. Chris left me outside the post office and went for a walk. I climbed a few steps up to a small veranda and glanced through the open door. Inside I could see a little window and a man sitting behind the counter.

'I've come to see Marion,' I said, trying to stop my voice from shaking.

'Are you Linda?' He smiled. 'I'm Peter. I'll just get Marion for you.'

I went onto the veranda to wait. A few minutes later a woman came out. She wore a simple floral summer dress and sandals. I wouldn't have looked twice at her if I'd passed her in the street. There was no family resemblance at all. This wasn't the blonde ice princess that I remembered. She was a middle-aged woman, with a figure to match.

'Hello, Linda,' she said, guardedly. She looked uncertain as she walked over and hugged me awkwardly. Neither of us knew what to do or say. Should I cry? Should I be angry? The only instinct I felt at all was the desire to get away. This had been a bad idea.

My mother held my hand and we sat side by side on two chairs on the veranda. She brought out cold drinks and fried bacon skins. I was grateful for something to do with my hands.

She didn't look directly at me as she talked. She looked down at her hands, as if insecure, or hiding something. She had thinning hair. I remembered her hair being shiny and full. I don't know what I expected. I think Chris thought there'd be a spark of recognition and sudden chemistry between mother and daughter. Instead, I felt nothing at all. I didn't know this woman. She didn't know me.

Without me asking she began telling me her version of what happened when she left. First she went to Bulawayo to stay with her family and then she tried to find a job.

'You probably think I'm a terrible mother,' she said, dabbing at her eyes with a handkerchief. 'I don't know how much you remember, but it was very difficult. In the end I didn't have any choice, however painful the decision. I would have taken you with me, but I was on my own. I didn't have any money. They were hard times.'

She didn't know that Annette had seen the letter from her attorney. I let her go on telling me things that I knew weren't true.

'The truth is, I had to leave,' she said. 'I couldn't stand his affairs. He used to sleep around with the black women in the villages. He couldn't keep his hands off them. You can see that, can't you? You only have to see *who* he married.'

I wanted to defend Dad. I wanted to refute what she was saying, but I couldn't find the words. I knew the grounds for divorce had been *her* adultery, not his. I also knew that a white man accused of sleeping with black women in the villages would never have been granted custody of the children. Nor would my mother have allowed herself to be sued for adultery under these circumstances.

I said nothing. It didn't make sense. Why did she say these things? Didn't she see that if everything she said was true, it made *her* worse? If Dad had been so terrible, how could she leave her children with him?

As if reading my mind, she said, 'I wanted to take all of you to Bulawayo, but I was a woman alone. I wouldn't have been able to earn enough to look after you.'

A woman alone? Her family lived in Bulawayo – a mother, father and five or six brothers and sisters. Did she take me for a fool? If she had taken us, Dad would have been forced to pay alimony and child support. She said she only met up with Peter Blake again by chance, when she went to work for the post office in Bulawayo. They renewed their 'friendship' after the divorce came through. 'We married and made a home for you in Bulawayo, but your father wouldn't give you up,' she said.

I didn't believe her.

Peter appeared on the veranda and locked the door behind him. It was lunchtime and the post office was closing for two hours. Over lunch, he and my mother convinced Chris and me to stay the night.

'We're having a Christmas party at the club,' she said. 'You'll have a great time.'

I looked at Chris. He smiled and nodded. As far as he could tell, I was getting on famously with my mother and we could catch up on all the lost years. I accepted apprehensively.

At the party that night I wore a black, figure-hugging outfit, with knee-high boots and a headband. I don't know what possessed me. Maybe I was trying to shock my mother. The outfit turned heads in a conservative town like Mtoko. When my mother began introducing me to her friends, I overheard a farmer muttering, 'She's a bloody hippie!'

My mother cut him dead with an icy stare. 'She is *not* a hippie. She's my daughter.'

Then a young girl of about nine pointed to me and asked, 'Who is she, Auntie Marion?'

'She's my little girl.'

'But she's not a little girl.'

'No, she's not a little girl, but she was once, just like you are now.' My mother cradled the young girl's face with her hands and ran her thumbs over her cheeks. My heart lurched. It was such a sweet, loving moment, but I felt nothing but confusion. Why did I have no recollection of my mother ever talking to me like that?

The post office and the social club were the two social hubs of Mtoko, which meant Peter and my mother were involved in everyone's lives. All the locals seemed to really like them. After the party we drove back to their modest house. There were blackout curtains and iron mesh covering the windows to stop hand grenades being thrown through them. Mtoko was in a 'hot' area in the war with nationalist rebels.

Chris slept in the lounge while I had a canvas camp stretcher in the dining room. For a long while I couldn't go to sleep. I kept going over what had happened during the day, trying to sort out what I felt about seeing my mother again.

I must have dozed off because I woke suddenly with the terrible feeling that someone was in the room with me. As I lay very still I heard a quiet shuffling close by. Moving my eyes, I could just make out the form of someone kneeling next to me, who began crying softly.

I half sat up and reached out with my hand. I touched my mother's hair and pulled her towards me. She put her head on

155

my chest and continued crying. They were deep, heartbreaking sobs that shook her whole body. 'It's all right,' I whispered. As I stroked her hair I remembered what Annette had said about it being baby-soft. She was right. It was the softest hair I have ever felt.

I don't know how long we stayed like that. As she calmed down she began to take short breaths between her sobs, just like a child who's been crying a lot. Then she slipped my arm off her shoulder and left. She hadn't said a word.

I took me a long time to go back to sleep. I kept wondering what it was all about. Was she trying to say sorry? Did she feel guilty for leaving us?

The next morning, I woke and went through to the kitchen. I stopped in the doorway and watched my mother get bread ready to be toasted. She had her back to me. I had a strong sense of knowing what was about to happen, as though it had happened before.

'Good morning,' I said. She turned around and said good morning back to me.

'Would you like some toast?' she asked.

I went cold inside. There was no hint in her face that anything had occurred during the night. No acknowledgement that she had cried in my arms. Instead, she turned away from me and continued cutting bread. I stood transfixed and watched her with feelings of total confusion. Had I just imagined or dreamt what happened? No, it was real. IT . . . WAS . . . REAL!

'Did you say anything to your mother?' asks Dr Royston.

I feel startled. The memories are so vivid that I've been lost in them, and I realize I almost shouted the last words, like an accusation. I feel as tense as a coiled spring.

Dr Royston sees my confusion and repeats his question: 'Did you speak to your mother about it?'

I shake my head. 'I wanted her to acknowledge what happened, but she never did. We sat and ate breakfast and made small talk. Afterwards Chris and I packed up and left. There were so many questions I wanted to ask her, Dr Royston. I wanted to know whether she was sorry for leaving us. Is that what she was trying to say to me?'

'Why didn't you ask her?'

'I couldn't. Maybe I was scared of the answers.'

'Did you stay in touch with her?' Dr Royston asks.

'Yes. I saw her a few times, but I always felt I was being disloyal to Dad. She spoke so badly about him. She started sending me birthday cards again and I wrote to her occasionally after we moved to England. I don't know why I kept in touch. She frightened me, but at the same time I wanted her to love me.'

Robin Royston

A pigeon flutters onto the window ledge and distracts Linda just enough to interrupt her train of thought. She lapses into silence, perhaps going over the events in her mind.

Linda has talked more about her mother in this one session than in all the others before it. Up until now her memories have been fleeting and disjointed, which has made it difficult for me to paint a mental picture of her mother. Even so, the woman she describes seems rather cold and hard. Apart from the lies, there is a lack of any guilt or doubt about her actions. It is very easy to mistake sentiment for genuine feeling, but when you find hard coldness it usually occurs in spades.

Sadly, the reunion created enormous confusion and uncertainty in Linda because of her desire for a mother. It is a confusion that has lasted her whole life and has affected how she views her own role as a wife and a mother. At her worst moments she has asked herself, 'Am I my mother's daughter?'

At our next session, two days later, she picks up the story again. She was living in a tiny flat in Lusaka with Annette, still traumatized by Mike's death. By her own admission, Linda became quite promiscuous. Partly this was due to not wanting to go back to the flat, but mostly because she hated being alone at night. Sex was the price she paid for company.

Linda doesn't feel comfortable talking about her promiscuity. I think she feels guilty for having sexual encounters so soon after Mike's death. But I am struck by how irrelevant and unimportant she regards these sexual encounters to be.

She visited Salisbury three times in the four months after Mike died. On the second of these trips, something took place which points strongly towards what I suspect lies at the heart of her difficulties. She and Chris had grown very close, but nothing had happened between them. The relationship was very different to the others she'd had.

'I knew that he had a crush on me, but I wasn't in a very good place,' says Linda. 'He was so sweet . . . he deserved better.'

'But something *did* happen?'

She nods. 'I was staying at Chris's parents' house in Highlands. Chris had a one-bedroom flat with its own entrance. One night we both had a lot to drink and we ended up in bed together . . .' She pauses, embarrassed about going on.

'Chris was still a virgin,' she whispers. 'He'd done pretty much everything else with a girl except intercourse. I could tell he was nervous. This was special to him. He started making love to me . . .' Her voice begins breaking. 'I'm sorry . . . I'm trying not to cry . . . but poor Chris . . . it wasn't his fault.'

'What happened?'

'I don't know . . .' She takes short breaths. 'One minute he was kissing me and the next thing I remember was his voice saying, "Are you OK? Are you OK?" I don't know what happened . . . I didn't faint . . . I just stopped sensing anything.'

She squeezes her hands hard between her knees and keeps raising and lowering her heels from the floor. 'Chris couldn't get through to me. It was as though I wasn't there. He said I just curled up on the bed and said nothing.'

'For how long?'

She looks at me wide-eyed. 'For hours.'

'And you don't remember anything?'

'No. According to Chris, a couple of times I said, "Everything is dead. Everything is dead." That's all. Poor Chris was beside himself. He didn't know whether to call a doctor or get his mother, who was a nurse. It must have been awful for him.'

Linda doesn't know what happened. Her only recollection is of being 'far away'.

'Did it ever happen with Mike?' I ask.

She shakes her head. 'Not really. Sometimes I just seemed to switch off, but I never blanked this completely. Sex was important to Mike. I didn't think of it in the same way.'

'What happens now when you and Chris make love?'

Linda falls silent. Her voice falls to barely a whisper.

'Sometimes when we're being intimate, I see a sudden image of a huge man looming over me. It frightens me so much that I have to turn on the light to make sure it's Chris who's touching me. He doesn't know that. I've never told him.'

Linda has just described three different experiences during sex, but all of them set alarm bells ringing in my head. Her description of becoming 'distant' and seeming to blank out reminds me of what happened when she lost her virginity and afterwards had no recollection of being penetrated or feeling any pain. Any therapist, psychologist or welfare officer who works with sexually abused children will tell you that 'distancing' is very common. The victims try to cut themselves off from the abuse, by becoming small or going far away in their minds. Now Linda admits to having flashes of 'a huge man' looming over her when she makes love to Chris. She feels small and helpless.

For a long while, I have wondered if this is what lies at the heart of her problems. The 'hallucinations' she describes having as a child; the bed-wetting and being scared of the dark; the dark-haired man in her dreams; the idea of something or someone coming for her in the night, the hand over her face . . .

I am beginning to feel a burgeoning unease, and a strong sense that we are looking at the tip of a huge iceberg. I am particularly apprehensive that at this stage I still have no idea where exactly all this is leading.

The notion that a major traumatic event can block out memory is the subject of enormous debate. There is still no international recognition that amnesia even exists. Despite more and more examples, the evidence hasn't been strong enough to be conclusive. Some of these cases date back to the First World War when soldiers disappeared and had no memory afterwards of what happened to them. Such disagreements within psychiatry and psychology are common. We know so little about the human mind.

My knowledge of blocked memories comes from practical experience. Early research tends to suggest that children are more likely to block things out than adults. Grown-ups have a greater ability to rationalize and understand the predicament they're in, whereas a child is often helpless.

Linda takes the view that if something had been so terrible, how could she forget it? Surely it would be branded on her mind and no amount of time could wipe it out. It isn't until she realizes there are gaps in her memory that she begins to ask me about the possibility. Linda describes to me how just before she became seriously depressed her father had a heart attack and nearly died in America. Her brother Clive called from California to break the news.

Linda's immediate response was to fly straight out there. Her family is spread over three continents. At that time, her father, Clive and her half-brothers Sean and Jemal were in America, Annette and Brendan in Africa, and herself in Britain. She wanted to show solidarity and offer support. Annette also flew out to join them.

'Dad opened the door to his apartment in Inglewood looking pale and gaunt, and puffing away on a cigarette,' she says.

' "This is absolutely crazy," I told him.

' "Why, Lindy?"

' "Because you'll die, you old fool."

' "And I could get hit by a bus tomorrow, or struck by lightning. Let me enjoy life while I'm here."

'That was just Dad, and I couldn't reason with him. But it was a curiously happy time. When Annette arrived two days later, it was the first time we'd lived under the same roof for fifteen years. Dad was no trouble at all. He pottered about with his patio plants and watched *Wheel of Fortune* on the TV. We made him cups of tea and made sure he took walks each day.

'In between times, Annette and I sat and swapped stories about growing up in Rhodesia. We had never reminisced about our childhoods before. Africa had been such a powerful backdrop that events seemed almost larger than life. The very sounds and smells were still vivid; the village drums that ebbed and flowed with the wind; the smell of wood smoke in the air; and the first raindrops on hot earth, exploding in the dust like miniature atomic bombs.'

Whenever Linda talks to me about Africa, I notice how she relaxes and becomes animated, immersed in her memories. More importantly, she is now beginning to give me a more detailed insight into her relationship with her father.

'When I was eight and Annette ten, Dad used to let us play outside in the rain, as long as there wasn't any thunder or lightning. Sometimes he'd play with us, chasing us through the puddles. At other times he'd sit and watch from the veranda as we made rivers and dams.

'We had to be careful of the water scorpions. It might not have rained for a month or more, but the puddles would bring them out again. The neighbours used to watch us from their windows. One old woman lectured Dad one day about letting us play in the rain. "They'll get sick," she scolded. "Pneumonia and terrible things."

'Dad politely ignored her. I think she was more offended by the fact that he let his daughters wear boys' swimsuits and no tops.' The corners of Linda's mouth curl upwards as she says this.

'If we looked particularly cheeky, Dad would tickle us and say: "What have you done, you wicked little wenches!"

'Giggling and squealing, we'd chorus: "Daddy, we are *not* wicked little wenches!"

' "Well then, you must be foolish little floozies!"

'More shrieks of laughter. "No! We're not foolish little floozies!"

' "Then you must be silly little sausages!"

'By then we'd be running away squealing our denials.'

I ask Linda how she felt, talking to Annette about their childhood.

'Well, that's just it,' she says, the ease of our conversation starting to ebb away. 'I discovered that our memories were completely different.'

'In what way?' I ask her.

'Annette and I were sitting at the kitchen table in Dad's apartment and I began talking about 5 Maple Avenue, the house we moved to after our mother left. It was a sturdy brick house, built on about an acre of land, in a middle-class area called Windsor Park. It was close to the showground where Prince was stabled, and had loads of space in the garden and lots of places to hide. It was a great house for kids, and we were only a few minutes' walk from open fields and paddocks, as well as the railway lines. On the far side of the railway line, through the bush, was the Gwelo river.

'Inside, the house was large and airy, and had a sort of circular design so that you could walk through most of the rooms and come back to where you started. There was Dad's room to the left of the hallway, and the lounge with an open fireplace to the right. You went through the lounge to the dining room, and then into a small hall with the pantry and kitchen on your left, and the scullery – leading to the back door – on your right. Further down the hall past Dad's bedroom was the housekeeper's room, and then Annette's and my bedroom at the back.

'The house had a sand and gravel driveway with two entrances onto Maple Avenue. Two cement pillars flanked each entrance, and a hedge ran around the remaining three sides of the garden. I loved the garden, which was full of fruit trees – mulberries, guavas, figs and oranges. Our bedroom looked out onto the orange orchard, and we could also see the animal pen and aviary that Dad built to house our menagerie.

'We always had loads of animals – cats, dogs, guinea pigs, rabbits, pigeons, a lamb. That night in the kitchen at Dad's with Annette, we were talking about them and how Dad had built cages for them all.

'Then while we were talking Annette reminded me that this was the second time we'd lived at the house.

' "What do you mean?" I asked her.

' "We lived there twice."

' "When?"

' "Before we moved to the Park Hotel and our mother left."

' "No we didn't!" I exclaimed.

' "Of course we did. For three years."

Telling me this is making Linda agitated. She is looking down and pinching her clothes.

'Dad confirmed what Annette said. We'd lived in the house for three years, from the time I was about four years old. How could I forget three years? And that's not all. For example, I can remember Annette starting school – I can picture her standing in her school uniform, when we lived at Riverside – but I can't remember *my* first day at school eighteen months later. It's all just a blank, as though somebody swept a duster across a blackboard and wiped my memories clean.

'Do you know the strangest thing?' Linda looks up at me and seems to be trying to make sense of something.

'When we moved back to 5 Maple Avenue – after our mother had gone – I used to feel sort of as though the house was haunting me.'

'How?' I ask her.

'Annette remembers how Dad used to say that I had hallucinations. I've told you about them. They were so bad sometimes that Dad told Annette not to let me out of her sight. But I still can't remember *anything* about the three years we lived there before, when our mother was still with us.'

What worried her most is that if she has forgotten three years of her childhood, what else is missing? What other events or relationships or confrontations?

'It's frightening to think that you don't know something is missing until you find it, or other people confirm that it happened.'

She has written in her notes:

'What difference will it make if I remember? Why let it affect me so much now? If I stopped therapy and I stopped searching and I tried to stop my mind thinking about anything from the past – would the flashes stop?'

She also questions whether she is trying to lay the blame at somebody else's feet rather than take responsibility herself. Trying to find a scapegoat and turn herself into a victim. These are common doubts.

Linda can understand the theory behind blocked memories, not the practice. If something really bad had happened to her then surely she'd remember. If she'd been suffering from amnesia caused by something sudden and traumatic like a car accident, it would have been easier to accept. But hers is like a selective amnesia. How can the mind simply choose what to remember? And why is it coming back to her now?

Without doubt, in addition to all the terrible things she has told me, something traumatic has happened to Linda – a dramatic, destructive episode which she has blocked out. I see this as a positive. The fact that something has been buried means we have a chance to dig it up. Even so, I don't look forward to the prospect. I have a deep, instinctive fear that whatever has been hidden from her all these years will be dangerous and difficult to contain.

13

SEPTEMBER 1989

Linda Caine

Things are getting better. I'm learning to cope with everyday life. I go shopping every week and try not to panic when I pick Christy up from school and one of the other mothers begins to make polite conversation.

I went to Gary's schoolhouse barbecue last week and on Friday night there was a charity fund-raiser organized by clients of Chris's. I managed to speak to a few people and occasionally find a pocket of quiet to calm my nerves. It might not sound like much, but it's a start.

Oh, *who* am I fooling?

The reality is that I want to hide from the world.

Gary and Christy hardly ever have friends over any more. Worse still, I'm teaching them to be deceitful. A week ago, when I was feeling shaky, I told Gary and Christy not to answer the door or the telephone. Gary forgot and picked up the phone.

'It's Mrs Jones,' he said.

I panicked and backed away.

'Tell her I'm in the bath,' I said, shaking my head.

Gary looked mystified. I had always taught him not to lie.

I ran into the bathroom and stood in the bathtub. 'Tell her I'm in the bath. You're telling the truth. I *am* in the bath.'

Now my 'cleverness' has come back to haunt me. For a little while, I've suspected Gary of smoking. He's only thirteen. I've asked him outright but he denied it completely. Today I confronted him again. 'I know you're smoking, Gary. You're normally so truthful.'

'Mum, I wasn't lying to you,' he said, sheepishly. 'When you asked me the question – whether I was smoking – I wasn't . . . not right at that moment.'

I've taught him how to manipulate the truth by playing with words. It's something else to feel guilty about.

A walk to the local shops is a major expedition. I keep hoping that I won't bump into anyone I know. Thankfully, our neighbours mostly keep to themselves.

In the shop, as I pay for the milk, the woman behind me smiles. My heart sinks. Her name is Margaret and she's in her mid-fifties. She lives over the road and often waves to me. Oh, help!

'How are you? I haven't seen you around for ages,' she says.

'I'm fine.'

'Have you been away? I noticed your car wasn't there.'

'I was in hospital for a while.'

'Nothing serious, I hope.'

I don't know why I tell her. It just comes blurting out. 'I've been suffering from depression.' Why can't I just keep my mouth shut?

'Oh, that happened to me a few years ago,' she says, sympathetically. 'It lasted for about three weeks. Do you know, I would rather break my legs and arms than go through that again. They were the worst three weeks of my life, waking up each morning and just mentally shutting down.'

I'm stunned.

'What are you doing now?' she asks.

'I'm just getting some milk.'

'Look, I'm about to walk my dog. Why don't you drop the milk off and come with me?'

I feel a surge of anxiety, but still say yes. We go for a walk through the woods and swap stories about life in general. It's about the first time since Ticehurst that I've been able to talk to someone for so long without panicking or becoming tearful.

For those few miles I feel like a normal human being again.

Gary and Christy are upstairs doing their homework. Christy has been going through a difficult patch and I can't seem to communicate with her. I keep thinking that it's adolescence, but she's only eleven. I know something's wrong. Normally, when Christy goes quiet, she's just thinking things through. But this time she seems to be struggling. She's fighting with her friends and she's constantly complaining about her teachers. It's as though she's angry at the world. When I'm struggling like I am now, I don't have the patience to deal with her moods.

Yesterday we fought because she refused to put her dirty clothes in the laundry. Then she complained that I hadn't washed some jeans she wanted to wear. Today she hasn't said more than a dozen words to me since I picked her up from school.

At dinner she announces that she's not hungry. I tell her that she has to eat something but she starts to argue.

'Look, I'm not going to discuss this. You must eat something.'

'I'm not hungry.' She gets up and begins to walk out of the room.

'*Christy*, come back to the table.'

She ignores me and keeps going. I get up and follow her. 'Christy! Come back to the table.'

'*No!*' She's already halfway up the stairs.

I follow her, with anger burning my cheeks. I can't deal with this today. I'm already struggling. As I reach Christy's room, she turns to face me defiantly.

'Just leave me alone!' she shouts.

'Don't talk to me like that, young lady. If you don't come downstairs this minute, I'll take . . . I'll take . . .' I look around the room and spy her doll's house. '. . . I'll take your doll's house away for a week.'

'Take it!' she flashes back.

I try to tell myself to calm down, but my blood is up. 'Don't make me do it,' I warn.

She looks at me coldly. 'Just take the doll's house. Do what you like. Just get out of my room.'

Something snaps inside me. I raise my foot and stamp down through the roof of the doll's house. Pieces of plastic shatter and fall

166

in colourful shards over the floor. I turn and walk out. By the time I reach the bottom of the stairs, I'm crying. I can't believe what I've done. She loved that doll's house.

I keep picturing the look on her face. She gets the same expression of defiance just before she starts to cry. I know I shouldn't have pushed it. I know I should have just let her go to her room for a while. She only needed time and space to calm down. Then maybe she would have told me what was wrong. Now she's crying in her room.

I've messed things up. I'm a terrible mother.

I'm still shocked and angry with myself when I tell Dr Royston about it on Monday. I'm relieved that he doesn't condemn me. He knows I'm not a saint.

'You reacted badly and we should look for the reasons,' he says. 'Where did the anger come from?'

'I don't know. I just don't have any patience. And Christy seems so bitter about things.'

'Is she bitter towards you?'

'I think so.'

'Why?'

'I don't know. Maybe she's angry that I went away to Ticehurst. She had a dreadful time with her grandparents. She gets into these moods that I can't cope with, but I should have known better.'

'Why do you say that?'

'Sometimes Christy just won't listen to reason until she has calmed down. You don't argue with her. I should have sent her to her room and given us both a chance to cool down.'

'Did you talk to her afterwards?'

'It's OK now. We've said sorry to each other. I think it shocked both of us.'

Robin Royston

Linda's row with Christy worries me. It shows how close she is to the edge and how easily she can lose control.

The more we peel away the layers of Linda's life, the more destructive become the forces it unleashes. There is no way of avoiding this. Linda has been on the receiving end of aggression and indifference as a child and an adult. We have to cope with the fallout.

'Don't be too hard on yourself,' I tell her. 'Just remember that Christy is struggling too.'

'I know. That's why I feel so terrible.'

'She'll forgive you.'

The past three months have taken their toll on Linda. She is underweight and exhausted from lack of sleep. There are nearly always dark rings bruising the skin under her eyes. And there is a remarkable duality about her. In her blackest moods she wants to die, but she also wants to live. In a sense I carry the same duality because I don't know how this process is going to end. I won't be surprised if Linda has been crushed beneath the wheels of a lorry on her way to Canterbury, but at the same time I would be very surprised indeed. This is the uncertainty we exist in.

Since leaving Ticehurst Linda's dreams have become darker and more menacing. The most recent is set on an aeroplane that is gaining speed down a runway. Linda is sitting by a window near the back and can see the full length of the aisle as the plane takes off. Suddenly she realizes that it has stopped rising and started to fall. She knows the jet can't avoid the mountains that lie ahead. It is definitely going to crash and she will die, but she feels relieved that it will all be over quickly. She shuts her eyes so that she can't see it coming.

This is a dream full of pessimism and helplessness. I have to ask myself whether the dream predicts the outcome, or whether it simply reflects her current emotional state. I have no way of knowing, but sometimes, in quiet moments when I'm tired and driving home at the end of the day, I have started to wonder if Linda can survive this. She has been my patient for eight months and there is still no sign of light. Whenever we seem to move closer to whatever lies at the core, Linda's condition grows worse. She begins to close down, becoming almost like a statue, with her hands covering her face. Often I spend a long time reaching her before the session ends. I don't want her driving home unless I know she is OK.

We need a breakthrough – some sign that we are on the right path. It comes on 25 September 1989, when Linda tells me about a dream from the previous night. She has written it out for me.

There is a large cavernous room made of mud, with a pool of soft mud that stretches from wall to wall. Chris and I are wading through the shallow edges with another person. I think it is you, Dr Royston. We are all trapped and trying to get out.

Chris stands knee-deep in the shallow end of the mud-pool and begins digging into the wall. Someone has tried to dig there before and Chris continues making the hole deeper. On his knees, he claws at the clay, tunnelling feverishly. But the wall is so thick that it risks collapsing on him before he can dig through to the other side.

Meanwhile, you begin wading deeper into the soft mud until it creeps up to your shoulders. I think you are going to die. Then I realize that you are trying to reach the far side of the pool. You've seen another place where someone has tried to dig. You start shovelling mud with your hands and it isn't long before you break through the wall and I can see light on the other side. You have found the way out.

I can see you silhouetted against the light and you motion for me to follow. I can't move. I don't want to wade deeper into the mud. What if I slip under? Nobody will reach me, or find me.

I almost sigh in relief and Linda can sense that something has happened.

'It's a good dream,' I say.

'Why?'

'Because it shows there is a way out of this ... that you *can* survive.'

I can see that Linda really wants to believe this, but she feels so depressed that she can't see anything positive.

'What if the dream is speaking to you and not me?' she asks. 'Maybe it's saying that you can get out if you leave me?'

'No. I think it's telling us that you have to go deeper into the muddy water; to immerse yourself in whatever is infecting your unconscious. So far your attempts to escape are reflected in the dream by Chris. He's trying to dig through the wall at the shallow end of the mud-pool. He doesn't want you to have to go through

169

the mud-pool either, but that isn't going to work – the dream says as much. Your only escape is through the muddy water. We have to go into the heart of this, whatever it is.'

Linda doesn't want to hear this, but she understands the rationale. The dream sees hope; there *is* a way out. And according to the dream *I* will be with her.

For the first time since Linda became my patient I have reason to be encouraged.

During our twice-weekly sessions Linda continues telling me about her life. It is a lot like finding the missing pieces of a jigsaw puzzle and putting them in place. She tells me about her father's sudden decision in 1972 to leave Africa and take the family to America. The experiment with living in Zambia had turned sour. President Kaunda had adopted a policy of Zambianizing businesses, which meant that whites like Keith Houston-Brown had to train black personnel to take over their positions.

'Dad wanted to start all over again on a new continent,' says Linda. 'He was sick and tired of the politics of racism. Dad's idea was to sell his properties and buy up African arts and craft. He would export them to America and open a gallery in Los Angeles. Meanwhile, Connie and the children would stay in Rhodesia until he had the money to send for them.

'A lot of this depended upon me. The insurance policy Mike had could be paid out in America, which would give us some money to live on over there. Dad also needed somebody to go ahead and establish an address in America to which to consign the shipment.'

Linda Caine

On my final visit to Salisbury I said goodbye to Chris. I hated the idea of leaving Africa, but Dad really needed my help.

Chris drove me back to the border. The Chirundu crossing consisted of a bridge that spanned a deep gorge carved out by the Zambezi river. It was about half a mile long and crossed the no-man's-land between the two countries.

'Can I talk to you for a second?' said Chris, as I was about to say goodbye.

'Sure.'

We sat in the car and he looked very serious and nervous. He held on to the steering wheel with both hands, staring at it intently, while he chose his words. He began slowly at first.

'I need to tell you something. I know maybe I shouldn't, but I just want you to know.' He looked up at me for a brief second, before turning back to frown at the steering wheel again. 'I've fallen in love with you.'

'Oh, Chris.' I rubbed his arm gently, and suddenly he turned and hugged me really tightly.

He kept talking, all in a rush, almost afraid to let me speak. 'I know because of your circumstances that you can't reciprocate. I'm not expecting you to. I'm not asking you to stay. I know you have to go. But I want you to know that I'm here for you and that I'm in love with you.'

I desperately wanted to give him something in return. I had never been treated with so much respect and gentleness. He had made me feel special. Yet I was coming from such a dark place, with so much emotional baggage. I was terrified that I'd poison his life, just like I'd poisoned mine. He was so together and I was such a failure. The world that Chris had grown up in had been ordered, clean and run on time by his military father. Mine had been a total mess. His life had been mapped out – school, university and the law. I had drifted. If I stayed around him too long then surely I'd infect him.

I stared out the windscreen at the Chirundu Bridge. 'I'll make you a promise, Chris. I promise that you will always know how I feel. I'll never lie to you. Right now, I care about you more deeply than anybody I've cared for in a long time, but I can't make any kind of commitment.'

He accepted that and we sat in silence for a long time. On the other side of the bridge a friend was due to meet me and drive me to Lusaka. Finally Chris walked with me to the boom gates. The guards stopped him and he handed me my heavy suitcase. I half carried and half dragged it along the road. A customs officer took pity on me and drove a car onto the bridge, giving me a lift to the halfway point where Rhodesia ended and Zambia began. I had to walk the final five hundred yards on my own. My last image of Chris was of him standing at the barrier. He raised his hand to wave.

Three months later, Dad and Annette drove me to the airport in Lusaka for my flight to America. I was desperate not to go. My stomach churned and I felt sick as I waited in the queue at the check-in. After going through passport control, I reached the departure lounge. Dad and Annette were on the other side of a large glass partition, ready to wave goodbye. I panicked. I wrote on the back of my cigarette box '*I DON'T WANT TO GO. PLEASE CAN I JUST GO HOME?*' I held it against the glass for Dad to read. He smiled and pointed to himself and the aeroplane, reminding me that he'd be coming to join me soon. I could see Annette arguing with him, but he remained strong. I found out later that he thought he was saving me. So much had happened in my life, he saw this as my chance for a new start.

Thirty-six hours after leaving Zambia, having flown via Rome and London, I reached Los Angeles late at night. The lights were like a sequined shawl stretching out to the horizon. Annette's new husband, a professional hunter, had telexed one of his clients and asked them to meet me at the airport. I collected my bags and waited and waited. The arrival hall slowly emptied until the only people left were the cleaners, pushing mops across the floor.

A TWA flight supervisor had been watching me. 'Are you OK?' he asked.

'No. Nobody has come to meet me.'

He introduced himself as Roy Kraal and told me not to worry. He had my name called over the public address system. Nobody responded. I had a telephone number for the family that was supposed to look after me. Roy helped me call and a woman answered.

'I'm Linda Louw. Did you receive a telex about me?'

'I can't collect you,' she said icily. 'My daughter is getting married next week.'

'Can you just take me for one night? I'm at the airport.'

'No. Find a hotel.'

I couldn't understand why she was being so rude to me. Much later I discovered that Annette's husband hadn't been entirely honest with us. A couple of years previously, he had slept with this woman while taking her and her husband on safari. A year later he had an affair with their daughter while visiting them in America. No wonder she was angry.

Exhausted and tearful, I thought about curling up on a seat at the airport until morning.

Roy wouldn't hear of it. 'I'm a flight supervisor, my job is to make sure all our people are OK.'

I told him the whole story about Dad and the gallery and needing a place to stay.

'OK, I have a plan,' he said. 'You can stay at my old apartment. There's nobody living there.'

Roy had just moved into a new studio apartment because his place had been too big for him. 'I'm always away flying, so I don't need much space,' he explained. 'If you like the place I'll talk to the landlord.'

It was after midnight by the time we reached the apartment. Roy gave me the keys and I lay down on the bed, too exhausted even to think about unpacking. It felt as though I'd only been asleep for a few minutes when I woke in a fright, knowing there was somebody in the room. Roy was standing at the end of my bed with a woman.

'I'm sorry. We were ringing the bell for ages,' he said. 'When you didn't answer the door we thought something was wrong. This is Judy, my fiancée.' It was mid-morning. They were carrying bags of groceries. 'We bought you a few things . . . just till you get to know your way around.'

Before I left Zambia, people had been giving me lectures about the perils of big cities and being careful of strangers. And yet I'd managed to meet two of the loveliest, most generous people in my first few hours.

Roy's old apartment in El Segundo became my address in LA. Dad was supposed to arrive in a couple of weeks, but it took him four months.

Because my family had originally come from the US, I knew that I had American relatives. One of them, my cousin Eleanor, had written letters to us in Africa over the years. I found out that her brother, Frank Snow, lived in El Segundo, just a few blocks away from my apartment. He had three stepsons, Rick, Chip and Michael, who were fascinated by the fact that I came from Africa.

It might not have been the summer of love in San Francisco, but the hippie culture was still alive and well in LA in 1973. Rick and Chip talked about things being 'far out' and 'cool'. Along with their friends they sat around smoking dope and playing guitars. Before I left Africa, I'd been told that anyone who took drugs was mad and a potential killer. Yet these people were all so nice to me I didn't know what to believe any more. By the time Dad arrived I had a steady boyfriend, Bill Mittie, who had long hair, a moustache and beard. Bill was a wonderfully laid-back guy, with a slow drawl.

Dad rented a gallery on La Cienega Boulevard and we began setting up our African art. We couldn't afford to keep the apartment so we slept in a back storage area at the gallery. Dad slept on a rickety fold-up sunbed. I slept on a shelf, sandwiched in a huge doubled-over quilt that Bill gave me.

The gallery and the restaurant above it were owned by a gay couple, Jerry and Cecil. These were the first homosexuals that Dad had ever met. Jerry terrified him because he was so effeminate and outrageous, but Cecil was quieter and less overtly gay.

'African Gallery' did really well at first. We were fresh and new. People would come in off the street and some of them I recognized from TV, but I couldn't remember their names. I did recognize Tony Franciosa. He came in with a woman on his arm, and began asking Dad about one of our more expensive soapstone sculptures. A woman I was serving turned around when he began to speak.

She suddenly rushed over to him, shrieking, 'I know you! Oh my God! You're Tony Franciosa.'

He smiled, but it didn't reach his eyes.

The woman continued hysterically, 'My friends won't believe this. Oh my God. You have to give me your autograph.' She rushed over to me, snatching the pen out of my hand. Behind her, I saw Tony and the lady with him turn and rush out of the gallery, into a large car parked outside.

174

The woman was distraught. 'Did you see that? Did you see that? It was Tony Franciosa.'

Dad was so angry he couldn't speak. High-profile buyers were like gold dust to a gallery and this woman had chased one of them away.

Once the gallery became successful, Dad planned to bring the rest of the family over. He needed enough money for the fares, a house and to pay school fees. In reality, I think his marriage to Connie was over before he even arrived in America.

My heart still lay in Africa. I would have flown back in an instant if Dad hadn't needed me so much. He couldn't run the gallery by himself. We were open seven days a week, for sixteen hours a day. Bill was very sweet and gentle but Dad felt that a 'hippie' hanging around the gallery would be bad for business. Bill eventually cut his hair and beard to please Dad.

Meanwhile, Chris was writing me letters every fortnight, giving me news of Rhodesia and telling me about university. I pictured him in his garden at home, sitting in the sun by the swimming pool, with his Labradors lying next to him as he wrote to me. He felt so clean and uncomplicated, whereas I was totally screwed up and could only drag him down. I didn't write back. I cared about him deeply, but I was still afraid of messing up his life. The sooner he forgot me the better. After five months without getting a reply, Chris wrote, 'I don't know if you are receiving my letters, but I'm not going to write again unless I hear from you. If I scared you, Linda, by saying I loved you, I need to know. And *you* need to know that if all you want me to be is your friend, I'll be your friend.'

That night I wrote a letter back to him. 'I can't offer you anything,' I said. 'But I would love to be your friend. Please keep writing to me.'

There were no recriminations. He wrote back straight away and from then on we kept writing to each other like pen pals on opposite sides of the world. Bill knew I was writing to Chris and, while I don't think he was entirely comfortable with it, he accepted the friendship and my need for it. I was incredibly fortunate to have met two such good men.

14

CHRISTMAS 1989, OUDTSHOORN, SOUTH AFRICA

Linda Caine

The rains have arrived and the days are warm and overcast. Everything seems suddenly to come alive, not just the new growth, but even the crickets and cicadas seem louder. Flowers and plants that were drooping yesterday are now open and upright.

My brother Brendan and his wife Sharon have a wonderful garden. The kapok trees are flowering and weaver birds are building teardrop-shaped nests in the branches overhanging the pond.

I should be getting out and doing more, showing Gary and Christy all the things I love about Africa. But since we arrived four days ago I've barely left the house. I'm nervous about being so far away from Dr Royston and Ticehurst. What if I have another breakdown?

Brendan hasn't changed much at all. It's been eight years since I last saw him. He's in the South African Army, stationed at a base in Oudtshoorn. On the first evening I tried to explain to him about being depressed and suicidal. He put his arms around me. 'You must hold on and be strong, Linda,' he said. 'Remember Jesus is watching over you.' His voice broke and I saw, with surprise, that he had tears in his eyes.

'Now look at what you've done. I'm crying too!' he said, laughing.

Although I'm trying not to let it show, I still panic when it comes to meeting new people or mixing with strangers. Thankfully, Brendan and Sharon understand.

Gary and Christy have never experienced a hot Christmas. Oudtshoorn is practically desert and it must be close to 100°F. Sharon is an incredible cook and on Christmas Day we have turkey, lamb and a ham. Unfortunately, it's so hot that nobody has much of an appetite. I feel guilty about leaving so much food.

There are wild tortoises roaming around the place. It sounds like a contradiction in terms. A 'wild' tortoise! There are also Red Roman spiders, which have bodies about the size and shape of a man's thumb with long legs. They can run very fast and if threatened, they stand on their back four legs and arch backwards as though ready to strike.

On Boxing Day I show Brendan and Sharon the notes I've written over the past eight months. Brendan is quite honest about not understanding depression. I get so frustrated that I don't have an answer to give him when he asks why. There *has* to be a reason for this. The best I can do is to tell them Dr Royston's story of the goat track. I just have to keep looking.

We spend New Year with Chris's brother and sister-in-law in Durban. Mike and Anne have a lovely, sprawling house with a thatched roof, and a separate cottage in the garden which is perfect for guests. They organize a party on New Year's Eve. The idea terrifies me, but why should they change their plans just because of me? I'm sick of having people make exceptions and excuses.

I manage to get dressed up and have every intention of joining the party. I can hear music playing and the hubbub of voices. Sitting on the bed, I will myself to get up and go outside. I can't do it. Anne brings me a plate of supper. 'Are you sure you won't come for just a little while?'

'No, I really can't. I'm sorry.'

'Don't apologize.'

Anne is so understanding that I feel even angrier with myself.

Gary and Christy come to check on me. They're both really excited about joining in such a large party.

'You should come out, Mum,' says Gary. 'Just for a little while.'

'I'm actually quite tired,' I tell him. 'I'd spoil the party if I fell asleep in front of everyone, wouldn't I!'

He and Christy giggle.

'You go and have fun.'

They give me a hug and run back outside.

This difficulty in mixing with people is slipping backwards. In our entire three-week holiday, I go out about five times. I suppose it could have been worse. We spend a few days at a safari camp in Zululand, and go on a game-viewing drive. I'm really pleased when I manage to join others in the camp one night, sitting around the campfire and having a barbecue. The rest of the time I stay in the lodge while Chris, Gary and Christy go out.

The English winter seems particularly bleak and cold when we fly home. The radio reports warn of freezing fog and there are pile-ups on the motorway. Dr Royston has been away, but I don't know where. I know so little about him. I know he has children. Once or twice he's mentioned having a baby girl. And I've heard him talking to Carol about buying a bike for his son's birthday. When I next see him, he gives me a big smile. I feel relieved. It's totally irrational, but I've been afraid that he wouldn't come back from his holiday. He ushers me into the consulting room and pulls up a chair. Raindrops are being driven hard against the windows.

I tell him about my time in Africa and how I'm becoming even more isolated and withdrawn. 'On some days I want everything to simply stop. I want to cease to exist – to have total oblivion.'

'You mean death?'

I flinch. Is that what I mean? I don't know. Before I became a Christian I thought death would be oblivion. I used to find that quite a comforting thought because it gave me a feeling of being in control of situations that I had no control over. I could always choose to die and be out of everybody's reach – to be totally at peace.

'So you don't think that any more?' asks Dr Royston.

I shake my head. 'As a Christian I believe in heaven and hell. Whatever happens after this life, oblivion isn't a choice. I can't choose to be switched off – to simply stop existing. God hasn't given me that choice. If I step out of this life, I go straight into *His* presence.'

'Most people find the idea of an afterlife quite comforting,' he says.

I shake my head. 'I don't want there to be a heaven or a hell. I just want to stop being.'

'Suicide isn't the answer,' he whispers, leaning closer and handing me a tissue.

'But I'm pulling those I love down with me. I want to save them.'

'Then worry about saving yourself.'

Robin Royston

Linda smiles stoically, but her eyes betray her fear. Even God seems to be hemming her in and she can't see a way out. I remind her about the mud-pool dream. She has to go deeper into the muddy water before she can reach safety. But unlike before, this doesn't comfort her.

Linda's faith is incredibly important to her. At times it is all she has. Her anchors in this world, such as her children or Chris, dim at times – so much so that occasionally they recede completely, leaving only her sense of God. This makes the therapy more difficult. A more expected, even healthy reaction towards her mother, for example, would be anger, but Linda's Christian beliefs preach forgiveness. She looks for good in people and makes excuses for everybody except herself. Ever since the mud-pool dream seemed to signal a way out, her dreams have been disturbing and bleak. I can see a crisis coming, but know that we have no choice but to carry on.

One dream involves a man who Linda knows has some sort of hold on her.

I sit on a seat at the end of a row in a large, crowded stadium. The man walks slowly down the stairs from the top of the stadium. I know he is coming to fetch me and I am afraid.

As the man reaches my row, another man – I'm sure it is Chris – comes over and tells me not to be afraid because he will help me. He hits the man very hard in the stomach a few times, but the man doesn't even flinch. Then I realize that nobody can help me.

179

Again we have a sinister man whom she doesn't recognize, and who this time seems to stalk and control her. But the real significance of dreams like this is how they signal that Linda is struggling to cope. The further we delve into her past, the more complicated the picture becomes. Equally, the closer she comes to unlocking whatever lies behind her difficulties, the greater her terror at confronting the truth. Now, despite feeling guilty, she is contemplating suicide again as a way out.

A week later, in early March, Linda writes down the details of another powerful and disturbing dream. The central character has changed.

> *Chris and I are driving through the countryside. A commotion in a field catches my eye and I turn to see a beautiful horse being mishandled by a lovely but hard-looking woman. The horse is magnificent but clearly terrified. It rears violently in a bid to break away from the woman. She holds on to the reins and begins to beat the horse with a whip.*
>
> *There are other men around them, but she and one particular man are in charge. The others watch without interfering. The horse's coat begins to glisten with blood. I can't bear to see it go on. Chris tries to stop me as I jump out of the car and begin to run to the horse.*
>
> *I can't see properly because I am crying. As I get nearer the gathering, I realize that the man who has been standing with the woman looks sad about what has happened, but he doesn't do anything to stop it.*
>
> *The woman stands over the horse, which now lies on a slatted wooden stretcher, covered by a blanket. Breathing heavily, its eyes are wide with shock and its sides are heaving. It doesn't move or try to lift its head as the stretcher begins to move. I feel a tremendous sense of sadness and helplessness. I can't stop it being hurt.*

When I finish reading, I look up at Linda. She has taken her coffee to the window. The light highlights her hair but also shows the worry lines etched around her eyes. She has aged a lot in the past year.

Linda turns, waiting for some explanation. I say nothing.

The silence grows until she mutters, 'I hate that dream. I woke up in tears.'

I nod sympathetically.

She continues, 'I thought it might be about Prince, but he didn't die like that. I hate seeing animals mistreated . . .'

'Apart from Chris, is there anyone else that you recognize?'

Linda shakes her head.

'I think the horse is you,' I say.

She looks surprised. 'Why?'

'Because that's how I feel about you sometimes. As though someone has broken your spirit.'

She thinks about this for a while as she watches steam from her coffee mist up the window.

I read the dream again, contemplating whether the dream figures represent real people, or are compilations of real people. Sometimes characters in a dream can reflect a part of the dreamer's own personality: their happy nature or angry side.

In particular I am fascinated by the cold, lovely woman in the dream. Linda's descriptions of her mother have given me the impression of a cold and powerful woman. It takes a special kind of ruthlessness to walk out on your children without even saying goodbye.

Her father, on the other hand, comes across to me as a big, strong, warm-hearted man, who has raised his children the best he can – making some mistakes along the way. He seems genuinely to love Linda and she loves him back.

Although Linda bears all the hallmarks of having been sexually abused, I am still no closer to discovering the identity of her abuser. Mike was certainly a violent, abusive husband, but does that explain it? Who else should I be looking at? As time goes on, I cannot help the awful but insidious thought that it might be her father. A safe, loving figure being an abuser could certainly explain the depths of her despair. Yet still she loves him. Could he perhaps have been both – the good, loving father and the violent, aggressive abuser?

If he has crossed a boundary and plunged her into this conflict, Linda may well end up with two sides to him in her mind. She might consciously only allow herself to see the good father and split off (bury, if you like) the bad part of him and their relationship. I have to be aware also of the possibility that she might be giving me an image of her father that is not true to him, an image 'through rose-tinted spectacles'. Discovering the truth means being patient. Can she ever look at this 'other' Dad, or will it be too overwhelming?

Although aware of all this, I want to believe that it isn't him. I like her father. He did a lot of good things when he raised Linda. He has nurtured and protected her, loved her and been both parents to her. He has helped her to remain warm, related and human. I respect that. I have a daughter too.

Linda picks up the thread of the story that she's been trying to tell me for weeks. I have a strong feeling that something happened to her in America which she finds difficult to talk about. Whenever she tries to broach the subject, she loses control, sobbing and gasping for breath.

Now I can see her steeling herself to try again.

'I don't know why I can't tell you . . . it happened so long ago . . .'

Linda Caine

I missed Africa. On some days I'd go to the beach and sit facing the sea so that I couldn't see the buildings or people. I wanted the sense of being alone and surrounded by open space. Dad knew I was homesick but he thought I'd fall in love with America. 'Just give it time,' he'd say. He needed my help to run the gallery. He also worried that I wouldn't be able to support myself if I went back to Rhodesia. I didn't have any qualifications or skills, but I *was* tall and slim.

'What if I did a modelling course?' I said.

'What good would that do?'

'There's a department store in Salisbury that employs models to give fashion parades in its coffee shop. If I do a modelling course in LA, they're sure to give me a job.'

Dad wasn't so sure, but he finally agreed. I looked in the yellow pages for a modelling agency. There were lots of advertisements but I chose one that had a photograph of a model who looked lovely. The agency was owned and run by a man called Paul Damon. When I called to arrange an interview the receptionist said the modelling courses were run in a mansion in the Hollywood Hills. The initial interviews were conducted in an office. Instead of giving me the address, she gave me a general location and a telephone number I had to call when I arrived.

The appointment was late afternoon. I wore a short black dress with yellow flowers and my gold sandals. I took great care with my make-up, hoping to make a good first impression. Calling from a public phone box, I was given directions to an attorney's office on the eighth floor of an office block. As I came out of the lift I was met by a striking-looking girl, even taller than I was. She introduced herself as Laurie and took me into a conference room with a long table.

The agency boss, Paul Damon, sat at the head and next to him was his fourteen-year-old son. Another beautiful girl sat next to Laurie. They were both obviously models. An Asian girl was also being interviewed.

Damon was in his late thirties and looked casually wealthy. He asked about my background and I told him about Africa. I wanted to know about the shortest course that he ran – something that would give me a grounding. I didn't want to go into acting, or appear in magazines.

We talked for a long while and I became more relaxed.

'Well, that's the general interview,' he said. 'Now I need to interview you separately.'

The Asian girl had come with her fiancé so he asked her to come back the following day. 'I'll interview you now, Linda, if that's OK.'

I looked around and realized the two models were also getting ready to leave. They were taking Damon's son home. For a brief moment it crossed my mind that I'd be alone with this man, but I thought nothing more about it. He was very businesslike and professional.

Damon suggested that we move to a smaller office because the conference room seemed too large and impersonal. He led me down a hall, away from the lifts, into a plush attorney's office, with a desk, a couch and two single chairs.

'I want to see how you move, Linda,' he said. 'Just walk up and down the room a few times.'

I felt stiff and nervous.

'Relax and slow down. Turn and come back.'

He stood up and put his hands on my shoulders. He was standing very close to me . . .

Robin Royston

'I'm sorry, Dr Royston . . . I'm sorry . . .' Linda covers her face and starts to cry. 'He said to me . . . he said . . .' She desperately tries to continue. 'He said that he liked to have . . . to have . . .'

Words come out between the broken sobs. For another five minutes Linda tries to continue. Then she grows quiet and distant. Physically she is still sitting in front of me, but her mind has left the building. She doesn't appear to recognize me, or even acknowledge my presence.

'Can you hear me, Linda?'

She doesn't answer.

'Linda, it's me, Dr Royston.'

Her eyes have glazed over.

'Listen to my voice. Talk to me, Linda.'

For the next twenty minutes I talk softly to her, hoping my voice will bring her back. It is important not to shake her or shout. In some way this has to be a defence mechanism. When things become too painful to talk about, she dissociates and escapes to a 'safe' place in her mind. I find this idea of 'mind sliding' alarming and intriguing in equal measure. I have never come across it before. Linda describes it as a 'dream-like far away feeling'. At other times she speaks of going 'so deep in my mind that nothing can reach me'.

Towards the end of the session, Linda finally begins to come back. She blinks rapidly and looks fearful.

'What is the last thing you remember?' I ask.

She shakes her head. 'I'm never going to manage this.'

'Yes, you will.'

As much as it distresses Linda, we can't simply move on. We have to keep visiting the same issue until hopefully she finds the strength to tell me more.

My mother holding Brendan, with me sitting alongside, in Riverside, Gwelo, in 1955.

LEFT: Annette (*right*) and me, at our home near Gwanda, Rhodesia, 1951.

RIGHT: My mother holding me, and Dad holding Annette, in Gwanda, Rhodesia, 1951.

TOP: Dad standing in the sea in Fishoek, South Africa, with Annette and me, in 1959.

LEFT: Me at the beach holding a cormorant in Fishoek, South Africa, in 1959.

BOTTOM: Annette, Brendan, me and Clive picnicking with Dad at Whitewaters Dam, Rhodesia, 1960.

OPPOSITE

ABOVE: Me reclining in a haystack, at Lagnaha Farm, Bindura, Rhodesia, in 1961.

BELOW: Annette and me on the beach in Fishoek, South Africa, in 1959.

ABOVE: Chris (*right*) and two friends on the beach, in Beira, Mozambique, in 1972.

LEFT: Chris and me at his home in Rhodesia in December 1971. I did not see him again until I returned from America in April 1973.

RIGHT: Chris and me on our wedding day with Vicar Norman Wood who married us in Salisbury, Rhodesia, on 17 November, 1973.

RIGHT: Chris and me riding in Nyanga in the Eastern Highlands of Rhodesia in 1973.

LEFT: Me resting on a journey through Swaziland to South Africa in 1974.

RIGHT: Prince and me, entering the showjumping arena at the Gwelo Agricultural Show, in 1964.

BELOW: Christy (*left*) and me on the top of Table Mountain in Cape Town in 1989.

Chris and me with the dogs, 2002.

FRIDAY, 9 MARCH 1990

Linda Caine

Happy birthday, Linda! Thirty-nine, going on eighty.

I can hear clattering downstairs in the kitchen. Gary wanders past the bedroom door, trying to look casual. 'Oh, you don't have to get up yet, Mum,' he announces.

'What's happening down there?'

'Nothing,' he says, a little too stridently.

Ten minutes later I hear him giggling on the stairs. Christy tells him to hush. The two of them appear at the door with a big 'Ta daaaa!' I feign complete surprise.

Christy is carrying a tray with orange juice, cereal, toast and marmalade. She's even tried to poach an egg, which seems to have rubberized on the plate. They sit on each side of me, sharing the toast and spilling crumbs on the sheets. Then the homemade cards are produced, along with presents.

It is an idyllic scene. Nobody watching from the outside would think anything was out of place. This simple ritual with its laughter and proud effort on the part of my children is just as it should be. I am happy and content in the moment – yet terrified, because I know how fragile it is. It could disintegrate at a moment's notice.

When the floor is littered with coloured paper and torn envelopes, it's time for Gary and Christy to get dressed for school. Downstairs in the kitchen, I organize their lunches. Chris is still talking about going out to dinner for my birthday. 'Only if you feel up to it,' he says, hopefully.

I don't want to disappoint him, but I can't face sitting in a restaurant. 'Maybe I'll just cook some pasta,' I say, not looking at his face.

It's a shame because he needs to relax. The law firm has to cut costs and that means letting some of the staff go. One of the first redundancies is a man whose wife is chronically ill, and Chris had to break the news to him last night. Chris was almost in tears when he came home. He wouldn't talk about it. He poured himself a drink and sat alone in the lounge.

I look at my watch and call up the stairs. 'It's time to leave, Christy. I'll be in the car.'

'I'm just fixing my hair.'

'You have two minutes.'

After dropping her at school I drive to the Chaucer. Along the way, I try to plan what I'm going to say to Dr Royston. Nowadays all I seem to give him are tears and soggy tissues. He keeps re-assuring me that we have plenty of time, but it's not true. I feel so tired. My mind keeps sliding. How many more sessions are we going to waste before he gives up on me? I get so angry with myself. America was seventeen years ago – almost half my lifetime. Why can't I tell him about it?

He has mentioned going back into Ticehurst. He said that it would give us more time instead of having to stop after fifty minutes because he has other patients waiting outside. He's prob-ably right. I'm not coping. But then I think about Chris, Gary and Christy. What will I tell them?

15

FRIDAY, 11 MAY 1990

Robin Royston

Linda arrives at the Chaucer carrying a box of photographs and photo albums. Some are old and faded, and the albums have dog-eared pages and frayed stitching. I sit on a low chair and Linda kneels on the floor. She spreads the photographs out on a coffee table, occasionally shuffling them around.

'I wanted to show you my life,' she says. 'I thought maybe if you could see the photographs, it would help you understand. You'd see the faces and places that go with the stories I've told you.

'This is Prince when he was all skin and bone.' She holds up a tattered black and white picture. 'And this is when Dad took us to the beach after Mum left. That's Brendan in the sunhat and Clive with the bucket and spade.'

On and on she goes, introducing me to the various characters in her life and the places that she's lived. All the key events of her childhood are here: her mother leaving at eight; her father's struggles; Prince's death; her mastectomy at fourteen; leaving Rhodesia; marrying Mike; his brother Robbie dying . . .

Linda is a natural storyteller, who has led a remarkable life and observed nature with a knowledge I have seldom experienced. It is a life full of richness and darkness, a life born out of the cruelty and beauty of the African bush.

She points to another image and says, 'Mike gave me this white bikini.' She looks young and carefree in the photograph, leaning on a car with her long legs crossed. 'That's when I was pregnant...' She doesn't finish the sentence. Suddenly, the innocence and warmth of the image fade away. I can see a young girl, barely sixteen, who has worn what her boyfriend wants because deep down he frightens her.

As the box empties, I can sense Linda's mood beginning to change. I begin to understand what she is trying to do. She hopes to pull it all together – her life in pictures – so that we can complete the jigsaw and come up with a reason for her urge for self-destruction. But now she begins to realize the answer isn't going to be there. She fumbles through the box, searching desperately for more pieces to the puzzle. There has to be some underlying pattern, some solution that explains everything.

'It's not here,' she whispers hollowly.

A jumble of photographs covers the table. Turning to me, she speaks in the same dull monotone that I remember from our very first meeting.

'What now?' she asks.

'We carry on.'

'But I've given you all of the pieces.'

'No, you haven't. There's still more. We've only scratched at the surface.'

'How can you say that?'

'Because we haven't made sense of things. The only way to understand your current problems is to see how they evolved.'

Linda clearly doesn't share my confidence.

'We can't rush this,' I explain. 'I know it's hard on Chris and the kids, but we're dealing with your life here. Right now you don't value your life, so for you it isn't important. For me it's crucial.'

I remind her about the goat track. 'That's what we're on. We have to trust it, wherever it goes, no matter how rocky or steep it becomes, or how many times it seems to be leading us away from our goal.'

I know that she isn't convinced. She has dared to lay things out, piece by piece, but nothing has come of it. The months of psycho-therapy were meant to climax today. It didn't happen and she despairs.

'Thank you for all your help, Dr Royston.' She speaks with a cold finality.

'So I'll see you on Monday?'

'I'm not coming any more.'

'Don't give up, Linda.'

'There's nothing you can do.'

'Well, I'll be here on Monday, same as usual. I'd like to see you.'

She won't look me in the eye. A part of me wishes that she'd cry. Her tears are far more reassuring than this cold finality. She collects the photographs and carries the box to the door. She waits while I open it for her and then walks out into the passage without a word. She has nothing left to say. After she's gone, I sit in the quiet, dimly lit room, certain that I'll never see her again. I am convinced that she has made up her mind to die. What should I do? Telephone Dr Stefani and get the social worker round to her home? Or should I have her sectioned and carted off to St Augustine's – confirming her worst fears about herself? At least she'll be alive and we can try again when the dust settles.

I know that none of these things will help Linda, although they'd probably make me feel better. She's been suicidal for a long time. This isn't a sudden, alien feeling, arising out of a depressive illness. Treating her in hospital isn't going to avert the crisis. By locking her up, I'd make it worse. I'd take away her escape route and she'd never trust me again. As hard as it is to accept, I don't have a choice. This has to be lived through without deviating from the path we've taken. Somehow we have to trust that it will lead us to safety.

Of course, however technically correct, this tenuous explanation is going to sound hopelessly inadequate if Linda decides to end her life and I have to explain it to a coroner – or, worse still, to Chris, Gary and Christy. As I drive home that night, the battle continues to rage in my head. I know I'm doing the right thing, but can't help worrying about the potential consequences. I wonder if Linda has made it to Chestfield. The headlights of my car seem too weak. I haven't cleaned the glass for a long time. This seems to sum up how ineffective I feel as the darkness presses in. It is a rare feeling that I can't shake as I reach home and eat dinner. I have a strange detached numbness that Lynn intuitively recognizes.

'Who is it?' she asks.

'Linda Caine.'

At that moment the telephone rings and my heart leaps. A dozen scenarios race through my head, all of them bad, all of them involving Linda. What has she done?

Lynn answers and turns to me.

'It's Frank. He wants a game of squash on Saturday.'

Linda Caine

I have nothing left. I thought that one day I would tell Dr Royston something that would be the 'key' and then he'd know how to help me. That's why I got my life together in photographs, so he could see the good and the bad. I thought it would fall into place as we looked at the photographs, but as I laid them out on the table and tried to tell him, it just drifted away and died.

I can't fight the blackness any more. I can't even honestly say if I want to or not. Last night I was sorting the washing, the whites in one pile, the colours in the other, but I ended up sitting in the middle of the lot, crying. Then this morning I wrote a single line in my diary: 'I am still here.' There was nothing else to say.

After lunch we take a walk through Chestfield Woods and I finally find the courage to tell Chris that I'm struggling.

'I don't know what to do,' I tell him.

'What do you mean?'

'I don't want to see anyone, I don't want to talk to anyone. I don't want to dream. I don't want to think. I don't want to do anything any more.'

The words come tumbling out. Chris puts his arm around me and I hate myself for being so selfish and full of self-pity.

'Surely it can't be that bad,' he says.

'I woke up this morning and I wondered why the sun was still shining.'

'Because it's a beautiful day.'

He doesn't understand. I'm not talking about the weather. How can he imagine the creeping shadows I see at the edges of things, the darkness that threatens to overwhelm even my good days?

'Sometimes I think you'd be better off if I had died,' I tell him.

'Don't say that.'

'At least you could be getting on with life.'

'You are my life.'

I'm trying to hold on to the moment and not let my mind slide away. How can I tell him how cold, numb and bleak it all seems? He's read books and watched TV programmes about depression, but he still can't fully understand. If I tell him how close I've come to suicide what good will it do? He'll just stay home from work and never let me out of his sight. That's what's so ironic. I can only talk to him like this on my good days, when I don't feel like dying. But on the bad days suicide overwhelms all the rational arguments.

Back at the house I go through the motions of making dinner and getting Gary and Christy to bed. I set up the ironing board in the kitchen and put the basket on the bench. Chris is in the TV room watching the nine o'clock news on the BBC.

I spray starch on the collar of one of his shirts. As the iron slips over the white cotton I feel my mind begin to slide. Oh no! Not here! Not now! I can't hold my thoughts together. They spill out in confusion. I want to hold myself in the real world . . . I can't think.

The smell of burning flesh brings me round. Wisps of smoke curl from my skin. The iron has left an imprint on my left forearm. I stare at the burn, still holding the iron in my right hand. Suddenly, the pain arrives. I know that I should put my arm under running water, but I don't move. I want the pain to keep me grounded.

Later I put on a blouse with long sleeves to hide the burn. The pain is terrible. I feel embarrassed. What am I capable of?

'I had a bit of an accident,' I say to Chris. I show him my arm. 'I was leaning over the ironing board and my arm brushed against the iron.'

I don't know if he believes me. He says the burn looks quite bad and I should see a doctor.

'It's OK.'

'Does it hurt?'

'Not much,' I lie.

For the next few days I feel as though I'm clinging on by my fingertips. The same sense of sliding away keeps threatening me. I wouldn't mind so much if it happened when I was alone in the house, but I'm scared that Gary and Christy might see me. On Thursday I spend an hour exercising, really pushing myself hard on the bike. I can feel my T-shirt clinging to my back. Afterwards, I do a few chores around the house and have a shower. Normally, I feel clean, fresh and invigorated, but not today.

I dice some onions and brown them in a heavy-based pan. As I stand over the stove, I stare into the blue flame of the gas. I feel it happening again . . . I'm sliding away. I pick up a knife and hold it over the gas flame. I turn the blade, watching the flame divide and embrace both sides. Turning my palm upwards, I press the knife against the original burn on my forearm so that Chris won't notice the new burn. For a few seconds the knife doesn't seem hot enough. Then I feel the pain. It brings everything into clear, sharp focus.

I can't go on like this. Burning myself with the iron had been a reflex action, like biting my lip. Using the knife had been far more calculated. That's what worries me. How far will I go? I have to go back to Ticehurst. I know it and Dr Royston knows it. The past few weeks have been like a blur. It's a vicious cycle. Sitting in front of my computer, I let my thoughts spill out.

I'm frightened.
– Of what?
I don't know.
– How can you be frightened of something if you don't know what it is?
There's something in my mind that can't come out. I know it's there. A part of my mind doesn't want to know what it is. That's why I can't grasp enough to pull it free and see it clearly . . .
– Give up, Linda. You can't explain it with words. Just don't let them reach you.
They can't really reach me anyway – I'm too far away.
– Where are you, Linda?
I go to a place, a place in my mind, a place I am safe.
– Are you really safe, Linda? Or is that where no-one can hear you screaming?
What a fool I am. What a fool, what a fool, what a fool, what a fool, what a fool . . .

*

Words look funny when you look at them for a long time. I remember a game we played at the church holiday camp after our mother left. We were sitting around a campfire at night, listening to stories. The camp leader gave us magic words to say.

'I want you to say the words very slowly at first,' he explained. 'And then get faster and faster. Are you ready?'

We all nodded.

'OK, the magic words are: Ohwa . . . tafoo . . . lye . . . am.'

I started shouting the words mindlessly with the others: 'Ohwa tafoo lye am. Ohwa tafoo lye am. Ohwa tafoo lye am . . .' Faster and faster I went, with the words blending together. Finally I realized the joke and fell silent.

It's happening to me now. My mind is laughing at me.

Where do I go from here? I've lost my balance again. This is so self-centred. My family is hurting and I'm thinking about me, me, me . . .

As I wait for Chris to get home from work I rehearse everything I want to say. I'll tell him my old ways of coping aren't working. That's why I have to go back to Ticehurst for a while. I listen to myself and it sounds pathetic.

I wish I could say, 'I'm just going to Ticehurst to sort things out and when I come home I'll be completely better.' But I can't give any guarantees. I can only promise to try my best.

That's his car in the driveway. Gary and Christy are watching *Neighbours* on TV. I let Chris shrug off his jacket and tie. He pours himself a drink and sinks into a lounge chair. First I show him my notes from the previous two weeks and then mention Ticehurst. Chris goes very quiet.

'I phoned Dr Royston this morning and asked if I could go back. I know this comes at a bad time. That's why I've waited until the absolute end.'

'Are you sure it's not just a bad day?' he asks.

He knows the answer – he's read my notes.

'Tomorrow might be better,' he says, hopefully.

'No.' I can't convey how I feel. I want to tell him that I won't give up. That I'll look at all the possibilities. Mostly, I want to say, 'I love you.'

He nurses his drink and stares at the fireplace.

'Why can't you just keep going to the Chaucer?' he asks.

'Because you were right. People bring their legal messes to you because you're a trained lawyer. Dr Royston is a mind specialist. He's the expert. And he thinks I should go back to Ticehurst.'

Chris wants to talk to Dr Royston. He uses the telephone in the kitchen and I don't hear what they say to each other. Afterwards, Chris seems reassured.

'We both agree that it should be your decision.'

I feel so relieved. He's been amazing, which is why I feel as though I'm letting him down. I'm the weak link in the family – the basket case.

On Saturday morning we break the news to Gary and Christy. Gary sits on his favourite red cushion in the lounge and Christy is cross-legged on the couch. I try to explain how hard it is to understand mental illness because sufferers can look absolutely fine on the outside. 'If I was physically scarred or crippled then people would understand more. I wouldn't have to explain things because they would be able to see *why* I was hurting. When you've been hurt mentally, people don't understand why it should sometimes still affect you.' I look at Gary. 'Remember when you grazed your knee, we had to examine the graze and clean it out in order for it to heal. That's what we are trying to do with my mind.' Gary and Christy are old enough and bright enough to understand where I'm going.

'How long will you be away for?' asks Gary.

'I'll try my best to be home every weekend. We'll spend them together.'

I look at Christy. She's sitting very quietly, saying nothing. Gary asks the questions.

'What's happened? Why now?'

'I don't know. I'm really struggling at the moment. I'm sorry . . .'

He ponders this for a moment. Then he bounces to his feet and gives me a hug. I can put my chin on the top of his head. 'It's all right, Mum. If that's what needs to happen.'

Christy takes my hand. 'It's going to be all right,' she says, in a matter-of-fact voice.

They both go upstairs and I feel relieved. I hear a few thuds from Gary's room and think that maybe he's dropped something. Later I notice that he's moved his Ferrari poster to a different spot on the wall. It neatly covers a hole that he has kicked in the plasterboard.

MONDAY, 21 MAY 1990

Chris is going to drive me to Ticehurst in the morning. I'm still trying to pack, but the feelings of panic keep rising in my throat. Is this my last chance? What if one day, as much as I trust him, Dr Royston says, 'Enough is enough.'

Every system has a cut-off point. Then what happens? I'll be sent off to St Augustine's and locked away for life. I couldn't let that happen. I'd want to die first. I start thinking about suicide being my friend again. I want my 'friend' to stay close to me. Glancing down at the open suitcase I notice the foam prosthesis that normally pads out the mastectomy side of my bra. There are two foam cups, one bigger than the other. They fit together neatly like spoons.

Taking a needle and thread, I sew the edges of the cups together, leaving a small gap to create a pocket between them. Then I slip a pair of nail scissors inside and sew up the gap. What if the scissors aren't sharp enough to cut my wrists?

I look around the room. I've been taking Temazepam to help me sleep. Ticehurst won't allow me to take my own medication into hospital. They want to keep check of what I'm taking. Retrieving the bottle, I tip the contents into the palm of my hand. I count them. Eighteen pills. Would that be enough? I sit on the bed and begin to unpick the hem of my dressing gown. I push the pills inside one by one.

I'm not planning to commit suicide. I haven't given up. I just don't want to lose control. I don't want to be locked away. I know it sounds paradoxical, but if I know there's a way out then I don't feel so trapped.

FRIDAY, 25 MAY 1990

Robin Royston

All morning I have outpatients in my first-floor office at Ticehurst. In between the sessions I catch up with paperwork and at noon I sit down with Linda McCormack to discuss Linda Caine. I am tremendously relieved that she is back at Ticehurst. The situation has become increasingly difficult to control, but in hospital we can give Linda the time and support she needs to contain whatever is in her mind.

'She's talking of suicide again and seems to have given up,' I tell Linda McCormack. 'There's something she wants to tell us, but she can't get it out. Every time we get close she gets too disturbed.'

'Do we know what it's about?'

'Only vaguely.'

'Is it something to do with her father?' Linda McCormack, as with several of the other staff who have grown close to Linda, has also picked up on the signs of likely abuse.

'Possibly, but it could be totally unrelated.'

'What about meds?'

'Just the usual.'

'How regularly do you want her monitored?'

'That's going to depend on what comes out in our talks. At the moment she's trying to tell me about something that happened to her in America. Whatever it is upset her terribly.'

When the meeting ends I go downstairs to see Linda in her room. She's set up her computer and brought her art books and supplies. The room looks spotless, with the bed neatly made and her art pencils lined up on a sketchbook. She also seems relieved to be back in hospital. Certain decisions are out of her hands. She doesn't have to worry about her 'absences' or 'mind-sliding'.

'How did you sleep?'

She shakes her head.

'What happened?'

'I don't know. Just as I was nodding off I suddenly began to panic. I tried to turn on the bedside light but the bulb flickered and died. Then I *really* panicked.' She tries to make the last sentence sound light-hearted, but isn't able to hide the fear in her voice.

'Why did the darkness bother you so much?' I ask.

She shrugs. 'I hate the dark.'

'Why?'

'Because I can be reached.'

'What can reach you?'

'I don't know. It's just a feeling I have.' She shivers and hugs her knees to her chest.

'What did you see?'

'At first I didn't know if I was dreaming or if it was real. I had trouble falling asleep, even though I was exhausted. Just as I began to drift off I heard a loud squeaking noise that sounded like the door. I opened my eyes, but the room was black. Whoever had come inside had shut the door. I sensed that someone was there.

' "Who's there?" I said. Then a voice moaned, "Oh no, oh no."

'I could see a figure crouched by the door. I tried to switch on my bedside light but it wouldn't go on. "Is that Joseph?" I said, trying not to panic. [Joseph is a night nurse.] Then the voice said, "No, I am not Joseph." It sounded sly.

'I tried to switch on the light, but it still wouldn't work. And I knew that I couldn't reach the door before "it" reached me. If I screamed then someone would come. But I was so scared, I didn't think I could scream loudly enough for anyone to hear. What if I made the person very angry?'

Wide-eyed with terror, Linda recounts the story. She stares at the end of the bed as though this figure is still in the room with her. I can sense that her mind is sliding away from me and I try to keep her grounded.

'Did you recognize the voice?' I ask.

She turns her head suddenly, startled by the sound. She shakes her head and stares at me for several seconds as though surprised to find me there.

'What happened next?'

'I opened my eyes and saw the room wasn't as dark. I could make out the shapes of the chairs so I knew I was facing away from the door. I threw myself towards the bedside light and switched it on.'

'So you were dreaming.'

'I guess so. But it seemed *so* real. I kept telling myself afterwards, "It was just a dream . . . just a dream." I got up and switched on the toilet light. And I searched the whole room, to make sure I was alone.'

I sense the story isn't over. Linda's voice drops to a whisper. 'I lay down and must have dozed off again. Some time later I opened my eyes and could see the glass on my bedside cabinet. I tried to wake up properly, but I couldn't. I really wanted to wake up, but it was like being paralysed. That's when the rushing sound came . . .'

'The rushing sound?'

'Yes. It whooshes through my head. It's the same sound I get when I'm put under anaesthetic. When they give me the injection I feel a cold sensation in my hand going up my arm. Then I hear the rushing sound in my head as I lose consciousness. It's a "SsshhshshshSHSHSSHSH" sound.'

'And this happens to you now?'

'Sometimes when I'm sliding into sleep or trying to stay awake. Last night I couldn't wake up and I couldn't move. I thought if I could just knock the glass over then somebody would come . . . one of the nurses. I managed to throw my arm out and it somehow broke the spell. The rushing sound faded.'

'Were you dreaming this?'

She nods. 'I think so. I woke up feeling very cold.'

'You mentioned trying to stay awake. Why were you scared of falling asleep?'

Linda shrugs. 'I'm scared that I might not be able to wake up . . . I'll be trapped.'

'In what way will you be trapped?'

'In the dream.'

I am fascinated by the idea of being caught in a dream and also her 'false awakenings'. Linda's dream imagery is exactly the same as reality. She imagines that she is awake in her room at Ticehurst, but she can't be sure. Where does the dream end and reality begin?

Even more frightening is the sense of paralysis; unable to raise the alarm, or turn on the bedside light. In one such 'waking dream' Linda describes being unable to speak. Her mouth has been clamped shut and she tries to force it open with her hands. Her whole body arches into a convulsion and she can't breathe.

'Last night it was more powerful. I heard the sound coming, felt it touch me. It was like a darkness that was so black and heavy that it was pulling me into it. I could see myself curled up on the bed, becoming less clear as the darkness surrounded me. Once I could no longer see myself, I knew that I wouldn't be able to get back. I'd be trapped.'

What Linda describes is to me a totally unknown sensation. I once saw something similar in a psychotic patient, but that doesn't apply to Linda. Clearly it has links to her past, but I can't explain its significance. Three days later I raise the subject of America again with Linda. She sits cross-legged on the bed, pushing her hair away from her eyes. She no longer tries to dismiss the story as unimportant. Now she just hopes to get through it.

Linda Caine

I don't bother about recapping things. Instead I go straight to the moment when I was in the attorney's office, walking up and down the room for Paul Damon.

'Relax and slow down,' he said. 'Turn and come back.'

Damon got up from a chair and moved closer to me.

'I like to have a casual, informal relationship with the people I work with,' he said. 'It helps put them at ease. That's the way I train my models and actresses. Do you think that you can be like that?'

'I'll try,' I said, not understanding what he meant.

He stood up and walked around me. Then he leaned closer and tried to kiss me. I pushed him away.

'I think there's been a misunderstanding,' I said urgently.

He kept moving towards me, backing me towards the desk.

'I want to leave now. I have to go.'

Damon stepped back, looking mildly surprised. I pushed past him and headed for the door. So that was what he'd meant by having 'casual, informal relationships' with his models. I cursed my stupidity.

As I reached the reception desk Damon stepped in front of me. 'What's wrong with you? Why are you behaving like this?'

'I have to go.'

'I'll take you home.'

'No, it's OK. I'll call my dad.'

I picked up the telephone and began to dial. He slammed his hand down hard, cutting me off. I spun towards him, ready to protest, but then I saw his face. His features had set in stone. His eyes were cold. That's the moment I realized that I was in big trouble. Glancing quickly around the room I saw the main door that led to the outer passages. Somewhere down one of the corridors were stairs and lifts. I had to get out.

My thoughts raced. The reception desk was U-shaped. I tried not to show any fear as I walked past him towards the large wooden doors leading to the elevators. As I reached for the handle, he attacked me. I don't know if he hit me. One moment I was standing up and the next I was lying on the floor. He lay on top of me, crushing the air from my lungs.

'Have you ever seen a film called *The Godfather*?' he asked in a low, menacing voice. His lips were pressed against my ear.

'Yes,' I stammered.

He grinned. 'It's not just a film – it's real. And if you ever go to the police I'll know first. I have contacts. If you try and report this, they'll tell me. Do you know what happens then?'

I shook my head.

'You're dead,' he whispered. 'And so is your dad. People get killed in this town for the price of a fix. That's how easy I can have it done.'

I knew he was telling the truth. He knew exactly where I lived. I'd told him all about Dad and the gallery. I lunged towards his eyes, but he caught my arm. Then I tried to knee him between the legs. Each time he anticipated me by a fraction of a second.

'Please don't do this,' I begged.

'Take your shoes off,' he said, glancing at the heels. He didn't want me using them as a weapon. Then he got up carefully and held my arm in his fist.

'Get up and go back to the office.'

'You don't want me. Please let me go.'

'Get undressed.'

'I've had a mastectomy.'

'I don't care.'

My hands shook as I slid my dress from my shoulders. It slipped down to my ankles and he motioned for me to kick it away. I stood in my underwear. I noticed a glass ashtray on the table. It had a heavy base. If I could just reach it, I could hit him. I knew that if I lunged he'd get there first. I had to wait for the right moment.

He made me sit down on the couch. Then he sat next to me and began touching me. As he lowered his head to my breasts, I turned towards him as though yielding to him. At the same time, I moved my hand behind me, feeling for the ashtray. My fingers closed around it. I brought the ashtray down hard on the side of his head. He crashed to the floor and turned over, dazed and disorientated. I should have hit him and hit him, but I hesitated and turned to run.

Suddenly, Damon reached up, grabbed my arm and twisted it until I fell to my knees. Then he took the ashtray and held it against my head. His voice had changed. He couldn't breathe or speak properly. Spit leaked from the corner of his mouth. He reached up and touched his head. His fingers came back covered in blood.

Gasping, his voice rattled as he said, 'Do you want me to kill you?' He looked insane. 'I'M GOING TO SMASH YOUR HEAD IN!' I felt the glass ashtray against my forehead. I knew that if I moved, I would die.

At that moment something happened. Damon was still talking, but he seemed further away. I was floating upwards, above the whole scene. I could see myself, with Damon holding the ashtray against my head. I watched him rape me, but it was as though it was happening to someone else. I couldn't feel a thing except the fear, knowing I was going to die.

Robin Royston

Linda crouches in the corner of the room, hiding behind the curtain. Halfway through the account she has covered her face and crawled towards the corner, as if trying to escape. Her whole body shakes with her sobbing and her words come out in broken sentences. I kneel nearby. Linda keeps talking through her hands, desperate to finish what she has started. Eventually, it becomes too much. It is as though she has been tamed and broken all over again by Damon. If there was any doubt about Linda's ability to dissociate this seems to be the final proof. During the attack her mind has broken away from her body. Her dreams have shown the same pattern: she flies above things, watching but not feeling.

A part of me wants to stop her talking, to ease her pain, but at the same time I know that we have to continue. Slowly Linda recounts the details of the rape. It is a long and painful process, with sentences sometimes coming minutes apart. Her memories are so vivid that she gags and covers her mouth.

In the early hours of the morning Damon told Linda to get dressed and took her downstairs to the underground parking area. As they waited for the lift, Linda looked down the long passage with a window at the far end. Convinced that she was going to die, she contemplated running and throwing herself through the window. As if reading her mind, Damon held tightly to her arm.

Once in the carpark, Linda was placed in the passenger seat of a black Cadillac and driven from the building. Damon chatted about modelling courses as though nothing had happened. Turning off the main road, he parked in a side street and raped her again on the front seat. Halfway through the attack, a couple came out of a nearby house and got into a car.

Damon pushed her head down, away from the beam of the head-lights. 'I was screaming for help inside my head, but no sound came out. We started driving again and he pulled up outside a House of Pies. As though nothing had happened, he said, "Let's get a coffee." He made sure my dress and hair were presentable and then he walked me inside.

'There was a telephone near the main door. Damon put his arm around my waist and whispered in my ear. "I want you to call your dad and tell him that you've had a really good evening. Say that you're sorry you didn't call him earlier."

'He stood next to me as I made the call. I could feel his breath on my face. Dad was furious. "Do you know what time it is?" he said. "I've been worried sick."

' "I'm really, really sorry," I told him.

'Damon whispered the words and I just repeated them. "It's gone really well. I've been having such a good time. Mr Damon thinks I have potential. He's going to train me. We're

202

just having coffee now. He's going to bring me home soon." '

Linda begins sobbing again. She hides her face in the folds of the curtains, unable to look at me. I don't try to rush her.

Afterwards Damon dropped Linda off about half a block from the gallery. 'I'll call you,' he said, as he leaned across her to open the passenger door. She stepped onto the pavement, convinced that he was going to shoot her. The Cadillac drove behind her as she walked to the gallery.

Her father and her boyfriend Bill were both waiting. Damon had primed Linda about what she should say. Time had just slipped by . . . she didn't realize it was so late, etc.

Her father retired to bed and Bill said goodnight coldly. 'I only stayed to make sure you were OK. I'm going home now.' Linda followed him out to his motorcycle and began to shake uncontrollably.

'What's wrong?'

She couldn't answer. She was almost hyperventilating. Bill took her back inside and poured her a stiff brandy. Linda told him about the rape.

'You have to call the police,' he said.

'I can't. He threatened to kill us.'

'He's bluffing.'

'No. He knows people.'

'At least tell your dad.'

Linda shook her head and swore Bill to secrecy. He reluctantly agreed. After he'd gone, she scoured her body in a hot shower, trying to take away the filth and the smell of the rape.

The next day Damon called the gallery, wanting to make arrangements to collect Linda.

'I told him I wasn't going,' she says.

' "We need to talk before you make that decision."

' "I don't want to talk. I'm not going to the police. I just want to be left alone."

'He kept calling every day after that. One time Dad answered the phone. Damon told him how good he thought I could be and how he was looking forward to training me. Dad couldn't understand why I had suddenly changed my mind about being a model.

' "I'm going to do a typing course instead."

' "Oh, come on, Linda. You're wasting an opportunity."

'He carried on cajoling me, until one day Bill snapped and said, "Just leave her alone."

' "You stay out of this," said Dad. "Linda *needs* something behind her. She could be a good model. This man believes in her."

' "You don't know what he did to her."

' "Bill, don't," I cried.

' "What did he do?" Dad's voice had a tinge of uncertainty.

' "Just leave it," I pleaded, starting to cry.

' "Did he touch you?" Dad demanded to know.

'I nodded.

' "Did he rape you?" His voice had grown very quiet.

' "Yes." '

Linda told her father what had happened – about the death threats and Damon's claim to have high-powered friends in the police force.

'We won't contact the police. We'll go straight to the FBI,' he said.

After meeting federal agents, Linda was reassured about her safety. She was then interviewed by detectives from the Los Angeles Police Department. There were no rape counsellors or special sexual assault teams. A woman officer took down the details, while men wandered in and out of the room.

A couple of days later, two detectives collected Linda from the gallery, and accompanied her to the District Attorney's office. While they were there, a detective called the telephone number that Linda had been given when she arranged her interview with the modelling agency. It was indeed a law firm. Within minutes Damon called the District Attorney's office, having obviously been tipped off by his lawyer.

Linda could only hear one side of the conversation. The DA took notes. Afterwards, his attitude changed. Although still polite, Linda sensed that he no longer believed her.

'Damon told the detective that he'd been expecting me to make a complaint,' says Linda. 'He said that I'd threatened to blackmail him. If I didn't get money and a modelling diploma, I'd accuse him of rape. From then on I was treated differently. Damon was a prominent businessman, always surrounded by beautiful women. Why would he need to rape anyone?'

Two days later, she heard from the DA's office that no further action would be taken on her complaint. It had come down to her word against Damon's.

'Within days the phone calls started,' says Linda. ' "I'm watching you. I know where you are." He used the same panting, hateful voice as when he held the ashtray to my head.'

Working in the gallery made Linda feel even more vulnerable. Every day she kept watch for anyone hanging about outside or cruising up and down the street in a car.

'The back room of the gallery had no curtains on the window. Anyone on the stairs to the restaurant could look directly inside. When it was dark I always had a feeling there was somebody on the stairs watching me.'

The gallery was struggling and Linda's father took another job selling vitamins. This left Linda on her own for most of the day. She began to secretly close the gallery after her father had left for work. Then she'd hide in the back room.

'I used to crawl onto my shelf, out of sight, and sit there for hours writing, reading and drawing. I felt terrible about deceiving Dad, but I was terrified. I relived the night of the rape over and over, trying to work out what I could have done differently. Should I have seen it coming? Could I have run? Was it my fault?'

Burying her head in her hands, Linda begins sobbing again. Her whole body seems to deflate. There have been times during the previous two hours when she has grown distant, but never totally dissociated. At the same time she hasn't just given me a factual, objective account of the rape. What she's done is to give me an insight into how it felt. Her ordeal hadn't been about sexual conquest. Damon was a man who knew how to get into a woman's mind, not for any positive purpose but out of perversion and the terrifying need for power. His aim was humiliation and he was utterly ruthless. He had taken a bright, vibrant young woman and broken her will.

Linda didn't have the physical powers to match him. Mentally, she also had no chance. She read the situation well enough, although too late. He may not have been a killer in the physical sense, but Damon had destroyed her mind just as effectively. When Linda describes what happened, she does so as someone who watched but didn't participate. The actual rape seems to be meaningless to her. By far the most potent memories are of the humiliation and depravity. Is this the trauma that has triggered her descent into suicidal depression? Could Damon be the dark-haired man who wants her dead?

In the fairy tale 'Rumpelstiltskin', the nasty-tempered wizard says to the Queen, 'If you know my name you can have your first-born child back, but unless you can name me, I will have the child.' When the Queen ultimately names him, Rumpelstiltskin flies into a rage and disappears. His power is broken.

This is what I hope will happen for Linda. By talking through the harrowing events she will stop them replaying over and over again in her mind. Traumatic memory will be turned into normal memory. She will never forget what happened but it won't have the same damaging impact.

When I leave Ticehurst that afternoon, I feel hopeful that we have achieved a breakthrough. Linda has named her Rumpelstiltskin. Now we have to wait and see if there has been a fundamental shift in her mind.

16

Linda Caine

I don't remember how the session with Dr Royston ended. I must have fallen asleep. It's late afternoon when I wake. I still feel exhausted and tearful. I keep thinking about Damon. I should have run, I should have run . . .

In the bathroom I splash water on my face and rub colour into my cheeks. My eyes are red and puffy. I've barely eaten all day, but I don't feel hungry. Chris phones and he can tell that I've been crying. He keeps asking me what's wrong.

'It's something I told Dr Royston about.'

'What is it?'

'Can we talk about something else?'

He sounds hurt. 'Why can't you tell me? I'm your husband.'

'I'm sorry.'

Chris has been so patient, but he can't understand how I can talk to Dr Royston and not to him. Couldn't we share everything? He knows about Damon, but not the details. There are things that you can't tell the man you love.

I start to cry and he feels guilty. 'I'll give you some time to calm down,' he says. 'I'll call you back. We can talk about it then.'

But he doesn't understand. I don't *want* to talk about it. I know he loves me. I know he wants to be able to help me. But if I tell him what really happened, it would tear him apart. My pain would be his pain, perhaps even more so. Why can't Chris see that?

I walk into the passage, forgetting that I'm not wearing shoes. As I reach the main door, it occurs to me that I should ask Martin, a duty nurse, if it's all right for me to go out for a while. I hesitate and panic. One line is echoing in my head. 'I should have run! I should have run!' There is no time to do this properly.

Outside, I notice an old man holding on to a wheelchair being pushed by a nurse. The geriatrics unit is upstairs and on sunny days the staff often take patients for walks. The old man stands on shaky legs and holds on to the chair to give his legs some exercise. Suddenly, he lets go and beetles off down the driveway in a geriatric shuffle. The nurse leaves the wheelchair behind and goes after him. She tries to take his arm but he pulls away and carries on. This is his burst for freedom.

Hearing her call for help, two male nurses take off down the long, sweeping driveway. I feel sorry for the confused old man. Instead of grabbing him and hauling him back, the nurses fall into step alongside him. One of them rubs his back.

'Where are you going, Joe?'

'Home.'

'But it's not time to go home.'

'I want to go home.'

'Why don't you come back and have a cup of tea? I think we have date scones today. You like date scones, don't you?'

Gradually the old man slows down, saying, 'Date scones?'

They turn him around and I'm glad to see he looks happy.

I decide to take the long walk around the grounds, to the end of the field, and then back towards the old summer house. I'm so glad they haven't pulled it down. I have to clear away fallen branches from near the door and lean on the rusty hinges to get inside. Weak sunlight slants through the trees, lengthening the shadows.

Once inside, I close the doors and sit down on a bench. I can look down the tree-lined path that leads back to the hospital. I don't want anyone to know I'm here. I want them to pass by and think the summer house is old and disused. That way it can be *my* special place. I don't want to go back. I can't face Chris's telephone call. I feel so tired. Lying down on the bench, I close my eyes.

It's almost dark. I can't move. It's as though I'm trapped – unable to wake. There's a ringing sound in my ears. I bite down hard on my lip, trying to clear my head. I can taste the blood and feel the pain, but it doesn't work. There's just enough light leaking through the shutters to pick out the shards of glass on the floor. If I cut myself, then I'll come back; my mind will stop sliding.

Willing my hand to move, I reach out and feel for the sharpest piece of glass. At that moment a sudden movement catches my eye. A tiny mouse in the centre of the room is looking up at me. We see each other at precisely the same time. It runs, scurrying over the broken glass and out the door. I lie completely still, hoping it might come back. Another movement makes me turn. A second little mouse creeps from a large crack in the floor. Hardly daring to breathe, I watch as it sniffs the air and twitches its whiskers. All its senses are telling it there is something wrong. Gaining in courage, it edges a few inches away from its hole then bolts back. A minute or so passes and it reappears. It creeps out and sits up, sniffing the air. This time it bravely scampers under the benches. I peer through the slats, hoping to glimpse it again. Emotion and fatigue wash over me.

Several times I half wake, unsure of where I am. Once I imagine that I'm back in the cooling tower behind our house in Zambia. Normally the dark frightens me, but my eyes have grown accustomed to the night. The scuffling beneath the bench reminds me of the mouse. It's a comforting sound. I wonder what time it is. If it's after ten o'clock the doors of Ticehurst will be locked. I'll have to ring the bell to get in. What will I say to them? Cold and stiff, I curl up and wrap my arms around my chest, trying to get warm. I'm so, so, so tired . . .

Robin Royston

The phone call arrives as I sit down to dinner at the Spa Hotel in Tunbridge Wells. It is a black-tie gathering for Ticehurst consultants, their guests, local doctors and other worthies. Most of us have gone searching for our dinner jackets at the back of wardrobes and found them smelling of mothballs. At least I've managed to get through the pre-dinner drinks without offending anybody or being asked to psychoanalyse their relatives. The nursing officer at Ticehurst breaks the news. Linda has been missing since 5.30 p.m.

I look at my watch. That was three hours ago.

'What's she wearing?' I know it is unseasonably cold outside.

'A light cotton top, light trousers, thin socks, no shoes.'

'Have you called the police?'

'Yes. Should we phone her husband?'

'Of course. You must tell him. I'm on my way.'

I make my apologies and quickly leave the hotel. As I drive to Ticehurst I have mixed emotions. Already I am questioning whether I pushed Linda too hard. Has recounting the rape been too much for her? Having dredged up such traumatic events and emotions, Linda is likely to be at her most vulnerable. Not only does she have to cope with her memories, but her ongoing feelings of self-destruction. She has never run away at night before. If she left the paths and went into the woods she won't be found easily.

What if she is already dead? What will I say to Chris? What about her children? The scenario begins playing out in my imagination. I can picture the coroner asking why a young mother of two committed suicide in the grounds of a mental hospital . . .

I turn through the large stone gates of Ticehurst House Hospital. Dark shapes weave among the trees and torches dance like fireflies on the distant paths. I count at least a dozen lights to my left. The heater blasts warm air against my feet and the inside of the windscreen. Leaning forward, I peer over the wheel. The headlights are on full beam and bleach the colour from the plane trees that line the drive. I see two people in conversation by the main entrance, and their breath mists in the cold air. Opening the window a few inches, I hear them calling Linda's name. I switch off the engine and listen, hoping for a response. The collar of my starched white shirt feels suddenly cold against my neck. The hospital looks almost deserted. Lights and police cars would have been more reassuring. Instead there is emptiness and silence.

Inside the acute unit, along the echoing corridor, a policeman stands near the nurses' station. A walkie-talkie buzzes and crackles on his belt.

Roger Smith looks up from the desk. 'Here's Dr Royston now.'

'I'll be with you in a moment,' I tell the senior constable. Then I take Roger to one side.

'What happened?' I ask.

'Something spooked her. It was just after you left. Dympna checked her at four and she was asleep. She had a phone call from her husband. He tried to phone her again at 8.20. Linda wasn't in her room and we couldn't find her anywhere.'

'Did anyone see her leave?'

Roger shakes his head.

'Has she anything sharp?'

'The windows and mirror haven't been broken.'

I turn to the policeman who briefs me on the search. A helicopter with heat-seeking equipment is on its way. In the meantime he needs more information about Linda. 'Is she suicidal?' he asks.

'Most definitely.'

'Is she dangerous?'

'Only to herself.'

I look at my watch again. It has been six hours.

'Have you tried the old summer house?'

Linda Caine

The darkness has swallowed me whole. I can't even see my hand in front of my face. It takes me a moment to remember where I am. Forcing myself to stand, I look out the window of the summer house towards the hospital. I can just make out the twin rows of trees silhouetted against the dark sky. It looks like a long, uneven passage. I just want to lie down and close my eyes again. Lights suddenly appear at the end of the trees. I move to the side of the summer house and press myself behind a section of the wall that juts out a little, beside the small window. Peering over the ledge I see torches flashing back and forth into the trees.

They're coming for me. I've left it too late to run. The torches are dancing. Voices are nearby. I press myself into the bench and the wall thinking maybe they won't see me. Light floods the summer house and I cover my face.

Someone takes my arm. 'Linda, it's Les. Come on. Let's go back to your room.' Les is a nurse who works nights sometimes. His voice is gentle and reassuring.

Dr Royston meets us just outside the main door. He holds my shoulders at arm's length and says softly, 'Linda, have you hurt yourself?'

I shake my head.

'Thank God you're all right.' He sounds relieved.

I'm confused and embarrassed. I don't want to see anyone. I keep my face covered as he leads me to my room. Dympna is there. She begins to clean the dirt off my hands. I wince as she holds my forearm. Dr Royston looks at me inquiringly.

'It's not from tonight,' I explain, urgently. I pull up my sleeve and show him the burns on my forearm.

'How did you do that?'

'With an iron.' I feel so ashamed.

'That was careless!' he says, trying to sound light-hearted. I expect him to chastise me, but instead he tries to cheer me up. 'Accidental, was it?'

I shake my head.

'What happened?'

'I was trying to clear my mind . . . to stop it sliding.'

'The same as before.'

I nod sadly. 'I'm sorry.'

Dympna has gone to get me a cup of frothy coffee. I don't deserve these people.

Robin Royston

Linda begins telling me why she ran away. The phone call from Chris upset her. There were things she couldn't tell him and she didn't have the energy or words to explain why. She hadn't intended to stay away. Nor did she contemplate suicide.

Recounting the rape has overwhelmed her emotionally. All the negative energy has dragged her down into the blackness. Her destructive response and the fairy-tale qualities of her 'rescue' are testament to the depth of her disturbance. The 'fairy-tale' feature was finding the mice in the summer house. When Linda cuts

212

herself, it is because she wants to focus her thoughts and stop her mind sliding away. But this time, as she searched for a sharp piece of glass to do this, she saw a mouse and the effect was the same. The mouse kept her safe.

Whether it was a dream or reality, I can't be sure. This line is often thin, and in Linda's case it sometimes disappears completely. There is a mythological dimension to what happened that, as often before, suggests we're looking at a small piece of something much larger. Several times during her account Linda calls herself 'weak' and 'hopeless'. She speaks with real hostility towards herself, which I find hard to comprehend. She has never aroused aggressive feelings in those around her. Yet in her notes she describes herself as being an 'arsenic-filled marshmallow' or harangues herself for 'being so pathetic'. With some people such feelings might be appropriate, but with Linda it is as though she has been taught to hate herself. If so, who by?

It is after midnight when I leave. Dympna offers to sit with Linda until she falls asleep. At the nurses' station, I write a note in large letters on Linda's chart: 'THIS LADY REMAINS A <u>HIGH SUICIDE RISK</u>!!! Continue on thirty-minute recorded observations day and night.' This means that someone will check on Linda every half-hour. Linda's mind-sliding and dissociating are getting worse, and I feel that the closer we get to what is buried in her mind, and therefore to saving her, the more likely she is to want to die before it reaches her.

The carpark is deserted as I walk to my car. On the drive home I contemplate how throughout her life Linda has always found places to hide, like the cooling tower and the old water tank in Zambia. Now she has the summer house. When she can't run, she looks for a safe place, dissociates, or – as happened during the rape – 'floats above' the whole scene, watching it happen. She separates her mind from what is happening to her body.

Linda will have to be watched even more closely in the days ahead. Her defences have been lowered and she is now more vulnerable than ever.

FRIDAY, 1 JUNE 1990

Linda Caine

It's a beautiful morning. I go jogging to clear my head. My mind has been in a dark place all night but now I'm feeling better. In a field over the laneway I see a little chestnut stallion and a lovely grey mare. They have a very young chestnut foal that occasionally leaps and gambols, happy to be alive. The countryside seems to be bursting with life on a perfect early summer day. It's such a contrast to how dark I feel inside. I want to soak up the beauty around me – to bring the light into my darkness.

Stopping at a hedge, I concentrate on a bee that is buzzing between the flowers. I feel almost invisible, as though I can see the world going on around me but can never be part of it. The bee flies off into the distance and I search for something else for my mind to hold on to. Where the path divides at the short walk, I find a pile of old, broken slate tiles that have been dumped. I pick out a few nicely shaped pieces. I want to use them for paintings.

Maybe I'll paint an orchid for Linda McCormack. That's her favourite flower. And I'll paint a frog-mouthed owl for Roger Smith. We were looking through photographs the other day and he pointed one out. 'That's one of the ugliest birds I've ever seen,' he said. 'It's so ugly, it's almost beautiful.'

I carry the pieces of slate past the nurses' station and back to my room.

Dr Royston arrives just before 7.30 p.m. I drag him outside to see the evening light over the field with the horses in the foreground. Just my luck – clouds are hiding the sun and it isn't nearly as dramatic as I hope. Back in my room, we talk about my thoughts, feelings and dreams. I'm even brave enough to get us both a cup of coffee from the lounge instead of ordering it from the kitchen. Little things like this mean more to Dr Royston than they do to me. He makes me feel as though every small step is a big achievement.

17

TUESDAY, 5 JUNE 1990

Linda Caine

Dr Royston asks me what happened after the police dropped the rape case. I tell him about the phone calls from Damon and hiding in the back room of the gallery. Then about three weeks later, I was in the storeroom when a man came in and asked for me. My blood ran cold. I peered through a crack in the door. The man showed Dad a police badge. 'My name is Sergeant Daryl Walker.'

Dad called me and I edged nervously into the gallery. The detective looked relieved to see me.

'I thought you might have gone back to Africa.'

'Not yet.'

'I need you to come down and make another statement.'

'Why?'

He said another girl had made a report. Paul Damon had attacked her the previous night, but she'd managed to get away. The story this girl, Annalese, from Holland, had told the police was almost identical to mine.

'How did she escape?' I whispered.

'She jumped out of his car and ran into a shop.'

Although Annalese had gone straight to the police, Damon had again been very shrewd. He went to the nearest police station and handed over her handbag. He told them he was tired of dealing with hysterical women. I didn't know it then, but almost everything Annalese had told the police matched my story except for the actual rape. Daryl Walker explained that the strength of the case rested on the fact that Annalese and I had never met. The chance of us fabricating the same story was remote. We had to be telling the truth. In addition to this, the police had also trawled the files and uncovered a similar complaint made by a sixteen-year-old girl several years earlier.

Daryl Walker took me to the San Vincente Police Station and I made a new statement. Within hours a warrant had been issued for Damon's arrest. He surrendered to the police and was charged with rape and attempted rape. Bail was set at US$100,000. Damon paid the money and was free within twenty-four hours.

I was terrified. Daryl Walker kept reassuring me that everything would be OK.

'You don't know this man,' I said. 'He won't give up.'

Within a week Damon had disappeared. Again Daryl Walker told me not to worry. More than ever I wanted to go back to Africa, to escape. But now I was trapped. The case against Damon rested on my evidence. In the weeks that followed I knew the police were discreetly watching me. Detectives would drop into the gallery and ask about any suspicious cars, or visitors. At Damon's mansion in the Hollywood Hills they had found a 'harem' of women who refused to co-operate. Daryl Walker described them as being like 'disciples'.

The gallery continued losing money and we had no choice but to close. Dad began renting out the African art to film studios and selling it privately. We moved into a two-bedroom apartment in West Hollywood, with a main window that overlooked the street outside. We had a full security system installed, with panic buttons linked to the nearest police station. I trusted Daryl Walker because he'd always been honest with me. Now he admitted that our safety couldn't be guaranteed. Police had uncovered a plot that was aimed at discrediting me as a witness.

Finally the District Attorney agreed to let Annalese return to Holland and me to Africa. This was on the understanding that we'd come back to give evidence once Damon had been caught.

'Maybe then he'll drop his guard and we'll catch him,' said Daryl, still confident of getting his man.

I arrived in Salisbury at the end of April 1973. I knew that Bill had wanted to come with me. We'd talked about it often, sharing our love of the wild, open spaces. But it could never be that simple for me. I felt that Bill would end up homesick for America as I had for Africa, and I was certain then that I'd never want to go back to a place that held such awful memories for me. And allowing Bill to return with me would, in itself, be a commitment to a long-term relationship with him that I didn't think I could make. In the end, hard as it was, I told Bill I needed to go by myself.

Chris knew I was coming home, but not the exact date. He'd been called up to do his compulsory national service and was still in boot camp.

I went to visit his mother and Chris phoned home while I was there.

'I'm glad you called,' she told him. 'There's someone here who wants to talk to you.'

She handed me the phone.

'Hello, Chris.'

'Hello,' he said, questioningly.

'Guess who this is?'

'Linda!' He sounded glad to hear me and I felt relieved.

Chris knew about the rape and the search for Damon. Nothing seemed to faze him or frighten him away from me. I found that amazing. I still worried that I'd shatter his illusions if he spent time with me, but I no longer tried to push him away. Chris said he would teach me how to play tennis and chess. I promised to teach him how to ride. We were going to take things slowly and see what happened.

Don't get me wrong, I cared deeply for him. That's why I didn't want to lead him along. Chris deserved better than that: someone who would commit to him totally, for ever. Until I was sure, we had to remain friends.

A few weeks after I returned we were in a nightclub called Bretts in Salisbury. I found myself staring across the table at him, thinking how special he was. He looked up and smiled at me. All my defences melted. I knew I loved this man. Trying to be heard above the music, I leaned over and shouted, 'I love you.'

'Don't say that unless you mean it,' he said, looking vulnerable.

'I do mean it.'

'Don't feel that you have to.'

'Hey, *listen* to me. I *love* you.'

Two days later we moved into a flat together and became engaged. My favourite stone is an amethyst and that's what I wanted in my engagement ring.

'It's not even a precious stone,' said Chris. 'Why don't you choose a diamond?'

'No, I want an amethyst.'

I wrote and told Bill what had happened, and he replied with a sweet letter. He told me he was hurt, but that he only wished me happiness.

We set the date for 27 October, but two weeks before the wedding I came down with hepatitis. We postponed the wedding, but then discovered I was pregnant. Quickly reorganizing things, Chris and I walked down the aisle at the Rhodesian Light Infantry Chapel in Salisbury on 17 November. My bright yellow skin was a beacon against my pale blue dress! We honeymooned in the Eastern Highlands of Rhodesia. Our room overlooked a small lake with pine trees all around it. My great uncle, William 'Curio' Harvey-Brown, planted the first pine forests in Rhodesia.

Weak from hepatitis and morning sickness, I lost the baby at sixteen weeks. Chris and I were devastated. In my mind I had already decorated a nursery and started choosing names. As soon as I was better, we decided to try again for a baby. Despite the loss, I can't remember ever being happier or more in love. Not even the war could touch us. The signs of it were everywhere and all the young men were being conscripted. Having finished boot camp, Chris would normally have had to spend a year doing basic training in the bush. Instead he was seconded to the Directorate of Legal Services at Airforce Headquarters in Salisbury. It meant that we were together.

A few months after we married we moved to Gatooma, a dusty little frontier town not much bigger than Kalomo in Zambia. Chris was the sole public prosecutor at the little courthouse. His cases ranged from chicken stealing to murdering someone for stealing chickens.

We had a three-bedroom house on a big block of land, with fruit trees and a pretty garden. With Chris beside me, I became more out-going, playing sport and meeting people. I fell pregnant again, but lost the baby after six weeks. We kept trying.

Early in 1975 we had a telephone call from Los Angeles. Chris answered and I knew something was wrong from the sound of his voice. Paul Damon had been recaptured. Daryl Walker had flown to New York and personally escorted him back to Los Angeles. Damon had been so confident that he'd never be caught that he took photographs of himself in all his different disguises. Some of them were amazing.

'I don't want you to go back,' said Chris, as we sat on the veranda that evening.

'But without me the police don't have a case.'

'You've been through enough. Let it go.'

'But what if he rapes someone else?'

Chris looked torn between doing what was right and wanting to protect me. He believed passionately in the law and seeing justice done, but he also knew that I'd have to relive the attack all over again in the witness box. The idea of facing Damon across a court-room terrified me, but I couldn't let him walk free. We agonized over the decision but finally agreed when the District Attorney arranged for Chris to accompany me back to America.

Our flight touched down in LA almost two years to the day since I left. I looked out the window at the sprawling urban landscape and felt a shiver of trepidation. I hated this place because of one man.

Dad met us at the airport. His marriage to Connie had broken up and he now had custody of my brother Clive and my half-brothers Sean and Jemal (Brendan was serving in the Rhodesian Army). They were all living in a three-bedroom house in Inglewood. Dad was back selling insurance.

A few days before the trial started, Daryl Walker took me to meet the District Attorney, Mr Savitt. They warned me to expect a diffi-cult time in the witness box and they weren't wrong. I spent three days being questioned. Damon's attorney tried to take my story apart, piece by piece, looking for any weakness and probing for uncertainty. Although I tried to be strong, if I wavered even slightly the defence attorney accused me of changing my story and making up lies.

I told him, 'I've spent the last two years trying to forget what happened. I don't remember every detail. But I do know that your client raped me . . .' I burst into tears and Judge Older asked if I needed a recess. He then stopped the attorney using transcripts in the cross-examination. Each time I walked in or out of the courtroom, I noticed a group of women staring at me with undisguised contempt. They were friends of Damon and it was clear they were trying to intimidate me. According to Daryl Walker, Judge Older eventually allowed only three of these women at a time in the public gallery because of their attempts to unnerve witnesses.

During one recess, I spotted Damon and his attorney in the foyer. Three of his 'women' followed me with their eyes. A few minutes later, upstairs in the restaurant, Damon arrived. He looked exactly the same as at our first meeting – relaxed and confident, as though nothing could ever touch him. It was the first and only time that Chris ever saw him. I don't think I've ever seen him so angry. His hands were shaking and I had to hold them tightly to stop him from going over to Damon's table.

I wasn't in court for the verdict. Daryl Walker phoned Dad's apartment.

'It's over,' he said. I sobbed.

Although Damon had been found guilty of rape, the jury had failed to reach a decision on the allegations of attempted rape. Judge Older, who had earlier been involved in the celebrated trial of Charles Manson, said that Damon had the same mesmeric and charismatic quality about him as Manson.

Chris and I flew back to Africa without waiting for the sentencing. Dad sent me a telegram that said simply, 'Johnny boy got five years.'

Robin Royston

Linda has managed to tell me the story without getting tearful or growing distant. Given how easily she dissociates at the moment,

220

this is a good sign. She has also written out a dream from the previous night that is full of positive images.

> *I am lying on the floor of the gym holding an electrical wire near the end. It is plugged in and switched on at the socket, but the appliance has been pulled off, leaving the wires exposed and 'live'.*
>
> *I know it is dangerous, but I can't keep the wires away from me, or move my body properly. I keep rolling around, throwing myself towards the socket, trying to switch it off.*
>
> *I roll towards the socket again and this time I manage to flick the switch. The wires aren't dangerous any more. I feel enormous relief.*

This dream of flicking the switch seems to confirm that Damon has largely been resolved. Linda has managed to turn off the unconscious destructive energy of her memories. However, I know how fragile any recovery can be. Only a few days earlier she ran away from Ticehurst and gave us all a terrible scare. If not for the 'fairy-tale' mouse, she would probably have hurt herself.

There are reasons to be hopeful, but it is still too early to say if we have achieved a decisive breakthrough.

The next two weeks prove to be a roller-coaster ride of good days and bad. I try to see Linda every few days and have regular briefings from staff at Ticehurst. Instead of her mind 'sliding' Linda now talks of it 'crashing'. She is caught in a vicious cycle, afraid of going to sleep in case she can't wake up from a nightmare, yet exhausted and desperate for sleep.

Some people have the ability to recognize they are asleep and dreaming and, if the dream becomes unpleasant, can either change the drama or wake themselves. This is called 'lucid dreaming'. Linda's problem is the reverse: she is never really sure if she is asleep or awake. Nor can she change anything in a dream.

221

WEDNESDAY, 6 JUNE 1990

Linda Caine

I had a nightmare last night. I dreamt Dympna heard me and came into my room. I tried to speak, but I couldn't open my mouth. My whole body arched off the bed.

I'm getting the old flashes again, of being held under water in the bath, with a hand covering my face. There is a new one as well, where the hand is replaced by a cushion pressed hard over my nose and mouth. I can't breathe and my body arches in the same way as it did in my dream. When this one comes I hear the rushing sound inside my head. I don't know if these are real memories. I am desperate to find out. Maybe my mind is just playing tricks. If they are real, who is behind the pillow? I can't see. I hate this.

When I tell Dr Royston about the pillow over my face, he says it makes sense. The rushing sound could be blood pounding in my ears.

'Are these memories?' I ask him, almost pleading.

'It's more important what you think,' he says.

'I don't know. The only way to stop the sensation is to wake up. But some nights I can't. I keep slipping back under and the rushing sound returns. I try to pray in my mind, but it's hard to form the words. They sound distorted and thick, as though I can't speak properly. In the end, I just think the name "Jesus", over and over again. He'll know I'm asking for help.'

After Dr Royston leaves I sit on my bed and try to get my mind to think past the pictures that keep flashing into it. I've become aware that the one in the bath has more detail than before. It's as though instead of a frame or two of an image, I'm starting to see a few feet of film, and maybe if I concentrate hard enough, the complete home movie might emerge.

I'm under water with a hand over my face. Then I see a fleeting image of Annette as a child. She's sitting in the bath with me, with a shocked look on her face. It lasts only a split second, but leaves me shaking. I shut my eyes again and try to return to it. It flashes into my mind and suddenly slows down. I'm under water. A hand covers my face, forcing me down. Looking up through the fingers I see furious eyes. I'm fighting for breath, swallowing water. The hand lets go and I'm pulled up by the back of my neck, coughing and spluttering. Annette is sitting in the bath, facing me. Her hands are jammed into her mouth and her eyes are wide with fright as she watches.

All the images have flowed together like watching a film – a film that doesn't have a beginning or an end. Is it real or just my imagination? Is it a memory or a dream? I want to ring Annette to ask her if she remembers such a thing happening. How did it begin? How did it end? I lie on my bed and close my eyes, trying to picture the scene again. I can't get it back. My mind keeps sliding away.

My life is like a fluid jigsaw. Each time I find a piece that might help complete the picture the whole image changes and I'm working on a completely new puzzle. It fills me with despair.

A knock on the door startles me. A nurse puts her head around the door. 'Sarah was asking how you are.'

'Tell her that I'm fine.'

'Can she come and see you?'

'Of course.'

I've seen Sarah in the corridor a few times since I've been back. She still has the same confused, shy look as before, but doesn't seem as highly medicated. Once or twice I've heard her screaming at night. It always makes me cry. I hear nervous shuffling in the corridor and a polite knock. Sarah comes inside and smiles shyly. She says hello, but her voice is so quiet I can barely hear her.

'You look pretty today,' I say, giving her a hug.

She beams. She's wearing a simple sundress, tied at the back with a bow. She notices my paintbrushes and paper. 'What are you painting?'

'An orchid. It's for Linda McCormack.'

She touches the picture. 'I love flowers.'

'Have you a favourite?'

'Lupins.'

'When I've finished the orchid, I'll paint you a lupin.'

She begins to protest but I put my finger to her lips. 'You gave me a tape of you playing the piano, which I love. I'll give you a painting in return.'

Sarah smiles and I feel as though I've touched her. She has certainly touched me.

Most of the patients at Ticehurst keep to themselves. Perhaps they're embarrassed about being here, or lost in their own world. I'm still very careful to avoid people. With my guitar, computer and art supplies, I'm almost self-sufficient. I don't take my sketchbooks on my walks. When you sit and draw out-of-doors you're like a magnet for every passer-by. They look over your shoulder and ask questions. Instead, I collect flowers and leaves and take them back to my room to draw.

Leonie is still running her keep-fit classes every morning. Normally I enjoy them, but I keep getting cornered by a patient called Verity. She saw the small cross on a chain around my neck and asked if I am a Christian. I said yes.

'So am I.'

Since then she's been telling me all about her church. It's nice meeting someone who understands my faith, but Verity is very intense.

As the keep-fit class ends, Verity asks if I'll go with her to the lounge.

'I won't, but thanks for asking.'

'Why not?'

I don't want to offend her, so I explain that I have difficulty being around people.

'That's OK. You can come to my room.'

'Thanks, but . . .'

'Or if you'd prefer, I'll come to your room.'

'I don't think patients are allowed in each other's rooms.'

'They are if we give each other permission.'

Leonie overhears the conversation and comes to my rescue.

'Come on, everyone, let's go and have coffee in the lounge!' she announces, giving me a wink. As she herds everyone up the passage, I slip into my room and sigh with relief.

Since then Verity hasn't let up. This morning she slipped a note under my door. 'I've been trying to come and visit you, but every time I get chased away by the nurses. Please tell them that you want me to come and see you.'

I asked Linda McCormack what I should do.

'Don't worry. We know what Verity is trying to do. That's actually part of her problem – she needs to learn not to be so dependent.'

'So what should I do?'

'Keep saying no.'

A day later Verity corners me at keep-fit class again. 'Please pray with me,' she asks, looking downcast. I don't have the heart to say no.

When everybody has left the old chapel, we sit down on folding chairs and I hold her hand. 'Lord, I don't know Verity well, but you do,' I say out loud. 'You also know her needs. People often become stronger when they go through difficulties. Please help Verity to feel your presence and your peace. Please heal her. Help us to remember that we are in your hands, and you will heal us in your way and in your time.'

Verity seems pleased. 'Can I come and see you whenever I feel down?' she asks.

My heart sinks. 'Verity, I'm here because I'm also in a bad place emotionally. I don't know how I'm going to be from one day to the next. I can't make any promises or give any guarantees. I really struggle.'

This goes straight over her head. 'I know God will give you the strength to be able to help me when I need you,' she says.

I know nothing short of letting Verity *move* into my room will satisfy her. From now on I'll have to avoid her completely. I'll work out at night, alone in the gym, listening to Roy Orbison on my headphones. I'll keep the lights off, so that nobody knows I'm there.

Chris is going to bring Gary and Christy to visit me today. I'm really excited. They've only been once before, during my first stay. I want them to come more often, but it's hard to plan anything. I never know when I'm going to have a bad day. I can also hear the reluctant tone in Chris's voice. 'They hate it here,' he says, but I know that he's speaking more for himself. Gary resents Ticehurst because he wants me to be at home. Christy does as well, but I think she finds it reassuring to see that I'm being well looked after.

When they arrive I meet them on the front steps. It's a lovely day and we walk around the grounds and sit under my favourite tree. Gary can't sit still. He picks up twigs and throws them at the trees. Christy is picking wildflowers and making me a posy. She tells me about taking Nibbles for walks around the garden with the harness we bought. 'He loves it. You should see him. It's so funny. He takes off as soon as I put him in the garden. I have to run to keep up with him.'

The barrage of twigs and stones hitting the trees is becoming more urgent.

'What about Squeaky, Gary? Does he still have tantrums if you wake him up?'

Squeaky is Gary's pet hamster. He earned his name because of his high-pitched squeals of indignation whenever he's woken. It's even worse if you try to touch him.

Gary holds up a bandaged finger.

'What happened?'

'Stacy wanted to pick him up. I told him it was too dangerous but he didn't believe me. So I decided to show him.'

I burst out laughing. 'That was pretty silly.'

'I know. Stacy thought it was hilarious too. I should have just let *him* pick Squeaky up – that would have stopped him laughing.'

Christy gets the giggles.

The summer holidays start in a few weeks. I really want to be home. Chris hasn't said anything, but I know he's under pressure at work. If the Canterbury office is closed he'll have to commute to London or find another job.

'I'm coming home for the weekend soon,' I declare, trying to cheer them up.

'For good?' asks Gary excitedly.

'Just for the weekend.'

His face drops.

'But if things go well . . .' I don't finish the sentence. Don't make promises, Linda.

After they've gone I arrange Christy's flowers in a vase and feel a dull ache in my chest. One way or another, I'm getting out of here . . . going home.

TUESDAY, 12 JUNE 1990

Last night I tried to phone Annette in America but she wasn't home. I left a message on her answering machine. I'm hoping she can remember some of the things that I've forgotten about our childhood. In particular, I want to ask her if she ever remembers me being held under water in the bath.

I'm still trying to avoid Verity, but she shadows me everywhere. Thankfully, she's only staying until Friday.

I fall asleep at 10 p.m. but wake up shaking. I'm so distressed that I even ring the bell beside my bed. Up until now I've never used it. It probably sounds silly, but I'm afraid that nobody will come if I ring it, so I don't.

Dympna sits with me until I fall asleep. She promises to wake me up in two hours, just to make sure I don't fall asleep too deeply and can't wake up.

I've written out a dream for Dr Royston. I wonder what he'll make of it.

I have to get from one room to another but it means having to cross an open space. I am frightened because there are two elephants standing under a tree a short distance from the rooms. I know that as soon as I leave the safety of the room, they will see me.

One of the elephants is standing quietly with its back to me. The other moves restlessly and is clearly agitated. I know this is because it has a wrong gene and is mad. I also know that it is somehow linked to me and it will charge as soon as it sees me.

Knowing that I have no choice, I step quickly and quietly across the open space. Although it is only a couple of steps from door to door, the disturbed elephant sees me and begins walking towards me. I stand in the room and wait. There are two other people with me. I can't see their faces and don't know them.

The elephant suddenly begins changing from its original shape into something resembling a plastic blow-up toy. I stand still and watch it as it burrows backwards into the sandy earth floor of the room. It burrows until its whole body is concealed and only its face can be seen. It is still moving in an agitated way and I lean down and rub its forehead softly. Although it lets me do this, I am still aware how dangerous it could be.

I also know no matter who or what disturbs the elephant it will go for me and nobody else.

Robin Royston

If ever a dream sent shivers down my spine, this is it. As I read the typewritten page, I try hard not to let my feelings show. Linda looks tired and careworn. She toys with a paintbrush, brushing the soft bristles across the back of her hand.

Although she seems to be managing, dreams like this one tell a very different story. The meaning is clear.

The fact that there are two elephants is important. The classical Jungian would see them as a symbol of the unconscious and a symbol of wisdom; however, Linda was brought up around elephants in Africa so they have a real and immediate association with her.

The first room in the dream is the place in Linda's mind where she retreats to protect herself. She feels safe and secure there, but knows that she can't stay there for ever. Deep in her psyche she wants to get out and confront whatever the danger is.

Once again I sense that something has happened in her childhood that has deeply disturbed the unconscious. Something dreadful has 'got into' her unconscious and has split the centre of it, or a significant part of the centre, into a good, normal part and a mad, dangerous part.

The bad elephant – the mad, dangerous part – then appears to take on a different form and hide itself beneath the sand, apparently harmless. But it is still just as malevolent as before. It is merely waiting. Woe betide anyone who dares to dig it up!

It is strange how compassionate Linda is towards it, stroking its head. This has to be part of herself, I think, or perhaps it relates to figures in her life that frighten her, yet she still shows affection towards them. Her father, or maybe her mother. She stroked her mother's hair, just as she strokes the elephant's forehead.

Although I sympathize enormously with Linda's pain, I don't ever assume that she *has* to be a victim of circumstances or a particular person. Jung called the dark side of a person's nature 'the shadow'. We all have one. It is possible that the wild horse and the mad elephant and the cold angry woman in Linda's dreams all reflect an aspect of her dark side – her unacknowledged rage and destructiveness.

On the other hand, the degree of her pain and the power of her dreams suggest I have to be very cautious before making her responsible. There are still too many missing pieces in her story.

Clearly, the 'outing' of Damon has not caused a fundamental shift in Linda's state of mind. It was such an obviously traumatic event, and Linda had so much difficulty in relating it, that I held out great hope of a turning point. And the dream with the electrical wire seemed to indicate just such a positive move. But now her dreams continue to be relentlessly negative, with no sense of everything working out in the end. Unlike the mud-pool dream, there doesn't appear to be a way out.

Despite the emergence of Damon, I can't shake the conviction that Linda has been sexually abused as a child, much earlier than the age of twenty-one. I have never mentioned this to Linda. On the contrary, I have always been careful to avoid putting ideas into her head.

In one of our earliest sessions, she told me how her father had gone to great lengths to explain to his daughters how they should wash themselves. 'Women smell,' he had told Linda and Annette. 'Which is why you have to clean yourself really well.' As a result both girls had always douched frequently and, if anything, over-washed.

Much later Linda recalled an incident in 1987 when her father was recuperating from his heart attack. He complained of a rash on his chest and thought it might possibly be an allergic reaction to his medication. As he showed Linda the spots he pulled down the blanket much further than necessary and exposed himself. Linda tried to dismiss the incident, yet she was shocked by the terrible sense of familiarity about it. It was almost as though she anticipated it happening.

Whenever I gently try to probe these feelings Linda's mind slides away. She isn't attempting to avoid the subject. Nor does she lack the courage to confront it. Her mind simply can't go there. If her father was her abuser, why does she love and defend him so passionately? Why was it so reassuring for her when she climbed into his bed after having nightmares? Victims of child abuse do sometimes have an ambivalent attitude towards their abuser, particularly when the abuser operates in a gentle, almost subtle way. But I can't sense any ambivalence in Linda. She truly loves her father.

Sitting on the bed, she watches me with her clear green eyes. I often feel the intensity of her gaze. Her sense of expectation can swing from hope to hopelessness in a matter of minutes.

'Let's leave the dreams today,' I say. 'Why don't you choose something we can talk about?'

She looks a little surprised and begins gathering her thoughts.

Linda Caine

I tell him the story of how we left Rhodesia. I don't know what was worse – having to leave my homeland, or watching it being torn apart by war and hatred.

Chris and I had left Gatooma and were back in Salisbury. Chris was doing his articles with a large firm of attorneys, Scanlen & Holderness. By then the 'bush war' had moved into the cities and urban terrorism was a reality. A lot of whites were growing nervous and many were leaving. Chris's father and mother had always talked about retiring to the Isle of Man, where they had been raised. The war gave them an added excuse.

Seven months before they were due to leave, Chris and I moved in with them. The idea was that we would eventually take over their house and the mortgage. It was a lovely place in Northwood, on a couple of acres, with a huge weeping willow in the garden.

I hated the war. I didn't believe in perpetuating the system of white majority rule. I wanted to live in a country where colour didn't matter; where politicians ruled for everyone and nobody had a privileged place.

The question of whether to stay or leave dominated every white dinner party and social gathering. People asked, what if the country blows up? How would we get out? Where would we go?

This drama was unfolding around us, but to me the war still seemed far away. I was pregnant. We had a lovely house and great friends. America was fading in my memory. I was really happy.

'What happened to change things?' asks Dr Royston.

Sometimes I forget he's listening to me. He seems to blend into the background. Maybe that's what psychotherapists are supposed to do.

I tell him how Chris's law firm had been hired by Amnesty International and Christian Aid to defend some of the black political prisoners being detained in Rhodesian jails by the government. Among them was Robert Mugabe, who was destined to become Zimbabwe's first President.

Part of Chris's job was to go into the prisons and interview detainees. The conditions were bad, and Chris sympathized with the plight of these people. He understood their anger at the injustice of white colonial rule.

Black majority rule was inevitable, we knew that. We hoped that when it finally happened there would be room for everyone, white and black, in Zimbabwe.

One day Chris had to interview one of the black independence leaders. They sat in a cramped cell that stank of sweat and stale air. Chris asked him whether there would ever be a place for white people in the future of the country.

'The white man has had his day,' said the leader. The hatred in his voice was so profound Chris realized it was too late for forgiveness and compromise. Instead, we were locked in an all-or-nothing war where both sides had fought themselves to a standstill. Just as the whites were wrong to cling to power in Rhodesia, the blacks were wrong to want absolute power.

When Chris received his next call-up, he was no longer posted in the Directorate of Legal Services. Instead he was sent to Mukumbura, one of the most dangerous areas in the war.

In command of a dozen men, he had to guard an isolated airstrip near the border where Rhodesia, Zambia and Mozambique converged. Units would come in from the bush after firefights, the casualties lying on trucks, ready to be airlifted out to hospitals or the morgue. Chris spent five weeks falling asleep at night not knowing if the landmines were being detonated by animals wandering into the minefield or terrorists coming across the border.

I hated knowing he was at the sharp end of the war. He was everything to me. A few months later he was called up again.

Seven and a half months pregnant, I was sitting under the willow tree in the garden when he came across the lawn with the envelope in his hand. He looked pale.

'I've been called up,' he said, without looking at my face.

'Another five weeks?'

He shook his head. 'This time it's indefinite.'

I didn't understand at first. 'How long . . . I mean . . . what do they mean?'

'At least eighteen months but probably for the duration of the war.'

'Where?'

'In the bush.'

'Oh, Chris.' I cradled my stomach and imagined terrible things happening to him.

'It's going to be OK,' he said. 'I'll sort things out.'

He went to Airforce HQ and they confirmed the papers. When he came home I met him at the door and knew from looking at his face that he hadn't succeeded.

'It's time to leave,' I said resolutely.

'Don't say that.'

'Listen to me, Chris. I'm not prepared to lose you for a system that I absolutely disagree with. We're having a child. What if . . . what if . . .' I couldn't finish.

Chris tried to find every reason to stay. He had lived in Salisbury for most of his life. This was his home. We had a beautiful house, good jobs and a baby on the way.

All the 'what ifs' were discussed. How violent would the changeover be to black rule? You can't hide your colour when mobs come chanting through the streets. I had experienced this in Zambia.

'Where will we go?' asked Chris.

'To England.'

'It means abandoning everything – this house, our furniture, our belongings . . .'

'We'll have each other . . . and the baby.'

Facing a call-up notice, it was potentially illegal for Chris to leave the country. He immediately asked for his call-up to be deferred because I was pregnant and had miscarried twice. A new date would be sent to him and until the new papers arrived we had a very small window of opportunity. Technically, Chris wouldn't be breaking the law if he left the country because his call-up papers hadn't been issued. Chris's father was ill, so we arranged for a friend in England to send us a telegram saying Chris should go over immediately. He then went to a travel agent and arranged a ticket.

We could tell nobody. Chris had to pack in secret and leave without saying goodbye to lifelong friends and workmates. Many would accuse him of deserting or taking 'the yellow route'.

But by far the hardest part for Chris was leaving me behind. I was so heavily pregnant I couldn't fly. Once the baby was born I planned to follow him.

Right up until the last minute Chris wavered. 'Maybe things will work out. We love this country,' he said as we sat in the car, staring at the terminal building.

'No, Chris. This way we have a future.'

We had to be careful how we said goodbye. There were military police everywhere and immigration officers were on the lookout for draft-dodgers. Full of fear, anger and regret, Chris waved goodbye and disappeared into passport control.

A senior officer stopped him at the immigration desk. It was the former chief of police of Gatooma, who recognized Chris. 'I know what you're doing and where you are going,' he whispered.

Chris expected to be slapped in handcuffs, but the officer leaned close to him and said, 'Good luck and God speed.'

Those words were the validation that helped Chris get on the flight and leave Rhodesia. I watched the plane take off and felt enormous relief, as well as fear. Now I could tell people the truth. How many of them would understand?

I moved in with friends down the road, who looked after me. Meanwhile, I arranged to auction all our furniture, which I might as well have given away. There was so much second-hand furniture on the market it raised less than a tenth of what it was worth.

On 2 August 1976, I spent the morning trying to arrange

insurance to ship three trunks of baby clothes to England. I waited in line, feeling very tired and suffering from cramps.

'When is the baby due?' asked a woman.

'A week ago.'

'You shouldn't have to wait in line.'

'That's OK.'

'No, really,' she insisted. 'Listen, this woman is pregnant. Can't you do something to help her?'

The insurance staff processed me quickly and a friend collected me outside. She saw me flinch as I sat in the front seat of her car.

'How far apart are they?'

'About fifteen minutes.'

'You're going to a doctor.'

Gary was born that evening at 6.30 at the Lady Chancellor Hospital.

The next morning an eight-word telegram was sent to Chris in London: 'You have a son. Mum and baby well.'

I spent ten days in hospital. Chris telephoned and it was wonderful to hear his voice. He was so excited and thrilled. I wanted to book tickets as soon as possible, but spent a month trying to get Gary stamped into my British passport. There were very few foreign embassies left in Rhodesia because of the international sanctions. The British Embassy in South Africa refused to do it, so I had no choice but to get Gary a Rhodesian passport.

He was five weeks old when we left. I felt a deep ache as the aircraft wheels left the tarmac. Jacaranda and acacia trees dotted the landscape and through the haze I could see the distant orchards and tea plantations. I remembered peering out of the broken back window of Dad's van and watching Gwelo disappear into the dusty haze ten years earlier.

'It won't be for ever,' I whispered to Gary, asleep in my arms. 'One day we'll come back.'

18

FRIDAY, 22 JUNE 1990

Linda Caine

I'm packed and I'm scared. I know I'm only going home for the weekend, but it's still a big step. It's been four weeks since I arrived.

After lunch I ask Roger if I can go for a walk in the grounds alone. I'm grateful when he says yes. I walk straight to the summer house and sit quietly on the bench, staring at the hole below. The mouse doesn't come out.

I sketch the entrance of the mouse hole with the broken glass and leaves all around it. I need a reminder of that night.

Back in my room I still have a few hours to wait before I go home. I start reading my notes from a year ago when I first came to Ticehurst. The four typewritten pages reveal how scared I was about leaving hospital. They were written just after I ran away from the group therapy session and cut my wrists on the barbed wire. It doesn't seem like I've come very far since then. At least I didn't cut myself this time. I'm also driving myself home.

I leave just after 3 p.m. so Gary and Christy are home from school by the time I arrive. There's a lot of catching up to do. Their lives are packed with the gossip and drama of school. There are new songs in the Top 40, new fads and fashions. I feel very out of touch.

Although I only have a weekend, I try to spend as much time with them as possible as well as doing everyday things.

I manage to go shopping on Saturday morning and that night there's a charity fund-raiser organized by one of Chris's clients. We stay a couple of hours and I speak to a few people.

On Sunday afternoon I start to feel shaky. Chris is at the office for a few hours and Gary and Christy are doing their own things. I tell them, as I often have before, not to answer the telephone if it rings.

'What's wrong?' asks Christy.

'Nothing. I just don't want to talk to anyone, not right now.'

I can see them swapping glances, but neither of them says anything. I hate myself for the obvious burden that this sign of my not coping places on them.

Later that night Annette calls from America. I'm disappointed that she can't clarify more things about my childhood. She doesn't remember seeing me being held under the water.

'You used to have nightmares about the gargle pipe,' she says. It was the name I gave to the deep gurgling sound that water made when it drained out of the bath. It was the same sound (only much louder) that Dad made when he gargled after brushing his teeth.

'And you hated being ducked under water,' she reminds me. 'Even if we were just playing around in the pool.'

We talk particularly about the years I don't remember at 5 Maple Avenue. When I first realized about the missing time, as Annette and I talked at Dad's kitchen table after his heart attack, it worried me but it didn't seem that important.

It didn't become an issue until I started telling Dr Royston about my life. Even now it doesn't seem that significant. I've lived in so many houses, what difference does it make?

Yet it still niggles me. It's like an itch I can't scratch. It's one thing to have absences, where hours disappear and I have to set alarm clocks to collect Christy from school, but now we're talking about *three years*!

For weeks I've been dipping in and out of *Memories, Dreams, Reflections* by Carl Jung. I want to understand more about psychotherapy.

236

I'm beginning to understand how the cure has to grow naturally out of the patient. Every patient is an individual and the solution to the problem is always an individual one.

Jung wrote: 'Analysis is a dialogue demanding two partners. Analyst and patient sit facing one another, eye to eye; the doctor has something to say, but so has the patient ... There are many cases which the doctor cannot cure without committing himself. When important matters are at stake, it makes all the difference whether the doctor sees himself as a part of the drama, or cloaks himself in his authority ...

'The doctor is effective only when he himself is affected. Only the wounded physician heals ... For psychotherapy to be effective a close rapport is needed, so close that the doctor cannot shut his eyes to the heights and depths of human suffering. Unless both doctor and patient become a problem to each other, no solution is found.'

Is that what Dr Royston is doing? Have we become a problem to each other? I know so little about him. I've tried asking him about his family once or twice, but he always changes the subject.

I once asked him why he didn't answer my questions and he replied that knowing about him could hinder my therapy. I could use it as a distraction to divert the conversation or as a way of trying to alter the balance of power. Or, for example, if I had a deep fear of getting cancer, I would have difficulty discussing it openly if I knew *his* mother was dying of cancer.

I've spoken to his wife on the telephone. It was when Dr Royston gave me his home number in case I was really struggling. I called one night and Lynn answered. 'Is that Linda?' she said. She knew my name. What else did she know? 'Robin isn't here, but he'll be back in about twenty minutes. Is everything OK?'

'Yes ... fine ... I'm so sorry to call.'

'That's OK.'

She was so sweet to me. She didn't sound angry or fussed about being disturbed. Perhaps it happened all the time. I was just another mad woman phoning her husband.

On Monday morning I drive Gary back to school. He seems quieter than usual.

'Is everything OK?' I ask.

'Yeah.'

'Did you have a nice weekend?'

'Yes.'

He picks at his fingernails and stares out the rain-spotted windscreen. The silence deepens until finally I press him. 'Please tell me what's bothering you.'

'Mum, do you go to a loony-bin?'

'Why do you say that?'

'It's just something one of the guys at school said. I told him you were in a mental hospital and then he started telling everyone that you were in a loony-bin. He thought it was a big joke.'

'Did he say anything else?'

Gary shrugs. 'He was saying that you were a loony.'

This is a horrible shock. Despite my efforts, I realize that my children don't fully understand what's wrong with me and what I'm going through.

'When somebody is physically sick they go to a doctor or a general hospital,' I say, trying to find the right words. 'But when they are struggling mentally they go to a psychotherapist and a mental hospital. The only difference between the two is that one is physical and one is mental.'

'Why do some people call it a loony-bin?' asks Gary.

'Because they're small-minded. They're the sort who call people names and make fun of mental illness or other people's disabilities. You know better than that.'

'Yeah.' He gives me a playful punch on the arm.

MONDAY, 25 JUNE 1990

Robin Royston

My weekend has been spent teaching Mike how to ride his new bike. I've been promising to take off the training wheels since his birthday in May.

The back garden became our test track. I ran alongside him, with one hand on the seat and the other hovering near the handlebars. He managed to keep himself upright for a few yards in a straight line. Learning to turn is next week's assignment.

Meanwhile, Emma thought it was a great game to have me chasing her on all fours around the garden, trying to catch her before she pulled up the flowers. At least my children are keeping me fit.

Now it is time to focus on work. I have eight consultations booked for the day, most of them outpatients. Eight different stories; eight people struggling to cope with their lives. People often ask me how I handle the emotional baggage that patients unload onto me. Normally this isn't too difficult, but occasionally someone comes along like Linda and the drama of his or her life becomes part of mine.

My relationship with Linda has been more fluid than with many patients. It has to be. Her situation is so on the edge and so raw it can't be solved by me being distant and 'proper'. I have to be more open and let her glimpse who I am if I am to win her trust. By being a mixture of doctor, friend, confidant, guardian, brother and priest, she is gradually allowing me into her inner world. Most of all I am just myself.

I see Linda late in the morning. She talks enthusiastically about her weekend, but I can tell that she's slept poorly.

I am anxious for Linda to look more closely at her father. This isn't a case of nudging or steering her to look. I have to be patient and wait until she can cope with it. Until then, I must help her to exist in her uncertainty and guide her towards her own path or solution.

In Linda's case there are so many themes, doubts, suspicions, fears and uncertainties in her dreams and flashbacks that she doesn't know which ones are important. A lot of them are simply background 'noise' that block out the real message.

I can't tell what parts are to do with real happenings and what are symbolic either, although often I have a sense that some elements are based in a real, historical past. Again, Linda has to decide these things for herself. Deep down Linda wants to know the truth but fears it in equal measure. She loves her father. She defends him. Yet a seed of doubt has been planted in her mind. Then, a few days later, a different main character appears in her dreams – a beautiful and dangerous woman.

I am inside a room, lying down next to a beautiful woman who seems kind, but is not. I think I am a child because I know she is a grown-up and I should listen to her. I am afraid and want to go home, but I know I can't. A tune keeps playing over and over in my head.

The dream triggers a memory from Linda's childhood about her mother.

'I remember her being really angry with me,' she says. 'I don't know what I'd done. She dragged me behind the cupboard at the Park Hotel and began hitting me. I refused to cry but this only made her angrier. She went out and came back with my dad's plaited leather belt. She doubled it over and began hitting me again. I was screaming and shouting, "I won't cry. I won't cry." She didn't stop until I cried. Then she walked out. I hated myself for crying.'

This last sentence is delivered with poisonous self-loathing.

It is more evidence of Linda's extraordinary duality. She can be caring and compassionate towards the smallest earthworm, lifting it from a footpath to stop it being squashed. Yet at the same time she can be harsh and unsympathetic towards herself.

Of course, we all have a duality. Our dark side may be an explosive temper, or a streak of meanness or jealousy. These might only surface every so often.

In Linda's case the duality is particularly extreme. She speaks about herself with real venom. She hates being dependent on people. She hates it when she can't control her emotions or pull herself together. It isn't a whingeing 'I'm-so-sick-of-myself' hatred. Hers is a vengeful, cold self-loathing.

In part this is the product of her mother's harsh voice. Her criticism has divided Linda against herself. She was brought up in an emotionally neglectful environment and has internalized the harsh feelings shown to her and become self-destructive.

Linda Caine

I start telling Dr Royston what happened when I arrived in England in 1976, one of the hottest, driest summers on record.

At Heathrow Airport I stood in front of the immigration desk and handed over my British passport, and Gary's Rhodesian one. The young officer kept turning the empty pages of Gary's passport, as though expecting to find something.

'This is not considered a legal document,' he said. 'It's not recognized in Britain.'

'What do you mean?'

'You have no papers for the baby.'

'My husband is waiting for us outside. He's been to the Home Office and sorted everything out. If you'll just let us through . . .'

'You can't bring the child into this country on this document.'

A stewardess who'd been helping me gave him a scathing look. 'You have to be joking.'

'That's the law.'

'So I'm allowed in?' I said.

'Yes, you have a British passport.'

I plonked Gary on his desk. 'You'll be needing this,' I said, handing him a bottle. 'He's in the middle of a feed.'

'Where are you going?' asked the officer, suddenly alarmed.

'To find my husband.'

He looked at Gary and then at the bottle of milk. Suddenly he had a change of heart. 'Just wait here.'

He chatted to his supervisor and then came back. 'I'm not going to stamp the passport because it isn't recognized in this country, but you can take your baby.'

Outside in the arrivals hall, Chris dodged under the barrier, put his arms around us, and held us for a long time. It was the first time he had glimpsed his son.

In the taxi from the airport, I gazed out the window at fields and houses that seemed quite spread out. But after a few miles they became closer until the houses joined to form street after street of terraces and tenements. Feeling claustrophobic, I closed my eyes and snuggled closer to Chris.

He had rented a ground-floor flat in a large old house in Hendon, North London. The area had been used to resettle many Asians who had been expelled from Uganda by Idi Amin. In the hot, dry summer the high ceilings and airy rooms seemed just perfect, but in winter we struggled to stay warm.

There were only two gas heaters in the flat and we had no

washing machine. I did all the washing by hand, including Gary's nappies. My hands were soon cracked and bleeding.

That first winter was a huge shock to the system. It was dark by four every afternoon and the streets seemed as bleak and sad as the people who huddled against the wind and rain.

Chris had managed to get a job as a legal executive with an old-established law firm in Westminster. He had done half his articles in Rhodesia but these weren't recognized in England. He had to start from scratch, studying at night after working all day. The firm agreed to give him time off and pay for his exams, but it meant spending three years earning very little money.

Although desperately homesick, I didn't regret the decision to leave Rhodesia. I just yearned for blue skies and open country. At the back of our flat was a tiny, overgrown garden. The only thing separating it from the M1 was a burnt-out house, with blackened and torn lace curtains fluttering in the windows. Beyond the motorway the hills were covered in houses, but at sunset as the urban landscape disappeared in darkness the hills would be silhouetted against the sky. It gave the illusion of vastness and space that I missed so desperately.

I hadn't anticipated such cold. I had a leather fitted jacket, which left no room for a jersey underneath. Pushing Gary in a pram outside meant almost freezing to death. My only regular appointment was at the local medical centre every fortnight where they weighed Gary. On those days I sat with a mother and toddler club, trying to make conversation with women I had nothing in common with except for our babies.

As the months went by I became incredibly lonely and unhappy. A cold, wet darkness seeped into my heart. I had no friends, or money, or places to go. I was alone all day and when Chris arrived home from work in the evening he was usually exhausted.

Elizabeth, the paediatrician at the medical centre, asked if I'd be interested in child-minding her baby daughter, Sally, who was Gary's age. I agreed and felt good about bringing in some extra money.

It proved to be a disaster. The gas fires in the flat were rickety and the electric sockets were old. The wires leading from them were tacked loosely along the floor and up the wall. I couldn't let the babies crawl around and the playpen was too small for both of them so they had to take turns. And without a double pram I couldn't take them outside. One day I looked at myself in the big rose-tinted mirror above the fireplace. I was holding a crying baby in each arm and I was crying too. When I told Elizabeth that I couldn't look after Sally, I felt as though I had let her down. I had also let Chris down because we needed the money.

As I left the medical centre that day I felt empty inside. For months I'd been going through the motions of living. Nothing seemed to work out or bring me any joy. At the mother and toddler group I sat with these people but didn't feel like one of them. Most of them were friends. Their babies were born at the same time in the same hospitals. They would sit and chat together, while I sat alone. The Indian women from Uganda did the same. Even without racist laws to divide them people still tend to form their own groups.

On the walk home I crossed an overpass above the M1. It was a bleak, grey day, with drizzling rain. I could smell the exhaust fumes and hear the swish of tyres on the wet road. Pausing to watch the traffic, I suddenly had a sense of there being no way out of this. I stared at the speeding traffic, almost mesmerized by the blurring colours and misty rain.

In the back of my mind I kept repeating, 'If things don't get better, I can always die.' It had been in the background ever since I could remember. 'If things don't get better, I can always die.'

But what about Gary? If I jumped now, what would happen to him? I could take him home and then come back. But what if nobody found him? What if Chris was late home from work, or had an accident? I had always vowed that I would never leave my children – not like my mother had done to me. My heart pounded and the blackness in my mind seemed so dark that no light would ever penetrate. I couldn't leave Gary. I would take him with me. I would hold him as I jumped. But what if he was thrown clear? What if I died and he lived? Worse still, what if he died and I survived? Or what if we survived with crippling injuries?

The only way to be certain was to drop Gary first and make sure he was dead before I jumped. I took him from the pram and held him in my arms, resting him on the railing. A lorry raced towards us, kicking up a cloud of spray. The lorry's headlights were blazing. I had a mental picture of the truck hitting my one-year-old boy. I couldn't do it. Clutching Gary tightly I stepped back, shaking all over.

Suicide had seemed like an option, an escape route. Now it had gone. Knowing that I had to go on, I felt absolute despair.

Robin Royston

Linda can't look at me. She clutches a handful of tissues and turns her face away. Her shame and sense of failure are profound, even though these things occurred more than twelve years earlier.

'Has anything like that ever happened again?' I ask gently.

She shakes her head.

'Did you talk to Chris?'

'Not until years later, not until all this started.'

'Your depression.'

She nods. 'I was trying to explain to him how bad it could be. He couldn't understand. That's when I told him about Gary and the motorway bridge.'

'What did he say?'

'He was shocked. He told me I should tell him if I ever felt like that again.' She smiles sadly. 'But he didn't know what to do. Nor did I.'

On the drive home that afternoon I ponder what Linda has told me. The sense of desperation that drove her to the verge of suicide in 1977 might have been symptomatic of postnatal depression, which can exist for a long while after the birth. In Linda's case this was made worse by arriving in a new country with no money and no friends.

Her reasons for contemplating suicide have been very altruistic. She decided it would be best for everyone, including Gary. Altruistic suicide motives are particularly worrying because people are more likely to carry them out than if they're motivated by feelings of persecution or worthlessness.

Linda's later breakdown, when she left home determined to die, was also altruistic. Again she had reasoned that her family would be better off without her.

244

This is clear from some of her diary entries. In one she wrote: 'There are people suffering and dying all over the world, and I'm sitting in my warm bed with my family safe around me. What reasons do I have to complain? You're pathetic, Linda.'

Linda instinctively sees the suffering in others and empathizes with it. This has nothing to do with self-pity. I have worked with many patients with self-destructive feelings who have been victims of major trauma or abuse, often in childhood. While their stories are invariably appalling, I've frequently found that fact begins to blur with fiction. The more you get to know them the more you realize they are wrapped up in themselves. Some are looking for reasons *not* to get better. Linda has never shown this.

A few weeks later, in mid-July, she has a dream that gives a powerful insight into her own condition.

I am in a bathroom and see a large spider running around on the floor. Although Red Romans have long bodies and this one is more rounded, I know that it is a Red Roman. They normally move very fast, but this one moves quite slowly and keeps going round in circles.

Looking at it more closely, I see that its left legs are injured. I open the bathroom door and find that it leads straight outside. The spider manages to crawl out the door, but can't walk straight for very long. Soon it begins going round in circles again.

Knowing that it won't be long before something kills the spider or it dies a slow death, I decide to kill it quickly. I hate killing things, but I also hate seeing creatures suffering.

To stop myself thinking, I react quickly, before I can change my mind. I walk up to the spider and stamp on it hard. Then I walk away.

I believe Linda sees, as I do, that the spider represents her. It can't leave the bathroom because in the outside world it is handicapped. This aptly expresses Linda's reality. She doesn't feel that the spider can recover and believes it would be better off dead. Although at times she seems to improve, Linda's underlying belief is that she is too badly damaged to have any hope of recovery. Rather than go round and round in circles she wants to be put out of her misery.

19

THURSDAY, 19 JULY 1990

Linda Caine

There are eighteen pills in the hem of my dressing gown. I can count the bumps inside the material by pinching them between my fingers. I feel guilty about keeping them hidden but they make me feel like I'm still in control.

I know I shouldn't think like that. I promised Chris that I wouldn't do anything silly. 'Never promise a lie,' that's what my dad used to say.

The staff at Ticehurst have been wonderful and I've come to rely on them. They've helped me realize that my thoughts of suicide are holding me back, stopping me getting well. Whenever I feel shaky and distressed, instead of thinking, 'OK, let them help me,' I say, 'Should I or shouldn't I? Is now the time to die?' I'm never going to get better if I keep thinking like that.

Linda McCormack can see when I'm struggling. That's when she pulls up a chair next to my bed and listens. I feel guilty about keeping secrets from her. I don't want to let her down.

'What's wrong?' she asks, sitting alongside me.

I glance at my dressing gown, hanging behind the door. I try to form the sentence in my head, but the words keep disappearing. She doesn't rush me.

I reach into my bra and pull out the prosthesis. I pull the thread and open up the pocket. The scissors slip out into the palm of my hand. Linda McCormack looks down at the scissors and then at my face.

Do I tell her about the pills?

– No. I have to keep something.

But I can't keep deceiving people.

– Not yet . . . tell her later.

It's like an internal dialogue in my head. I can feel myself trying to hold the information back, but suddenly it blurts out.

'I am sorry, so sorry. I know it's silly. You're all trying so hard.'

I get my dressing gown and open up the hem. It's almost like a ceremony, the handing over of the scissors and pills.

Linda McCormack doesn't say very much as she takes them from me.

'What were you going to do with them?' she asks softly.

I'm fighting back tears. 'They were my escape route, just in case people gave up on me, or it got too hard.'

'What exactly was the plan?'

I shrug. 'Use them when I went to bed at night, or run away and hide in the grounds. If I took an overdose and cut myself, I'd be dead before anyone could find me.'

My hands are shaking. What if she's angry or disappointed?

She smiles. 'This is a big, big breakthrough.'

I haven't expected this. She hands me back the scissors.

'Don't you want to keep them?'

'No, I'm not going to take them away from you.'

'I don't understand.'

'I don't want you to regret confiding in me. And I don't want you to feel trapped.'

I think she's telling me that the scissors are a symbol of what I could do to myself. She wants me to be reminded of this every day.

'But I will take the pills,' she says, putting them in her pocket. 'Hospital rules. They're too easy to use in a moment of panic.'

I'm overwhelmed with a sense of relief and also tiredness. I can't remember the last time I had a proper night's sleep. Every time my eyes begin to close I suddenly get scared. What if I can't wake up? What if I get trapped?

Linda McCormack glances at her watch. 'You should get some rest.'

'Will you come and wake me later?' I ask.

'OK.'

'You have to make sure that I'm fully awake. Don't let me fall back to sleep.'

'I'll make sure.'

Robin Royston

Linda McCormack tells me about the scissors and pills at our regular supervision session the next day.

'What else has she in the room?' I ask.

'The main thing is her craft knife, which is far more dangerous than a pair of nail scissors.'

I ponder this. 'When Linda offered you the scissors, did she *want* you to take them away?'

'No, but she expected I would.'

This is an important distinction. When Linda surrendered the scissors it wasn't because she needed to be protected from herself. She didn't say, 'Look, take these away because I'm frightened I'm going to use them.' Instead she gave them up because she accepted that she wanted to live, regardless of the consequences.

Linda McCormack has handled the situation perfectly. We have to treat Linda's 'escape route' with respect.

This logic might sound strange to an outsider. It would certainly be hard to justify if Linda cuts her wrists with the nail scissors or her craft knife.

Even so, there is a growing body of opinion among experts in the treatment of self-harm that patients should be allowed to keep their knives and razor blades; and even be allowed to suture themselves.

The rationale behind this is quite simple. By giving patients this latitude there is a strong expectation placed upon them to stop harming themselves. They are given control, but are expected to exercise control.

Most patients who harm themselves have a sense of powerlessness in their lives. This being so, the last thing you want to do is to render them even more powerless. Force won't work – they just fight back. By giving them the power to control their own destiny, the choice comes from within.

For this strategy to work, you must be sure that the patient doesn't truly *want* to die. Otherwise it's like handing a drowning man an anchor instead of a life jacket.

Linda is a voluntary patient. I can't lock her in her room, or stop her going home. Similarly, at a place like Ticehurst, it isn't possible to eliminate all sources of self-harm. Even if I could remove every pill, sharp object and belt from Linda's reach, she could still find ways to die. A leap from the roof, a smashed cup, a broken windowpane, an electric power point – there are any number of ways.

I can't hope to remove all the dangers and have no intention of trying. Instead, this becomes part of an unspoken, unwritten contract between us. I will do everything in my power to make Linda better. But she has to stay alive.

'She's going to be under even more pressure now,' I say to Linda McCormack. 'If she's really given up suicide as an option, it means that she's shackled to life and all the horrors that it throws up.'

'What's likely to happen?'

'Her only "escape" will be into her mind.'

WEDNESDAY, 5 SEPTEMBER 1990

Linda Caine

Annette has sent me a tape about our childhood. I'm surprised because some things I remember far more clearly than she does but other things I don't remember at all. I know she feels guilty about not taking good enough care of me after Mum left. She thinks she let me down. Poor Nettie, she was only ten years old.

I want to know about living at 5 Maple Avenue before our mother left. Why can't I remember *anything* about this time? Annette remembers some things, but not a lot of detail. And yet we both have clear memories of Riverside, our previous home. Maybe nothing happened at Maple Avenue that was memorable enough during that time? Yet the second time we lived there, I remember feeling so incredibly threatened and frightened that I sat in the window so that if anything happened inside, I could jump out, or if anything happened outside, I could jump in. But I didn't know why.

That's how I've lived my whole life – sitting on the edge, ready to jump, wondering which way to go. Will I jump into death, or will I dip into life and let it touch me?

The past few weeks have been terrible, but I can't pinpoint exactly when I started losing touch. I fear what lies ahead, but I'm prepared to try. I want to look at *all* the possibilities, not skip around things that I'd rather not see.

I keep having these terrible 'awake' dreams where I don't know if I'm dreaming or not. They seem so real. Sometimes I wake in the dark, convinced there are shadows in my room that shouldn't be there.

Things seem to be sliding out of control. It's like tonight. I'm talking to Linda McCormack and telling her how sometimes, when Chris and I are being intimate, I have to turn on the light to make sure it's him who's touching me.

Just at that moment the bedside light flickers. It's one of my recurring nightmares: trying to turn on a light but having the bulb flicker and go out, leaving me in the dark.

My heart is racing and Linda tries to calm me down. But the light flickers again and this time it dies completely. I totally lose control and nearly demolish the desk light trying to find the switch. I can feel myself crashing. That's all it needs – a flickering bulb.

It takes me ages to calm down and finally get to sleep. In the middle of the night I wake with a scream filling my head. It grows louder until I think it must be coming out of my mouth. But it isn't me. It's someone down the corridor. I can hear two of the night nurses running to her.

I fall back to sleep, but wake again with a start. There's someone in my room. I can see the outline of a figure kneeling next to my bed. I try to switch the light on, but the figure stops me. I recognize the outline as my dad.

'You know I'm frightened,' I say, reaching for the lamp.

Annette answers, 'Just leave the light, Lindy.' She's standing near the door.

Looking back at my father, I see that his outline isn't clear any more. I know that he's dying. I'm frightened because I don't want him to die.

Later still, I wake again. My head is pounding and my throat is so tight I can barely breathe. I press the bell and Katrina, one of the nurses, comes to my room. I don't know what to say or do. I keep my face covered and try to breathe. 'It's a dream,' I say, gasping. 'When I fall asleep they're coming to fetch me.'

She sits next to me and puts her hand on my arm. It seems to stop my mind from sliding.

'Did someone scream down the corridor earlier?' I ask.

'No.'

'So you didn't run down to her?'

Katrina shakes her head. 'Maybe it was the TV.'

For goodness' sake, what's happening to me?

Dr Royston comes to see me on Thursday. As always he asks about the last few days and then I tell him about my dreams. Lately, they always seem to be about me swimming in revolting water and scrubbing myself clean.

'I hate this. I hate this. I hate this.'

'What do you hate?' he asks. He's sitting in the armchair with his legs crossed and his trousers riding up to the top of his socks.

'The possibility that I've forgotten something or blocked it out. It must be bad, why else would I block it out? But whenever I think about the worst thing that could have happened to me, I . . . I . . . can't. My mind won't let me.'

'I think you're trying too hard,' he says. 'You're trying to force everything to come up. Take your time.'

He uses the analogy of childbirth. When a woman goes into labour she can't push the baby out immediately. She has to wait until everything is ready. 'This process is the same. Your mind will deliver when it's ready.'

Later that day I have the strangest dream. I'm watching a girl walking away from me and as I look carefully she begins getting younger and younger. Soon she is a little girl. I'm being pulled towards her and I realize that she's me as a child.

I wander around a corner and I recognize the park in Gwelo. It is

251

really pretty. I notice some jigsaw puzzles lying around. Some are in piles of pieces, some are partly done and others are almost complete. A lot of pieces are lying scattered on the grass waiting to be put together. I squat next to one (African-style, sitting on my haunches, with my feet flat on the ground). It's the way a child squats. I begin trying to put the pieces together but I get upset and then distressed. My eyes are so full of tears that I can't see the pieces of the puzzle properly. A policeman walks up to me, but I am too 'far away' for him to reach me. I try to tell him that something is wrong. I shouldn't be a little girl – I'm really grown up.

I cover my eyes because I don't want to see any more.

When I wake from the dream I can't get back to sleep. One part of my mind tells me not to let a stupid dream affect me, while the other part is flooded with childish feelings of confusion and grief. When I try to work it out in my head my emotions come out in verse:

> *Grow up Linda.*
> *I'm trying. I'm trying.*
> *But there's a child in my head*
> *And she won't stop crying.*
> *She covered her eyes*
> *And she got left behind.*
> *And now she won't see*
> *And she's lost in my mind.*

I can't get the image out of my head of a little girl squatting next to an unfinished jigsaw puzzle. She's covering her face because she doesn't want to see any more.

I decide to draw the image, hoping it will break the hold that it has on my thoughts. I relax and let the picture of the child come back into my mind. But instead of the little girl squatting empty-handed over the jigsaw puzzles, she's standing and holding a teddy bear.

I tell myself it's wrong and try to separate the teddy from the dream, but I can't. The more I try to erase it from the image, the more important it becomes.

252

Why?

I remember my old teddy bear being replaced by a brand new one, Dumpy. Because of him, I never saw my old teddy again. That's why I used to turn on Dumpy and beat him up, or punish him by leaving him on the dark side of the room behind the cupboards at the Park Hotel.

I look at the image in my mind and can see why she's clutching the teddy so tightly. She doesn't want it taken away. Then another image appears – a teddy bear being held under water. I suddenly remember that this was one of the ways that I used to punish Dumpy. I scribble a note for Dr Royston, 'I used to drown my teddy.'

As I sketch the picture of the girl and her teddy something jars inside me. At first I can't put my finger on it, but then it dawns on me: I used to drown my teddy in the drain outside our kitchen at Riverside. The drain was slightly blocked, which meant that there was always a pool of water at the top. We lived at Riverside before 5 Maple Avenue, and before the Park Hotel. I only got Dumpy at the Park Hotel, when I was almost eight years old. So it was my old teddy I drowned!

I must have been four years old, maybe younger. I remember holding him under the water for a long while one day. I stood in the hot African sun holding his soggy wet head, wondering whether he'd be dry by bedtime. I tried to squeeze the water out of him, but my teddy looked even more bedraggled.

When I next see Dr Royston, I tell him the story. I ask him why a child would drown a toy she loved.

'Children sometimes punish their toys the same way they are punished,' he says. 'You've already worked that out for yourself, haven't you?'

'Yes.' It's true. Children do exactly that. I've often heard Gary and Christy send toys to their room, or tell them to behave. They mimic the things I say and do.

Suddenly, my mind struggles to hold on to this. Does that mean my mother really held me under water?

Marion, Mother, Mum – I don't know what to call you – did you do such a thing? Would you tell me if you did?

It explains so much; my fear of the bathroom; the flashbacks of being held under water; my terror at being ducked in the swimming pool; drowning my teddy bear . . .

'I need to know I'm not mad, Dr Royston. That all this fear and confusion has a reason and it's not just my mind playing tricks on me. I wish you could tell me.'

'Why is it so important what I think?'

'Because I'm frightened. What if it's all in my mind? What if none of it's true? I'm sorry. I'm crying again. For goodness' sake! Even if it did happen it was over thirty years ago. Why is it affecting me now?'

Robin Royston

I can't answer her questions although I feel sure it isn't all in her mind. Something has happened to Linda and out of the formlessness of our therapy sessions her 'forgotten years' have become a central issue.

It emerges gradually as Linda tries to crystallize her childhood. The jigsaw dream clearly relates to the present, and her despair at not being able to finish the puzzle mirrors her desire to put all the pieces of her life together. It is like the day she came into the Chaucer with all her photograph albums. She hoped that if she could set out all the pieces in front of me, we could somehow make sense of her problem. The policeman, like so many similar men in her dreams, apparently could not help.

The dream is an allegory of her search for the truth. And the missing pieces of the jigsaw represent the years she has forgotten.

Now that Linda is sure something is missing, she wonders what will happen if she can't, or chooses not to, remember. This really frightens her. 'Will I be able to leave the past behind or will I become like a pressure-cooker about to explode?'

Linda also questions whether she is trying to lay the blame at somebody else's feet rather than take responsibility herself. Is she trying to find a scapegoat and turn herself into a victim?

These are common doubts. One of the biggest problems I face is trying to confront the inner certainty that people like Linda have that *they* are to blame. They feel themselves to be bad or deserving of what happens to them. Their inner world has turned against them and voices from within constantly undermine any attempts to free them from guilt and blame. Linda has to be more honest and courageous soon. Yet every time she seems to get closer to the heart of the problem, she starts to withdraw. Her hands come up to her mouth and hair falls over her face. It is as though a 'Vacant' sign goes on behind her eyes.

SATURDAY, 15 SEPTEMBER 1990

Linda Caine

I'm home again until Tuesday. It should give me a good idea of how I'm coping, being away from Ticehurst. As much as I hate to admit it, I'm not getting any better. I feel as though there's something inside me that wants me dead – something evil.

At home on Sunday evening, I set up the ironing board in the kitchen. Chris is sitting in the lounge and the kids are upstairs. I've had a nice weekend, although I've slept poorly. I can never truly relax.

As I iron a shirt, I feel my mind start to slide. Chris walks into the kitchen and says something. I don't hear him. I see his lips moving. 'Are you OK?'

'I don't know.'

'How come you can't tell me what's wrong?' he asks impatiently.

'Because I don't *know* what's wrong.'

The sharp tone in my voice makes him flinch. I go back to ironing and Chris sits in the lounge. Every so often he comes into the kitchen and asks if I'm OK. When it happens the third time I get annoyed.

'Just leave me alone,' I say, getting angry.

But he won't do it. He stands at the door and watches me. I can feel his eyes on me, boring into me.

'Get out! Get out! Get out!' I scream. 'Just leave me alone.'

Still he doesn't move.

There's a milk bottle on the sink. I pick it up and smash it down against the counter. Broken glass scatters across the floor and I hold the jagged end in my hand. I point it towards Chris, who looks horrified.

As he backs out, he collides with Gary who's heading for the kitchen. He sees me standing at the ironing board clutching the jagged bottle. Chris pushes him backwards. 'Get up the stairs,' he tells him. I can hear the fear in his voice.

I slam the kitchen door and try to barricade it by jamming the rubbish bin and laundry basket between the fridge and the door. Broken glass crunches under my shoes. Then I begin picking up the glass and putting it in the bin. I feel the edges of each piece, looking for the sharpest. I slip it into my pocket . . . just in case. My hands are shaking. How could I have done that? What thoughts have I put into my son's mind?

Chris manages to push open the door by about an inch. He peers through. 'Are you all right?'

'Yes. Just go away.'

He opens the door a bit wider.

'Are you sure you're all right? Have you cut yourself?'

'No. Just go away.'

'Have you burned yourself?'

'NO! GO AWAY! Why won't you leave me alone?'

'Because I'm concerned.' His voice breaks. 'You burnt your arm last time you were upset.'

His words begin to penetrate my stupid mind. Now I realize why he can't leave me alone. All this time I thought he'd been irritated at me because I can't tell him what's wrong. Instead, he's been worried sick.

I feel terrible. 'I'm not going to burn myself, but I need to be left alone.'

He nods. 'Can I just leave the door and the hatch open? Is that OK?'

'Yes.'

I can't believe what I've done. I feel numb. I put the bigger pieces of broken bottle in the bin. Then I sweep the floor for the slivers of glass. I finish the ironing and get ready for bed. In the bathroom I take enough sleeping pills to knock me out. Then I slide into bed and hide my face in my pillow. I don't care if I don't wake up. It would serve me right.

Poor Chris. I sometimes wonder why he's still here. He must be sick and tired of the worry and stress, of not knowing from one day to the next whether I'll be OK. He hates leaving me alone, but he has to work. He always says, 'Just give me a call if you're struggling. I'll drop everything and come straight home.'

But I can't call him. He has enough on his plate and I know he'll just worry about me. I feel guilty enough already.

'At least you can never say that life with me is boring,' I used to tell him, trying to make light of things. But the joke has worn thin for all of us.

20

OCTOBER 1990

Robin Royston

Fallen leaves swirl in the wind as I drive along the narrow country roads to the hospital. It has been a wonderful day. I spent Saturday tidying the garden for winter, collecting huge piles of leaves and dead plants. Today we lit a bonfire, Mike and Emma wrapped up against the autumn chill, their excited faces glowing from the warmth of the fire. They danced around it like Indian braves, the tang of woodsmoke invading their clothes and hair.

Roger Smith left me a message. Linda isn't coping well. The past few weeks have been terrible for her. She seems to be sliding out of control, with endless broken nights, silent screams and sudden 'leaps' from the grip of nightmares. When not at the hospital, I am being briefed each day by Linda McCormack or Roger. One of the things they tell me is that Linda is over-washing her body and hair – showering twice and sometimes three times a day. This isn't a compulsive or ritualistic thing, but more a wish to get clean. She also struggles to keep any food down.

I have told the staff to contact me day or night if a problem arises. Thankfully, the roads were clear when Roger called, although there were weather warnings on the radio. I park near the side entrance and go straight to the nurses' station. Roger is busy in the lounge, so I take the opportunity to read Linda's nursing notes for the previous thirty-six hours.

Monday:
Relaxed evening in room. Poor night troubled with dreams. Hears screaming in her head.

This woman is really frightened to go to sleep. Did so but when checked at 0400 called out, obviously dreaming. She became very frightened when n/staff tried to rouse her. Started thrashing around and finally slid off her bed onto the floor.

Very disturbed. Spoke of her nightmares recurring. Feels if she could remember the worst of these it would reveal her problem.

Talked about period of promiscuity after the death of her first husband . . . not interested in sex but desperate not to be alone. Said that her first husband predicted she would 'become a whore just like her mother' . . .

Tuesday:
Linda went to sleep until 7 p.m. then bolted out of the door barefoot wearing very little. Was found lying on the grass and persuaded to come back in. Robin Royston is coming to see Linda at 9 p.m. tonight.

The most striking feature of Linda's plight is the sense of something pursuing her when she sleeps. Rarely a night has passed without her suddenly 'leaping' from her bed, or 'silently' screaming. Sometimes she slides to the floor but more often she dashes for the door or window, trying to escape.

Each time she 'jumps' she seems to have no idea of where she is. Nor can she acknowledge the people around her. Sometimes she 'comes back' within minutes, or it can take hours.

I knock on Linda's door and wait for her to answer. She gives me a weak smile and apologizes with her eyes. Her hair is still wet from the bath.

'What happened?' I ask.

She presses her hands together and shakes her head. 'I had another one of those "awake" dreams . . . And I heard the rushing sound.'

'Tell me about it.'

She takes a deep breath. 'Well, I was asleep – or at least I thought I was asleep – and I woke feeling anxious. Roger came in to check on me and I felt relieved. He sat on my bed and patted my leg through the blankets. I tried to tell him about the dream, but his touch changed and became more urgent. His hand moved further up my leg getting higher and higher. I screamed inside my head but no sound came out.'

'What happened next?'

'I woke up and Roger had come in to check on me. "Are you OK?" he asked, as he sat on the bed. He put his hand on my leg. I began telling him about the dream but his touch changed. His hand moved further up my leg, getting higher and higher . . . I screamed and woke up. But it happened all over again . . . Roger came in and sat on the bed. He put his hand on my leg . . .'

This is one of the most striking and horrible examples of false awakenings that I've ever encountered. Yet for the first time in weeks, Linda seems to be telling me things without her mind slipping away. It amazes me that she can seem so sane and balanced, yet can change so quickly.

'I can't remember if I've ever told you this,' she says, 'but when we lived at 5 Maple Avenue, I used to fall asleep holding Annette's hand. Our beds were next to each other, with a little table in between. If I reached out across the gap I could hold her hand.'

'Did that make you feel better?'

'I didn't want to let her go. I was afraid of going to sleep.'

'Why?'

She shook her head. 'I was frightened that someone would come and take me if I fell asleep.'

'Take you where?'

'I don't know . . . I can't remember.'

She starts to cry. She lowers her head and her hair drops in the habitual curtain over her face.

'Just as I fell asleep I would get a flash in my mind of a hand coming over my face. It was like a snake striking. Have you ever seen a cobra strike, Dr Royston?'

She doesn't wait for an answer. 'That's when I used to jump awake. Annette said it was a nightmare. I think she

260

thought I was a neurotic child, just like everyone else.'

Linda has curled up in a foetal position and is shaking. I can see her chest heaving.

'I get those same flashes now,' she sobs. 'That's why I jump awake. I feel Annette's hand getting heavier . . . I don't want to let it go. I jump awake and tell myself not to fall asleep. But after a while I feel my eyelids getting heavy. "Don't fall asleep. Don't fall asleep. That's when they'll come." '

Linda's hand covers her mouth and nose. She can't breathe. She seems to be stifling her own scream. Perhaps that's what she means when she talks of screaming inside her head?

In broken sobs she blurts out, 'What if my father took me away to do things to me?'

Over and over she repeats, 'I want to die and take the children with me. I want to die and take the children with me.'

This time I can sense her sliding away. My voice can't bring her back. She falls silent, alone in a place that I can't reach. I sit with her for another forty minutes, trying to get through to her. She lies curled up on her bed, with her face hidden in a pillow. When I am sure she has fallen asleep, I close the door quietly and walk along the passage to the nurses' station.

I write in the medical notes a recommendation that a close eye be kept on Linda. Reading them over my shoulder, Roger raises the issue of 'specialling'. This means putting a twenty-four-hour watch on Linda, with a member of staff in her room at all times.

'I don't know if it's justified,' I say uncertainly.

'Well, if you don't want to specify, we can do something anyway,' he suggests, with a nod and a wink. Roger doesn't pay much heed to rulebooks. As a counsellor he dives straight into a patient's problem and then fights his way out afterwards.

'How about a Par-4?' I suggest. This means checking on Linda every fifteen minutes.

'Not a problem,' says Roger.

I debate whether I should stay or leave. I am deeply concerned about where this is taking us. Linda seems on the verge of remembering something that threatens to destroy her: she has finally given voice to the unspoken fear that both of us have, but what are the consequences for Linda if she confronts the truth? What if her father did do something to her?

The question is now out there. The answer still lies within her. But what will happen when she finds it? Again I ask myself, how will she cope if the truth is that her father abused her? Linda has no recollection of her father sexually abusing her, but she seems to be accepting the fact without having the recall.

The figure in her dreams doesn't seem to have a face. During the dream she can recognize him, but when she wakes his face vanishes. There are brain diseases where a patient can have a selective loss of function, such as the ability to see faces. The condition is called prosopagnosia. Perhaps Linda has a psychological version of this, maybe involving just one face? Equally, it could be called a highly selective hysterical blindness. We know so little about the mind and the consequences of major trauma.

In the early hours of the following morning Linda is found asleep curled up in the corner of her room. Staff wake her and return her to bed. At 5.15 a.m. she bolts for the side door and collapses crying. When I see her later in the morning, she is still distressed. Our session lasts only a few minutes before her mind begins to slide and I can no longer reach her.

I don't see her again until the following evening. In the intervening period she has experienced 'patches of calm', according to the nurses who check on her every fifteen minutes. Twice she tries to flee but the staff manage to get to her before she reaches the outer doors.

I find her sitting on her bed staring at the wall. She looks almost shell-shocked. I pull a chair alongside her and try to establish how much she remembers of the previous few days. She has little recollection of the 'leaps' or trying to run.

'I want to ask you about when you used to hold Annette's hand.'
Linda doesn't answer.
I carry on. 'Why were you frightened of falling asleep?'
'I knew they'd come and fetch me,' she whispers.
'Who would come and fetch you?'
Linda's mood changes suddenly. Her eyes flitter from the door to the window and back again. She wants to run. I can see it in her eyes and the way her muscles are tensed. I try to use my voice to

reach her, but she seems to have little conscious ability to control this flight response. After a while she calms down and excuses herself to go to the bathroom. She walks as though her muscles have grown stiff. I can hear water running in the basin. Then the unmistakable sound of breaking glass.

Running for the door I push it open. Linda is standing in front of the window, staring at her hands. She has smashed two window-panes with her fists. Blood drips between her fingers onto the tiled floor. Glass crunches under my shoes as I stand beside her. I put my arm around her shoulders.

'Are you OK?'

She doesn't answer.

There are cuts to her left palm and wrist. She has punched through the glass with her fists and then dragged her hands back over the sharp edges. She looks up at the window and down at her hands as though she is trying to remember what happened. Pressing the bell, I summon a nurse. Linda's cuts are washed and bandaged with steristrips. Throughout this she says nothing, but I sense her shame and embarrassment at what she's done.

The glass is swept away and wooden panels replace the broken panes. I order coffee and sit with Linda, trying to gauge what sort of danger she represents to herself.

'I had a dream,' she says softly. 'I was in Ticehurst, standing in the grounds, looking back towards the far-side door. I knew I had to run. That's why I was outside. But I couldn't run far away because I wanted to be near Ticehurst.

'As I stood among some trees and faced the buildings, I noticed a high round table standing on a pedestal in front of me. I walked over to it. The table had a circular top made of transparent ice, about three inches thick. Putting my hands on the surface, I watched as it began to melt. Then I ran my hands around the side and saw it begin to change shape as my warmth melted the ice.

'I began to feel cold and realized that the ice had taken away my warmth. Looking up, I could see Ticehurst and the side door just across the lawn in front of me. It looked warm and safe and I knew I should go back. I wanted to. But the cold was inside me now and I couldn't.'

This is a deeply significant dream. I strongly believe that it refers to the gap in Linda's memories of her childhood. The three inches of ice represent the three missing years that are frozen in her mind. Now the cold is inside her.

Whatever lies behind her difficulties has been frozen, according to the dream. In other words, it has been forgotten or blocked out. Ticehurst is her safe haven, but the cold inside her is stopping her from getting back to safety.

I have to help her, but know we are running out of time. She is very close to remembering something important, but can we keep her safe?

I sit down with Roger Smith and we discuss our options. I ask about the possibility of having someone stay in Linda's room at night. I don't want her officially 'specialled' because of the ramifications. Her insurance company won't be prepared to fund this for long and it would hasten the end of her cover.

'There are ways of doing it,' says Roger. 'We could have someone sit in the corridor outside her door. That way she wouldn't *officially* have someone with her.'

'That's what we need.'

'I don't know how long we can keep it going.'

'I understand.'

I know that Linda has become very reliant on the staff at Ticehurst. She has developed close relationships, particularly with Linda McCormack, and with Roger and Dympna who work the night shifts. Because Linda is terrified of being trapped in her dreams, the nights are when she most needs help and I know that she has become dependent on their support. As I talk to Roger now, I realize that the involvement of the staff has deepened. They are living with her fear on a daily basis and they are being drawn much further into her plight than might usually be the case.

I can see that Roger is not entirely happy with how things are going. He can sense Linda slipping away from us and feels helpless. Her internal struggle is having a profound effect on those around her and there is a danger of people giving up hope. We are treading a dangerous line.

That night Linda bolts twice. Roger catches her the first time before she reaches the door and holds her in a bear hug until she recognizes his voice. During the second 'jump' she goes straight for

264

the window in her room and puts her fists through the glass. Again, she isn't seriously injured.

With the weekend approaching, I decide to stop probing. I write in the medical notes: 'I feel that Linda has had enough at present and needs to leave it alone so that she can rest and get herself together for the weekend. If she continues to be troubled I will have to re-think. I will be available on the phone day and night.'

On Saturday Linda sleeps until 9 a.m. and seems much better. She wanders into the nurses' station and announces that she is going to her room to paint. Ten minutes later staff hear her screaming. They find her behind the dressing table, banging on the windows. Two panes are broken and she is screaming, 'They're coming to get me.'

Roger writes a letter to me the next morning, spelling out his fears.

Dear Robin,

I don't know how you regard gut feelings, but I have very strong ones about Linda and they aren't good. The last few nights (three) we have been able to offer constant supervision – i.e. an unofficial 'special' – but despite this we had quite a few hairy moments.

Last night Linda appeared superficially calm and I took the chance to explain to her about specialling, the costs etc . . . I emphasized that so far she had not been charged, but my concerns are for the future. What happens on the nights when Dympna and/or I are off duty?

After explaining this to Linda she became very frightened and her mind 'slipped' . . .

She is still planning to commit suicide. She also hinted at taking her children with her. She would do this, she said, 'Without their knowing it was me and without hurting them.'

My main concerns are these:

1. Her flights from panic are headlong and immediate and the lass really takes some stopping.

2. We cannot guarantee her safety during these times.

3. Determination – she has dragged my night staff across the room attempting to get out of the door. Also you know about the broken windows.

4. Having explained 'specialling' to Linda and the cost, she now feels –

despite my reassurance – that she will be left on her own and is very fearful.

'Even though you'll be looking in on me every fifteen minutes that won't do,' she said. 'I don't want to fight any more – something inside me has died.'

There is something about this girl that really frightens me.

Roger

The last sentence is the most telling. Roger has spent more than twenty years as a psych nurse and for him to say that Linda 'frightens' him is a rare admission. It is also clear that Linda's 'leaping' and fleeing are creating a major problem for the staff and hospital. She is taking up enormous amounts of time and resources. The fact that she is well liked adds to the pressure. I know that the staff have an emotional investment in Linda as well as a professional one.

How can we make her safe? As a voluntary patient, she can't be locked in her room or handcuffed to her bed. Nor have I been successful in getting perspex put in the windows. It is still being organized by management. Because Roger is working nights I don't get to see him until a few days later. We sit down again and discuss what can be done to keep Linda safe.

'She leaped three times last night and broke another window,' he says. He cannot hide his frustration, but is at pains to point out that this stems from his wish to keep her safe, not from the disruption she causes.

'We all care so much about Linda – maybe too much,' he says, rubbing his face tiredly.

'I know it's difficult. I really appreciate what you're all doing.'

'There must be something else we can do. Can't we change her medication to help her sleep?'

'The risk is that she might become "trapped" in her dreams.'

Roger knows what I mean.

'And if we physically try to hold her by locking doors we're likely to increase her fear and sense of being trapped. That's only going to make things worse.'

The concern on Roger's face speaks volumes about how far he is being drawn into Linda's drama, but I can't say anything without it sounding like a criticism.

'Linda only tries to flee at night. She's not aiming to kill herself; she's dissociating,' I say, thinking out loud.

'But she's still a danger to herself,' says Roger.

'That's true. The outer doors of the hospital are locked at night. Maybe that's part of the problem. She feels trapped and that just increases her determination to get out.'

'We can't leave all the doors open,' says Roger. 'There has to be some security.'

'What about just one?'

'What do you mean?'

'What if we left the side door open – near the nurses' station?'

'And let her go?'

'If necessary. By giving her more freedom we might reduce the pressure on her. If this happens, she'd be less likely to run.'

'Just like with the scissors?' says Roger.

'Yes. We give her an escape route and hope that she doesn't use it.'

If we leave the side door open, somebody is likely to see Linda if she runs. It wouldn't be a case of her sneaking out or going missing for hours without anybody knowing.

Roger understands the logic and also the risk. If Linda runs off, a lot of questions are going to be asked.

'If we let her run, where will she go?' I ask.

'Probably to the summer house.'

'At least we'll know where she is.'

'Hopefully.'

Roger and I agree it is worth trying. He arranges to leave the side door open.

When I sit down to tell Linda she looks defeated. Her eyes are bloodshot and ringed with dark circles. She is sitting staring at her notes.

'I know you've been feeling trapped,' I say. 'You think someone or something is coming to get you.'

She nods.

'I don't want you breaking any more windows. I don't want you hurting yourself. So if you want to run, I want you to know that you *can* get out. We're going to leave the ramp door open, at the side – near the nurses' station.'

Linda knows the risk I am taking without me having to spell it out.

'If you do have to run, I want you to go to the summer house,' I say.

Both of us know that she can't give any guarantees. When she flees she is in a dissociated state. I can only hope that enough of her mind remains in this world to remember the summer house. With any luck the cold will wake her before she gets too far. She might even come back of her own accord.

I have a meeting with Linda McCormack in my office and explain the experiment with the open side door. She also thinks it is worth a try. Then she takes something out of a folder.

'I want you to see this,' she says, opening a folded sheet of paper.

It is a drawing of a swirling black whirlpool. Reaching out from the centre is a white hand and arm. The rest of the body has clearly been sucked into the blackness.

'Linda drew this?' I ask.

She nods.

The drawing is tremendously powerful. Here is the very essence of Linda's plight. The black, swirling vortex symbolizing the terrible dark energy of those three missing years. The hand that reaches out, still desperately trying to hold on to her sister. If I had any doubts about the enormity of what we are balanced on the edge of, they are gone as I look down at this flimsy sheet of paper. The awful, malignant force that it represents is very frightening. I am certain that if the hand disappears it will mean death.

Linda McCormack is sitting very quietly, and I am profoundly aware in that moment of how other people will be affected by the grasping hand. All the staff are now wrapped into Linda's fight to live, but if the vortex wins, who else will be sucked into its black depths?

21

FRIDAY, 9 NOVEMBER 1990

Linda Caine

Dr Royston came to see me this morning. We spent an hour talking about dreams but he didn't press me to remember too much. I'm going home for the weekend and he wants things to settle down. It's a lovely day and I go for a walk in the grounds, which are still beautiful, even in the winter. A couple of gunshots echo in the distance. Farmers are probably shooting at rabbits. I stop to look at the fat sheep grazing in the central field. The ivy on the hedges is strong and healthy. I make a mental note to take some home with me. I'd like to see it cover our garage.

I sit down on my favourite log. It's one of the trees that Ticehurst lost in the big storm of 1987. Some of the trunks were cut up, but a few were left where they fell. When my feet start to grow numb with cold, I decide to keep moving. I follow the path past the summer house, which looks like a fairy-tale cottage amid the trees. In the field beyond I see two spent shotgun cartridges. Poor rabbits.

Heading back towards the hospital, I walk fast to get my blood circulating. Occasionally, I stop to pick up interesting pine cones. As I pass the sheep in the field one of them strikes me as odd. She lifts her head slightly and I see that she has a pink nose instead of a black one. Her eyes are also lighter. I've never seen an albino sheep. Gazing upwards, I look at the lovely blue sky, with misty patches. That's how I feel today – just happy, in the same way that the sky is 'just blue'.

On Saturday morning I leave Ticehurst for the drive home. As the miles pass I try to switch my confused mind from being a patient to being a wife and mother. I'm nervous about going home. What if I 'leap'? What if the children see me doing it?

That night it comes true. In the early hours of the morning I bolt for the door and Chris catches me. I only realize when I 'come to' standing in the middle of the floor with his arms around me.

He leads me back to the bed. We sit and listen to see whether Gary or Christy has woken.

'I don't think they heard you,' he says.

'I'm glad.'

I go downstairs to make us some coffee, but when I come back up I hear Gary talking to Chris.

'Is Mum all right?' he asks.

'She woke up with a fright but she's all right now.'

'Did you catch her before she reached the door?'

'Yes.'

'Good for you, Dad,' Gary says. 'I would have caught her in the hallway.'

I don't know whether to laugh or cry. My fourteen-year-old son has become my protector. Later I joke to Chris, 'Thank goodness I wasn't going to the toilet – I'd have been rugby tackled.'

On Sunday night I have another 'awake' dream. I'm paralysed, unable to move. I can hear the sound of Chris breathing next to me, but I can't wake him. Desperately, I try to roll off the bed. Eventually I manage to move my bottom half. As I begin to fall I grab hold of Chris's arm, hoping he'll wake up. He stays asleep. When I open my eyes I realize that it's a dream. I'm still lying on the bed and Chris is asleep beside me, breathing softly. Again I try to move, but the tiredness is overwhelming. My body feels heavy. I'm falling asleep . . .

The rushing sound is coming. It's too strong for me to fight. Please wake up, Chris! Help me! Willing my body to move, I manage to reach the bedside lamp. I turn on the switch but nothing happens. The screaming inside my head changes to a muffled groaning sound, like an 'Uh-uh-uh . . .'

Coming awake, I roll off the bed and kneel on the floor. The cold begins to force my mind to wake up.

Although I'm exhausted I can't risk falling into the 'dream' again. I take the top blanket off the bed knowing the cold will stop me falling too deeply asleep. Then I prop myself up with pillows until I'm half sitting. I test the bedside light to make sure it's working.

Chris stirs and puts his hand on my shoulder. 'Are you all right?' he asks sleepily. His hand feels warm on my cold skin.

'It's OK,' I whisper.

When I wake I'm surprised to find it's morning.

MONDAY, 12 NOVEMBER 1990

Robin Royston

It is always much more reassuring to have Linda in Ticehurst, but I can understand completely why she wanted to be home. From the moment she returns, the pattern of 'leaping' and fleeing begins again. Three times she shatters windows. Twice she manages to get outside in the depths of winter. Both times we find her quickly.

I feel we are taking a collective deep breath as the tremendous drama I foresaw begins unfolding. She is slowly and agonizingly reliving something, piece by piece. When she falls asleep she drops into another reality – falling back into her childhood and the nightmare that awaits her.

I have grown accustomed to her mind sliding. I can recognize the signs in her eyes and face. For a brief moment, she has a foot in both worlds and I can sometimes bring her back. The 'jumps' are more difficult to predict. Unable to recognize me any more, her eyes are full of fear and distrust. Suddenly, she bolts for freedom, hurling herself towards the door or windows. I try to stop her hurting herself, holding her back and using my voice to reach into her mind. The vivid flashbacks are just as powerful, bringing fear and repulsion. Linda tries to hold on to them, to see if they are real memories, but her mind keeps sliding.

'It's me, Linda. You're at Ticehurst.'

She is crouching on the floor, huddled in the corner. As I put my hand on her shoulder she flinches. 'Don't hurt me. Don't hurt me.'

'I'm not going to hurt you.'

'They're coming to fetch me!'

'Who are "they"?'

'Don't hurt me, don't hurt me.' Her whole body has gone stiff. She looks at me with sheer terror.

'What is my name?' I ask her.

'You know I never knew your name.'

'Look at my hair – it's not dark.'

She doesn't react. 'Linda, look at my hair. It's me, Dr Royston.' Her eyes are desperate and pleading.

'Linda doesn't tell stories. Linda doesn't tell stories.' She repeats this phrase over and over again, sobbing and choking.

After almost half an hour, she returns. I help her back to the bed, where she curls up and cries.

'You were repeating something,' I say. 'You kept saying, "Linda doesn't tell stories. Linda doesn't tell stories." Do you remember?'

She shakes her head.

'Does that sentence mean anything to you?'

She struggles to remember. If the answer was ever there it has gone.

After a while Linda blurts, 'You know that Annette used to say I hallucinated. Nightmares, hallucinations, stories . . . what if they were real?'

'What do you think?'

'I don't know. I can't remember.'

She wants me to *give* her the answers, but I can't do that. This is one of the central paradoxes of psychotherapy. Analysis is born from a certain sense of trying *not* to make a judgement but simply questioning over and over until the individual is ready.

Immersed in feelings, images and ideas, Linda struggles to find anything solid to hold on to. She can't separate dream from reality and memory from fact. So far I have tried to define the boundaries of the problem by gently probing and questioning, but never offering her simple answers. But I know that if I carry this too far there is a risk that Linda won't survive. She will drown in her own sea of uncertainty. At some point, I will have to plant certain posts and tell her what I feel is real and not real. I can only make such judgements with the weight of evidence and information behind me.

She lies on her side, staring at the window. The moon has risen above the trees and cast wintry shadows on the paths. Linda watches the moon and tries hard to remember a lost thought.

'When Dad used to go away on business I was always afraid that he wouldn't come back,' she says. 'That's why he told me to look at the moon and say goodnight to him. "I'll be looking at the same moon as you," he said, "and saying goodnight to you." '

I have heard her tell this story before. 'How long were his business trips?' I ask.

She shrugs. 'They seemed to last for ever, but they were probably only a week or so.'

'Who looked after you?'

'Our mother . . . and later the different housekeepers.' Linda pauses. 'Dad knew she was having affairs while he was away.'

'How did he know?'

'Whenever he came home from Bulawayo our mother used to insist that he collected a cake from *her* mother – about an hour's drive from Gwelo. He forgot one day and my mother was furious. Dad couldn't understand why she was so upset.

'Then he put two and two together. Collecting the cake had been a signal, and my mother would get a phone call. According to Dad it was her early warning system. Once he realized, he deliberately didn't fetch the cake again, and arrived home much earlier than expected. He caught her with another man.'

FRIDAY, 16 NOVEMBER 1990

Linda Caine

Only two 'leaps' today. The first time I make it all the way down the passage to the side door before Dympna stops me. Roger catches me the second time.

'Why do you always cover your face?' he asks when I settle down.

'I hate not being able to breathe,' I say.

'Then why do you cover your own face? I had to prise your fingers away from your mouth and nose.'

Without even thinking, I answer, 'If I cover my own face, then nobody can cover it for me and stop me breathing.'

It stops me in my tracks. Is that really why I do it? Why?

Later in the day Linda McCormack drops in to see me. We start talking about the 'uh-uh-uh' sound I make just before I 'leap'. Dr Royston and Dympna have heard it too. So has Chris.

'Maybe it has something to do with the scream that stays inside my head,' I say, thinking out loud. Then I wonder if it could be because my mouth is covered.

I experiment, covering my mouth with my hand, but I can still make a screaming noise. Then I cover my nose as well, so that I can't breathe. I can only make an 'uh-uh' sound deep in my throat. I can't scream. It's exactly the same noise as the one I hear when I'm trying to wake up.

MONDAY, 19 NOVEMBER 1990

Robin Royston

Last night Linda fled barefoot down the passage and burst through the side door. Noel kept pace with her as she ran down the long walk towards the summer house. Clearly frightened, she kept repeating, 'I don't tell stories. Linda doesn't tell stories.'

Back in her room she was given frothy coffee and Noel stayed with her until she fell asleep.

I arrive just before midday and Linda seems very focused and ready to talk.

'Coffee is on the way,' she says, giving me a smile. She has dressed in a pair of slacks and a loose-fitting checked shirt.

I sit in the armchair by her bed and she gives me her notes from the previous two days. She has written down several more dreams and also some notes to remind herself of what she wants to tell me.

I wait as she searches for the words. Linda tells me how the flashes in her mind are beginning to splice together, like pieces of old film. She remembers clutching Annette's hand across the gap between their beds. She was frightened of going to sleep because 'that's when he comes'.

Her voice is shaking and she squeezes her hands between her knees to stop them covering her mouth. She drops her head. Hair falls across her face and she begins to cry.

I have come to realize that Linda is always a lot further through the journey than me. I have reached the border while she is already deep into the next country.

'He's coming to fetch me,' she whispers.

'Who?'

'I don't know. A dark-haired man.'

'Has he been before?'

She takes a deep breath and nods. 'He comes to fetch me in the night. He puts his hand over my mouth so I can't make a noise and wake Annette. I hold Annette's hand across the table between our beds. But when I fall asleep, my hand falls. That's when he comes.'

Linda rocks slightly as she hugs her knees and her voice cracks with soft sobs. She is back there now, at 5 Maple Avenue. Even her voice seems to have become childlike and fearful.

This is extraordinary. I have waited so long for this moment, and now we're here I wonder if it's real. Everything in the room seems to sharpen in focus. There is a sense of elation, followed by extreme fear. For a moment, I want to turn back. I'm acutely aware of my role as guide – if I handle this wrong the consequences could be cataclysmic. And if I help Linda give voice to the truth, will she survive?

'Where does he take you to?' I ask. My voice sounds firm and calm, belying my fear.

'Through the house. He opens the door into my parents' bedroom. "No, no, no, no," I try to say, but his hand is over my mouth. The arm around my chest is squeezing the air out of my lungs. When he sets me down I try to run, but he catches me before the door. He laughs as he carries me back to the bed.'

Linda's sobs are so deep they shake her entire frame. I can see her fighting for breath, as though drowning or being rolled over and over in the surf.

'Do you see his face?'

She nods.

'Do you recognize him?'

She shakes her head. I can't tell if she means no, or simply can't bring herself to say. Her misery seems absolute. Her face has contorted in pain and fear.

'He lays me on the bed and lifts my nightdress. I think about the blanket . . . it's soft against my cheek. So soft. The soft blanket doesn't hurt . . .'

Linda's mind begins to separate. Her eyes, although open, are fixed and not focused. I realize that this particular dissociation is part of what she is reliving. This is how she had coped. She fell deeper into her mind and found a safe place. A similar thing happened during the Damon rape. She found a place where nothing could hurt her, regardless of what happened to her body.

I can't let her slip away again. I have to hold her in the real world – in her room at Ticehurst – for just a little longer. Too often in the past she has 'escaped' into her mind. Too often the dark-haired man has escaped with her.

At the same time, I have to be careful. How hard can I push her? How much can she take? Linda has always been much braver and more determined than I am. She has more to gain or lose.

'Please, don't hurt me. Please, don't hurt me,' she sobs.

I sit on the bed next to her and put my hand on her shoulder. I hope that physical contact will help anchor her in the real world. Perhaps if she has a greater sense of me being there, she won't be so frightened.

'There is a man . . .'

'Yes?'

'I'm screaming, but no sound comes out.'

Her fingers are pressed over her mouth and nose. I can hear a deep 'uh-uh' sound in her throat.

'They . . . they . . . t-t-told me . . . to shut up,' she stammers.

She uses the word 'they'. I ask her, 'Is there somebody else in the room?'

Linda shakes her head. 'I can't look.'

'Yes, you can.'

With my arm around her shoulders I can feel her racking sobs. She shakes her head from side to side.

'I can't feel anything,' she cries. 'Just the soft blanket taking my mind away.'

'Where is the other person?'

'Beside the door.'

'Can you look now?'

'No! No!'

'Yes, you can.'

Linda lifts her head from her knees and her fingers draw aside the curtain of hair by just a crack. Her eyes are clamped shut.

Suddenly, her entire body goes rigid with shock. Her hand flies to her mouth and her face fills with the most profound horror.

'Who is it, Linda? *You have to say.*'

She opens her mouth but no sound comes out.

'Who can you see?'

She stares right through me.

'Who else is in the room?'

She mouths the words, 'My mother.'

The silence is absolute. Linda is still with me – normally by now her mind has slipped away. It is as though she is standing on the edge of an abyss and could go either way. I am so stunned by what I've heard that for a second I don't move. It's taken us two years. Two years of struggling to piece together so many fragments of information. It finally makes sense. But it doesn't. I'm left with only an empty horror inside.

I still have my arm around her shoulders, but the shaking has stopped. I have to bring Linda back from the edge. I can't leave her like this. Equally, I have no idea how she will react to the revelations. All her defences have been breached.

Stroking her hair, I begin telling her a story that I remember reading to Mike and Emma. It is a fairy tale about a boy made of iron and a girl made of sandalwood.

'On the roof of an old house in the middle of a town, there was a clock that belonged to an old magician. The clock had a little bell tower and underneath was a boy made of iron. He had a silver hammer and at one o'clock he lifted his silver hammer and struck the bell once. Dong!

'He struck the clock every hour and every day for many years . . .'

Linda's sobs have grown softer and I sense that she is listening.

'But one night everything changed. The sun had set and the moon shone down on the old house. The hands of the clock moved on to twelve. The iron boy lifted the hammer. But instead of striking the bell twelve times for midnight he lifted his silver hammer and struck the bell again!

'Suddenly he was free. He lifted one foot. Then he lifted the other. He could move! All his life he had been fastened to the bell tower. He had never done anything except strike the bell.'

Linda has fallen silent.

'The iron boy talked to the old magician. Even though he was free, what he really wanted was to be a normal child. The magician told him that it was only possible if he travelled to a far-off country and bathed in the Silver River.

'Meanwhile, in a room in the same house where the magician lived, a pile of toys lay forgotten, gathering dust. Among them lay a pretty doll made of sandalwood. Sadly, the children had grown up and no longer played with her.

'The sandalwood girl was very lonely. Every night she'd listen to the iron boy up on the roof, striking his silver hammer on the bell. But one night he struck the bell thirteen times.

'She was so surprised that she sat up and realized she could move her arms and legs. She climbed down from her shelf and went to the magician. "I've been sitting on a shelf for years and years," she whispered. "Now I really want to be alive. I want to be free."

'She, too, was told to go to a far-off country and bathe in the Silver River.

'At the edge of a forest, within sight of the Blue Mountains, the sandalwood girl and the iron boy met each other. Their journey was very dangerous. They were attacked by fire dragons that set fire to the grass. The iron boy carried the sandalwood girl over his head to keep her away from the flames.

'When they finally reached the Silver River, it lay at the bottom of huge cliffs. They were both very frightened.

'Standing high above the river, the iron boy said, "Suppose the

278

magician was wrong? If I jump in the river, I'll sink to the bottom and that will be the end of me."

' "If he's wrong, I shall still be made of wood," said the sandal-wood girl. "I can hold you up."

'They stood on the ledge, held hands and jumped into the river. As they plunged into the water a great change came over them. The iron boy kicked his legs and came up to the surface. He could swim! The sandalwood girl also became real and swam alongside him.

'They were so happy they danced on the banks of the river. They were alive!'

22

WEDNESDAY, 21 NOVEMBER 1990

Robin Royston

Linda wakes with a scream late in the afternoon. She is found with a blanket over her head, curled up in a corner, saying, 'I can't breathe. I can't swallow . . .'

That night she 'leaps' twice. Staff hear her scream and manage to catch her the first time. During the second 'leap', in the early hours of the morning, she puts her fists through a window, cutting her hands and feet. She is given 10mg of Diazepam to help her settle down.

Linda's pain is so raw that I can't shake it. I keep picturing the moment of realization when she saw her mother's face, watching her being abused. It is an image now branded on both our minds and one she will never block out again.

Being a witness to Linda's pain and struggle, now that we know the whole truth, has a new and appalling dimension. I know that everybody who has been involved feels it acutely, and we are watching her more closely than ever.

The truth was there all along – locked within Linda's unconscious – but it was too horrifying for her to confront. Now we know why, and yet the suddenness has come as a surprise to both of us.

Although all these pieces of evidence have fallen into place, it isn't simply a case of accepting what Linda told me as being the truth. From a professional viewpoint I must try to distance myself from the daily drama and question everything very carefully, like a neurologist would examine a patient's nervous system. Sometimes sitting with Linda in her room, trying to reach her and calm her shattered mind, and at other times while driving and sorting the pieces in my own head, I go back over the dreams and stories she recounted looking for any details that jar or contradict what she's revealed. Could the evidence be interpreted differently? Does it all fit too neatly together? Ultimately, I am left in no doubt about what she remembered.

Linda's mother brought the dark-haired man into 5 Maple Avenue. And this man sexually abused Linda while her mother watched and took part. This happened when Linda's father was away on business. That's why she'd been so desperate for him to come home – poetically saying goodnight to the same moon.

When he headed home he dropped in to pick up a cake from his mother-in-law, Linda's grandmother. Mother and daughter had a system worked out and a phone call warned Linda's mother that he was on his way home. This gave her time to get her lover out of the house and remove all trace of what had happened.

The 'dark-haired man' was there all along in Linda's dreams. He was beside the swimming pool, offering her iced lollies that tasted strange. At various times he was the figure without a face, the malevolent black horse and the evil presence that she sensed was watching her at night.

I now realize that her mother also featured throughout Linda's dreams. She was a dangerous lioness, a cruel abuser of horses and a cold distant beauty. In one of the dreams Linda even described lying down next to a beautiful woman 'who seemed kind, but was not'. The woman frightened her and she wanted to go home, but knew she couldn't. The harshness of her mother is evident not just in the dreams, but also in the way Linda criticizes herself. There were other clues, such as Linda's flashbacks of a hand over her face and of being held under water in the bath. She 'drowned' her teddy in a copycat punishment.

In all the memories of her mother, she never once recounted how she brushed her hair, or read her bedtime stories, or cuddled her when she was sick. Instead, she remembers only her mother's anger and neglect. Annette confirms this. She also is unable to remember a single incident of their mother touching her in a loving way, or doing any of the things a normal mother would do for her child. This is the same woman who deserted her children without saying goodbye, and made very little effort to stay in touch with them.

We'll never know the truth, but perhaps remorse was the reason that she wept beside Linda's bed all those years later when they met again. Maybe she was trying to say sorry. Yet by morning she acted as though it had never happened. This is why Linda felt a horrible sense of *déjà vu*. She remembered what it was like as a child, waking up after being abused and finding her mother standing in the kitchen making breakfast as though nothing had happened.

It is hard to imagine that a mother could be capable of such deeds, but the sad truth is that my own experiences, and stories I've heard from child psychiatrists and community paediatricians, prove that such things are all too common.

The thing that now occupies me exclusively, however, is what to do next. How will Linda react now? Will the poison be removed, or will it destroy her?

I keep telling myself that when Linda first came to me she wanted to die. Given the nature of the truth she has uncovered, I cannot be sure that this doesn't remain the case; at the very least, we still have a way to go. And what will happen during that time? Whatever the rights and wrongs of the situation, a lot of people, including myself, have grown deeply fond of Linda. Her awful, black vortex encompasses all the people who care, and if she were to die, especially now, the effect would be devastating.

Linda makes people smile and they care about her. She has never been manipulative or a 'professional' psychiatric patient. I've had patients who sought to drag me into their chaos and mischief, or who wanted to spread their negative energy to those around them. But never Linda. She has a strong, stable home life and *wants* to get better. She is on our side rather than fighting against us. Members of staff like Roger and Dympna are quite open about how much they like her. They consistently bend the rules to keep watch on her. At one point, during a 'leap', Roger had to hold Linda for nearly two hours. He couldn't reach the bell to summon help and couldn't risk letting her go. These are the sorts of sacrifices that people here are making on a daily basis to keep her safe. And they do so because they want to.

I have always been aware that discovering the source of Linda's pain might also remove her defences to cope with it. She blocked out these memories for a reason, perhaps to protect herself. Having trusted the process and followed the 'goat track', I don't know if she can survive the truth. Ultimately, this rests with her unconscious. Hopefully, something will now change within her mind. If not, she is lost.

As though to highlight my fears, on Thursday morning I have a call from Roger. It has been another difficult night. Linda has smashed a window and had to be restrained by two nurses.

'She was desperate to get out,' says Roger. 'I finally let her go and she ran to the summer house. I found her huddled under a bench, whimpering. She kept saying, "Don't let them find me." It took me almost an hour to coax her out. She was freezing. She wouldn't take my sweater at first. She was worried that she'd make it dirty. That's what she kept saying, "I'm dirty. I'm dirty . . ." '

'How is she now?'

'She's in her room. Dympna is keeping an eye on her.'

'OK. I'll be there in the morning.'

I go to sleep that night with a growing sense of unease. We've unearthed the mad elephant. Now we have to find some way of coping with it.

FRIDAY, 23 NOVEMBER 1990

Linda Caine

My mother's face keeps appearing to me like a jack-in-the-box. I want to run and hide. No, I want to be dead so nobody can take me. I can't keep any food down. I vomit as soon as I start to swallow. But the worst time is when I close my eyes. The dark-haired man comes for me again. He puts his hand over my mouth and nose and carries me down the passage. I scream, trying to wake Annette, but the sound doesn't leave my head.

How could my mother allow it to happen? How could she watch?

I've started to remember all the places I used to hide. There was a hole in a conifer hedge at 5 Maple Avenue. I would crawl inside where nobody could see me, but I could see them coming. That's where I want to be now, safe in my hedge. They won't find me there.

Run, Linda, run!

There's a man in the doorway. He won't let me leave. I spin around and try to crash through the window. I hear the tinkling sound of breaking glass. Someone has pinned my arms to my side. My head feels like it's going to explode.

'Listen to me, Linda. You're in your room at Ticehurst.' It's Roger's voice. He's holding me tightly, trying to calm me down.

'Don't let them take me.'

'I won't.'

'Please don't let them hurt me.'

'I won't.'

I start to recognize where I am. They've moved me to the observation room next to the nurses' station. It's so they can watch me through the glass observation window in the door. They don't trust me. Who can blame them?

Dr Royston comes to see me in the morning. We have a long session but I don't remember much about it. I try to explain why I get these sudden urges to run. I don't know where I am. I can't recognize people around me. I just have to get out . . . to hide.

'Even when I let them take me back to my room, I'm just waiting for the chance to run again. If they let go of my arms, I'll be gone.'

'Do you understand why we can't let you run?' Dr Royston asks.

'I do now – when I'm sitting here talking to you – but not at the time.'

'When you tried to run last night, when did you realize where you were?'

'When they caught me. I heard one of the nurses say that I had to stop running up the passages because I might knock over the old people and hurt them. It was like a switch being suddenly flicked in my head. I felt ashamed. At that moment I went from being a child to being a very embarrassed forty-year-old. It was like jumping from the past to the present, but not knowing which of them was real.

'The adult me kept saying what a fool I'd been, but the frightened child was saying, "Oh, no. Oh, no. Run, Linda, run." '

I look at Dr Royston and wonder if he understands. Sometimes I wish he could get inside my head and see what it's like. I don't have the words to explain how it feels. Whenever I try to tell him my words dry up. It's as though I'm a child and I don't have the vocabulary to explain.

FRIDAY, 30 NOVEMBER 1990

I dream about a slightly overweight girl with long hair. She's lying on a slope and I can see that she's hurt. She's naked and her body is limp. She begins to slide down the slope to the ground below. Her legs are apart and there is deep red blood between her thighs. The blood has been smeared down to her knees and up to her waist.

Suddenly I look into her eyes. It's like looking in the mirror. I can see her terror and her mouth is open as though she's screaming but no sound is coming out.

Drifting away from her slightly, I see that her head has come apart from her body but both are still alive. Her body is still leaning back against the slope and her head is higher up the incline. Although the ground is quite steep the head doesn't roll down. Instead it lies there, with fixed eyes and mouth open in a desperate attempt to scream.

My own scream wakes me. I don't know if it makes a sound. A part of me knows I'm safe in the observation room at Ticehurst, but my forty-year-old logic can't outweigh my five-year-old panic. I want to run. The only way out is through the nurses' station. The five-year-old wants to blindly throw herself at the door, but the forty-year-old keeps saying, 'If you run they'll catch you.

Just open the door and walk quietly past anyone in the room.'

I open the door and walk into the nurses' station. Dr Goorney raises his head from a clipboard and then looks down again. I walk quickly around him. Dr Mills is on the phone and glances up at me. He lowers the receiver and begins to stand. My heart is pounding.

'Is everything OK, Linda?'

I bolt towards the front door. He makes a grab at me but he's too late. Steve, one of the nurses, is walking down the corridor from the reception area. I duck into a side passage. Dr Mills catches up with me. Someone touches me from behind. My mind crashes and I drop like a stone.

The next thing I remember is being held up. I can hear a voice and I try to concentrate on the words. It's Sheila, another one of the nurses. The five-year-old me clings to her, but the forty-year-old me is so embarrassed that I want the floor to swallow me up. How can I be two people at once?

I fall back to sleep and wake quietly at about 5 a.m. I glance at the observation window in the door. If I lie very still then nobody will know that I'm awake. I look carefully around the room. How can I escape? Even if I did get out, where would I go? People know about the summer house. What about my hole in the hedge? Don't be ridiculous, Linda, that was in the past. Get it into your head – there's nowhere to run to. Running doesn't work. Getting up, I go to the bathroom and splash water on my face, trying to clear my mind. I still can't think clearly. I can feel the panic rising in my chest, squeezing my throat.

If I can't get away, then I have to stop them from reaching me. Act now, Linda! Outside the bathroom, I grab the big armchair and throw it against the observation-room door. I can't get the back of the chair under the door handle properly. Then I remember the other door! I run and jam a chair against it, then spin round looking for more furniture to use as a barricade. In that instant I catch sight of myself in the mirror. I see the face of the decapitated girl in my dream. I want to destroy her. I hate her! I hit the mirror very hard, but it refuses to break. Raising my fists, I try again and again.

I can hear somebody outside trying to shoulder open the door. Run, Linda, run! Turning to the window, I try to lift it open.

286

Wooden blocks stop it sliding more than a few inches. I can't fit through the gap. I smash two of the panes with my fists. The right one breaks but doesn't shatter into pieces. It has some sort of plastic coating. I pull the windowpane out and look through the gap. Run, Linda, run!

If I can squeeze my top half through the window sideways, I can use the scaffolding on the outside of the building to pull myself through. There's a crash and the sound of splintering wood behind me. Somebody has smashed down the door. Strong hands grip my arms. I drop and curl up as my mind begins to slide.

Some time later, I hear Noel's voice. It seems a long way off. He's telling me that I'm safe, that nobody can reach me.

'Please let me go.'

He's rubbing my back.

'I can't do that. I don't want you to hurt yourself.'

'Please.'

'Where are you, Linda? Do you know where you are?'

I shake my head.

'Who am I?' he asks in a soft Irish accent.

'Noel. You're Noel.'

'And where are you?'

'I'm at Ticehurst.'

'Good girl.'

Robin Royston

The pattern of Linda's days becomes more and more disturbed, with the 'leaping' occurring every time she sleeps. She can start some days seeming relaxed and confident and change within minutes. As she falls asleep she seems to slip through a portal into her childhood and become five years old again, caught within the 'missing' years when the sexual abuse began. She fights sleep and exists on the edge of exhaustion.

'It's all very well somebody sitting with me in my room,' she says, 'but they can't come with me when I fall asleep. They can't follow me into my dreams. That's when he comes . . .'

After two years of terrible tension and stress, of false trails and

287

dead ends, we have finally named her Rumpelstiltskin, yet Linda doesn't seem capable of coping with the energy released. There is no sign of healing; no connection between the head and body in her dream. My fears are becoming real, and now I sense that Linda is slipping away. Eighteen months earlier, after she brought the photo albums to the Chaucer, I thought I had lost her when she left my office having abandoned all hope. Now I have the same feeling again. Knowing the truth wasn't ever going to be enough. Linda has to cope with it. And right at this moment it is proving to be stronger than she is.

In the past Linda's suicidal feelings have ebbed and flowed but now they have hardened into a firm resolve. Even more worrying is her acceptance that it is going to happen anyway. 'They're coming to fetch me.' This profoundly negative conviction seems to infect everyone around her, as I dreaded it would. I can feel it in myself and see it in the faces and hear it in the voices of the staff. It is as though we are all being contaminated by Linda's despair and hopelessness.

From the very beginning we have lived with the potentiality of Linda killing herself. In both formal and informal meetings at Ticehurst we have discussed the possible outcomes. In corridors and over coffee I have chatted to staff and listened to their concerns for Linda. There were disagreements, of course, but now they are growing more strident. An Australian nurse, Liz, confronts me in a corridor after Linda has barricaded herself in the observation room.

'You have to stop this immediately,' she says angrily. 'You've got to medicate.'

'Look, I understand your concern, but . . .'

She won't let me finish. 'Can't you see that she's going to die? You have to do something. You're killing her.'

'She has always wanted to die.'

'Stop her, then.'

'I can't. Firstly, it wouldn't work. Secondly, this is our only chance to save her. She has to know what happened to her and confront it. If I medicate her now, she'll never know. What do we do then? Do we medicate her for the rest of her life? She has a husband and children. They want their wife and mother back.'

Liz shakes her head furiously. She can't understand. As I slip past her, she challenges me one last time. 'It's going to be your fault, Dr Royston. I hope you realize that.'

If only she knew how heavily it weighs on me. I question my decisions every day. I go over the options and debate the pros and cons. Yes, I could sedate Linda. But what would happen then? Would she be trapped in the dream at 5 Maple Avenue with the dark-haired man? At the very best it is a short-term solution. She might never get better. I know how much Linda hates the idea of being sectioned and medicated. She won't thank me.

Weighed against this is the knowledge that people are beginning to give up hope for her. Her internal struggle is having such an impact on those around her. Night after night, people like Roger and Dympna watch while she falls asleep and drops through the portal into 5 Maple Avenue, and then fight to keep her alive. How long can they keep going with no sign of light?

I remember, yet again, Linda's drawing of the black whirlpool with the outstretched hand. Linda is trapped inside the vortex. Remembering these childhood events has been like letting a genie out of a bottle. It is now alive within Linda, actively sucking everything into itself. We are being dragged into the darkness with her.

I go looking for Linda McCormack and find her between sessions. I ask her to look at the drawing again. She takes the page and looks at the hand stretching out of the blackness.

'I know what it means,' I say. 'We've all started to give up hope. We don't think Linda is going to make it. She's dragging us into the vortex, infecting us with her negativity.'

'But what can we do?'

'We can't afford to go down with her. We have to stand on the edge and hold her, but we can't let her drag us in. If Linda's fate is to die, then we cannot prevent it. We just have to accept that fact.'

'But we must . . .'

'Try, yes. That's all we can do. We're like climbers who are roped together, but somewhere above us the rope *has* to be secured. This isn't about caring too much or too little, it's about finding the balance so we don't go down with Linda.'

Linda McCormack can see what I mean, but also knows it will take enormous courage to step back. We have to realize that a doctor is no good to the patient if he dies of the disease. We can't go down with Linda and we can't cut her adrift. We have to stand on the edge of the vortex and hold her. And, if necessary, we have to be prepared to let her go and accept the outcome – even if that means her death.

'What are we going to do?' asks Linda McCormack.

'We'll have to talk to the staff. We have to make them aware of what's happening.'

'One-on-one?'

'That's probably best. Let's see if we can pull them aside over the next few days.'

I go home that night feeling a strange sense of relief. It is like being lost in a foreign country and suddenly finding a signpost. I can see the way ahead, even if I'm not sure about arriving there safely.

At the same time I feel an enormous weight of expectation from Chris, Gary and Christy. They are relying on me to keep Linda safe and help her recover.

I turn a corner on the dark, wet road and realize something else. It's amazing how often a patient can begin to sense that they have become responsible for others. Linda has started apologizing and telling people that it isn't their fault if she dies. Perhaps she has known, even before I did, that she is dragging people into the blackness with her.

23

WEDNESDAY, 12 DECEMBER 1990

Linda Caine

I've been sleeping a little better these last few days. I didn't scream at all last night, which is the first time for a while. All the windows that I've broken in the observation room have been boarded up. According to Roger I jumped six times one night. He joked with me yesterday that he didn't believe in levitation until he saw me trying to fall asleep.

The sun came out this morning. The snow has melted and the paths are starting to dry. Linda McCormack asks if I'd like to walk into town. The hospital is less than half a mile from Ticehurst village. We follow the gently curving lane down the hill and I can feel the colour coming back to my cheeks. Linda McCormack laughs when I pick earthworms off the path and put them back on the soil of the flowerbeds. 'I used to put them in the shade in Africa,' I tell her. 'The sun used to scorch them quickly in the open.'

'Is there *any* animal that you don't like?' she asks.

'They're all God's creatures.'

Ticehurst village is little more than a main street with a few houses, a grocer, a couple of pubs, an estate agent, an antiques shop and a café. Linda McCormack has a house in the village and knows most of the locals.

We stop for a coffee and the waitress gives her a smile. She motions towards the hospital, arching an eyebrow. 'How is it going with those people up there?'

Linda winks at me. 'Just fine, thank you.'

It's our little joke. I wonder if the locals regard Ticehurst House Hospital as being full of dangerous loonies. Do their children tell each other stories about the big house on the hill?

Chris comes to see me in the afternoon. He brings me a letter from Christy. She's now at boarding school during the week and home at weekends. It's a private girls' school, St Stephen's College in Broadstairs, about thirty minutes from Canterbury.

I read her letter as we walk in the grounds. After being incredibly homesick at first, Christy seems to be settling in. She's luckier than the overseas students, who only manage to get home once or twice a year.

'This girl Callie seems to be a new friend.'

Chris looks over my shoulder. 'Is she the one who is allowed to keep her own horse at school?'

'Yes. Christy is spending all her free time at the stables.'

'That sounds like our daughter.'

'And she's also adopted the stable cats and dogs.' We both laugh, relieved that she's starting to enjoy school.

'How's Gary?'

'Good. He's still playing a lot of squash. He's a real natural.'

'He gets that from you.'

Chris sounds more relaxed and less worried about things. He doesn't talk about work and wants to know about me. I don't know how much I should tell him. I don't want him to know about my mother . . . not yet. I'm not strong enough to deal with that. We walk on in silence, each breath condensing in the cold air. I pick up a smooth branch from the path and strip off the last remnants of bark. I love the texture and contours of wood. Chris wants to ask me something. I can sense it. He's trying to find the right words.

'Is anything wrong?' I ask.

'No.'

'Are you sure?'

'Do you think the psychotherapy is helping?' he asks. 'It's just that you keep going over all this and it seems to do nothing but reopen old wounds. Can't you put things aside now and just . . . just forget about the past?'

I know he doesn't mean to be critical. He's simply had enough.

'I'm not choosing for this to happen, Chris. If I could put it aside I would, believe me.'

'So why don't you?'

'Because I can't.' I turn to face him. 'Do you remember that TV commercial for Jolly Green Giant frozen peas?'

He nods.

'The voice-over says, "Our peas are snap frozen so they stay as fresh as the day we picked them." Well, that's what happens to me. When these memories come into my mind they're still as fresh as the day they happened, with all the same emotions, shock and pain.'

I don't blame him for having doubts. He can't see me getting better. On top of this, all his training and his very nature equip him to deal with facts rather than emotions.

That evening I call Annette in California. I know about the affair our mother had at the Park Hotel, but I want to know if Annette can remember her having any earlier boyfriends.

'There was one guy when we were living at 5 Maple Avenue,' she says. 'He used to really irritate Dad, who called him "some lover-boy" and used to complain about how much attention Mum paid to him.'

'Do you remember his name?'

'No.'

'What did he look like?'

'He had dark hair and he was always grooming himself.'

I keep pressing for more details. Finally, Annette says, 'Listen, Lindy, whatever happened, can't you just leave it behind?' She doesn't say it in a nasty way. Like Chris, she just wants me to look forward instead of backwards.

Settled back in the observation room, I try to make sense of what she has told me. Both of us have talked about our mother's film-star looks and how distant and cold she had been. I always thought I'd understand my mother more when I had children of my own, but I understand her less.

Next morning, I decide that I'm going to write down what happened to me. I want to have some sort of record, so it doesn't slip away again.

Sitting at my computer, I close my eyes and think about the session with Dr Royston when I remembered what happened. It was as though the different flashbacks had been spliced together and put in order. But now as I try to put them down, they fragment all over again.

Angry with myself, I try once more. I imagine that Dr Royston is with me. He's sitting on the bed, touching my shoulder. My mind begins to slide and I let myself go with it . . . all the way back.

It's dark inside the cupboard. The door is locked and I can't get out. I hate the dark, but I don't want them to come for me. If I cover my face with my hands I can pretend that it's light and I'm outside. I can pretend that it's only dark because I have my hands over my eyes. There are shoes at the bottom of the cupboard and clothes hanging above my head. I can smell my dad's aftershave.

This is what I remember . . .

The Child

The child didn't know how long she had been in the cupboard. It seemed like a very long time since the door had shut behind her. She knew that she mustn't cry, otherwise they'd make her stay in the cupboard. She didn't mean to be naughty – she just didn't want to do those things any more.

It was best not to struggle or try to run. The man seemed to like her to run. Sometimes, if she curled quietly on the floor or in a corner, hoping they would leave her alone, he would stamp on the floor next to her or growl in her ear. If she bolted and ran for the door, he always caught her.

Sometimes he would laugh at her when he carried her to the bed. She knew not to make a noise, so she just whispered, 'No, no, no, no, no . . .' over and over again very quietly, but loud enough for them to hear.

They got angry and told her to shut up.

The first few times they took her she thought that she was going to die. Now she tried to make herself die. She wished it, but that didn't work. So she learned to take her mind away from the things they did.

How long would he leave her in the cupboard this time? Her heart began to beat so loudly that she could hear it in her head. What if he forgot about her and left her there all night? With her hands still tightly over her eyes, she listened at the cupboard door. Maybe if she kept very quiet they would just do things with each other and leave her alone.

The cupboard was stuffy and smelt of clothes and shoes. Some of the smell was her father's. She could picture him in her mind – tall and strong and laughing in the sun. And she wanted to scream and scream for him to come; to open the cupboard door and pick her up and hold her tight; to never let her go.

The cupboard door opened. 'Are you going to be a good girl now?' said the man.

The child nodded. She stumbled to her feet and walked over to the bed. The man's hand became urgent as he lifted up her nightdress. The child began to take her mind away from that part of her body. She concentrated on the blanket against her cheek. It was soft. The blanket against her cheek didn't hurt.

She went deeper into her mind – so deep inside that nothing could reach her, not even feelings. She was safe and far away. Her eyes, although open, didn't focus any more. He could do what he liked, but he couldn't touch her – not the real her in her mind.

When it was over, her mother took her to the bathroom and watched while she washed herself. She made sure that she went to the toilet so she didn't wet the bed. The child then walked down the passage to her bedroom while her mother watched.

She climbed beneath the sheets and looked across at her sister sleeping in the bed opposite. Her hand hung over the side and the child wanted to reach out and hold it again. That's when she felt safest . . . when she held Annette's hand. Then the man wouldn't be able to fetch her any more.

But it didn't matter any more. It had already happened. Even if they fetched her again her mind would go far away where they couldn't reach her. She shut her eyes and wished that she were dead.

In the morning the sun streamed through the window. She opened her eyes slowly and smelled the urine as she moved. She felt ashamed. She stood up and began to peel off her wet nightclothes. The ache inside her and the soreness between her legs reminded her of what had happened.

The sun shone and birds sang in the fruit trees outside her window. She could hear noises in the kitchen as the cook prepared breakfast and packed lunches for school. On such a beautiful day, the night seemed a long while ago. But it hurt when she walked and her stomach ached.

She washed herself and changed into her school uniform. Then she sat at the breakfast table with her sister, watching her mother feed their baby brother. Her mother's face showed nothing. Everything was normal.

At school she watched the children play in the playground at break time. Sometimes she joined in, but not often. She preferred sitting quietly by herself. She was different from them. She lived on the other side of an invisible wall.

School finished and she went home, knowing that the nightmare would either begin again, or her father would be home and she'd be safe.

But he wasn't home. The realization made her mind spin and her thoughts race. She couldn't hold on to them. She backed quietly out the front door and ran down the steps. Looking over her shoulder she made sure nobody was watching – not even the gardener. She found the hole in the thick conifer hedge and crawled inside on her hands and knees. There was just enough room for her to sit between the branches. Nobody could see her. It was cool, quiet and safe. She could hear the sounds of children playing and people going up and down the road. It let her know that she wasn't completely alone.

She sat there watching the spiders spinning their webs, weaving silken threads between the branches. If she blew gently at them, they rushed away. She didn't like it when they caught insects. It was OK if they were already wrapped in silk.

'You've had all morning to catch your dinner,' she told the spiders. 'So don't do it now.'

She drew pictures and patterns in the sand with twigs, brushing over them and starting again. This was her world. Time stood still until the darkness came.

As the shadows lengthened and merged, she knew that she couldn't escape any more. Fear caught in her throat. What should she do? Images flashed through her mind . . . holding Annette's hand between the beds . . . feeling it grow heavy as she fell asleep . . . desperately holding tighter, not wanting to let go . . . growing more and more tired . . . sleep was coming . . . and so was the dark-haired man.

She thought of running far away. She had thought about it many times before, but she had nowhere to run. Who could she tell?

Once before she had tried to tell someone – a very pretty lady with kind eyes. She sat on a chair with her legs crossed and her floral skirt fell beautifully from her knees. She smiled at the child and leaned over to talk to her.

The child desperately tried to put into words things she was too young to have words for. 'A man comes and takes me at night . . . he puts his hand over my face and I can't breathe . . . he takes me to my mummy's room . . . he hurts me . . . Mummy watches . . .'

The lady's face changed. She looked at her with uncertainty, then disbelief.

The child felt a hand grip her shoulder like a vice. She flinched at the sound of her mother's voice.

'I'm sorry,' said her mother. 'Linda has a very vivid imagination. She has nightmares. And she's always telling stories.'

The lady nodded and smiled kindly. Then she glanced at the child with irritation. The child shrank away in confusion and fear. Now she knew that she was totally alone. Nobody could save her.

That night she tried not to fall asleep. She held Annette's hand between their beds and jumped each time it slipped from her fingers. She dozed and jumped, dozed and jumped. Suddenly, her eyes flew open. A hand covered her mouth and nose. Unable to breathe, the scream stayed inside her head.

With her head exploding and her body convulsing, she fought for breath as he carried her down the passage. A loud rushing sound roared in her ears. She was losing consciousness. Please let me die, she wished.

But she lived. And it happened again and again . . .

Days later, from her hiding place in the hedge, she heard her father's car pull up. She crawled out and ran to him, throwing her arms around his neck. He tickled her and said,

'How have you been, my wicked little wench?'

She giggled and said, 'I'm not a wicked little wench!'

'Well then, you must be a foolish little floozie!'

She laughed. 'No! I'm not a foolish little floozie!'

'Then you must be a silly little sausage!'

She wanted to tell him what had happened, but her mother arrived. She looked concerned and shook her head.

The child heard some of her words. 'Terrible nightmares . . . bed-wetting . . . telling stories . . .'

She wanted to scream, 'No, Daddy, they're not nightmares. It's real!' But she hesitated. What if he didn't believe her? She would have no-one left. She clung to him while he stroked her hair.

Maybe time eroded the knowledge. Maybe she went so far into her *mind that she left the memories buried there. Whatever happened, the child began to lose track of what was real and not real. In the daylight everything seemed to be normal. Only at night, when her father was away, did it all start again.*

The child sat in the hedge and watched the shadows lengthen. Her father had not come home. She could hear her mother calling her for supper. Her throat closed with fear. She wouldn't be able to swallow her food again and her mother would be angry.

She wanted to jump out of the hedge and run and run and run. But there was nowhere to run to and nobody to tell. So the child climbed carefully out of her hole and walked up the driveway towards the house.

24

Linda Caine

I don't realize until afterwards that I've written 'The Child' in the third person. I don't know why. Maybe that's how I cope – by pretending it happened to someone else.

'What does it prove now that it's on paper?' I ask myself, feeling exhausted. 'Does it make it real?'

No, but my reaction is real. That counts for something.

Dr Royston comes to see me at about 7 p.m. and I show him the story.

'All the feelings and images came spilling out,' I explain. 'It was like having all the pieces of the jigsaw.'

He says it's a good sign because I'm confronting things rather than trying to deny them or pushing them away. The problem is that I don't feel unburdened or cleansed. The child in the hedge still wants to die.

Dr Royston doesn't know about the piece of glass in my pyjama pocket, wrapped in a tissue. I found it on one of my walks. It gives me my old feeling of having a little control over my life. I can stop living any time I choose to. A part of me feels ashamed because I promised Chris and Dr Royston that I wouldn't use this way of coping any more. I hope they forgive me.

Dr Royston has always said that psychotherapy can't be rushed.

It's like running a marathon. Now I want the race to be finished. I want to stop running.

Desperately tired, I fall asleep early, hoping for an unbroken night without any 'leaps'. At 3 a.m. my eyes open and my heart pounds. Lying on my side, I lift my head slightly and peer over my legs. The observation curtain is open. Roger is talking to someone in the nurses' station. If I move he'll see me. I contemplate jamming the doors again and getting out of the window. Then I remember the piece of glass. Moving very slowly, I pull the tissue from my pocket. Holding the glass makes me feel better. I run it across my tongue, feeling for the sharpest edge. Then I test it lightly on my arm. Nothing happens.

It's hot under the blankets. Perspiration leaks into the small of my back. The veins on my wrists and inner arms are standing out. I slide the glass over one of them, using more pressure this time. A line of red appears and a drop of blood runs down my arm. I run the glass over the vein three or four times. It bleeds freely and I feel elated. People can sit right outside my door but I can still 'escape'. They can sit there and check on me through the window, but I'll be gone by morning.

I swap the glass into my left hand and try to cut across the vein in my other wrist. My hands are shaking. In dismay I look at the blood on my left wrist and it's starting to congeal and stop flowing. I try to open the wound wider, but the numbness has worn off. I jump at the sharpness of the pain. Lying very still, I wait to see if anyone has noticed. Then reality begins to leak in. What am I doing? I'm a wife and mother. I promised my husband and children that I wouldn't leave them this way. I lie very still, trying to decide what to do. Finally, I spit on a tissue and clean my arm as best I can, while still hiding beneath the covers. I spend the next few hours drifting in and out of sleep until Roger brings my coffee at 7 a.m.

'Look at the time,' he says, smiling. 'You've slept all night.'

I don't know what to say. Sensing something is wrong, he pulls down the blanket and sees the blood. His face drops.

'Oh dear,' he says quietly.

'I'm so sorry.'

Poor Roger. He spent all night looking after me and this is how I repay his kindness.

Robin Royston

I had no idea that Linda was writing the story 'The Child', but I see it as a positive exercise. By writing things down she recalls events with far more clarity and detail. And until we can bring it all into the open, we can't begin dealing with the emotional fallout. Linda hates the child intensely. This is the fundamental reason she has written the story in the third person. She needs to distance herself from the young girl otherwise she will have to *own* all of the things this child has been through.

The child lives as a separate person. This is what often happens to adults who are traumatized as children. They split it off in a very literal way. They talk about the child as being somebody else, as though he or she exists in a separate state and time, with thoughts and feelings that are totally separate from the adult. This in part explains why Linda dissociates. To her the child *is* someone else.

At the same time her poetry and journals are full of self-loathing and statements like 'You're pathetic! Why don't you just kill yourself and be done with it?' If she kills the child, she kills herself. Deep down Linda knows this.

I know that, having remembered events from her childhood, Linda is never going to be instantly better. She has been traumatized. My task is to take these traumatic memories and turn them into narrative memories. We all have them but rarely do they impact so dramatically on our lives.

By talking about her memories, bringing them into the open, we can hopefully take the energy out of them. That is the theory anyway. They will still be just as horrible, but they won't have the same emotional power. 'And if they don't have the same power, they won't impact upon you in the same way,' I tell her. 'You won't be perfect, but nobody is perfect. We all have things to deal with. We just need to find a way for you to accommodate these memories into your life – to give you your life back.'

From the night when Linda used the broken glass to cut her wrists, the vicious cycle seems to break. It isn't just a case of Linda pulling back from the brink. We all do. It is as though the vortex is slowing down and losing its power. Perhaps the writing of 'The Child' was the final nailing of the disturbance. It has the effect of changing the balance of power. From being severely suicidal Linda slowly becomes more positive and determined to survive. It proves to be a turning point.

A week later Linda shows me a verse that she's rewritten. I read the original version soon after she began coming to the Chaucer as a day patient in February 1989.

I'm reaching the end of this –
I know I will find
Release from the darkness
That once filled my mind
A darkness so black
It smothered my soul
But could not take away
The fact that I'm whole

FRIDAY, 21 DECEMBER 1990

Linda Caine

Since writing 'The Child' I've been feeling a lot more positive. It is as though a burden has been taken from me and put onto the page. The same thing often happens when I draw what I feel.

The story captures what happened. It's set down in black and white and can't slide away from me any more. I still question whether these memories are real, but when I read the story the same powerful feelings swamp me all over again.

My bags are packed and I'm ready to leave. I'm going home for Christmas but I'll be back in the New Year. Please God, may next year be better than this one. I want to be 'normal' again. It's time I put the past behind me.

At home the Christmas tree has been up since early December. Christy did most of the decorating this year. I call her my Christmas girl. She loves the little rituals of putting up lights, wrapping presents and setting the table for Christmas dinner.

Gary doesn't mind helping to decorate the tree between being on the computer and playing squash, but he's happy to leave it to Christy and me.

I steal a glance at Chris. He's sitting across the lounge, chuckling at Christy and me fussing over where the new star should go on the tree. With his army and boys' boarding school background, he is essentially a 'no-frills' man. He says Christmas has been over-commercialized, and that too much fuss is made over birthdays. I sometimes think he could quite happily do without either – until I see the look in his eyes when he watches the children excitedly opening their presents.

All the general family gifts are under the tree, but we don't put the special presents out until Christmas Eve, when the kids are asleep. Christy prefers to get a smaller main present and a huge stocking full of bits and pieces. It isn't easy getting a big stocking into her room without waking her because some of the floorboards squeak. Her stocking crinkles and crackles in my arms as I nudge open her door and creep into her room. A floorboard squeaks loudly and I drop to the floor, clutching the stocking and trying not to make a sound. Christy rolls over and murmurs. I lie very still until she settles back to sleep. Ten minutes later I'm numb with cold as I get up stiffly and put her stocking at the foot of her bed.

Next morning, just after sunrise, I hear her excited squeal. She comes into our bedroom carrying her stocking. Smiling from ear to ear, she sits cross-legged at the end of the bed, unwrapping each gift carefully and showing them to us one by one. Gary munches a bag of fruit gums and watches us. His own stocking is smaller because he wants a larger main present.

After breakfast we go to the Christmas service. As we begin singing the familiar carols, the thought jumps into my mind that I almost wasn't here for this moment. I almost committed suicide and left my family. I blink back tears and fight the urge to turn and hold them. The pianist begins playing 'Silent Night', and I close my eyes and let the peace of the carol soak into me as I thank God that I am here.

Lunch is traditional, with turkey and all the trimmings. I cook loads of vegetables for Christy. Then it's time to open the presents under the tree. Now it's Gary's turn to be excited. There's a flurry of ripping paper. I chuckle inwardly at how different my children are as I watch them. Christy opens her presents painstakingly slowly, trying not to tear the paper. Gary dives among his presents, ripping the paper off with cries of 'Oh, *wow*! Thanks, Dad!' at his new squash racquet, and 'Thanks, Mum – no more cuts!' at skateboard pads for his elbows and knees. Then he yells with delight and I know we've lost him for a while. Holding aloft a computer game he shouts triumphantly, 'Eat your heart out, Stacy,' already out of the door and up the stairs.

Chris gives me a card with a gift voucher inside. He knows that I want some new watercolour paints and paper. I give him a new snooker cue and a squash glove. Christy is in a world of her own, outfitting her Barbie and Sindy dolls in their new clothes. Chris brings me a sherry and sits down. I feel relaxed, tired and happy.

Snuggling up in a warm bed a little later, I close my eyes and think about what a special day it's been. I tell myself I must hold on to it tightly in my mind, and remember it when I have bad days. I must remember my children's excitement, our family time around the table at lunch, and around the Christmas tree afterwards. I must remember my happiness, and the love I feel for them all. I must remember that I *will* get better. I drift off to sleep holding on to that thought. Desperately.

That night I dream that I'm standing in a field and I see a horse galloping towards me. It's beautiful and wild and doesn't want to be caught. But I know that it has to be contained or it will hurt itself.

The horse is very quick and evasive. It races past me into a corner of the field. I edge closer from the left, but know I can't do this on my own. It is sure to escape. Then a man – I think it is Dr Royston – appears on my right and starts helping me. The horse swings back and stands with its head thrown up, watching our every step. It's trembling with fear. I know that if we make one wrong move it will bolt and we'll lose it.

I don't remember how the dream ends, but at least I don't wake screaming or gasping for breath. In the morning I write it out on my computer for Dr Royston.

I still haven't been able to tell Chris about my mother. I get as far as mentioning her name and can never finish. He keeps asking me why I won't tell him, but when he presses me I start to cry.

Just after New Year, when I'm packing to go back to Ticehurst, he tells me that he's telephoned her.

'Who?'

'Your mother.'

'When?'

'A few weeks ago. I asked her whether anything had happened to you when you were living at 5 Maple Avenue. I told her about the breakdown.'

My voice is shaking. 'What did she say?'

'She couldn't think of anything. She said that you had a vivid imagination and used to annoy her by telling stories.'

My blood runs cold. 'Is that all?'

'She sent her love and hoped that you'd get well soon.'

For the next few hours I struggle to control my emotions. Maybe she's right. Maybe it's all in my mind.

I print out a copy of 'The Child' and give it to Chris. Then I switch off the computer and follow him through to the bedroom. I sit quietly as he reads the story.

'Are you trying to say that this is what happened to you?' he asks, clearly shocked.

'Yes.'

There's no suggestion that he doubts me, but I can see he's struggling. He believes and disbelieves all at once. He remembers how she cried beside my bed that night in Mtoko.

'I thought you might have been abused,' he says very calmly. 'But I thought it would turn out to be your dad.'

'I know.'

'How long have you known?'

'About a month.'

'Why didn't you tell me earlier?'

'It was already stuck in my mind – I didn't want it stuck in yours.'

He looks hurt. 'You must talk to me. I need to understand.'

His calmness is a real comfort, but I'm struggling to hold myself together. Chris makes us both a coffee and reads the story again.

'Don't you think it's quite suspicious that my mother hasn't contacted me at all since you phoned her?' I ask.

'Maybe she doesn't know what a state you're in,' he says.

'But she didn't even send me a Christmas card. She's sent one every year since I met her again in Mtoko.'

'Maybe she thought it would upset you,' he says defensively.

I can see a look in his eyes.

'Have you spoken to her again?' I ask.

'No.' He seems uncomfortable. I'm not sure if he's telling the truth.

Finally he sighs and says, 'She wrote me a letter.'

'When?'

'After I telephoned her. I knew you were struggling. That's why I didn't tell you.'

'I want to see the letter.'

'I don't think that's a good idea.'

'Chris, I want to see it.'

'You're upset already. Maybe it's best to calm down. I'll show you the letter when you're feeling better.'

'No, I want to see it now.'

He retrieves three handwritten pages from his study, next to my art room. My hands are shaking as I read. Chris had obviously asked her to write down what she could remember of my childhood and the places we lived. She's written little excerpts, a paragraph on each place. The paragraph about 5 Maple Avenue has no details. It just states that we lived there for about three years.

She describes how she and Dad had struggled financially during the first few years of their marriage. The conditions were very rough and isolated. Dad ran a mine in those days and lived out in the bush. It must have been hard for them. The African heat was relentless and dust blew into every nook and cranny.

As she recalls the hardship, I begin to feel sorry for her. Yet she's made a couple of mistakes in the letter. We moved to Riverside first, not 5 Maple Avenue. Brendan was born at Riverside because I remember our mother feeding him in the bedroom.

Later I call Annette and check these details. I'm right. It proves that I have a good memory.

I sit down at my computer and read the letter again and again. When the sentences don't give up enough I try to read between the lines. I keep thinking about what I'd say to her if she were here now. I find myself writing it down.

Do you know how much my memories haunt me? How much they've always haunted me? I still question myself – are they memories or nightmares?

One side of me argues that it can't be real, but the other side asks why the fragments come back to me with such force – even when I'm wide awake.

But it has *to be real. It can't be my imagination. Where would images like this come from? I wouldn't know about them and exactly how they feel if I hadn't experienced them.*

Yet you say that you're mystified; that you have no idea what could have upset me so much; that maybe what upset me happened after you left.

You're wrong! It happened before *you left – when we first lived at 5 Maple Avenue.*

You say, 'I am still at a loss to understand why something that may or may not have happened 30–35 years ago should be troubling Linda to the extent that she wants to take her own life.'

How could you think it wouldn't trouble me? Did you think that because I survived physically, because I eventually stopped crying and struggling, that it didn't affect me? Well, the truth is that it affected me so profoundly that I blocked it out.

I buried it so deeply that it only came up in nightmares or when I unconsciously reacted in panic to certain smells or situations.

Do you know I still can't sleep alone without feeling panicky? That I have to touch someone because I'm frightened that if I let them go I'll be 'fetched' from my bed and taken away?

Do you know that I still have to fight panic if someone walks into a room and shuts the door? It can take all my self-control not to run.

You ask, among other things, if they can inject me with a drug that will take me back in time and make me talk. If there is such a drug, would you be prepared to take it as well?

And you say: 'Linda really must try and pull herself together and think of her family . . .'

You're right, I must pull myself together. That's what I am trying to do. I think of my family all the time and I feel guilty for what I've put them through in the past two years. Did you feel guilty about leaving us? Do you feel guilty about me?

I look at your last paragraph again. You wrote: 'Please let us know how she is, Chris. I feel very deeply for what you are going through and only wish I could be of more help. If there is anything you think of please don't hesitate to contact me and I will do all I can to assist. Does Linda know you have contacted me? If she does, please give her my love and tell her we are praying for her. Keep strong, Chris. Our love to the children. God bless. Fond love.

Marion and Peter.'

It sounds so plausible and caring. I want to believe you. That's why I keep questioning myself. Is it me? Is it all in my mind?

I don't want it to be real. I don't want to believe that you could have been involved in something like this. It's a terrible thing to accuse a mother of doing such a thing to her child.

Dr Royston and the specialists at Ticehurst have never doubted me. They tell me to trust my mind. Can they all be mistaken?

Strangely, I feel no malice towards you. My own life and experience have taught me that we are all capable of doing horrible things, especially if we are (or have been) hurt and confused. You, too, had a difficult life.

I'd like to talk to you about it – just to bring it into the open. I suppose mainly for my own sake, but also for you. It must be a difficult thing to carry such knowledge around with you for all these years. For me, I just want to be certain that it happened. Do you know what peace that would give me?

I print what I've written and read it over and over again. The questions keep pouring into my mind. What do I do now? Do I send this to my mother? What if she denies it? Why would she do otherwise? She knows that I have no evidence to prove anything.

I look at her letter again. As I read the phrases 'vivid imagination' and that I 'used to tell stories', I feel my stomach churn with fear. These are the same words she used all those years ago when I tried to tell the lady with the kind eyes what was happening. My mother's hand had squeezed my shoulder like a vice as she'd made excuses for me. I was terrified. I feel the same way now. I'm almost forty years old, and I'm terrified of my mother being angry with me. I know I can't confront her yet. Maybe in time, but not yet.

THURSDAY, 3 JANUARY 1991

Robin Royston

Rain has fallen all morning and daylight struggles to penetrate the low cloud. The long, empty halls of Ticehurst are cast in a warm yellow light that seems almost cheerful. A grey-haired cleaner opens the door for me as I dash through the rain. I shake out my umbrella and walk along the passage to the nurses' station. The air is thick and warm from the central heating, but for once I don't mind. Linda's door is half open. She has just spent an hour playing 'Ticehurst Squash' in the old chapel and her cheeks are flushed.

'How was Christmas?'

'Not bad,' she says with conviction.

She is holding a letter. I think she's written down another dream.

'It's from my mother,' she says.

'Really.' I'm shocked and surprised.

'She wrote to Chris.' There is a determined edge to Linda's voice – as though she is doggedly trying to keep her emotions in check. When I read the letter I understand why. Linda doesn't want to give her mother the satisfaction of crying over her words. She also shows me the response she has written. I am fascinated by how her initial doubts turned to anger as she went through her mother's letter paragraph by paragraph. It is a very good sign. She is challenging her mother's account, refusing to be fobbed off or intimidated. This cold, hard, uncompromising woman has given Linda nothing, yet for years Linda made excuses for her and forgave her. She was never challenged, nor had her anger directed back at her by her daughter.

'Do you know what line really makes me angry?' Linda says. 'It's where she says that I should pull myself together and think about my family. That's all I've been thinking about for these past two years.'

'I know.'

Linda has clearly tried to decipher every word and phrase of the letter. She wants to find some sign of guilt, or contrition, or defensiveness. The fact that she hasn't found anything disappoints her.

'You didn't really expect a death-bed confession, did you?' I say wryly, trying to lighten her mood.

'I guess not.'

'You must expect a reaction from her – either from the real her or from within yourself – but she's not going to say, "Oh sorry, Linda," and let you go. There's too much at stake.'

Linda looks at the letter again and begins to understand this.

The tentative sense of her getting better has been undermined by this contact with her mother, but at the same time it has galvanized her growing indignation and helped her gain strength. She is standing up to her mother, which to some degree she has been gradually doing ever since the story emerged.

Even so, her mother is still very powerful.

'Sometimes I feel as though I'm trying to protect a five-year-old Linda Caine,' I say.

'Well, you can have her,' she replies with venom.

'No change there then.' I smile gently.

Linda suddenly relaxes and her shoulders slump. 'I'm sorry.'

'Don't worry. Things are easing, but they'll take time. You are not suddenly going to love the child, but you might be able to begin approaching her soon.'

Linda gives me a look that says she isn't so sure.

It has been six weeks since she remembered what happened to her. Although she sometimes still 'leaps' at night, it has been three weeks since she broke a window or tried to flee from her room. The power of the imagery has weakened and we both begin to feel that the hard work has been done. I suggest to Linda that perhaps it is time for us to be working towards her leaving Ticehurst again. She is anxious, but agrees, which in itself is also a good sign.

In general her dreams have a more positive tone. For instance, her dream after Christmas about the runaway horse shows that together we are beginning to contain the horse despite its fear and desire to bolt.

Another of her dreams suggests that the dark-haired man has lost his destructive power.

I am under water and there are dismembered parts of bodies floating around me. I can breathe and see quite clearly. A movement catches my

eye. I turn to see the dark-haired man. Although I can see no visible
wounds on him I know that he is dying.

I feel sorry for him. I think that no-one should be left to die in such a
horrible, slow way. I wish I could reach him so that I could kill him and
put him out of his misery.

This dream comes as an immense relief. Not since the mud-pool dream, where Linda saw a way out of her problems, have I felt so positive about the ultimate outcome. The dark-haired man is dying. She will survive.

Another of Linda's dreams is even more self-explanatory. It seems to be a continuation of her earlier jigsaw puzzle dream, but this time she has a scrapbook in front of her. She is sitting at a table surrounded by scraps of paper that are her memories. As she tries to put them into the right order before gluing them into the book, a man keeps taking them and mixing them up. Although this dream shows Linda's frustration, there is a much greater sense of the process being organized. Her memories are being put into their proper place and stuck down. They are being stripped of their destructive energy. In essence, this is what psychotherapy is all about.

'But why is someone trying to mess up my memories?' Linda asks.

'I don't know. Do you recognize him?'

She shakes her head.

'Maybe he just represents a component of the mental process,' I say. 'He's making you work hard to put things in order.'

In truth, I suspect that he is the dark-haired man. He is like a computer virus that has infected the innermost corners of Linda's mind, corrupting all files. He doesn't want her to remember.

25

SATURDAY, 9 MARCH 1991

Linda Caine

Forty years old today! Happy birthday to me.

I've been home from Ticehurst for nearly three weeks and already it has faded into a strange vagueness. Now, if it wasn't for my notes and Dr Royston, I'm afraid it would slip into the same place in my mind as the three missing years. I still question how much of it was real. If what I've written in 'The Child' is true, why don't I remember it as clearly as I do the other horrible things in my life? Why does it have a dream-like, evasive quality? The difference, of course, is that I have no witnesses. For all the other events – even the rape in America – there were people who could confirm that they happened.

As a child at 5 Maple Avenue I woke each morning and found my mother standing at the kitchen sink, acting as though nothing had happened. When I asked questions it was denied or put down to nightmares. 'Linda tells stories.'

I'm reading a few books about child abuse and I've discovered that most survivors have no access to proof. One woman convinced herself that it was a dream. I have reacted differently. One part of me recognizes the truth, but another part fights to deny that it happened. I still 'leap' sometimes at night but I 'come to' almost immediately. It helps having Chris lying beside me. I listen to him gently snoring and it brings me back.

'This is for you,' he says, handing me a birthday card. 'I can't believe that I'm sleeping with a middle-aged woman – even though she doesn't look a day over twenty-one.'

'I wish.'

Inside the card is a gift voucher for £50 from M & S. 'A pound for each year of your life – plus a £10 bonus,' Chris says.

Gary and Christy are both awake. Christy has bought me perfumed soaps in a wicker basket, while Gary gives me a homemade card, with a note inside inviting me to lunch at the Barn, our favourite restaurant. I give them both a hug as we sit up in bed together. They're both so grown-up. I feel as though I've missed a year or two.

Gary is nearly fifteen and has just started to get tall. He'll be pleased when he outgrows Christy. It's not easy having a little sister who's as tall as him. His life seems to revolve around sport, with tennis and cricket for his school and squash over the weekend. He has become so much more independent – doing things like catching the bus to town and meeting up with friends. I used to be the one who ferried him around the place and I knew exactly where he was and what time he'd be home. Now he pops his head around the door on his way out and says, 'Bye, Mum. Gotta run.'

'Hey, come back. Where are you going?'

'I'm meeting Graham in town. We're going to the movies. Dad said he'd drive us home.'

I knew Chris was working late, but didn't know what plans had been made. I know it sounds foolish but I feel a pang of regret. I've been away so much that Gary has become used to making his arrangements without me. Sensing my sadness, Gary comes back and gives me a hug.

'Off you go now or you'll miss the bus,' I say, trying not to let him see my eyes.

My family has learned to cope without me. Isn't that what I wanted . . . to make them more self-sufficient . . . just in case?

Chris is encouraged by my improvement. But he's still going through a difficult time at work. It's almost certain that the Canterbury branch of the firm is going to be scaled down to just one small office. Chris will have to decide whether to leave and branch out on his own, or commute to the London office four days a week, with just one day in Canterbury. We also have another option that we're considering. Because of my family links, we have the chance to live in America, but only while Dad is alive. Over the years we've talked about the possibility, particularly since Dad had his heart attack.

It would be a major step. Chris would have to resit all his bar exams and start all over again. Gary and Christy would have to leave all their friends and start at new schools. The main reason for going would be the lifestyle. We all love the outdoors and sunshine. California could give us that. It's pretty much now or never. The older we get the harder it becomes to start again. We've done it once before when we arrived in England with just a few suitcases. At least this time we'll have a little more money, if we sell the house and Chris gets a pay-out from the partnership. And we wouldn't be totally alone. Clive and Annette and their families are living in Turlock in California. Dad has moved there as well.

We've mentioned the possibility to Gary and Christy, who were quite excited. But so much depends upon me getting better. For the moment we've decided to lodge an application, which the American Immigration Department should take a few months to process. Hopefully by then we'll have a better idea of what we should do.

My stay at Ticehurst seems like it happened a long while ago. I didn't think I'd ever be able to forget the nightmares and the running. Some things are getting easier. I've stopped taking scalding showers and baths, trying to get clean, and the haunted feeling isn't as strong. I still feel embarrassed and ashamed about what happened. I met up with a friend yesterday for coffee. I hadn't seen her for ages.

'How are you?' she asked tentatively.

Suddenly, I blurted out that I'd been abused as a child. I don't know why I told her. I don't want anybody to know. She took it very well and didn't turn away. As we kept talking she said, 'I read somewhere that one in every ten children is sexually abused. I can't believe that. I've never heard them screaming for help.'

I grew annoyed. 'If a child is being abused by their own parents, who do they scream for?' I asked. 'Who are they going to tell? And even if they could tell someone, they don't have the words or knowledge to articulate what is happening to them.'

She looked surprised, then thoughtful as she said, 'I'd never thought about it too deeply before. I suppose I didn't want to really . . .'

Afterwards, I wondered if most people thought like she did. If a child came to her and complained, what would she do? Would she be like the lady in the floral dress?

I still see Dr Royston twice a week at the Chaucer and tell him my dreams. I'm getting quite good at interpreting them. Last night I dreamt that I was standing in front of a vast expanse of water. I started to walk slowly into it and the water began lapping over my feet. I paddled for a while, but it wasn't very clean and I didn't want to go any deeper.

A man standing in the water, just behind me, tried to encourage me to continue. 'It's OK,' he said, but I didn't want to go in any further. Finally, I lifted my arms into the air and let the wind take me high into the sky, above it all. My elation at leaving the water and the man behind was mixed with apprehension. I didn't know how long the wind would hold me up.

I know that Dr Royston was the man in the dream. I also suspect that he won't like the idea that I'm trying to avoid the deep water. 'Sometimes we have to swim through the dirty water,' he'll say. 'Learn to trust the depth.'

MAY–JUNE 1991

Robin Royston

For two months Linda's state of mind has improved. She still has some bad nights and bleak days, but she is now strong enough to cope. That's all I have ever sought to do. Psychotherapy doesn't create perfect people with perfect lives. It just helps us cope with what we have. I enjoy seeing Linda every week. On her good days she has a real sparkle in her eyes and is polite enough to laugh at my jokes. We continue talking about her life – trying to tie up the loose ends.

'I don't know if this is doing any good,' she says after a session in late June. She puts her hands on the windowsill and looks out at the children playing in the school grounds. 'Am I perpetuating all this by coming to see you?'

'What makes you say that?'

'If I stopped coming would it force me to stand on my own two feet? Would I pull myself together instead of looking for re-assurance, like a child, whenever I feel shaky?'

I have asked myself these same questions. I am always happy to see patients move on, but it's often a difficult decision knowing when to step back. Patients can become too dependent and therapists can risk probing too deeply and finding new issues that were never a problem in the first place. Once Linda is capable of coping with life then my job is done.

'What about having a break?' I suggest.

Linda looks anxious.

'I'll be available if you want to see me, or you can still call Ticehurst,' I reassure her. 'We'll try it for a couple of weeks and see how we go.'

The timing seems perfect. I have promised to take Mike and Emma to Spain for the summer holidays and Linda has mentioned possibly going away. We could have a break until August.

A week later we have our last session before the holidays. Linda arrives wearing light summer clothes, with her hair tied up and just the faintest hint of make-up. She asks me about my Spanish holiday and talks about her own plans. 'I'm going to take things one step at a time,' she says. 'I'm still pretty panicky around people.'

'That's OK. Do only what you feel comfortable with for now. You said that you had a few dreams for me to look at.'

She nods and hands me her diary. Immediately I sense that whatever she is about to show me has disturbed her more than she wants to admit. I start to read with growing unease.

There is an evil force in the house hiding behind the beam on the ceiling of the living room. It has no shape, but is pitch black – like a dark shadow against the white beam.

I am alone and it is getting dark. I want to make sure that the french windows leading to the garden are locked. As I begin to walk towards

them, the black, evil thing drops part of itself in front of me in the shape
of two hands. My left arm reaches up towards the hands and they catch
me. They are immensely powerful and hold me in a vice-like grip.

Struggling desperately, I break free and run to the door. I lock it and
turn to run upstairs to the sanctuary of my bedroom. Halfway across the
living room, I realize that the formless, black thing is no longer on
the beam. It now fills the entire house. Turning again, I run back to the
french windows, trying to escape outside. But I know that the presence
has closed the house around me.

'I hated that dream,' she says, the denial she initially exhibited
starting to slip as she expresses her emotions.

'Why?'

'Because it's in our house, in Chestfield. I've always felt safe
there. It's a happy place.'

Of course. Linda almost expects the dark-haired man to be
haunting 5 Maple Avenue when sleep takes her back there, but in
this dream he has followed her into the present . . . into *her* home.

I, too, dislike the dream. What concerns me most is that Linda's
dark thoughts of being pursued are still so strong. The dark-haired
man was dying in one of her dreams, but now he is hunting her
down again.

Her second dream is very short but equally powerful. I ask her
to tell me in her own words, so that I can try to gauge how she is
dealing with this new apparent threat.

'Chris was holding me in his arms and I was enjoying the close-
ness,' she says. 'Suddenly I pulled away because I realized a large
shard of glass was sticking out of my forehead. The glass was so
sharp that I couldn't hold it without cutting my hands.'

This, very literally, seems to indicate there is still something
stuck in Linda's mind; something dangerous and destructive.

Images such as this could simply be reflecting what she has been
through. At the same time, there is also the possibility they are
warnings. Linda has learned enough about analysing dreams to
realize when the signs aren't entirely good. I know she is worried
about this development, but at the same time she doesn't want to
deny the progress we've made. Both of us want to keep a positive
outlook. I am anxious not to spoil this for her, so I bury my concern

and we end the session, wishing each other well for our holidays.

AUGUST 1991

Linda Caine

With Gary and Christy home for the summer, we've planned a holiday at Center Parcs in Elveden Forest. It's one of those all-inclusive resorts where cars stay outside and everybody rides bicycles or walks. There's a massive indoor bubble with pools and water slides.

Gary and Christy are each bringing a friend along to keep them company.

We load up the car on Sunday morning and circle London on the M25. The fields are a patchwork of yellow and green as we head north. It's harvest time and they are dotted with rolls of straw.

When we arrive at the resort, Gary and Christy head straight for the water slides with their friends. Chris and I play tennis and have a swim afterwards. I'm feeling really pleased with myself. Things are getting back to normal, or at least I'm not falling apart. Maybe we can go to America after all.

'Hey, Mum, they have badminton,' says Gary, dashing into the chalet, breathless with excitement.

'And they have ten-pin bowling,' echoes his friend Graham.

Chris teases them, 'And I thought you'd be hanging around the pool looking at the girls.'

'Aw, Dad,' says Gary, before they dash out again.

Chris and I go for a long walk, chatting and planning all the things we want to do.

'How are you feeling?' he asks. It's a question I'm getting used to.

'Really good,' I say sincerely.

His smile says it all. He looks happy and light-hearted. We've been through a terrible ordeal, but we've survived. We both want to do nothing but enjoy being together and relaxing. We need this holiday badly.

On Monday night I go to bed early and read. When I finally fall asleep I have a deeply unpleasant dream. I'm in a dense wood and

I'm standing facing Chris. I'm wearing a long fox-fur coat that comes down to my ankles. Chris thinks it is fake fur, but it's a real one. I found it buried in the ground.

Suddenly, I realize the dark-haired man is coming. I have to get away. I shouldn't have found the coat. Now he'll make me die.

In the morning I can remember the dream vividly, but it seems so strange and nonsensical. I'm so certain I'm getting better that I don't want it to have a special meaning. I decide that if I am getting better, then I don't need to know.

Two days later, as I leave the chalet to play badminton, I get a sudden flash in my mind. I picture myself wearing the fox-fur coat. The power of the image leaves me breathless with my heart pounding. It's just like I used to feel when I had the flashes of being held under water.

'I've been over this. Let it go,' I tell myself.

'But it won't go away.'

'Yes, it will. It was just a silly dream.'

I continue lecturing myself inwardly, determined not to dwell on the coat. This is a holiday with my family. I have so much to be thankful for. I have confronted my childhood and accepted the content of those missing years. I will now think positively and put it behind me.

After a family and friends badminton challenge, we're all in high spirits. Gary and Graham decide to play squash and Christy and her friend, Vicky, go swimming. Chris and I take a stroll around the grounds.

We walk round the lake and come back through the woods to reach our chalet. It's a wonderful setting, with doves cooing in the trees and blue jays claiming their territory loudly.

'Isn't this beautiful?' I say, turning to Chris. He smiles and my mind crashes. It's like stepping back into my dream of Monday night. I'm in a dense wood and I'm standing facing Chris. I'm wearing the fox-fur coat.

The next thing I remember is Chris talking to me. 'Are you OK? You've gone as white as a sheet.' His smile has gone.

'Yes . . . Yes . . . I'm fine . . . It's beautiful here, isn't it?'

I struggle to hold my mind together.

'Something is wrong,' he says, taking my arm to steady me.

'I think I'm just tired. We've had a lot of exercise today.'

'Maybe you should lie down.'

'No. Let's have a jacuzzi. I'll bet that's where Christy and Vicky will be.'

I squeeze his hand and we head for our chalet to get changed.

Sitting in the hot water a few minutes later, I close my eyes and try to stop my heart from pounding.

I tell myself, 'Don't over-react. It's been a long day. All I need is a good night's sleep.'

Opening my eyes, I see Chris watching me. He smiles and I smile back. Inside I have the same safe feeling that I used to get when Dad watched over us when he took us swimming in rivers in Africa. He would sit on a rock, nursing a rifle and watching for crocodiles.

That's the thing about rivers. The water might sparkle and splash over rocks, looking refreshing and idyllic, but danger can lie unseen beneath the surface.

The next morning as I'm getting dressed, I get the flash again. The coolness of the blouse slipping over my shoulders feels like the fox-fur coat around me. The image knocks me sideways. I sit on the bed and try to get my breath back.

This is starting to really frighten me. The horror that, after all this, I might be returning to the nightmare is overwhelming. I *cannot* do this to Chris and the children again. I write something in my diary to try and ground my thoughts:

> *I am having flashes in my mind again and they seem to be connected to the dream I had on Monday. I'm trying to push the flashes aside but they're becoming more detailed. They're disturbing me more and more. I'm beginning to feel like I did when I went back to Ticehurst last time. Why?*

WEDNESDAY, 4 SEPTEMBER 1991

Robin Royston

From the moment I set eyes on Linda I know something is wrong. She has the same haunted look that I remember so well. And her body language seems almost apologetic, as though she is expecting me to throw my hands up in disbelief.

We chat about our respective holidays, but I know she has something else on her mind. She is holding several sheets of paper – normally a sign that she's typed out some dreams.

She doesn't flag the fox-fur coat dream as being important. Instead it is buried among many others as though she is consciously trying to conceal it because she hopes it isn't important. Yet it stands out immediately because of the dark-haired man. He is still so powerful.

I don't ask Linda about the dream but carry on reading. I am very concerned, but have to respect Linda's obvious desire to play this down. It isn't until our next session that she tells me about having flashes again.

'They started after I had one of the dreams I showed you.'

'The one about the fox-fur coat.'

'How did you know?'

'Because it was so powerful.'

Linda still seems to be quite dismissive, but she tells me about the flashes of her wearing the coat and her growing sense that the dark-haired man is coming for her.

'Have you ever owned a fox-fur coat?'

'No.'

'Do you know anyone who has one?'

'I think my mother had one . . . but I'm not sure.'

As Linda tries to remember more about the flashes, her mind begins sliding away. She is desperately trying to hold on, but her eyes grow wide with panic and fear. 'Please, God, don't let this happen again,' she says, before I lose her.

'Linda, can you hear me?'

Her eyes are fixed and unseeing.

'Linda, it's Dr Royston. You're in the Chaucer.'

She doesn't respond.

'Look around you. You recognize this place. You've been here before.'

I keep this up for half an hour. When she finally begins coming back, her whole body is trembling with fear. This has taken me very much by surprise. Linda genuinely seemed to be getting better. If anything, I had envisaged that any problems we encountered now would stem from her mother. But the dark-haired man is back, and his sheer power shocks me. The threat appears to be overwhelming Linda all over again. And there's something new: what does the fur coat signify? Why has it suddenly appeared now?

FRIDAY, 6 SEPTEMBER 1991

Linda Caine

My mind seems to be stuck on 'replay' and I can't shake this sense of dread. The same images keep bursting into my mind like the flashgun of a camera. The scene is frozen in white light. I'm standing, wearing the fox-fur coat. He's angry with me. He's coming. After lunch I phone the Chaucer, hoping Dr Royston might be between patients. Janet, his secretary, asks if he can call me back when he's free. At this point, my mind crashes. I keep repeating, 'I don't know what to do. I don't know what to do.'

Janet tries to calm me down. 'Hold on, Linda, Penny has just come in – will you talk to her?'

But I can't pull my thoughts together. 'No, it's all right,' I say, hanging up on her. Afraid that Penny might call back, I take the receiver off the hook. I don't want to explain everything to her. It's too confusing.

He's coming for me. I have to stop him. I close all the curtains and lock the doors and windows. Then I lie in bed upstairs, hugging a pillow and staring blankly at the ceiling. Time stands still, then the alarm goes off, reminding me that I have to fetch Christy from school. Splashing cold water on my face, I brush my hair and make myself presentable. Driving the car seems to focus my mind and stop it sliding. It also helps having Christy alongside me for the drive home.

We reach the house and she goes upstairs to change. Suddenly the front door opens and Chris comes running inside.

'What are you doing home?' I ask, surprised.

'We couldn't reach you on the phone,' he says, sighing with relief. 'Dr Royston called me. We were worried. Nobody could get through to you.'

I suddenly remember taking the phone off the hook. 'I'm so sorry.'

'What happened?'

I shake my head and can't answer. 'Can we talk later?' I ask shakily. 'I have to fetch Gary.'

'I'll do that.'

'No. It helps me to keep busy. It stops me thinking.'

Poor Chris looks shattered. He's raced all the way from Canterbury, convinced that something terrible has happened. He must have relived the agony he went through when I first disappeared from Chestfield.

The rest of the afternoon passes in a blur. I can't talk to Chris with Gary and Christy around. I still don't know what to tell him.

After supper I call Annette in California. 'Do you remember if our mother had a long fox-fur coat?'

'Yes, I think so,' she says, 'but I don't think it was long. She had a short one.'

The coat in my dream had been long – at least down to my ankles. I tell Annette about the image that keeps flashing into my mind and how shaky I've become.

'Just try to think about all the good things you have,' she says. 'Why don't you just tell yourself, "OK, it happened over thirty years ago, but it's over now"?'

She doesn't understand what it's like. This thing has *me* – I don't have it. It won't let me go. How can I explain how I feel? It seems like it's all happening again . . . just like before when I had flashes of a hand over my face. Maybe the coat seems long on me because I was a child. But why would a small child be wearing a fur coat? And why do I think the dark-haired man is coming?

That night, just as I'm falling asleep, I get the flash again. I see my mother wearing the same coat. It fits her well. Then I see the dark-haired man holding the coat for me to put on. I keep pushing the images away. I don't want to look. The coat feels cold on my body. I'm naked underneath.

'Dr Royston, I'm frightened – I don't want this to be happening again.'

THURSDAY, 19 SEPTEMBER 1991

Robin Royston

Over the previous two weeks Linda's state of mind has collapsed almost completely. Each time I try to talk to her about the fox-fur coat dream, her mind slides and it takes longer to reach into her dissociation and bring her back.

On each occasion she is embarrassed about wasting my time. 'Why do I have to get so involved and emotional?' she asks. 'Why can't I just discuss it rationally? So what if the dark-haired man made me wear this coat? It's just a coat . . .'

She can't finish. Again her memory slides away. Talking about things – saying them out loud – still makes her react badly. Yet if she doesn't talk about them, it is even worse. She begins arriving at the Chaucer fifteen minutes early to give herself time to gather her thoughts. She also brings notes to help her, but it doesn't seem to make any difference. As soon as she starts trying to tell me about the flashes in her mind, her breathing changes and the tears begin to flow.

It is clear to me that Linda needs to go back into Ticehurst, but I know the ramifications are enormous. Linda has promised her family that she won't go back to the hospital again. Her marriage has endured enormous strain, and now this . . .

First I have to clear the admission with Linda's medical insurance company. After everything that has gone before, we discover that she has only twenty-eight days left of cover. This is our deadline. I have no beds on the NHS. If Linda has to leave Ticehurst and be admitted to St Augustine's she will go in as somebody else's patient. All the people she has learned to trust will be gone. After two and a half years of psychotherapy it has come down to four weeks. What are our chances? What if we fail?

I have always been a believer that the unconscious stage-manages things in its own way. It's a very Jungian idea. My only hope is that Linda's unconscious will hear the clock ticking down and show us the way.

26

FRIDAY, 20 SEPTEMBER 1991

Linda Caine

Light rain is falling as I walk down the steps and cross the carpark of the Chaucer. I glance up and let it fall on my eyelids. When I start moving again, my feet seem heavy, as though I'm walking through water. On the drive home the showers sweep over the natural bowls created by the hills. It's misty and hazy, just like the inside of my head. The only thing I can really be certain of is that I need to go back to Ticehurst.

That night I try to tell Chris, but the words catch in my throat. 'I've spoken to Dr Royston. I need to go back to hospital. There's something . . .'

'No! No!' His voice is full of anguish. 'You can't do this to us again. Don't give in to this again.'

'I'm not giving in. I'm trying to fight.'

'But you were doing so much better. We had a great holiday. You were so happy. Why can't you just get over this?' He turns away from me, but I catch his arm.

'Please, Chris, listen to me. I've started remembering something else, getting flashes in my mind again. I've been trying to ignore them but they won't go away.' I tell him about the fox-fur coat dream. He listens quietly, his face a picture of misery.

'And you think going to Ticehurst will help.' It's more a statement than a question. The look in his eyes is almost one of betrayal. Before I can answer, he walks out of the room and stays in his office until dinner.

As we sit down to eat the atmosphere is tense. Gary and Christy sense something is wrong and go quiet. I try to act normally, asking questions about school. Suddenly Chris interrupts in a stern voice. 'Mum has something she needs to tell you.' He looks at me across the table. Gary and Christy turn to me.

'Yes. Well, ah, I do want to say something . . . It's about me going away again . . . to Ticehurst.'

The look on their faces says everything.

'But why?' asks Gary, with a hint of accusation in his voice.

'I'm not doing so well . . . I need some help.'

He looks at Chris as if hoping he might talk me out of it.

'When will you go?' asks Christy.

'Tomorrow morning.'

The hurt in their eyes cuts through my numbness. I almost want them to scream with frustration and anger. Anything but this silent acceptance of my betrayal.

Christy pushes her plate away. 'I'm not very hungry tonight, may I be excused?'

'Yes. Wait. Listen. You all need to know that I'm really trying to get through this.'

'But you were so much better,' says Gary.

'I know. That's why I hope that it won't take long.' The words sound so empty. They've heard it all before. I sound like a politician trying to avoid giving a straight answer.

Christy gets up and begins to clear the table. It's so hard to know what she's thinking. Does she hate me? Is she angry?

That night, as I tuck her into bed and listen to her prayers I ask if she has any questions. She shakes her head. I wish I knew what she was thinking.

Going to Gary's room, I sit on his bed and ask him what he's reading. He's not in the mood to talk. When I mention his prayers, he says angrily, 'I'll pray by myself tonight.' It's as though he blames God for what's happened to me.

'It's nobody's fault,' I tell him.

'Mum, you say God loves us all more than we love each other.'

'That's right.'

'Well, I've prayed night after night for God to make you well and he hasn't. What kind of love is *that*?'

I sigh and brush hair from his forehead. 'If God hasn't healed me yet, it's for a reason. A broken leg doesn't heal overnight. It takes time. And if you try to walk on a broken leg before it has healed, you'll hurt it again. Maybe that's what I've done – tried to cope before I'm ready.'

He hugs me and I kiss him on the forehead.

'Just be careful in Ticehurst,' he says. 'You seem to get worse when you go there.'

Later that night, as I lie in bed, I reach over and touch Chris's shoulder. He turns around and holds me. I can feel his body shaking. I think he's crying. He must believe that this will never end. I lie awake for a long time after he has fallen asleep.

In the morning all my prayers seem pointless. The darkness is overwhelming. I search for the tiny spark of hope, but can't find it. It's as though my decision to return to Ticehurst has allowed me to let go. Everything I do is just delaying the inevitable. I'm going to die.

THURSDAY, 3 OCTOBER 1991

Robin Royston

From the very beginning this admission feels different. Linda has changed. Her level of fear remains the same, but now there is a ruthless element – an emotional detachment that goes far beyond what I have seen in the past. I can sense it from the moment I first see her. Sitting on the bed with her legs curled beneath her, she wears an old black cardigan and toys absent-mindedly with the buttons. Yet in her eyes I see determination and conviction. She has come to a decision.

'How did you sleep?'

She doesn't seem to hear me.

'Have you settled in?'

She nods and doesn't elaborate. I try to keep the conversation moving by asking if she's caught up with people like Roger and

Linda McCormack. Finally Linda softens and begins to open up a little.

'You know why we're here?' I ask.

She shivers. 'We have to talk about the dream.'

'What can you remember?'

Linda takes a deep breath and looks down at her hands. She begins telling me a story that has many similarities with her memories of being taken from her bed. She woke when the hand covered her mouth and nose. She couldn't breathe and heard the rushing sound in her ears. Then she blacked out.

'I woke up and I was lying on the floor,' she says, calmly. 'The dark-haired man pulled me up and put the fur coat around my shoulders. It came down to my ankles. He stroked the front of the coat. Then he put his hands inside . . . No, no, no, uh-uh . . . uh-uh . . . uh-uh . . .'

She is groaning over and over. Her mind is sliding away.

'Listen to me, Linda. Stay with me.'

She has covered her face with her hands. 'I don't want to die,' she murmurs. 'I don't want to die.'

'You don't have to die.'

'Yes, I do. He's coming.'

'Linda, where are you?'

'Uh-uh, uh-uh, uh-uh . . .'

For a long while I can't reach her. I sit next to her on the bed, with my arm around her shoulders. She rocks slightly and groans. As she comes back, I decide to press ahead.

'Why did you have the coat on, Linda?'

'Because of the lady.'

'What lady?'

'The one in the floral dress. The lady I tried to talk to. I tried to tell. I haven't been good. That's why he's so angry. "But I don't tell stories. I don't make things up" . . .'

Linda's mind begins to dissociate again. But whereas in the past when her mind separated, she ran to the corner of the room or hid behind the curtains, now there is a detached acceptance of what happened to her.

The following morning, I have a phone call from Roger. Linda was found in her room hyperventilating. She appeared to be screaming inside her head and was digging her fingernails into her forehead. She threw herself at the window and had to be restrained. Later she cut herself in the bathroom, using a piece of glass on her wrists. She was moved to the observation room and 'specialled' throughout the day. In between broken sleep, she groaned and muttered, 'I don't want to die . . . I can't tell . . . Linda doesn't tell tales.'

In periods when she is lucid, she talks to the staff and thanks them for all they have done. When challenged, she says, 'I'm not saying goodbye tonight, but I am just saying goodbye.' Linda is convinced that she will die. It is as though she has no choice in the matter.

On Friday morning I have two separate discussions with Noel and Linda McCormack. Both are convinced that Linda is severely suicidal. What frightens all of us this time is Linda's emotional detachment. She doesn't want to feel anything any more. She wants to stop feeling. Her only regret is that others might blame themselves for what happens to her.

Jung called this 'snake' behaviour. If you hit certain areas in the nervous system, there is no feeling, just action. The snake is cold-blooded and purely instinctive, with no emotional attachment to anything. A person in this state will do things without reflection or consideration. It will be impulsive and immediate.

Many years ago I was lecturing on a psychotherapy training weekend. One of the students was an extremely beautiful American airline hostess, who struck me as being very bright and articulate. A few days later, she flew back to America and found her boyfriend in bed with another woman. She drove immediately to a suspension bridge and threw herself off. This was classic 'snake' behaviour. There was no reflection or consideration. She simply acted. In this sort of mood Linda is capable of committing suicide regardless of how closely she is supervised. She will simply bide her time and then find a way out.

As each day passes I constantly review her condition. Could I do anything differently? Have I missed something? I go over every-thing she has told me, hoping for some sign that the power of the dark-haired man is diminishing. I can find none. Her fate is in *her* hands, not mine.

MONDAY, 10 OCTOBER 1991

Through all our next sessions, some of which last more than two hours, I try to ferret out more detail about the abuse Linda suffered. In almost every session her mind splits off and she dissociates. Often she stares at me with a mixture of terror and loathing.

I ask her, 'Who am I?'

And she repeats, 'You know I never knew your name.'

In today's session she dissociates for more than five hours. Staff keep watch over her until she falls asleep. However, when Linda wakes she slips quietly from her room and out through the side door. It is twenty minutes before anyone realizes she is missing.

I have a phone call and drive immediately to Ticehurst to help with the search. Although Linda has run off before, this time I can't shake my growing sense of dread. She has never left the hospital in such a calculated and premeditated way. Normally she panics and runs, making it easy for someone to see and hear her. This time she has deliberately crept away. What is she planning to do?

Linda Caine

It's dark and the silhouettes of the trees and shrubs have a dream-like quality. It's like being back in Africa except that it's cold, so very cold. Pressing my cheek against the earth, I curl up against the upturned roots of a fallen tree. I wanted to find my hole in the hedge, my special hiding place, but I couldn't see it anywhere. Then I realized that I was being silly. The hedge was in Gwelo. I must think clearly, otherwise they'll catch me.

I hear a noise and lie very still. After a few minutes I ease my face from the dirt and peep through a small gap in the roots of the tree. I recognize Linda McCormack, walking away from me. Part of me wants to scream for her to come back and get me, but the scream stays inside my head. The earth feels cold and damp against my cheek. My eyelids are heavy. I *can't* fall asleep . . . that's when he comes for me. But I'm so tired . . .

When I open my eyes again, it's dark. I'm so cold I find it hard to move, but I manage to sit up. The moonlight plucks a piece of glass from the blackness. I reach out and scoop it closer with my fingertips. Holding it, I run my tongue along each side to find the sharpest edge. Then I make a small cut across my wrist – watching the red line blur at the edges as blood leaks across my skin.

My hands are so numb I have difficulty gripping the glass. I begin sawing it back and forth across my wrist, hoping I can cut in the same place. It's not bleeding enough. I hold the glass in my left hand, jamming it between my legs to minimize the shaking of my hand. I run my wrist across the edge, but it doesn't work. In desperation, I cut hard into the inside of my left elbow. The pain seems to explode inside my head. White spots dance before my eyes. My mind jolts.

What on earth am I doing? I promised Chris I wouldn't do this again!

Then a voice inside me says, 'Go ahead. Nobody will care. You are insignificant . . . a speck of dust in a dust storm.'

I remember the dust storms in Africa – choking things that would seep into every crack and crevice. Sometimes the storms would sweep across the landscape as a wall of dust that swallowed everything in its path. At other times the wind whipped up 'dust devils' that swirled and skipped across the dry earth, sucking up debris and spitting it out again. As the wind died, the dust would settle and become just dust again.

Thinking about Africa seems to break the mental loop that's been playing over and over in my mind. I let the piece of glass fall from my fingers. Get up, Linda! Go back to Ticehurst. You can't run from something inside your mind. There is no hole in the hedge any more. You've got nowhere to hide. I try to stand and disentangle myself from the roots. Clouds have hidden the moon and I can't see anything. Fighting my way through thorny branches, the spikes tug at my clothes and scratch my skin. The brambles won't let me go.

Finally I stumble free, emerging onto the tree-lined path. My feet are so cold I can't feel them and it's hard to keep my balance. I can see the main hospital building in front of me. A woman appears from the front door and walks towards me. I panic and stand like a statue. She stops and looks directly at me. A voice inside my head says, 'Run!'

'Where will I run to?'

'Run!'

'There's nowhere to go.'

'Run!'

The woman hesitates and begins walking towards me. I force myself to carry on.

She reaches me and asks quietly, 'Are you all right?'

I try to answer but can't find the words. She touches my arm and talks to me gently. My mind is sliding. I can't hold on to her words. I can hear dogs barking and see a police car parked outside the main door. Spinning on my heels, I try to run, but I crash headlong into two dark figures in neon vests.

'Please don't hurt me.'

'We won't hurt you.'

They walk on either side of me, holding my arms gently.

The light in the reception area seems too bright. I look down the passage towards my room and see instead the passage that ran from mine and Annette's bedroom to our mother's, at 5 Maple Avenue. I turn to run, but can't get away.

'Please. Let me go. You don't know what will happen . . .'

A policeman looks at me. His eyes are kind. '*What* will happen? Tell me what will happen.'

My mind is swimming. I see Dr Royston walking towards me. He sees the smears of dried blood on my wrists. I cover my face with my hands, feeling ashamed.

'Let's get you cleaned up and have that coffee,' he says. 'I need one.' He tries to cheer me up by being light-hearted, but I'm past caring.

I don't feel the pain as they bathe and bandage the cuts. Afterwards I sip a coffee and listen to Dr Royston talking without hearing what he says. I don't remember him leaving.

WEDNESDAY, 12 OCTOBER 1991

Since I ran away they've moved me back to the observation room. I keep throwing myself at the windows when I 'leap' and it takes me longer each time to realize where I am. Maybe one day I won't come back at all. I'll be trapped at 5 Maple Avenue.

When I come back, I find myself sitting on the bed with Sheila, one of the nurses, rubbing my neck.

'Linda, how old are you?' she asks.

I can't remember. I rack my brain. Then the answer comes to me. 'I'm forty years old.' It doesn't sound right, but Sheila seems happy.

'You should try to get some sleep,' she says.

But I don't want to sleep. I want to stay away from 5 Maple Avenue. That's where he's waiting for me . . .

I'm so tired. Soon I'll lose the battle and fall asleep. He knows that. I can't run any more. There's nowhere to hide.

All of my art things are in the observation room – my sketchpads, pencils, crayons, charcoals, an art knife and scrapbook. My eyelids feel weighted down. I force them open. I can't go back . . . he's waiting for me there.

I pick up the art knife and run my thumb gently along the sharp edge. A wooden shaving from a pencil is caught in the handle. I puff out my cheeks and blow it away. On my left wrist I can see where I tried to cut myself with the glass. If I cut over the same place, I'll be able to hide the wound. Nobody will know what I've done. I can't go back . . . he's waiting for me . . .

In the bathroom, I sit down and feel the weight of the knife in my hands. Taking it in my right hand I watch the blade press against my left wrist. The flesh opens and then blooms red. It doesn't clear my mind so I cut again. Still it doesn't work, so I cut again, deeper and longer. I've cut all the way down my arm from my wrist to my elbow, but I'm not feeling anything. I cut again until I hit my bone. When I hold my arm up the whole section of flesh falls away and flaps loosely. Blood is dripping onto the floor.

Finally the pain clears my head. I try to close the wound by squeezing both sides of the cut with my other hand. Then I wrap toilet paper round and round my arm, watching it soak up the blood like a sponge. I pull my jersey on, putting wads of toilet paper up the sleeve. The blood is leaking through the paper.

I'm thinking clearly and I know it's serious. I have to stop the bleeding.

Noel is in the nurses' station. I put my head around the door.

'Can I have some Savlon?' I ask.

'Why?'

'I cut myself.'

He fetches the Savlon, but instead of giving it to me, he leads me back into my room.

'Let's have a look.'

'It's not bad. I just need to clean it.'

'Linda, show me.' His voice is gentle but firm.

I sigh, and hold out my arm. Noel helps me take off the jersey. The toilet paper is soaked with blood and breaks apart in his fingers.

'Jesus Christ!'

When he reaches the wound he lets out a little whistle between his teeth. 'Put your hand here,' he says, showing me how to put pressure on the wound. Then he goes to the first aid cupboard and brings back rolls of bandages and tape.

'What did you use?'

I motion to the craft knife, lying on the bathroom floor. He picks it up and puts it on the coffee table, with the bandages.

'This is going to need stitches,' he says. 'We'll have to take you to hospital.'

'Please don't tell Dr Royston.'

'I'm sorry, Linda, but I have to.'

Roger and Linda McCormack arrive as Noel finishes bandaging my arm. I can hear them talking about getting me to the hospital. My mind starts to slide. I've gone too far this time. They'll give up on me. They'll send me to St Augustine's. I must clear my mind.

The craft knife is still on the table. I reach over and my fingers close around it. 'I just have to go to the toilet,' I say, slipping quickly into the bathroom. The bandage on my arm matches the white of my T-shirt. I can't focus my thoughts. Everything is starting to blur. My back is braced against the door and my legs are levered against the shower. I lift the T-shirt above my stomach and slice downward between my rib cage. I want to cut in a place where nobody will look. I cut once and don't feel a thing.

Linda McCormack is knocking on the door. She tries to push it open, but can't get in.

'Have you got the knife, Linda?'

I don't answer.

'What are you doing, Linda? Where is the knife?' I can hear the urgency in her voice.

Holding the blade against the wound, I cut again. It isn't a long cut – about two inches. The flesh opens.

Roger tries to shoulder the door open. 'Linda, where is the knife?'

'Just leave me alone.'

'Linda, stand away from the door. Stand away because I'm going to break it down.'

My mind starts to clear. I lean forward, taking my back from the door. It swings open and Roger bursts inside, kneeling beside me. I hear someone say, 'Get the knife!'

I raise my hand and Linda McCormack prises the blade from between my fingers. I feel complete and utter despair.

At the Accident and Emergency room of Tunbridge Wells Hospital they're playing *Mr Bean* videos on the television. Roger and I laugh out loud. My arm and abdomen are aching and the whole scene feels surreal. For two hours they keep us waiting. Then Roger discovers the staff are doing it on purpose because they want to teach me a lesson for cutting myself. Roger is furious. He demands to see the supervisor and calls him a prat. I sit quietly on my seat, embarrassed about causing so much trouble.

Finally a doctor comes to do my sutures. She gives me a local anaesthetic, but I can still feel the pain as she begins stitching. I concentrate on a spot on the ceiling, and my mind floats away.

'What did you do it with?' asks the doctor.

'I beg your pardon?'

'What did you cut yourself with?'

'An art knife.'

'Was it dirty?'

'Yes.'

Robin Royston

I feel a mixture of shock and disbelief when I hear the news. Linda has really done it this time. Linda's bid to commit suicide has always been very serious, but the fact that she often talked about it took away some of the immediacy of the danger. By sharing her secret, she eased the pressure on herself. I also drew comfort from knowing that Linda's knowledge of suicide was rather naïve. She imagined that if she cut herself and blood began dripping out of her veins, then she'd soon be dead. It was a misconception that, for obvious reasons, I didn't seek to correct. Now she has cut herself very badly. I know that we are now dealing with something quite different.

On the drive to Ticehurst I find myself thinking about Chris, Gary and Christy. This news will be devastating for them. When I last spoke to Chris on the phone he sounded near to breaking point.

'Is she going to get better?' he asked.

'I do honestly believe so, yes.'

'When? How much longer?'

'I don't know.'

I sensed the pessimism in him. Perhaps he was the realist. What will he say now that his wife has sliced open her arm and abdomen?

I meet Linda McCormack in the corridor as I arrive, and we share the gravity of the situation without having to exchange a word. She gives me a full briefing and shows me the nursing notes.

'So what now, coach?' she asks.

'We've gone one goal down in the final,' I say, trying to lift the gloom.

'How much is left on the clock?' she asks.

'We're in injury time.'

MONDAY, 21 OCTOBER 1991

Linda Caine

This is my last chance. In ten days Ticehurst will no longer be my safe haven. I can't keep running back here.

'I don't want to have to think about these things again,' I say to Noel. 'I want to be able to go home and leave these memories here.'

'You make it sound as though we toss them into the incinerator,' he says in his lilting Irish accent. I can tell that he doesn't think this will happen.

The nurses have put the wardrobe in front of one window and the dressing table in front of the other. I think they're trying to slow me down so they can reach me before I hurt myself.

Last night Joseph caught me at the window when I woke screaming. My mind was alive with snatched and broken images. Afterwards I began trying to write them down. I thought that maybe – like when I wrote 'The Child' – it would help me get things clear in my head. I didn't get very far before my mind began to slide, but it was a start. I tried to sleep again, but had another 'leap'. After a hot drink I managed to doze until 7.30 a.m. Bliss!

I can hear cheerful voices in the corridor. The staff are changing over. Linda McCormack is on the day shift. Sitting back down at the desk, I write a little more about the flashbacks. I want to have enough to show Dr Royston. I know that time is running out. It's now or never.

I know Dr Royston has arrived because I can hear him talking in the nurses' station. He and Roger share a black sense of humour and they're always bantering and swapping stories.

'Good morning,' he says brightly. 'Did you order a shrink?'

'Yes, that would be me.'

'Oh, good.'

He takes a seat and leans back with his hands behind his head. He always seems so relaxed, as if nothing fazes him.

'I think the pieces are falling into place,' I tell him. 'I'm having that sense again, of the broken images starting to run together like a film reel.'

'What can you remember?'

'The lady in the floral skirt.'

'The one you tried to tell?'

'Yes.'

'Tell me about her.'

'I didn't know her name. She was very beautiful. She had kind eyes . . . I tried to tell her . . .' I'm starting to slip away. I look at my notes, hoping to find help. 'But she doesn't believe me. She believes my mother . . .'

Robin Royston

Although I try to hold her in the present, Linda slips through the portal into 5 Maple Avenue. She covers her face with her hands.

'They're coming! They're coming!'

'Who?'

She shakes her head desperately from side to side, unable to breathe. She is reliving what happened, being carried down the passage with a hand clamped over her nose and mouth. The rushing sound fills her head.

'What can you see?' I ask.

'He puts me down and my legs won't hold me. He's angry with me, but he doesn't shout. His voice is cold. He whispers close to my ear. "Look at me. Look at my face."

'He puts his hand under my chin. He jerks my head up so I look into his face . . . at his eyes . . . "I know what you told her," he says. "And I'm going to show you what happens to silly little girls who tell stories . . . they don't grow up."

'My mother is standing on the other side of the bed. I look at her briefly. She looks frightened. Why won't she help me? The man jerks my head around. "Look at me!" '

For a brief moment, Linda raises her head from her hands and looks at me. There is no hint of recognition in her eyes, only fear. She looks away again.

'He holds my chin tight. His fingers are digging into my cheeks. He pulls my mouth out of shape. I can feel my teeth cutting my mouth. I don't want to look at his eyes. They frighten me. I try to concentrate on a spot just above them. "You shouldn't tell tales," he says. "You might get people into trouble. Just because we let you do grown-up things, it doesn't mean you can talk to grown-ups."

' "Look at me," he orders. But I can't . . . I can't look . . . His hand is crushing my face. He won't let me look away. His face is next to mine. His eyes go right into my head . . . deep inside. He's watching me now. He's always been watching me . . .'

Linda takes big gulps of air between her sobs. She has rolled off the bed and is curled up on the floor beside it, shielding her face with her hands.

338

I can hear Dr Royston's voice. 'I'm still here, Linda. Look at my hair – it's not dark.'

He keeps saying it over and over. I look at him between my fingers. He doesn't have angry eyes. He's crouching next to me. How did I get on the floor?

'Go with it, Linda,' he says. 'What happened next?'

'I can't.'

'Yes, you can. What do you see?'

It's not a case of 'seeing'. I feel everything. It's happening again. The man is moving slowly behind me. I dare not move. Maybe if I stand very still, he'll leave me alone. Suddenly, his hand snakes around my head and covers my mouth and nose. My head snaps back. I can't breathe. I claw at his hands. The rushing sound fills my head . . . until the blackness comes . . .'

Dr Royston is speaking to me. 'Don't leave me, Linda. Tell me about the coat,' he says.

'I'm too frightened.'

'I'll help you.'

Nobody can help me. The man's voice is quiet and cold. He tells me to open my eyes. I don't know where I am at first. He pulls me to my feet and tells me to stand. My knees are shaking, but I mustn't fall down. I'm naked and shivering. The man picks up a fox-fur coat from the bed and puts it around my shoulders. It's too big for me. The coat feels cold, but soft like the blanket on the bed. I hold it tight around me. For a second, the softness is all I'm aware of. I begin to escape, sinking into it, away from the man, away from the pain.

'Keep looking at me,' he says, cupping my chin violently with his fist. He forces me back. I dare not look away.

'It's lovely and soft, isn't it?' he whispers. 'Feel how soft it is.'

I drop my eyes, but he makes me look up again.

'Such a lovely coat . . . so soft and warm. Just stroke it with your fingertips,' he says. I hesitate. I want the softness to take me away, so I lift my hands tentatively. He grabs my wrists and forces them onto the fur.

'It's a pity that it's made of dead animals. Little dead animals –

all sewn together. Just their skin, with no eyes. How does it feel to be wrapped in dead animals?'

I scream inside, but only a deep gasping noise escapes from my throat. I hold my hands away from the dead animals, but the man pushes them back onto the fur.

'Feel the dead animals,' he says, looking into my eyes. I cannot turn away. I've never seen such anger. 'If you ever tell anybody about this again then you will die. If anyone asks you about what you said, tell them it was just nightmares. If you say it's real – you are dead. Remember the little animals, all dead and sewn together. Remember the coat . . .'

His face is only inches away. His eyes are inside my head. 'Remember, I can find you. YOU WILL BE DEAD – just like the animals, only I'll put you in a box under the ground. In a dark place full of dead people in boxes under the ground. And you'll stay there for ever . . . in the dark . . . dead. *Look* at me! Do you understand? If you ever say this is real, I will find you. Wherever you are. I'll put you in a box deep underground. All I have to do is to stop you breathing for a little bit longer. Then you won't wake up. You *will* be *dead*!'

I can see myself there, curled up in a box under the ground, with all the other dead people. It will be like being locked in the cupboard, but no one will come and open the door to let me out. Will I be able to think if I'm dead? Will I still be frightened?

He takes me to the cupboard and opens the door. His hand is against my back, pushing me forwards. But as the musty smell hits me, something breaks deep inside me. I can't go in there any more. I half turn and lean against the man. He turns me around and crouches down. His hand slips beneath the coat. My mind is screaming, but I try to focus on something else. I want to cut my mind off, but all I can feel are the little dead animals . . . all sewn together . . . touching me.

Something splits inside my head. I feel myself falling deep into my mind. It's warm and hazy – like a cotton-wool world. I don't feel the pain. Nothing can reach me. I've found my hiding place.

27

Robin Royston

Walking into the sunlight is like emerging from a darkened cinema after watching a movie of immense power. Outside it seems like an ordinary day. Squirrels dart across the lawn between the trees; two nurses sit on a log bench, sharing a cigarette; a tractor ploughs a field, the mud spinning from its wheels. Nothing has changed, yet the world feels different. I have seen and heard some terrible things in my working life. Each time I immerse myself in a patient's life I have to be prepared to go into the mud-pool. It's not a pleasant task but life is complex and the dark illuminates the light. But this is a real drama, a piece of experience over and above the everyday.

At this moment I am acutely aware of the beauty in the hospital grounds and surrounding countryside. The idyllic rural scenery hasn't changed, only my ability to appreciate such things. Perhaps I am simply more grateful. Poor Linda. No wonder she tried so hard to die. What she endured, I have now truly been a part of. I have just been a witness to Linda reliving events with all the horror and fear that she experienced the first time.

We captured the very moment of severe dissociation in her childhood. The 'heart of darkness', as Joseph Conrad described it a century ago, when her mind split and the shutters came down.

This is why Linda blocked the memories. She didn't want to die.

The use of the fox-fur coat was a brilliant device. Her abuser knew how much Linda loved animals. He let her feel the warmth of the coat. He let her become seduced by the softness and then he made his move. He watched her make her habitual escape into the soft, warm fabric then he trapped her by telling her she was wrapped in death – surrounded by all those little dead animals sewn together.

At that precise moment, having tracked Linda into her secret hiding place, he forced her to look into his eyes and drove something into her head. Like the shard of glass that Linda dreamed was sticking out of her forehead, he broke her mind as he broke her body with his abuse. She would never tell because if she did, he would find her.

I've never known such evil. I've never been so close to it. Now, at last, I know why Linda is so resigned to dying. She did the very thing that he told her not to – she told someone. She told *me*. Deep in her unconscious mind, she knew what this meant . . . he was coming to kill her. Linda once told me that in Africa young children are taught to be frightened of the Tokolosh, which is like our bogeyman. The thing with the Tokolosh is that you mustn't think about him because if you do he will come. The dark-haired man is Linda's Tokolosh. She dared to speak his name.

I've left Linda sleeping in her room with Linda McCormack watching over her. I stand in the sunshine trying to find some warmth. A part of me feels relief at having discovered the core of Linda's dissociation. There is also a sense of achievement. All the dream images have come together – the ice, the angry eyes, the mad elephant . . .

Yet having fitted all these pieces together, I realize that instead of healing Linda's mind we have, in all likelihood, made things worse. We have woken the dark-haired man. Never before have I had such a sense of evil coming. Turning and walking back into the hospital I ask Roger if there is a spare room.

'Twenty-three is vacant.'

'I'm going to stay tonight.'

Roger doesn't ask why. He knows we have reached a crucial

stage. Partly I want to support the staff. They have coped with Linda night after night, while I go off to my wife and children and warm bed. But I also can't shake the feeling that the dark-haired man is coming. Roger feels it too. A part of me wants to lock the doors and windows to stop him getting inside. At the same time I know that he doesn't need a physical presence – he waits in Linda's dreams. Is there any way to stop him coming?

Linda 'leaps' at 3 a.m. and goes for the window. She breaks the glass and cuts her hands. I sit and have a coffee with her while they are bandaged. I don't know who I am trying to reassure, Linda or myself. Both of us perhaps. In the morning nothing has changed. Linda looks as though she has given up completely. Death would come as a relief. I encourage her outside for a walk and we sit on the log bench near the tennis court. Weak sunlight filters through the bare branches.

The theory was always that by talking through traumatic events in her past she would rid herself of the energy they contained. This is all very well, but with the truth we've discovered, this has back-fired completely.

'All I want to do is die,' she says, fingering the ugly red scars on her forearm. 'The more I talk about it, the more hopeless I feel. It's not getting any better. It's not helping.'

There it is. I feel as though time is slowing down and a great weight settles over me. I realize suddenly that there is nothing more I can do for Linda. We can talk about these things until we're blue in the face, but it won't make a scrap of difference. Linda's black vortex has been reactivated so powerfully that I can almost hear it churning. I have no notion of how to defuse the power, how to switch off its dark energy. However hard I try, I have run out of ideas.

That evening I have a phone call at home. Linda has taken an over-dose of between twelve and sixteen Temazepam and two Nitrazepam tablets. The amounts aren't enough to be fatal, although Linda hasn't realized that. I debate with Roger whether to send her to Accident and Emergency to have her stomach pumped, and we decide it won't be necessary. The medical staff at the hospital made her feel humiliated when she cut her arm. She feels bad enough already.

I try to be positive, but in reality I know that Linda's future is far less certain than when she arrived four weeks earlier. Psychotherapy is a process where we often exist in uncertainty. Psychotherapists *don't* have all the answers. The very essence of the process is for the therapist *not* to know and to help the patient find their own path out of his or her difficulties.

Linda and I have done this from the very beginning. We have trusted the process. Now I realize that unless Linda can shake off the destructive power of the dark-haired man and rid herself of the belief that she *has* to die, I can see no way forward.

Has the process failed? No. Would it have been better to have never started psychotherapy? Again the answer is no. When Linda first walked into my office she was seriously suicidal. Doing nothing wasn't an option. Linda's final nights at Ticehurst are typified by 'leaps', screams and severe dissociation. During the days she is exhausted, but too frightened to sleep. Knowing that she has to leave hospital, I sit down with her to discuss our options.

'How do you feel about leaving?' I ask.

'Scared.'

'I've never asked you this before, but I know you've always been very honest with me: are you planning to do anything terrible?'

'If you mean killing myself, I don't have the energy.'

I feel relieved and encouraged. I know Linda will do everything in her power to be 'all right' for her family. Hopefully, this might bring a change.

'I had a dream,' she says vaguely.

'Yes?'

'I was on a crippled plane that was about to crash-land into water. I jumped clear and found myself in the dirty water, with reeds wrapping around my ankles. The shore seemed a long way off but I began to swim towards it. Suddenly, a wave from the crashing plane overtook me. I went somersaulting under the water and seemed to be dragged down. But instead of drowning, I bobbed up and noticed that the wave had carried me closer to shore.'

Linda can see nothing positive in the dream. She lacks the energy. But I see it as a continuation of the mud-pool dream. Here is a real indication that she *could* survive. From being completely submerged in the muddy water, convinced she will drown, she emerges nearer the land and safety. I say this to Linda but she doesn't seem very reassured. Nothing I can say will change her mood. I can't bear to leave her like this. It is our last session before she leaves, and I know she's not ready.

'I know you're afraid of going home,' I say as our session ends. 'But I'll be waiting for you at the Chaucer on Wednesday.'

Linda nods and gives me a brave smile. 'I want to thank you for all that you've done.' She is on the verge of tears. I leave quickly, walking down the empty corridor feeling hollow with sadness. At the same time, I draw comfort from the dream she's told me about. The crippled plane has crashed, but a wave carried her closer to shore. I cling to the hope that if she can only get herself there, it will be the end of her journey.

FRIDAY, 1 NOVEMBER 1991

Linda Caine

It's six in the morning and I've already been awake for an hour. I want to leave Ticehurst early before traffic builds up on the roads. For a while I contemplate leaving straight away, but I still have to say goodbye to people. I 'leapt' twice last night. The second time I 'came to' I found myself wedged between the window and the wardrobe. I was trying to tear the newspaper that had been taped over the glass. The wardrobe began toppling over and Roger stopped it. It fell back onto my foot. I'm lucky my ankle was only bruised.

My two suitcases are on the bed and I've put my sketchpads and pencils in a folder. Chris wanted to come and pick me up, but I told him that I'd prefer to drive myself home. That way I can take my time saying goodbye. I decide to surprise Dympna and Linda McCormack by having coffee in the lounge. I can also say goodbye to Sarah. I know what's going to happen. Everybody will say nice, positive things about never wanting to see me again. Roger will joke about the glazier losing half his business. Then I'll start crying. Look at me! I'm crying already. Maybe I'll just sneak out quietly. I'm too emotional to drag this out.

I put my suitcases in the car and go back to get my art folder. As I walk down the passage I see Linda McCormack standing in the doorway to the lounge. Thankfully, she hasn't seen me. I turn the corner and bump into Dympna.

'Aren't you coming for a cup of coffee?' she asks.

I try to say that I can't, but the words won't come out. I just shake my head and keep walking. What a fool! I reach my car but Linda McCormack comes running out.

'Please, come back and have some coffee. I don't want you leaving when you're upset.'

I almost agree but no matter when I leave I'll be upset. Why delay the inevitable? I tell her I'm sorry and say a quick goodbye. The first few miles are the most difficult. I can't see the road properly through my tears. Finally, I manage to pull myself together and concentrate. Yet I can't shake the feeling that I should be dead. It isn't a whingeing, self-pitying, poor-old-me reaction. I *really* believe it.

The rational part of me knows the dark-haired man can't get me any more. It all happened a long time ago. How could he know where I am now? But somewhere deep inside me I know he's coming.

I arrive home just after 9.30 a.m. Chris is at work and Gary and Christy are at school. The sky is blue with scattered clouds and the morning sun streams through the windows of the living room and our bedroom. I enjoy the quiet as I unpack and put my suitcases away. Then I wander from room to room. The vestiges of hurried breakfasts are lying in the sink. I stack the dishwasher, pleased to do something useful.

Upstairs in Gary's room, I straighten up his desk. Paper and felt pens lie next to his computer. I love the fact that he and Christy draw and write poetry. They have different styles that match their personalities. Bending down I pick up a single sock from the floor . . . and then another and another. I once told Gary that dirty socks multiply if left lying around. I guess he's forgotten.

In Christy's room I pick up her nightdress which is lying on her bed. It's her pink one with white sheep on it. I have one exactly the same – we bought them together, so we could look the same. As I lift her pillow to put the nightdress underneath it, I find my nightdress already there. When I'm away she always keeps something of mine under her pillow. And she gives me something of hers to take with me, like the bunny soft toys.

On top of the nightdress is an envelope addressed to Chris in my handwriting. It's a letter that I wrote to him when he first arrived in London. Underneath is a second letter, this one from Chris to me, written while I waited in Africa for Gary to be born. I sit on the bed and read the letters. They are so full of love and hope. We were telling each other that we'd be together again soon; and that we'd start a new life in England. I don't know where Christy found them. I leave them under the pillow and straighten the covers.

Opening her curtains to the morning sun, I gaze down at the garden. It looks lovely and peaceful. I can see Nibbles's hutch through the window of the summer house. The fruit trees are looking . . . My mind crashes into blackness. It happens so suddenly that I lose my balance and grab hold of the windowsill. I'm a child looking out the window of 5 Maple Avenue. It's a beautiful day and the sun is shining on the fruit trees. I hear dishes clattering in the kitchen as the cook prepares breakfast. There's a pain between my legs . . . my stomach is sore . . . Suddenly I'm back in Christy's room, blinking into the bright sunlight. I'm forty years old. Glancing around the room I shudder. I feel as though I'm tainting Christy's room by being here.

As I walk down the stairs, I stumble and begin running for my room. The dark-haired man is watching me . . . and waiting. I hear his words echoing in my mind. 'Remember, I can find you. You will be dead – just like the animals . . .' For an hour I crouch in the corner, listening to my heartbeat. As I calm down, I scold myself for being so foolish. How can I be frightened of a man who existed so long ago?

Pulling myself together, I go downstairs and try to keep my mind occupied by doing chores. I'm making tacos for dinner, with oat flapjacks for dessert – Gary's favourite. Chris is coming home early today and collecting Gary and Christy on his way. I glance at my watch. They'll be here soon. Why am I so nervous? The scar on my forearm looks horrible. The stitches have come out, but it looks as though someone has taken a red crayon and drawn a line from my wrist to my elbow. Gary and Christy know about what happened, but I don't want it to be the first thing they see. I quickly go upstairs and put on a long-sleeved shirt.

Suddenly, the front door flies open and Gary tears in. 'Yehaaaaa! I thought I could smell flapjacks!' He gives me a hug and lifts me off my feet.

'Hey, be careful with your mum,' says Chris. Christy is beside him. Gary puts me down as though I might break.

I try to ruffle his hair, but it's stiff and stuck together. 'What's that?'

'Hair gel,' he explains, looking a little embarrassed. 'It just keeps it in place.'

I try not to laugh, but Gary gets defensive.

'Hey, listen, I've seen photos of Dad when he was at school. Look at all that grease he wore in *his* hair.'

'It was called Brylcreem,' says Chris.

'Well, at least this isn't greasy.'

I laugh. 'You're absolutely right.'

Christy comes forward and gives me a hug. 'Not you too,' I say, feeling her hair.

'Gel stops it coming out of the ponytail,' she says. 'I hate it coming loose and tickling my face.'

'Goodness me! I turn my back for five minutes and look what happens.'

'It was more than five minutes,' says Gary, but then he reprimands himself. The silence is uncomfortable and I try to change the subject. 'Why don't you two go and get changed? I'll put the kettle on.'

After Gary and Christy have gone, Chris puts his arms around me. 'They're so glad that you're home,' he says.

'I know.'

'And I think they're a little scared because they don't know how long it's going to be for.'

'I'm scared too, but I won't be going back to Ticehurst.'

We all sit around the kitchen table, drinking tea and hot chocolate. Gary and Christy tell me about school and all their latest news. Christy wants me to take her shopping on Saturday and Gary says we should all play badminton.

'Steady on,' says Chris. 'She's only just come home.'

After dinner I curl up on the sofa next to Christy.

'I found some letters under your pillow today,' I say. 'I was just tidying up.'

Christy thinks she's in trouble.

'It's OK. I'm not angry. Where did you find them?'

'I was doing my homework in your art room and I needed some paper. I looked in one of the drawers and I found a bundle of old letters. I know I shouldn't have read them. But I did. I thought they were beautiful.'

'Why did you put those two under your pillow?'

She glances at me self-consciously. 'It sort of made me feel that you *would* come home; that we really *would* be together again. Like before.'

She puts her head on my shoulder and I stroke her hair.

'Well, I'm home now.'

'I'm so glad, Mum.'

After Gary and Christy have gone to bed, I start folding the washing on our bed. As I close the curtains I notice the moon. It's almost full. I feel very small and frightened. I remember saying goodnight to the moon when my dad used to go away. A voice inside my head whispers the poem, as my mind slides away. The dark-haired man is waiting for me . . .

Chris is standing in the doorway holding a basket of washing.

'The tumble-drier stopped,' he says. 'I brought these up for you. Are you all right?'

'Yes. I just got a fright, that's all.'

He's not convinced. I know he's watching me closely . . . looking for signs. What can I say? All the things I've remembered keep coming alive in my mind. I seem to be living almost parallel lives – I'm Linda Caine, aged forty, and Linda Houston-Brown, aged five. It makes me angry. I don't want to be the child. She was left behind thirty-five years ago. She shouldn't exist any more. I don't want her to be part of me. I'm afraid of her. Stupid child! Why didn't she just destroy herself? It would have saved all this from happening.

In bed that night Chris puts his arms around me. I feel warm and safe. As I fall asleep I jump awake with my heart racing. Chris holds me tightly.

'Linda. It's all right. You're at home.'

After a minute or two, I realize where I am. 'I'm sorry. I hope I didn't scare you.'

'That's OK.'

We both lie awake for a long time before I drift off. Some time later I'm aware of a strange moaning sound. It takes me a while to realize the sound is coming from deep in my throat. I feel as though I'm being held down – crushed under a weight. I can't move. Panic overwhelms me. My vision clears and I see Chris's face. He's leaning over me, holding me down. He looks distraught. 'Linda. Linda. It's me. You're at home.'

'Chris,' I gasp.

He takes his weight off me, but keeps hold of my arm. He leans over to turn on the bedside light. I see the dark rings under his eyes. How long have I been like this?

'Are you OK now?'

I nod.

'Would you like some coffee?'

I nod again.

I watch him go downstairs and my heart sinks. How much longer can he put up with this?

28

SUNDAY, 17 NOVEMBER 1991

Linda Caine

Chris and I have been married for eighteen years today. I wonder if he regrets it.

As I stare out of the kitchen window, a cooing sound and the flutter of wings penetrate my thoughts. The doves have come back. I'm so pleased. They're beautiful, gentle birds and they pick so delicately at the food I leave on the lawn for them. They seem oblivious to the starlings who squabble and fight each other for every morsel. The starlings will end up going hungry because of their bickering. Silly birds. I'm not doing very well. I'm trying to hold on to all the good there is around me. I envy the doves. How wonderful it must be to have such freedom. In the blink of an eye they can fly away and watch the world from high above.

A few years ago I read a story about Jesus asking a lame man at the pool if he wanted to be healed. It seemed a rather strange question to ask a cripple because I thought the answer would be an obvious yes. Now I've come to realize that it isn't quite that simple. When you're crippled – whether it be physically or emotionally – people make allowances for you. You do the same for yourself. The lame man knew that once he could walk, he'd be expected to join the healthy people and work for his living. His whole way of life would change – probably for the better in the long run, but in the short term everything would be strange and new. He'd no longer have any excuses.

What would I say if Jesus asked me that? I don't honestly know. I am afraid. Right now everyone leaves me alone. Nothing is expected of me. If I have a bad day I have an excuse. But what happens if I ever get 'better'? Will I be able to cope with what's expected of me?

That night after dinner Chris and I watch a film about Africa. It makes us nostalgic because the scenery is so beautiful. In spite of all that happened there I would love to go back, but the Africa I remember doesn't exist any more. I don't want any more dreams – only reality.

We should hear about our application to move to America in the next couple of months. Once or twice I've mentioned it to Chris, but he hasn't responded. When I raise the subject again, he turns on me. 'Be realistic, Linda. We're not going anywhere. You're lucky if you manage to sleep through one night without jumping awake. We'll have no medical cover over there. If you get sick, we could lose everything we have. I won't take that risk.' He stops and takes a deep breath. Then his shoulders slump and he sits down. 'I'm sorry, I can't even think about leaving. There's too much I'm trying to hold together here. Day *and* night.'

I feel as though he's slapped me. I stand in shocked silence.

Suddenly, all the tension comes flooding out in a torrent of words. 'Great! You tell me to be positive. You say, "Look forward, Linda, instead of backward." And when I do, you shoot me down in flames. You talk as though everything we have now is safe and stable. Well, your firm is tearing itself apart and your career is at a crossroads. Our lives are changing *anyway*, regardless of whether we go to America or stay here. We're forty years old. We have the chance to do this but it won't last. If we're going to begin a new life, *now* is the time to do it.'

He challenges me angrily: 'And what about you?'

'I don't know. I wish I did. But I don't need reminding that it's *my* fault. And I *don't* need to be told that *you're* holding everything together day and night.'

I push past him and go upstairs. By the time I've showered and got ready for bed, Chris arrives with coffee.

'I'm sorry,' I say, giving him a hug.

'No. I'm the one who should apologize.'

'You're right to be scared about leaving here.'

'I'm scared for you.'

'I know it's naïve to think I'll just leave all my difficulties behind if we go, but maybe it *will* help. Maybe all that Californian sunshine and the open spaces and a horse of my own will be the medicine I need.'

Chris laughs and says he can imagine me riding the range. Then he looks at me seriously. 'Right now you see Dr Royston once or twice a week. And even though you can't go back to Ticehurst, you can still phone Roger Smith and Linda McCormack whenever you need to talk. What's going to happen if we go to America? What if you don't improve? We can't just pack up and come back.'

I don't have answers for him. The truth is, I don't know.

THURSDAY, 21 NOVEMBER 1991

The best times and the worst times are when Gary and Christy are at school and Chris is at the office. I enjoy being alone, but I can't stop the doubts creeping in.

Sometimes I manage to do some drawing or painting. I've almost finished a snowy owl that I'm painting on a piece of the slate that I picked up at Ticehurst. I want to give it to Dympna for Christmas.

Today I decide to force myself out of the house. I have to make a start somewhere. Jenny Walker is a friend from church and I arrange to visit her for a coffee. We've known each other for about ten years and I've seen her once or twice in between my admissions to Ticehurst. Jenny is about my age and has two sons, both a little older than Gary. She makes us coffee and we sit chatting in the lounge. 'I read something this morning, and I knew it was for you,' she says, picking up her Bible. She finds the page and reads the passage: '*Because you have said we have made a covenant with death and with Sheol* [the place of the dead] *we have an agreement . . .*'

I go cold inside. She's right. I *have* made a pact with death.

Jenny carries on. 'I kept reading and then another passage jumped out at me: *"And your covenant with death shall be annulled and your agreement with Sheol shall not stand . . ."* ' She looks up at me and smiles. ' *"Your covenant with death shall be annulled."* '

I feel stunned. It's as though God is talking directly to me.

Jenny asks me lots of questions about my breakdown and I tell her how death has been my friend for a long while. She nods and squeezes my hand. 'Have you ever heard about the Lydia women's prayer group in England?'

I nod my head. 'A little.'

'I'm the co-ordinator for East Kent. There's a lady I know called Lu Sunderland, who used to be the head of the Lydias. She's become more and more involved in specific prayer for healing.'

Jenny explains to me how Lu found her ministry in praying for the inner healing of people who suffer from mental, emotional and spiritual problems.

'Would she pray for me?' I ask, feeling a spark of hope.

'I can ask her. A lot of people make requests and Lu asks God who she should pray with.'

When I leave Jenny's house I feel more hopeful than I have for a long time. My faith has been sorely tested these past few years, but it's still intact. I couldn't have survived without God. For me faith and prayer are like living and breathing.

A few days later, Jenny calls to say she's heard from Lu. A meeting has been arranged for Monday 2 December.

'She lives in Bury St Edmunds. We'll drive there together,' says Jenny. I'm relieved that she's coming with me.

'Lu likes people to be very focused and serious about praying,' says Jenny. 'She wants us to fast and pray for three days beforehand. Hunger will help focus our minds and show God that we're serious about our prayer.'

The longest I've ever fasted is for twenty-four hours, but I know what Jenny means. Every hunger pain and tummy rumble is a reminder to pray.

FRIDAY, 29 NOVEMBER 1991

Robin Royston

Linda is ten minutes late for our session at the Chaucer. She apologizes for keeping me waiting and then stares distractedly out the window.

'Everything is taking me so much longer nowadays,' she says. 'I lose track of time.'

We chat about her difficulties at home and how she struggles to cope with the simplest of chores. 'I'm trying to keep myself busy all day. Things are OK when I keep my eyes open. But when the night comes I get tired . . .'

She doesn't finish the sentence. She doesn't have to.

Linda sighs in resignation. 'You don't know how many times I've wanted to phone you and ask if you could somehow put me back in Ticehurst. I want to go back there and hide.'

I find myself wishing that she'd cry. Instead she sounds cold and numb. She feels as though time has run out and so has people's patience. I keep trying to reassure her that I am still there for her.

'What if I leap in the middle of the night? What if I have a bad dream?'

'Phone me. You have my number.'

'I can't.'

'Yes, you can.'

'And what if it's two o'clock in the morning? What do I say? "Dr Royston, it's Linda. I've had a bad dream." What are you going to say to that?'

'I'll ask you about the dream.'

Linda laughs. 'You would, wouldn't you?' It is nice to see her smile.

She has written out two dreams for me. The first begins as many previous ones have.

I am at 5 Maple Avenue in the passage. There is something incredibly evil in the house. It is massive and black and does not have human form. It moves through the house and stops in the dining room. I know it wants me.

A man confronts the evil. I think he is you, Dr Royston. He drags it

outside and smashes it onto the ground again and again. At first I think
he has overpowered it, but then I notice that he is getting tired. I go cold
and realize that he isn't damaging it at all. It is just waiting until he
becomes exhausted.

Once the man becomes too tired to struggle, the evil will finish me off.

At that moment I sense there is another presence more powerful than
the evil. I don't know if it will arrive in time to save me. I look down
the driveway to the road, but can't see anyone coming . . .

Linda doesn't need me to explain the first half of the dream. It
portrays almost exactly what is happening to her. Her mind is still
stuck in 5 Maple Avenue with the evil. She feels like she is standing by passively, letting me fight her battle for her. But I can only
do so much. Her fear is that I will get tired, or give up on her. She
has to stand up for herself.

The idea of someone else coming to save her is new.

'What do you think is coming to save you?' I ask.

She shrugs. 'When I woke up from the dream I wondered if it
might be Jesus. Maybe God is going to heal me. I started fasting
today,' says Linda.

'Why?'

'On Monday I'm going to see the woman I told you about. She's
going to pray with me.'

'How do you feel about that?'

'Excited. Nervous. Apprehensive. Scared. All of them . . .'

Linda's decision to visit a Christian healer doesn't surprise me.
Her faith has always been an important part of her life and it has
helped her to survive some of her bleakest moments. Although I
don't share her beliefs, I have always felt there is a force that flows
through each of us and directs our lives. In this sense Linda and I
aren't so very different. We both believe that help can come from
within or without. In either case we have to be open and ready to
accept it.

Although I don't try to dissuade Linda from seeing Lu, I am not
optimistic about the chances of success. My reservations are to
do with naivety and false hope. I wonder if the people she will pray
with have any idea of the destructive power that Linda has been
exposed to.

356

She looks at me, clearly wondering if I think she is doing the right thing.

'I'm not being negative,' I say. 'I think it's worth trying. The power of the mind is an amazing thing.'

'And so is the power of prayer,' she says.

After Linda has gone, I look at the second dream. It is short and simple.

I am standing on a ship, waiting for it to move. I start to feel impatient that nothing is happening, but then I see the captain talking to another man. As I watch, this second man begins to take authority, and I realize that the old captain is handing over to him. I feel nervous at the thought of a new captain sailing the ship.

Here is another dream in which someone else is taking over Linda's situation. Whatever my anxieties about what Linda is going to do, one thing is clear to me now: I have gone as far as I can go with her; something – or someone – new will have to intervene if she is to survive.

MONDAY, 2 DECEMBER 1991

Linda Caine

I started fasting three days ago. Because I can't take my medication on an empty stomach, I've been having weak vegetable soup at meal times. There is a dull ache of hunger in my stomach which reminds me to pray.

I went to church yesterday. During the time for open prayer any-body could contribute. A middle-aged man stood up on the far side of the church and said, 'God has a message for someone here this morning. He wants to tell them, "I'm walking with you. I'm holding your hand and, if necessary, I'll carry you. Whatever is happening in your life, you *will* make it because I am leading you there."' As he prayed, I felt warm inside. I knew the message was for me.

After the service the same man came up to me and introduced

himself. 'When I was praying, you kept coming into my mind,' he said. 'God wants you to know that you *will* be all right.' I felt awed. I didn't deserve such love and support.

Jenny Walker's car pulls into the driveway. She's with Jill Poulson, a mutual friend. It's a three-hour drive to Bury St Edmunds. Jenny and Jill are in a happy mood. We sing praise songs and chat about children and church.

In the silences I alternate between apprehension and stillness. I look across the patchwork fields and realize that, after all these years, it's still a foreign country to me compared to Africa. As we arrive in Bury St Edmunds my apprehension turns to fear. What if this doesn't work? 'For goodness' sake, Linda, where is your faith?' I tell myself.

'But I've prayed to be healed for years. Why should it suddenly happen now?'

'I don't know. Maybe it won't. Everything happens in God's timing. Maybe today is His day.'

The internal monologue is interrupted as we pull into Lu's driveway. Her garden is neat and well loved.

Jenny rings the front-door bell and a white-haired woman appears with a wide smile. She's slightly older than I'd expected, with reassuring wrinkles around her eyes.

'You made good time,' she says, waving us inside. 'So you're Linda. I thought so.' It's as though she can see right inside me.

We sit down in an open, sunny lounge that overlooks the garden. Jenny is next to me and Jill and Lu are opposite. I can feel my palms getting damp as they make small talk.

Eventually Lu turns to me. 'My Lydia group are meeting today in another house,' she says. 'They're going to spend the day praying for me to have wisdom and insight, and for God to heal you.' Her eyes are full of compassion. 'If the telephone rings I'll answer it because sometimes they need to tell me what they feel God is saying,' she says, squeezing my hand.

It's amazing. All these people are putting aside their day to pray for me.

Lu continues talking. 'I want you to tell me what has happened. Just give me an overview of your life and what's upsetting you right now. Why have you come here? What are you hoping for?'

My first few sentences are disjointed and I can't hide my anxiety. Finally I settle down and tell her about my life. I give her the highlights and lowlights, as well as the three missing years. I don't know how long it takes. Lu hangs on every word, occasionally asking questions or nodding to show she understands. I tell her about my breakdown, the thoughts of suicide and of Dr Royston and how much he's done for me.

'Other Christians have criticized me because Dr Royston isn't a Christian psychotherapist,' I say quietly.

Lu replies that it doesn't matter. 'God uses everyone. This man has done a fine job. He has brought you to a place where you know what has happened to you.'

'But I'm still not . . .'

'I know,' she says. 'You're still not healed.'

As I tell her about being locked in the cupboard by the dark-haired man, I suddenly fall apart. The rest of the story comes out in sobs and tearful bursts. I can't look at her. My hands are covering my face.

Sometimes I'm vaguely aware of Lu talking to me. It's as though I'm a child and she's gently stroking my back and my hair.

'That was a terrible thing to happen, but it's all right now,' she whispers.

She asks God very softly for the damaged child inside of me to be healed. 'Lord, I ask that you bring this child into the life of the adult so that Linda can be the whole person you intended her to be.'

The words settle gently into my mind. I can feel them leaking into the dark corners and the deep chasms. And as they spread I can feel the darkness beginning to lighten. My hands are still covering my face. I stare through the gaps in my fingers and see the texture of the carpet. My mind is becoming clearer. It isn't the same cold clarity I felt when I hit Christy while cleaning her rabbit hutch. Instead, it feels as though the world has been out of focus and suddenly has come into focus again. Colours are brighter. Sights are more distinct. What an amazing feeling!

Lu is still leading me through some prayers. She is sitting next to me with her hand on my shoulder. 'Now when you go home, read your Bible every day and keep praying,' she says. 'Ask God to guide you. Don't expect giant steps.'

I nod and lower my hands. My cheeks are wet from my tears.

'I'll just call my prayer group and let them know we've finished,' she says, sounding very matter-of-fact. 'Then I'll make us some tea. You must be famished after your fast.'

I look up at Jill and Jenny. They both smile at me and start re-arranging the chairs. I glance out the window at the garden. I feel as though the world has been made afresh. It looks brand new. Lu pours the tea into delicate china cups. What faith she has, I think. As if reading my mind, she looks at me and smiles.

Later, when we say goodbye, Lu hugs me and kisses my cheek. 'Just take one day at a time, Linda, and keep praying.'

On the way home Jenny, Jill and I stop at a hamburger bar, because we're all still hungry. In the rest room I glance in the mirror and notice that my hair is oily. I only washed it last night.

Back at the table Jenny and Jill laugh when I mention it.

'Lu anointed you with oil as she prayed. Didn't you feel it?'

'No.'

I remember very little. All I know is that something strange and wonderful has happened. I can't put it into words, but it's a lovely feeling. I don't feel haunted any more. I don't know where the feeling has gone. I don't know if it's coming back.

I'm not used to this. It's like having lost a limb and I keep feeling for it even though it's not there any more. My mind is clear. I want to hold on to this feeling for as long as I can.

I arrive home quite late to find Chris has waited up for me. He looks up questioningly as I walk in. I hug him and tell him about my incredible day. 'I really think it helped . . . something has happened.'

He looks pleased, but apprehensive. He knows the danger of false hopes and expectations.

I go to sleep without any feeling of dread. And for the first time in months I don't 'leap' or scream during the night. At 7.30 a.m. I open my eyes and the sun is brightening the curtains. I feel a sense of expectancy. It's a new day. I can't wait to get started.

29

WEDNESDAY, 4 DECEMBER 1991

Robin Royston

Pulling into the staff carpark in front of the main hospital entrance, I grab my briefcase from the passenger seat and enter through the double doors.

'Hi, Janet. What's on for today?'

She glances up from her desk and hands me a file crammed with folders. 'Mostly regulars. There are two referrals. Do you want me to make them an appointment?'

I glance at the notes. 'OK, I'll see this one, but I want you to arrange for Mrs Davis to see a neurologist first. Thanks.'

I walk down the corridor, turn the corner and quickly check that my consulting room is in order. I have appointments all morning with private patients. With no waiting room, they sit on a chair outside the door until it is their turn.

Linda is early as usual. She's been sitting in the cafeteria collecting her thoughts. I poke my head around the door at 10 a.m. 'Hi, do you want to come in?' The moment I see her I know that something has happened. Instead of the troubled, dark visage that she normally wears, she smiles brilliantly and lights up the room. Her shoulders are back and she walks with a lightness of step.

I have seen many shifts in her moods. There are days when she laughs and seems in love with life. But this look is different again.

It is as though a light has been turned on behind her eyes.

She sits down and simply smiles.

'It's gone, hasn't it?' I say.

She nods.

I feel both relieved and completely shocked. Where has all the negative energy gone?

'Where? How? Tell me all about it.'

Breathlessly, she tells me about Lu and the prayer meeting. She can't explain what happened and neither can I. Whatever the reason, there has been a shift in Linda. Somehow the dark-haired man's hypnotic effect has been switched off. Lu quite intuitively picked up many things in Linda's background. In particular, she recognized how Linda's mind had split off as a child. Also how she seemed to slip between two different time periods. I am fascinated by every detail and have her tell me the story several times. The transformation in Linda is amazing.

In the Chinese game mah-jong, played with white tiles like dominoes, when you win a game on the last tile it's called 'Plucking the moon from the bottom of the sea'. That is what Lu has done. She has succeeded on the last tile, or the last throw of the dice, or the last ball of the innings, whatever analogy you want to use. I think back to Linda's most recent dreams about the powerful presence that was coming to save her. Everything has fallen into place. I might not have seen Linda's salvation coming, but her dreams have foreshadowed her rescue. It is a continuum.

I have always known that the answer lay within Linda. She has been leading the way from the outset and I could, only accompany her on the journey. Now, just as I'd hoped, her unconscious has stage-managed her survival. In Linda's mind, when all else had failed, God prevailed. It proves that you should never discount the power of prayer or underestimate the complexity of the mind and beyond.

I travelled with Linda as far as I could, weathering the storm, but it needed something or someone else to take charge and steer the ship into port. Lu understood this. I remember a story Linda told me about a man who fell into a river and was being carried down-stream towards a waterfall. A fisherman held out his rod and said, 'Grab hold, I'll pull you in.'

But the man replied, 'It's OK, God will save me.'

He drifted onwards, and further down the river a hiker leaned over the railing of a bridge and said, 'Grab my hand, I'll lift you out.'

'That's OK. God will save me,' said the drowning man, who drifted onwards.

Closer still to the waterfall, a helicopter hovered overhead and threw down a rope ladder.

'Don't worry. God will save me,' yelled the drowning man.

Seconds later he went crashing over the waterfall and perished on the rocks below. Later, as he reached the gates of heaven he said to God, 'Hey, didn't you see me down there? How come you didn't save me?'

And God said, 'I tried three times. Didn't you see all those people I sent to help you?'

This is what saved Linda. By trusting the process she learned to grab hold of the outstretched hand.

MONDAY, 16 DECEMBER 1991

Linda Caine

I haven't jumped awake at night for two weeks. It's incredible, although I'm not getting my hopes up too high. Just like Lu said, I'm taking things step by step. My good days are different from before. They used to be fragile, as if I was living on borrowed time. Now my mind is clear. The 'undercurrent' – as I used to call it – has ebbed and flowed and determined my life. On good days I held it back for a while. On bad days it overwhelmed me. Now that awful haunted feeling has gone, as well as the sense that the dark-haired man is coming for me.

I'm still trying to come to terms with what's happened. It doesn't say much for my faith that I'm so surprised and amazed that my prayers have been so totally answered. Thank you, God. Thank you, Dr Royston. I know I'm getting better because I can read 'The Child' and accept what happened to her . . . to me. The images still upset me but don't come alive in my mind any more. Just as Dr Royston said they would, they're becoming normal memories. I keep finding myself in situations that I couldn't have coped with a few weeks ago. I've been visiting friends and going shopping. At church I greet people and chat instead of hanging back.

I know Chris worries about me. It's as though my anxiety has passed to him. I see him watching me, waiting for the bad nights or the flashbacks to begin again. But I don't feel worried any more. I have a strange sense of peace. Somewhere deep down, I know it's over. I can't explain it. I just know that everything is all right. Gary and Christy can feel it as well. It's wonderful to see them relax again, instead of tiptoeing around me.

Tonight we're going into Canterbury to do some last-minute Christmas shopping. Chris and I have promised Gary and Christy that we'll take them to The Crêperie for a pancake dinner. It's been snowing during the day and the hedgerows are dusted with white. As we crest the hill near St Edmund's School, the city of Canterbury lies stretched out below us. The cathedral rises out of a blanket of white, lit dramatically by spotlights. The snow is falling lightly around it in a winter wonderland scene. I have always loved this view, but like everything else in my life now it seems different. I try to think why. Then it dawns on me. I suddenly realize why everything seems so new and exciting. In the past I've always been on the outside looking in. Now I'm inside – I'm part of the scene.

A few minutes later we park the car outside Chris's office in the cathedral precincts. With snow crunching beneath our feet, we walk towards the cathedral gate. The bell begins to toll for six o'clock. I glance upwards, blinking small snowflakes from my eyes as they tumble towards me like falling stars. Chris, Gary and Christy look at me quizzically. I'm standing on the footpath, staring up into the sky.

'Isn't it beautiful,' I exclaim.

Inside I want to dance and shout, 'I'm here! I'm alive and I don't have to die.' But I just smile and put my arms around Gary and Christy. We walk across the Buttermarket, past Debenham's department store, down the narrow street into the main street. A group of choristers are singing 'Silent Night'. I want to cry and laugh at the same time. I'm so happy. It's contagious. We spend the entire evening smiling and laughing about everything and nothing.

That night I dream that I'm standing at a railway station when a train arrives. Instead of stopping at the platform, the train carries on and stops at a deep pit full of clear water. I dive in and swim to the bottom. There are thousands of beautiful pebbles of all shapes, colours and sizes. I begin collecting them, but there are too many to hold in my hands. Suddenly, everything goes dark. I look up and see a huge car parking over the pit where the train had once been. It has a flat bottom that seals the top of the pit like a lid. I'm trapped. I swim for the surface and bang on the bottom of the car. I can feel myself starting to panic but then the car moves and day-light floods into the pit again. I'm OK. I'm free.

It's morning when I wake from the dream. I open the curtains and sunshine streams into the room on a crisp, clear day. I feel a real sense of anticipation. I'm just happy, like the sky is just blue – there's no other way to describe it.

Robin Royston

Over the next few weeks I watch Linda arrive for our sessions, half expecting to see her relapse. Perhaps there have been too many false dawns in the past for me to accept there has been a shift. Yet as I wait I see how she rediscovers the joys of living, and I begin to feel more confident. This isn't simply a lull in the storm. She has come through the other side. She doesn't have the same vulner-ability. Nor does she have the same aggression towards herself. The harshness of her mother's voice has disappeared.

Now, during our sessions, we are able to sit and bask in the warmth of reflection. We can take out each piece of the jigsaw, examine it, discuss it and then return it to its place. There are no signs of panic, frustration or Linda's mind sliding away.

'I used to feel that you'd disintegrate if I touched you,' I tell her. 'And if we dared to tread too hard, the ground under you would give way and you'd fall into the depths. Now we can jump up and down, stamp, pound . . . and it holds.'

She smiles. 'It does feel like that.'

The profound shift is mirrored in Linda's dreams. Some of the imagery remains the same, but the power has diminished and the outcomes are more positive. The water is clear and she is no longer trapped.

In January Linda arrives in my office with another startling dream. Again the water is crystal clear and full of pebbles. We have come full circle from the mud-pool.

She has written:

I am in a large building helping look after a group of children who have been abused. They are very wary of adults and watch me suspiciously.

I walk over to two large double doors and push them open. Light floods inside and the doors reveal a beautiful sunny day with blue skies. Waves break onto a beach with rock pools. I walk to the shore and begin picking up smooth pebbles and stones.

I call out to the children to come and see. One child comes over and tentatively kneels beside me. She dips her hand in the water and chooses pebbles to show me. We look at them one by one, captivated by their colours and patterns.

I feel wonderful because I know she is beginning to trust me.

This beautiful dream seems to symbolize how far Linda has come. She no longer hates 'the child' or wants to destroy her. The split in her mind is being healed.

WEDNESDAY, 6 MAY 1992

Linda Caine

Whenever I think about leaving this house I feel pangs of regret. Even after all that's happened here over the past three years, I love this place. It's full of wonderful memories. I've packed up most of the boxes to be shipped to California. We're leaving all the electrical equipment because of the different voltage in America, and most of the furniture is too bulky and costly to ship.

Saying goodbye to people has been hard. We broke the news to our church friends last Sunday before the evening service. Initially it came as a shock to them, but then they became really positive for us. Everybody wants us to stay in touch, which means a *lot* of letter-writing.

It's been almost four months since we were accepted to

immigrate to America. In the beginning I was nervous and excited, but now it seems even more daunting. Today, I drive to the Chaucer for the last time to see Dr Royston. Our final session is difficult because neither of us can look past the fact that this is goodbye. We've watched the clock tick down many times in our sessions, but never with the same sense of finality.

At eleven o'clock it's all over. 'So goodbye, Dr Royston. I'll miss you.' We hug and I feel the tears coming. 'You must promise you won't forget me. And if you're ever in America, you know you'd *always* be welcome to stay with us.'

He smiles. 'No, I'll not forget you, and I may just come over and see you one day. I've often thought of visiting America.'

'I'll keep you to that.'

'Let me know all about your new life.'

'I will.'

Words like this don't seem enough. There should be something more after what we've been through. This man knows more about me than anybody else. He has shared my darkest secrets and seen me at my very worst. Just as he said he would, he accompanied me on my 'goat track' until we came to the end of it. I owe him so much, and feel I can never repay him.

It's been over six months since I left Ticehurst. I haven't been back there since, although I've kept in touch with Linda McCormack and Roger Smith. Now I want to say goodbye to them, along with Dympna, Noel and all the others.

When I turn in at the gates and see the whitewashed buildings through the trees, I have the same sense of warmth and peace as before. I imagine it's like going back to a place where you grew up, where people understood and cared for you. Some things feel different. In the past I've been desperate to stay and terrified of leaving Ticehurst. Now I know I just want to visit. I don't want to hide away any more.

As I walk into the reception area, Tina looks up from behind the desk and smiles. She's talking on the phone and mouths 'hello' as I wave. Further down the passage, I look into the lounge and see a handful of patients. A few of them are watching TV, but most are lost in their own worlds.

Jimmy looks up at me with eyes that are wide with surprise. 'Linda!' It's almost as if he expects me to bolt from the lounge at any moment. I take a seat next to him and start telling him about going to America.

'I've just come to say goodbye to everyone.'

'You look incredible,' he says.

'I *feel* incredible. I'm so much better.'

Jimmy is happy for me, although a little bemused. The last time he saw me I was hurling myself at windows and running in the middle of the night.

'How are *you*?' I ask.

His face clouds over for a brief moment. 'Sometimes good, sometimes bad. OK today.'

A movement catches my eye and I look up. Sarah passes the doorway with a nurse holding her arm. She turns to look at me, but her eyes are vacant and her face is expressionless.

Suddenly, I feel guilty. Sarah and Jimmy were admitted to Ticehurst within a week of me – three years ago. They're both so young, with their whole lives ahead of them. Why am I well, while they continue to struggle?

I want to shout at them, 'Please, don't give up. *Fight* to get better.'

Linda McCormack's voice breaks into my thoughts.

'Sorry I'm late,' she says, giving me a hug. 'Let's go.'

I stand and turn towards Jimmy, not sure of what to say. All the faces in the lounge seem to have focused on mine. I give them a smile and a wave.

That's when it dawns on me that I used to identify with these patients far more than I did with 'normal' people. 'Normal' people used to scare me because they could think clearly. 'Normal' people couldn't understand how I was struggling with flashbacks. 'Normal' people were probably frightened of me. People like Jimmy and Sarah know what it's like to struggle with your mind. They are kindred spirits, comrades, fellow lost souls. I wish I could take them with me.

I follow Linda out into the passage and along the corridors to a lounge on the far side of the hospital.

'It's so good to see you,' she says, squeezing my hand.

'It's amazing! At first I was frightened that it wouldn't last, but now I *know* I'm better. I've only jumped awake twice in the past four months. And each time I knew where I was immediately.'

'Do you still have nightmares?'

'Sometimes, but when I wake up I can think clearly. I don't get trapped.'

My story comes out in an excited rush. 'I don't know what I expected when I used to pray for God to heal me. I just didn't expect everything to be taken away so completely.'

Linda McCormack smiles at me, but can't hide the concern in her eyes.

'You do believe me, don't you?' I whisper.

'Oh yes,' she says immediately, 'I can see the change in you, but . . .' She hesitates and picks her words carefully. 'I just don't want you to be disappointed if you begin to struggle again.' Although Linda has always been supportive of my faith, I know she doesn't share my beliefs.

'I'm not saying I'll *never* struggle again,' I explain. 'All I can say is that I'm different. I'm happy. I'm in love with life.'

We're meeting Roger for lunch at the Cherry Tree Inn in forty-five minutes. In the meantime Linda has a patient to see.

'What are you going to do?' she asks.

'Go for a walk.'

'Still saving earthworms, are you?'

'Of course.'

Crossing the parking lot, I follow the tree-lined path leading to the summer house . . . *my* summer house. It still looks sad and neglected. The doors are closed and squeak loudly as I pull at them. I open them just wide enough to slip inside, then close them after me. Leaves have blown through the broken windows and litter the floor. Spider webs hang from the beams and the wooden bench is grey and full of splinters. It must look desolate to an outsider but to me it's a haven. When I sit on the bench I feel peace wash over me. I love this place.

Roger is already at the Cherry Tree Inn when I arrive. He waves me over to a high stool at the bar and orders me a soft drink.

'Well, Linda Caine, look at you! You're looking good,' he says, sipping a beer.

'I *am* better, it's incredible.'

Again it's clear that someone is not entirely convinced.

'There are still things I have to deal with,' I tell him. 'I still get upset sometimes, but it doesn't overwhelm me like it used to. I *am* different now. I don't know why God chose this time to heal me. I just know he did.'

Roger's brow furrows and he says sternly, 'Well, I know someone who's not going to be pleased about this.'

'Who?'

'The glaziers, for starters. Look at all those windows they won't have to replace.' He gives me a grin and I burst out laughing.

Linda McCormack arrives and we have a wonderful lunch. It seems strange to be sitting chatting away like old friends, with me hearing about their own lives. Up until now I've only known them in hospital when they've been on duty, looking after me. Now I realize they have their own hopes and dreams and struggles.

After lunch, we walk into the parking lot. I feel sad because I don't know if I'll ever see them again. Hugging each of them tightly, I try not to cry. For a moment I'm a child again, clinging to my dad and wishing he wouldn't go away.

'I love you,' I whisper.

'We love you too,' says Roger, giving me a bear hug that lifts me off my feet.

'Make sure you keep in touch,' shouts Linda McCormack, as I drive away.

I call back to her, 'Look after my summer house!'

I can see them in my rear-vision mirror, standing and waving. The road lies ahead. The sky is blue. My mind is clear. I'm going to America to start a new life.

Epilogue

AUGUST 2002

Gary still sleeps through his alarm clock. Unfortunately, he's a little too big to be 'gated' nowadays. He's spent three years in the US Navy – in cramped quarters with his companions constantly going on and off duty – so he's now even better at staying asleep. I wonder if they sell air-raid sirens at Costco?

Fortunately he has jobs that are flexible and allow him to juggle his hours around his college classes and his many other interests. He works part time doing criminal investigating, while pursuing a degree in communications and marketing at our local city college. A gifted musician and song-writer, he is constantly frustrated by the fact that there are only twenty-four hours in a day.

After a difficult start in America – she was homesick for England for years – Christy has found her niche. Now a certified massage therapist and aesthetician, she lives in a lovely city near the ocean, working part time for an exclusive athletics club, and part time for a chiropractic office.

I feel an ache when I think about the fact that she worked at minimum wage jobs for two years to help put herself through college. But, like Chris, she sets goals and stays focused until she achieves them. In the next two years she plans to open her own private practice. I'm confident she will accomplish this as well.

The move to California cost us almost everything financially, but we made the right decision. In the beginning we had to live on our savings while Chris studied for the California bar exam. He passed at his first attempt – I was *so* proud of him. He took a job in Fresno for a few years, to become accustomed to the practice of law over here. Then two years ago he opened his own law firm. It was a wonderful and exciting time. Gary left the company he was with to implement a marketing system for Chris, while Annette helped him set up his front office and billing systems. Chris was told recently that his firm has become one of the most respected in the city, in his field of law.

And me? For a while I worked for a bankruptcy attorney, running the front office and doing the filing. It was pretty scary setting foot in an office after nineteen years of raising children and running a household. I moved on to work part time for a calligraphy shop in the Bay Area for a while. Now I'm a freelance artist and calligrapher, and I display and sell my paintings and calligraphy in local galleries and shops in Fresno and the Bay Area.

As for my state of mind, that too is reason to be thankful. I have good days and bad days, just like everybody else. Occasionally, I get 'flashes' when I remember a sight, sound or smell, but I'm not overwhelmed by them. The bad things that happened are still there, but I can live with them. I've learned to trust that the water will be shallow, and the ground firm beneath it. I think we all have to stop and take stock of our lives at times. We need to make a conscious effort to see where we are going and what we need. And never be too afraid or too proud to ask for help.

When I began writing this book I saw myself as a weak individual who was falling apart and could never be a proper wife and mother. But after putting all that happened down on paper, I know I'm not weak. I'm actually a very strong person who took a lot of knocks before falling over for a while. And perhaps 'falling' was the best thing that could have happened to me. It forced me to stop struggling and trying to pretend I was all right, and accept help. Thanks to God, the love and support of my family, and the help of Dr Royston and Lu, I came through it all. There were many times during my stints at Ticehurst when I asked Dr Royston why he was so sure that I'd get better. His reply was, 'Because you're a survivor.' He was right. I *am* a survivor!

I still have little recollection of the three years we lived at 5 Maple Avenue with my mother, yet I remember so much of what happened before that time. The gap has been filled by the 'flashes' which are like jigsaw pieces that still fall into place. It's amazing how often I make a connection or find a new piece of the puzzle. In the past few years I've told quite a few people about what happened to me as a child. A lot of them are very sceptical – especially about the concept of repressed or blocked memories. I've done a lot of reading and I know that even the experts are divided over whether repressed memories exist.

I have no witnesses to prove that what happened to me was real. There are a lot of questions only my mother – and the dark-haired man – could answer. But my mother is dead now, and she took what secrets she had with her to the grave. All I can tell people is that I've talked to my siblings and cross-checked what facts I can. I may never know exactly how or why these things happened to me, but I am confident 'beyond reasonable doubt' that it all really took place.

If the sun keeps shining we may go camping at Bass Lake this weekend, in the mountains north of Fresno. I took Dr Royston there a few years ago when he came to visit. He was in San Francisco to present a paper to the Association for the Study of Dreams.

It was a beautiful day and the high clouds were reflected on the stillness of the lake. We paddled in the water with our shoes off and trousers rolled up. Every so often I bent down to pick up a smooth pebble from beneath the surface. I held it up to the light and watched how the colours changed.

'You don't have to call me Dr Royston any more,' he said. 'Call me Robin.'

'OK . . . Robin.'

He must have noticed my slight look of concern, for he added, almost immediately, 'But Dr Royston will always be there if you need him.'

I laughed and dropped the pebble back into the water.

We had both stepped out of the past. Instead of being doctor and patient, we were now just two people – equals – sharing a beautiful day and a friendship.

Both of us love the outdoors and we chatted about wonderful places we'd seen. Robin talked about the Pyrenees in Spain and walking in the Pennines in the north of England, while I spoke of Californian redwoods and African plains.

I know that day was also special for Robin. There had been times, during the worst of my nightmare, despite all of his optimistic encouragement and gentle humour, when I know he doubted that I would ever reach this point. Now I am healed and happy, largely thanks to him and his refusal to give up on me.

Back in Fresno, before Robin left for San Francisco and then England, Christy made a point of telling him how she felt. She put her arms around him and said, 'Thank you for saving my mother's life.'

I knew this meant a lot to Robin, and I was so glad to see it myself. It was still all too easy to bring to mind the closed doors, the holes in the wall strategically covered by posters, and the bewildered, angry faces of my children as I left them yet again to be in Ticehurst. They had tried so hard to understand, but often it was easier to blame Robin, and I know there were times when Gary and Christy had resented and mistrusted him. They had seen him as being somehow responsible for my suffering. Now they knew the truth and Christy's embrace was like a final seal of approval.

Gary was only five weeks old when I fled Rhodesia twenty-six years ago. I promised him as the plane took off that one day he'd go back. Three years ago, it happened. He discovered a new country, Zimbabwe, but it was just as magical and exciting as the place I remember. He went bungee jumping off the Victoria Falls bridge and white-water rafting down the Zambezi. He saw wild elephants and lions in Hwange and watched hippos fighting at Mana Pools. I'm so envious.

With the help of my brothers Brendan and Clive, Gary retraced some of my childhood steps. He visited my cousin's farm in Bindura and saw the junior school that Chris and I had both attended. Chris's old high school is now an army barracks. He also went to see 5 Maple Avenue. In a cement rainwater drain that my dad had built, Gary found a set of tiny handprints. All of us kids had made our marks more than thirty-five years ago.

I can picture Gary squatting down and measuring his own hand against mine as a child. He also measured the stories that I had told him of that time in my life. During the bleakest times at Ticehurst when I wanted so much to die, I couldn't shield Gary and Christy from my pain. Chris told them certain things about my past and tried to explain how the sadness had suddenly overwhelmed me. Much later, when I was well again, they learned about 5 Maple Avenue and what happened to me there. Not surprisingly, it came as an awful shock.

Looking at my handprint, Gary found it difficult to picture me as a little girl. Only later, as they drove towards the Selukwe Road, did he finally make the connection.

'That's where Linda used to ride Prince,' Brendan said, pointing to the stretch of scrubby land between the road and the railway line.

'That's when you came alive in my mind,' Gary told me later. 'I could see you there – racing through the trees on that wild chestnut horse. You were fourteen years old and you were flying. The train didn't stand a chance . . .'

Afterwards, he wrote a poem for me that I will cherish for ever.

Where was I? Eleven years away,
When the wind caught your hair
And your horse beneath you
Gave freedom you alone could understand.

'Prince': what a fine name for a Princess's release.
I could only imagine the view from your eyes,
As your horse took flight
From a world that in the moment could not catch you.

To know such peace, to feel such passion,
While your heart beat as furiously
As the hooves beneath you.
As I think of you, riding through these sunset plains,
I know, now and for ever,
That you will always be a Princess to me.
My mentor, my guide, my mother to be.

It is a mystery to me, that you, my mother,
Could bestow on me such love –
From a world which offered it so sparingly to you.
It is one thing to repeat a kindness,
Yet to give what you never had
Is nothing short of a miracle.
And that miracle is you.